Capacity Planning and Performance Modeling

From Mainframes To Client-Server Systems

Daniel A. Menascé

George Mason University

Virgílio A. F. Almeida

Universidade Federal de Minas Gerais

Larry W. Dowdy

Vanderbilt University

P T R Prentice Hall, Englewood Cliffs, New Jersey 07632

Library of Congress Cataloging-in-Publication Data

Menascé, Daniel A.
   Capacity planning and performance modeling: from mainframes to
client-server systems / Daniel A. Menascé, Virgilio A.F. Almeida,
Larry W. Dowdy.
      p.   cm.
   Includes bibliographical references and index.
   ISBN 0-13-035494-5
   1. Computer capacity—planning. 2. Electronic digital computers-
-Evaluation. I. Almeida, Virgilio A. F. II. Dowdy, Larry.
III. Title.
   QA76.9.C63M46   1994
   004.2'4–dc20   93-43464
                                                                           CIP

Editorial/production supervision: *Dit Mosco*
Cover design: *Wanda Lubelska*
Cover Photo: *Masterfile©Mark Tomalty*
Manufacturing manager: *Alexis R. Heydt*
Acquisitions editor: *Paul Becker*

© 1994 by PTR Prentice Hall
Prentice-Hall, Inc.
A Paramount Communications Company
Englewood Cliffs, New Jersey 07632

The publisher offers discounts on this book when ordered
in bulk quantities. For more information, contact:

Corporate Sales Department
PTR Prentice Hall
113 Sylvan Avenue
Englewood Cliffs, NJ 07632

Phone: 201-592-2863
Fax: 201-592-2249

Printed in the United States of America
10 9 8 7 6 5 4 3 2 1

ISBN 0-13-035494-5

Prentice-Hall International (UK) Limited, *London*
Prentice-Hall of Australia Pty. Limited, *Sydney*
Prentice-Hall Canada Inc., *Toronto*
Prentice-Hall Hispanoamericana, S.A., *Mexico*
Prentice-Hall of India Private Limited, *New Delhi*
Prentice-Hall of Japan, Inc., *Tokyo*
Simon & Schuster Asia Pte. Ltd., *Singapore*
Editora Prentice-Hall do Brasil, Ltda., *Rio de Janeiro*

Contents

FOREWORD   xi

PREFACE   xv

1   THE CAPACITY PLANNING PROBLEM   1

    1.1   Introduction   1
    1.2   The Bank Problem   2
    1.3   Some Capacity Planning Situations   3
              1.3.1   Case 1: Increasing the Number of ATM Terminals, 4
              1.3.2   Case 2: Increase in Transaction Volume, 4
              1.3.3   Case 3: New Applications, 7
    1.4   The Capacity Planning Concept   7
    1.5   Why is Capacity Planning Important?   10
    1.6   Some Common Mistakes in Capacity Planning   11
    1.7   The Bank Problem Revisited   13
    1.8   Concluding Remarks   17

1.9   Exercises   17

         Bibliography   18

2   A CAPACITY PLANNING METHODOLOGY   19

2.1   Introduction   19

2.2   The Retail Company Problem   20

2.3   Methodology Overview   23

2.4   Understanding the Current Environment   25

         2.4.1   The Computing Environment Structure, 25
         2.4.2   What Is Capacity? 26
         2.4.3   Time Windows, 30
         2.4.4   Service Levels, 32
         2.4.5   Overall Description, 35

2.5   The Problem of Workload Characterization   37

         2.5.1   First Approach to the Problem, 38
         2.5.2   Simple Example, 40
         2.5.3   Workload Model, 43

2.6   Workload Characterization Methodology   46

         2.6.1   Identification of the Basic Component, 46
         2.6.2   Choice of the Characterizing Parameters, 46
         2.6.3   Data Collection, 47
         2.6.4   Partitioning the Workload, 47
         2.6.5   Calculating the Class Parameters, 51

2.7   Workload Forecasting   60

         2.7.1   From Business Plans to Computer
                 Demands, 61
         2.7.2   Forecasting Techniques, 63

2.8   Performance Prediction   68

         2.8.1   Rules of Thumb, 70
         2.8.2   Trend Analysis, 71
         2.8.3   Benchmarks, 72

2.9   Concluding Remarks   73

2.10   Exercises   73

         Bibliography   74

3   PERFORMANCE MODELS   76

3.1   Introduction   76

3.2   Building a Performance Model of a Simple Computer
         System   77

3.3   Performance Model of an Interactive System   84

3.4   Performance Model of a Batch System   88

3.5   Multiple-Class Performance Models   89

    3.5.1   Aggregation of Classes, 90
    3.5.2   Priorities, 93
    3.5.3   Shared Domains, 95
    *3.5.4   Summary of Parameter Types for Multiclass
          Performance Models, 97*

3.6   Baseline Model and Modification Analysis   97

    3.6.1   Baseline Model, 98
    3.6.2   Using a Database Management System, 98
    3.6.3   Using a DBMS and an Optimizing Compiler, 99
    3.6.4   Increasing Buffer Pool Size, 100
    3.6.5   Using the Log Option for Crash Recovery, 101
    3.6.6   Summary of Modification Analysis Results, 101

3.7   Performance Model of a Client-Server System   102

3.8   Multiprocessing   106

3.9   Types of Models   108

3.10   Concluding Remarks   109

3.11   Exercises   110

    Bibliography   112

**4   INTUITIVE SOLUTIONS FOR A SINGLE-PROCESSOR
   COMPUTER SYSTEM PERFORMANCE MODEL   113**

4.1   Introduction   113

4.2   Alternative View of the Modeling Paradigm   113

4.3   Simple Server System I   117

    4.3.1   Model Solution, 118
    4.3.2   Little's Result, 123
    4.3.3   Model Predictions, 126

4.4   Simple Server System II   128

4.5   Generalized Birth–Death Models   131

4.6   Alternative Approach: Operational Analysis   133

4.7   Concluding Remarks   136

4.8   Exercises   136

    Bibliography   138

5 EFFICIENT SOLUTIONS FOR COMPUTER SYSTEM MODELS   140

5.1   Introduction   140

5.2   First-Principles Approach Review   141

5.3   Basic Central Server System   143

     5.3.1   *State Description Specification, 145*
     5.3.2   *State Enumeration, 145*
     5.3.3   *Transition Rate Specification, 147*
     5.3.4   *Balance Equation Formulation, 147*
     5.3.5   *Balance Equation Solution, 149*
     5.3.6   *Performance Metric Derivation, 153*

5.4   Simple Convolution   155

5.5   Simple Mean Value Analysis   159

5.6   Simple Decomposition/Aggregation   163

5.7   Simple Bounding Techniques   167

5.8   Concluding Remarks   171

5.9   Exercises   173

     Bibliography   174

6 MULTIPLE-CLASS MODELS   176

6.1   Introduction   176

6.2   Simple Two-Class Model   177

6.3   Notation and Assumptions   180

6.4   Closed Models   182

     6.4.1   *Exact Solution Algorithm, 185*
     6.4.2   *Approximate Solution Algorithms, 189*

6.5   Open Models   192

     6.5.1   *Analysis of Multiclass Open Models, 193*
     6.5.2   *Open Model Example, 195*

6.6   Mixed Models   199

6.7   Concluding Remarks   202

6.8   Exercises   202

     Bibliography   203

7 PERFORMANCE OF CLIENT-SERVER ARCHITECTURES   205

7.1   Introduction   205

7.2   The Telemarketing Company Problem   206

7.3   Performance Considerations in the CS
Paradigm   207

7.4   Workload Characterization for CS
Architectures   209

7.5   Solving the Telemarketing Company Problem   210
      7.5.1   *Birth–Death Model, 213*
      7.5.2   *CS Model, 215*

7.6   Categories of CS Performance Models   219
      7.6.1   *Single-Request Clients and Homogeneous
Workloads, 220*
      7.6.2   *Single-Request Clients and Heterogeneous
Workloads, 221*
      7.6.3   *Multiple-Request Clients and Homogeneous
Workloads, 221*
      7.6.4   *Multiple-Request Clients and Heterogeneous
Workloads, 221*

7.7   Multiclass MVA with Load-Dependent Devices   222

7.8   Multiclass Open Queueing Networks with
Load-Dependent Servers   226

7.9   Concluding Remarks   230

7.10   Exercises   230

        Bibliography   232

8   MODELS OF PRACTICAL COMPUTER SYSTEMS   234

8.1   Introduction   234

8.2   Modeling Memory Queueing   235
      8.2.1   *Flow-Equivalent Method, 236*
      8.2.2   *Single Class, 237*
      8.2.3   *Multiple Classes, 240*

8.3   Modeling Disk Subsystems   243
      8.3.1   *I/O Subsystem Architecture, 244*
      8.3.2   *I/O Service Time, 246*
      8.3.3   *Estimating Delays within the I/O
Subsystem, 247*
      8.3.4   *Modeling I/O Contention in Closed
Systems, 252*

8.4   Modeling CPU Scheduling Priorities   254
      8.4.1   *Two-Priority Example, 254*
      8.4.2   *SWIC Priority Algorithm, 257*

8.5   Modeling Paging Activity   259

8.6   Modeling Multiprocessing   262

      8.6.1   Tightly Coupled Multiprocessors, 263
      8.6.2   Loosely Coupled Multiprocessors, 264

8.7   Concluding Remarks   266

8.8   Exercises   266

      Bibliography   268

9   OBTAINING INPUT PARAMETERS   **270**

9.1   Introduction   270

9.2   Measurement Techniques   272

      9.2.1   Monitor Tools, 274
      9.2.2   Monitoring Modes, 277

9.3   Input Parameter Description   278

      9.3.1   Workload Intensity, 279
      9.3.2   Service Demands, 280
      9.3.3   Overhead Representation, 287

9.4   Parameter Estimation   287

      9.4.1   Steps in Obtaining Input Parameters, 288
      9.4.2   Arrival Rate, 288
      9.4.3   Multiprogramming Level, 289
      *9.4.4   Number of Active Terminals and Think
             Time, 290*
      9.4.5   CPU Service Demand, 291
      9.4.6   I/O Service Demands, 294

9.5   Order Processing System Example   297

      9.5.1   Average Arrival Rate, 298
      9.5.2   CPU Demand, 298
      9.5.3   Disk Demands, 299

9.6   Concluding Remarks   301

9.7   Exercises   302

      Bibliography   302

10 MODEL CALIBRATION AND VALIDATION   **304**

10.1   Introduction   304

      10.1.1 Review of the Basic Modeling Paradigm, 305

10.2   Calibration Example   305

10.3   Types of Calibrations   309

10.4   Effect of Calibrations   311
          10.4.1 Percent and Absolute Difference, 312
          10.4.2 Calibration on the Mean Multiprogramming
                  Level, 313
          10.4.3 Multiprogramming Level Distribution, 314
          10.4.4 Multiclass Calibration, 315
          10.4.5 Absolute Demand Calibration, 315
          10.4.6 Calibration on the Bottleneck Device, 316
          10.4.7 Ghost Server Calibration, 316
10.5   Case Study of a Theoretical System   316
          10.5.1 Calibrated Models, 318
          10.5.2 Prediction Tasks, 321
10.6   Rules of Thumb   333
10.7   A More Formal View   334
10.8   Concluding Remarks   336
10.9   Exercises   336
          Bibliography   339

11 PERFORMANCE OF NEW APPLICATIONS   **340**

11.1   Introduction   340
11.2   The Credit Card Problem   342
11.3   Sizing the Credit Card Application   344
11.4   Techniques for SPE   352
          11.4.1 Software Development Life Cycle and SPE, 352
          11.4.2 Obtaining Data for SPE, 354
11.5   Environment for SPE   356
11.6   Credit Card Problem Revisited   360
11.7   Concluding Remarks   365
11.8   Exercises   366
          Bibliography   368

12 CONCLUDING REMARKS   **369**

APPENDIX A. GLOSSARY OF TERMS   **373**

APPENDIX B. GLOSSARY OF NOTATION   **382**

APPENDIX C. FORMULAS   **386**

APPENDIX D. QUICK MANUAL FOR *QSolver/1*   **393**

INDEX   **398**

Foreword

Reengineer the corporation! This battle cry resonates with a growing and widespread concern for effective design of the materiel, information and human processes of organizations. A firm's reputation, credibility, trustworthiness, and competitive position all depend on its ability to fulfill its promises to its customers, on time and with satisfaction. In the past decade, a firm's ability to fulfill promises, to accomplish more with the same staff, and to shorten cycle times, have all come to rest critically on its ability to deploy computing systems and networks with adequate power and response time. As the complexity of those systems has grown, so has the difficulty of answering questions about their capacities to perform their functions. The performance evaluation of computer systems and networks has thus become a permanent concern of all who use them.

Around 1980, the field in which this concern was addressed was known as performance evaluation, and sometimes as performance modeling or performance analysis. What was then an esoteric field of interesting mathematics, fascinating algorithms, elegant theorems, practical models, and creative measurements has become now a critical technology used routinely by organizations. This transformation has been marked by a change of terminology for the field, now called capacity planning.

It is useful to examine the way in which performance evaluation evolved into capacity planning, for the same stages will be observed as the field becomes more closely tied to the reengineering of organizational processes. The first evolutionary stage, "mapping," began around 1965. In this stage, analysts developed basic notations and diagrams that allowed them to observe jobs, servers, flow paths, and queues in computer systems. These maps were heavily inspired by classical queuing network theory and operations research, but eventually took on their own unique forms. Even though they were not good for predicting the future, the maps were quite useful for locating bottlenecks and allowing system administrators to relieve them.

The second stage, "instrumentation," began around 1975. In this stage analysts developed operating system probes, accounting systems, and measurement packages whose reports could be used to annotate maps quantitatively: the queuing network diagrams could be labeled with service times, queue lengths, job-flow rates, and response times. Measured parameters were used to test whether queuing network models could reproduce measured throughputs and response times, a process of model validation. Learning what to measure and how to measure it also facilitated the development of standard benchmarks for evaluating systems.

The third stage, "anticipation," began emerging around 1980. It was characterized by the commercial acceptance of analyzer packages that would take parameters derived from system measurements (typically service times and visit ratios for each job class) and compute congestion, throughput, and response time at any point in the system. These packages enabled performance analysts to routinely forecast system performance. At first, real systems contained characteristics that were not represented in the models, but today most commercial packages for capacity planning cover most of the cases encountered in practice.

The three stages just outlined do not have clear starting times. They are modern interpretations of actions and concerns of performance analysts over various intervals during the past three decades. Much useful theory has been developed over the same thirty years, extending considerably the older theories of queuing and operations research.

The new wave of interest in business process engineering is not a continuation of the current evolution. Its quantitative side will draw heavily on everything known about capacity planning. It is a discontinuity because it is based on a new notion of work.

For most of the past century, work has been regarded as motions and manipulations that carry out tasks and, since the 1950s, work has included movement and manipulation of information. In this context, the work of an organization could always be represented in, and sometimes performed by, computers. But in the 1980s a new interpretation of work began to appear: the fulfillment of commitments made by some people in response to requests made by others. Commitments are not items of information, and machines cannot make them. Reengineering the corporation does not mean reengineering software or information systems. It means examining the recurrent patterns of requests and promises in the network of conversations of an organization. The exploding "workflow" industry, expected to gross $2.5 billion in the United States by mid 90s, is busy trying to invent and supply tools that allow observation, measurement, and reconfiguration of the networks of request-promise loops constituting an organization. This new field is still in the mapping stage – developing the notations and diagramming conventions for observing the network of loops in and between organizations. Progress with the maps will stimulate progress in measurement, which in turn will stimulate progress in our ability to predict cycle times and throughputs of human processes supported by information processes. I expect that the instrumentation stage will be well under way by the year 2000, and the anticipation stage not long thereafter. Many of the quantitative methods used will be direct descendants of the methods now used in the capacity planning field.

The authors of this book have a clear sense of these impending changes. They understand that performance evaluation has evolved to a set of critical standard practices. They understand that the older methods must extend to sprawling networks of machines, and they go to considerable effort to demonstrate how this works. They understand that approximations are good enough for many practical situations where the exact models do not apply. They understand that the standard practices of today are the foundation for continued improvement of models, algorithms, and theory for the world of business processes that will be the focus of information technology in the future.

Peter J. Denning
Rosslyn, Virginia
January 1994

Preface

Often, in the systems analysis field, questions occur such as "What will happen to the response time of the mainframe when the arrival rate of transactions goes from the current 10 transactions per second to 20 transactions per second?" or "Will the file server support an additional 15 workstations?" or "What will happen to the response time of the existing applications when the new accounts payable application under development goes into production four months from now?" or even "Should I buy a new disk or add more memory to my workstation?" These are typical examples in which the performance level of a computer system has to be predicted under new situations (e.g., increased transaction volume, more terminals, new applications, new operating environments). The ability to predict whether or not a computer system will be able to support the growth of existing applications, a change in system parameters and configurations, or the addition of new applications without violating user-specified service levels (e.g., response time under 3 seconds, processor utilization under 60%) is called *capacity planning* and is the subject of this book.

Unfortunately, the answers to the questions above are often "I *think* that a CPU upgrade will be required to support the increase in transaction volume" or "The manufacturer recommends that we move to a multiprocessor file server to be able to support more workstations" or "My experience tells me that the new application will not affect too much the response time of existing applications when it goes into production" or even "Uncle Joe told me that getting more memory is better than adding a new disk." Unfortunately, these are also typical example answers to capacity planning questions. The goal of this book is to show that capacity planning questions can be answered in a scientific manner. One aspect of this is to be able to *predict* the future performance of computer systems under different scenarios and parameter values. Analytical models (i.e., a collection of formulas and computational algorithms) form the basis of the performance prediction models developed in this book.

UNIQUE BOOK FEATURES

This book is example driven. Instead of following a more traditional sequence of presenting the theory and then giving examples, each chapter starts by presenting a motivating problem. First principles and intuition are used to explore the solution to the problem. Only then is the theory necessary to generalize the solution formally presented. The original problem is then revisited. Many examples are used throughout the book to illustrate the concepts introduced. Each chapter includes a list of exercises to help develop further confidence in the techniques presented.

Included with this book is a disk that contains the source code, in Pascal, of programs that implement most of the performance modeling algorithms described in the book. These programs can be used to solve real performance problems that can be cast as networks of queues with multiple classes of customers. The algorithms implemented in these programs also handle the more general situation where the service rate of a server is a function of the number of customers queuing for the server.

Also included in the disk, is the executable of *QSolver/1*, a PC-based capacity planning software. Through a friendly spreadsheet-like interface, users can define workloads and the devices that make up a computer system. Workloads may be of three different types: transaction processing, interactive, and batch. For each workload, the user has to provide parameters that describe the workload intensity (e.g., transaction arrival rate, number of terminals, think time, degree of multiprogramming, priority, etc.), as well as parameters that describe the resource demands placed by each workload on each device. The package then generates the corresponding performance model and solves it. Several graphs and reports (e.g., response time and throughput per workload, response time and queue length per device and workload, utilization per workload and device, etc.) may be generated. The version of *QSolver/1* provided with this book is appropriate for educational purposes but has some implementation restrictions. *QSolver/1* gives the reader a flavor of the power of performance models in obtaining insight into the behavior of complex computer systems. None of the programs provided with this book can be used in part or as a whole for commercial purposes, nor should they be included as part of other programs without written consent of the first author of this book. For more information about the nonrestricted version of *Qsolver/1*, contact:

Prof. Daniel A. Menascé
Department of Computer Science
George Mason University
Fairfax, VA 22030-4444
(703) 993-1537
email: menasce@cs.gmu.edu

INTENDED AUDIENCE

This book is intended for use as a textbook or as a book for further individual professional development. As a textbook it can be used in a first course in performance evaluation at the graduate level or at the advanced undergraduate level. A recommended sequence of chapters for an undergraduate course on performance modeling is 1, 3, 4, 5, 6, 7, and 8. The book is also valuable for professionals working in the area of capacity planning, performance analysis, and system management. Professionals with previous knowledge in performance modeling may be more interested in Chapters 2, 7, 8, 9, 10, and 11.

BOOK ORGANIZATION

In *Chapter 1* we introduce the concepts and terminology for capacity planning. Notions of service levels, service demands, and performance metrics are presented.

In *Chapter 2* we describe the various steps of a methodology for capacity planning with emphasis on techniques for workload characterization and workload forecasting.

In *Chapter 3* we describe the various components of performance prediction models based on queuing networks. Servers, queues, and passive resources are given. It also introduces the notions of multiple-class models, aggregation of classes, priorities, shared domains, multiple resource possession, models of client-server architectures, models of multiprocessor systems, the baseline model, and modification analysis.

In *Chapter 4* we present intuitive solutions to simple performance models based on the solution of state-space diagrams (Markov chains). Little's result and the generalized birth–death system are discussed in this chapter.

Operational analysis as an alternative approach to performance model solution is introduced.

In *Chapter 5* we introduce efficient solution techniques to single-class performance models. Among these techniques are convolution, mean value analysis (MVA), decomposition/aggregation, and bounding techniques.

In *Chapter 6* we generalize the solution of performance models to multiple-class systems. The basic solution technique considered is mean value analysis (MVA) for closed queuing networks. The following algorithms are presented: exact MVA for closed queuing networks, approximate MVA for closed queuing networks, analysis of multiclass open queuing network models, and analysis of multiclass mixed queuing network models.

In *Chapter 7* we develop techniques for the use of queuing network models to analyze the performance of client-server architectures. The solution of open and closed queuing networks with load-dependent servers is presented. Different categories of client-server models are presented, including single-request clients and homogeneous workloads, single-request clients and heterogeneous workloads, multiple-request clients and homogeneous workloads, and multiple-request clients and heterogeneous workloads.

In *Chapter 8* we develop techniques to solve performance models of practical computer systems. Issues such as paging, memory queuing, CPU priority scheduling, complex I/O subsystems, and multiprocessing are considered.

In *Chapter 9* we deal with the issue of obtaining input parameters for performance models of existing computing systems. The techniques presented discuss how these parameters may be obtained in various types of environments, such as virtual machines and on-line transaction monitors.

In *Chapter 10* we present the techniques that may be used to calibrate and validate a performance model. Among the techniques discussed are percent and absolute difference, calibration on the mean multiprogramming level, multiprogramming level distribution, multiclass calibration, absolute demand calibration, calibration on the bottleneck device, and ghost server calibration.

In *Chapter 11* we introduce software performance engineering. A set of techniques is given that can be used to predict the values of service demands and workload intensity of applications under development.

In *Chapter 12* we present a historical perspective of the field citing the theoretical milestones and the main commercial products that emerged as a result of the theory. *Appendices A through D* contain a glossary of terms introduced in the book, a glossary of notation, a list of formulas, and a brief manual on the use of the package *QSolver/1*, respectively.

ACKNOWLEDGMENTS

The authors would like to thank the many students at George Mason University, Federal University of Minas Gerais (Brazil), and Vanderbilt University for having read and suffered through early drafts and having contributed with comments on some of the chapters. In particular, they would like to thank Gerry Blais and Ravindra Sanapala for their useful comments. The bulk of Chapter 10 is due to Craig Lowery, whose dissertation was on calibration techniques. We gratefully acknowledge his efforts and also the efforts of Amy Apon who was instrumental in helping to edit this material. Special thanks are due to the Internet that made it possible for three people thousands of miles apart to write a book. Finally, we would like to express our gratitude to our publisher, Paul Becker, for his support and flexibility.

Daniel A. Menascé, Virginia, menasce@cs.gmu.edu
Virgílio A. F. Almeida, Minas Gerais, Brazil, virgilio@dcc.ufmg.br,
Larry W. Dowdy, Tennessee, lwd@vuse.vanderbilt.edu.

To my parents,
my wife Gilda, and my children Flavio and Juliana.

To my parents (in memoriam),
my wife Rejane, and my children Pedro and André.

To my parents,
my wife Sharon, and my children David and Erin.

Chapter 1

The Capacity Planning Problem

1.1 INTRODUCTION

Planning is the process of elaborating methods to achieve certain preestablished goals. Planning is a rather common activity in many areas of human activity. In business administration, for instance, the process of planning is vital for the success of a company. The capacity of any system is its maximum performance or output. For instance, the capacity of a factory may be measured in terms of the number of parts manufactured daily. The capacity of an elevator may be measured by the number of kilograms it is able to lift.

Planning the capacity of any system is a common activity in many areas. For example, when engineers design an automobile engine, they should plan or calculate the capacity of the engine when subject to various loads and operating conditions. Farmers should be able to plan the capacity of their farms, measured, for example, in terms of head of cattle grown per year, as a function of several conditions, such as expected pasture availability, worm concentrations, and expected birth weights of calves.

In the situations mentioned above, it is also at least as important to consider the ability of the system to perform correctly (functionality) as it is to know its capacity or performance. It is not enough to guarantee that the automobile will accelerate from 0 to 150 km/hour in 12 sec, but a more

1

important question is: Will the car be able to sustain a load of 1500 kg at 90 km/hour at an appropriate fuel consumption rate?

There is usually a strong concern about the functionality of a computer system, and very little concern about its performance [1]. In general, performance becomes an issue only when the performance becomes perceived as being poor by the users. Very seldom do computer scientists and professionals worry about planning the capacity of the systems they are designing or managing. In this chapter we describe the concept of *capacity planning* of computer systems through several examples. First, a situation is described that calls for capacity planning decisions. Then, before a solution to the problem is discussed, several smaller, but related problems are presented. Finally, various solution methods are applied to the original problem.

1.2 THE BANK PROBLEM

Suppose that a local bank has three fully automated branch offices, all located in the same city. Each teller (i.e., clerk) at each branch has access to a terminal connected to the central information systems (IS) facility of the bank. The central facility consists of two mainframe computers that share a disk farm. Automated teller machines (ATMs) are available at 10 locations throughout the city, at shopping malls, supermarkets, and the local airport. The internal offices of the bank are also automated and supported by an office automation system (OAS), a software application program, which also runs on the central IS facility.

One of the two mainframes handles all on-line transaction processing, such as ATM transactions and transactions from the human tellers. The other mainframe runs the OAS, which takes care of all batch processing jobs, such as generation of managerial and operational reports, execution of large decision support system models, issuance of statements to customers, and issuance of paychecks to bank employees.

The bank branches are open to the public from 9:00 a.m. to 3:00 p.m. There are 24 tellers in the three branch offices, and each teller serves an average of 20 customers per hour in the peak period from 11:30 a.m. to 1:30 p.m. During the remaining banking hours, an average of 12 customers per hour are served by each teller. On average, each customer generates two on-line transactions. Thus, during the peak period, the IS facility receives an average of 960 (24 tellers × 20 customers/hour/teller × 2 transactions/customer) teller originated transactions per hour. ATMs have a different profile. They are active 24 hours a day, but are used more heavily when the branch offices are closed. In particular, peak volume for ATMs is observed in the period that goes from 8:00 a.m. to 9:00 a.m. and from 3:00 p.m. to 9:00 p.m. During these hours, each ATM serves an average of 15 customers per hour. Each ATM customer generates an average of 1.2 transactions. Thus, in the peak period for ATMs, the

IS facility receives an average of 180 (10 ATMs × 15 customers/hour/ATM × 1.2 transactions/customer) ATM transactions per hour. During bank business hours, ATM transaction traffic is about 50% of that observed during ATM peak hours.

Some measurements have been made on the current computer system. One measurement is concerned with the average *response time* (i.e., the average time interval elapsed between the instant a transaction is submitted to the system for processing until the answer begins to appear at the user's terminal). The average response time at the branch tellers was found to be 1.23 sec during peak hours. The bank manager considers 3 sec to be the maximum average response time to be tolerated at the tellers. The ATM average response time was found to be equal to 1.02 sec during the peak hours. An average of 4 sec would still be considered acceptable.

The board of directors of the bank decided that the bank should expand its operations to other cities. They approved a plan that included opening one new branch every two months during the next five years. These 30 new branches would be distributed over 20 cities located in several states. Each city would have one new ATM installed every two months.

The board of directors requires answers to several questions that are posed to the IS facility manager.

- Will the current central IS facility allow for the expected growth of the bank while maintaining the average response time figures at the tellers and at the ATMs within the stated acceptable limits?
- If not, when will it be necessary to upgrade the current IS environment?
- Of several possible upgrades (e.g., adding more disks, adding memory, replacing the central processor boards), which represents the best cost–performance trade-off?
- Should the data processing facility of the bank remain centralized, or should the bank consider a distributed processing alternative?

The foregoing questions are typical capacity planning issues. Before addressing these issues directly, in the next section we present related example situations that require capacity planning decisions. Through these examples it will be possible to introduce important issues related to the concept of capacity planning. These related issues include service level, saturation, service demand, workload, and workload characterization.

1.3 SOME CAPACITY PLANNING SITUATIONS

In this section three case situations are presented that will introduce several important concepts in capacity planning. These cases come from the banking profession, a profession in continual need of good capacity planning.

1.3.1 Case 1: Increasing the Number of ATM Terminals

A banking system runs on a mainframe and supports 100 ATM terminals with an average response time of 2.5 sec. The number of ATMs will be increased to 150 in the next six months. The average response time at these terminals is not supposed to exceed 3.5 sec. This is a limit imposed by the installation management based on the observed user tolerance for response time. Such a limit is called the desired *service level*. The capacity of the system is said to have reached *saturation* if the service level is violated.

In the banking example of Sec. 1.2, the following desired service levels were imposed:

- 3 sec maximum average response time at the teller terminal
- 4 sec maximum average response time at an ATM

Other examples of response time related service level specifications are: "The response time for 90% of the transactions should not exceed 3.5 sec." Or, the "maximum response time in a radar system processing collision-avoidance data should be 1 sec."

Service levels may also be specified in terms of other performance metrics such as average *throughput* (i.e., the average number of transactions or jobs executed per unit time). For instance, in the banking example the operations manager might have specified that the IS facility should be able to issue at least 150 customer statements per hour. In general, service levels are specified for the different types of transactions and/or jobs being processed by the IS facility.

The value of a desired service level depends on the type of application. For instance, 4 seconds may be an acceptable value for average response time for an airline reservation system but may be a rather unacceptable value for an airport check-in system.

1.3.2 Case 2: Increase in Transaction Volume

In some cases, it may not be possible to characterize an increase in the load offered to a computer system as an increase in the number of terminals connected to it. Consider, for instance, that the bank decided to offer to some customers a new service called personal banking. Through this service, customers can dial directly to the bank IS facility from their personal computers to perform several transactions. Since the number of terminals or users connected to the system varies with time, one must characterize the average load that is generated as the average number of transactions submitted to the system per unit time, also known as the *average transaction arrival rate*.

Suppose that the computer system used to support the personal banking application is composed of a CPU and two disks. Suppose that the types of transactions allowed by the system are divided into two types:

- *Query transactions.* These are rather fast transactions that account for 70% of all transactions submitted. The maximum average response time (service level) allowed for this type of transaction is 3 sec.
- *Update transactions.* These are rather complex transactions that update records in several files of the banking database. The established service level for this type of transaction is 10 sec as the maximum average response time.

Table 1.1 shows some values obtained from measurements taken with the help of software monitors. These values reflect the average total service time (in seconds) spent by each type of transaction at the CPU and at each of the disks. Such values are called *average service demands*. It is important to note that the service demand does not include the time spent waiting to gain access to a resource if there is contention for it, as is usual in multiprogrammed systems. Since the demand is the total service time at a device, it can be thought of as a product of the average number of "visits" (i.e., requests per transaction) to the device and the average amount of time required at the device per visit. Thus, in this example, each query transaction has a CPU demand of 0.20 sec and update transactions have an average service demand of 0.30 sec at the CPU. These are average values over the set of observed query and update transactions, respectively.

Table 1.1 Average Service Demands (in Seconds) for Case 2.

	Query	Update
CPU	0.20	0.30
Disk 1	0.30	0.80
Disk 2	0.25	0.45

The system currently executes an average of 700 query transactions per hour and 300 update transactions per hour. The current response times are 2.3 and 9 sec, respectively. The arrival rate of query transactions is expected to grow 30%. The question is: Will the system support this growth without violating the established service levels?

The set of transactions or jobs submitted to a computer system is called its *global workload*. In this particular example, the global workload of this system is composed by the query and update transactions taken together. Many times, it is desirable to partition the global workload into smaller sets, known as *workload components*, sometimes referred to as *customer classes*, which are composed of transactions or jobs that have similar characteristics. This process is called *workload characterization*. To carry out a capacity planning study, one must characterize the various workload components, referred to hereafter simply as workloads. This process entails separating the jobs or transactions into components with similar characteristics and resource usage demands, and assigning numbers to these demands, as well as to the intensity of the workload. In the banking example, the global workload has been decomposed into two different workloads: query and update transactions. These two workloads have different characteristics with respect to the use of system resources. For instance, from Table 1.1 query transactions are much less I/O intensive than update transactions.

Each workload may be characterized by two types of parameters:

- *Average service demands* at each device.
- *Workload intensity,* which gives an indication of the number of transactions and/or jobs that will be contending for the computer system resources. An example of a workload intensity parameter is the average transaction arrival rate. In this example, the average arrival rate for query transactions is 700 transactions/hour and for the update workload is 300 transactions/hour.

Even if query and update transactions had similar service demands, they would need to be considered as two separate workloads since a growth forecast is desired on one of the transaction types: query transactions. One of the stated goals is to predict system performance as a function of this particular growth. Thus, the motivations for partitioning a global workload into more specific workloads are:

- The workloads are of different nature (e.g., batch jobs versus interactive transactions, query versus update requests).
- One is interested in performance metrics on different types of transactions or jobs of different natures. For instance, one might be interested in studying the evolution of the response time of debit–credit transactions separately from all other on-line transactions in the banking system of Sec. 1.2.
- There is an expected growth in intensity in some of the workloads, or an expected change in the service demands of certain workload types.

In the banking problem, several workloads can be identified: teller on-line transactions, ATM transactions, decision support system model execution, payroll checks processing, and statement processing. Depending on the purpose of the capacity planning study, workloads may be further refined (partitioned) or aggregated. In Chap. 2 we discuss the workload characterization process in more detail.

1.3.3 Case 3: New Applications

Reconsider the personal banking application discussed in Sec. 1.3.2. Assume that the application is in the process of being developed. The bank expects to receive 1000 transactions a day in the first month of operation of the service. This number is expected to grow 10% a month during the following three months and is expected to stabilize at approximately 1330 transactions a day. The maximum tolerated average response time for transactions of this application is 4 sec.

This new application will share a computing facility with the existing global workload. One question that arises is: Will the system be able to deliver an average response time for the new application within the desired service level without violating the service levels of the already existing workloads?

Thus, *workload evolution* may occur due to two distinct situations:

- *Normal growth of existing applications.* In this case, the intensity of existing workloads is expected to vary, generally increase, with time. Cases 1 and 2 above are examples of this type of workload evolution. In these situations, service demands can, in principle, be measured since the applications already exist.
- *Implementation of new applications.* In this case, one must estimate the service demands at the various devices, since the application is still being developed. Techniques that can be applied to these cases are discussed in Chap. 11.

1.4 THE CAPACITY PLANNING CONCEPT

Having discussed some typical capacity planning examples, it is now possible to introduce the concept of capacity planning in more general terms. *Capacity planning* is the determination of the *predicted* time in the future when system saturation is going to occur, and of the most cost-effective way of delaying system saturation as long as possible. The prediction must take into consideration the evolution of the workload, due to existing and new applications, and the desired service levels.

Prediction is an important keyword in capacity planning. It is impossible to perform capacity planning without being able to predict system performance. Techniques to predict system performance will be described when we discuss models and/or tools in later chapters.

When a saturation point is predicted, one should be able to answer the following types of questions:

- Why is saturation occurring?

- In which parts of the system (CPU, disks, memory queues) will a transaction or job be spending most of its execution time at the saturation point?
- Which are the best cost-effective alternatives for avoiding (or, at least, delaying) saturation?

Figure 1.1 shows a graphical representation of the concept of capacity planning. The solid curve in the graph shows the predicted evolution of the response time, R, as a function of transaction arrival rate. The models needed to make such predictions are discussed in detail in subsequent chapters. The maximum acceptable response time is 4 sec. Currently, the system executes 1000 transactions/hour, and there is a prediction of reaching 3000 transactions/hour in the next six months. As seen from the figure, saturation is expected to occur at about 2600 transactions/hour. In other words, the system is not going to be able to support the expected growth in the workload.

Response time (sec)

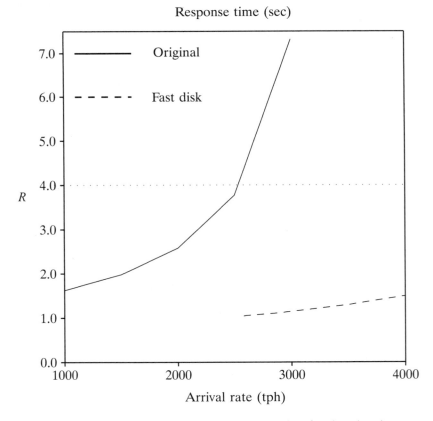

Figure 1.1 Graphical representation of a capacity planning situation.

It is interesting to note the nonlinear behavior of the response time curve. It starts off flat and after a certain value of the transaction arrival rate, the curve rises sharply. This is a typical evolution of the response time curve. The performance of computer systems is not linear!

The same models as those used to predict the evolution of response time can be used to answer the capacity planning questions above, so that several possible scenarios of system configuration alternatives may be evaluated. Reconsider Fig. 1.1, and assume that the predictive models indicate that the bottleneck—the component of the system with the highest service demand—is one of the system disks. The utilization of a bottleneck device approaches 100% before any other device, as the workload intensity increases. This is called *device saturation*. The dashed curve in the figure illustrates the effect of replacing the bottleneck disk by another disk that is twice as fast. As seen in the figure, the new disk solves the problem (at least temporarily). It allows the transaction arrival rate to grow to 3000 transactions/hour while keeping the average response time well below the desired level of 4 sec. Note that these conclusions may only be reached with the use of predictive models since the *future* behavior of the system is being considered. In other words, measurements made with software or hardware monitors can only give insight into the current state of the system.

In summary, the input variables of a capacity planning process are the workload evolution, system parameters, and desired service levels; the output variables are the saturation points and determination of cost-effective alternatives to avoid saturation, as indicated in Fig. 1.2.

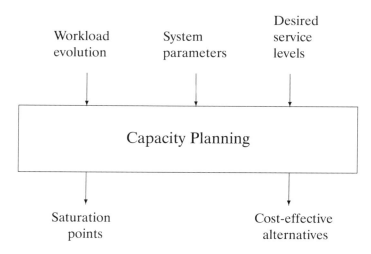

Figure 1.2 Capacity planning input and output variables.

1.5 WHY IS CAPACITY PLANNING IMPORTANT?

Consider the example of Sec. 1.4. If someone had not planned ahead of time, a situation would have been reached where the response time would become greater than the acceptable 4 sec. Users would start to complain. By using monitors, one could measure transaction response time and would find out that the disk is to blame. Also, this measurement task may not be trivial, depending on the type of monitor available in the system.

The next issue is to convince the IS manager that the disk is the problem and (even more difficult) get budget approval for buying a new disk. Often, it is discovered that this year's budget was prepared and approved last year (as is normally the case with most companies) and that there is no room for extra expenses of this order of magnitude. Since the problem with the computer system is getting worse, the board of directors may approve, from emergency funds, acquisition of the new disk. But chances are that you might be reminded that in other areas of the company people do not act in such an irresponsible manner and that "next time you should plan ahead of time, or *at least* warn the directors and users of bad things to come." This illustrates the use of capacity planning.

As seen, capacity planning is quite important. The primary reasons for capacity planning include the following.

- *User dissatisfaction.* If no one plans the capacity of the IS installation, situations will probably arise where the desired service levels are violated. Solving the problem may take longer than can be tolerated. In the meantime, users will have to cope with a degraded system. Depending on the type of workload (and the clout of the disgruntled customers), this degradation may range from a nuisance up to serious organizational problems and user dissatisfaction.

- *External image of the company.* In many situations, the performance of the IS facility of a company is perceived directly by its customers. Some examples include response times at ATMs in banking systems and response times at airline reservation system terminals. The lack of planning may lead to situations of degraded performance felt directly by the company's customers. In extreme cases, this may cause the loss of customers.

- *Productivity decrease.* Consider, for instance, the R&D department of an automobile manufacturer whose engineers are in the process of designing a new car, with the support of sophisticated computer-aided-design (CAD) software that runs on a large mainframe. A poor performance of the CAD system application will directly affect the engineers' productivity, with possible negative effects on the quality of their work or on not meeting established schedule deadlines.

- *Budgetary constraints.* In most cases, when performance reaches a degradation point, the solution involves hardware expansion or software rewrite with associated expenditures, which may be difficult to accommodate in a previously approved and constrained budget.

- *Risk of financial losses.* The life of most companies depends on their data processing facilities for managing and controlling routine operations and for supporting short-term and long-term managerial decisions with the help of decision support systems. A degraded computer system may lead to certain company actions and decisions that are made in an untimely fashion with possible negative financial effects.

- *IS environment control.* Assume that a company has a centralized IS facility that is supposed to serve the majority of its users. As service becomes degraded, user dissatisfaction increases and many users will tend to move toward alternative solutions, such as buying personal computers and workstations up to the limit of their budgets. These actions, if not coordinated, may lead to unnecessary replication of software development efforts for the new environments, difficulty of integration of information between departments, and at the bottom-line, more expenses to the company, which will be paying for maintenance contracts for the central facility and for a myriad of small systems.

1.6 SOME COMMON MISTAKES IN CAPACITY PLANNING

Once the importance and value of capacity planning are recognized, it is instructive to examine some common mistakes. Consider the following situation. A company has characterized its global workload and has decided that it should be partitioned into three different workloads: A, B, and C. The installation has been measuring the total CPU consumption for each workload in the past six months, as shown in Table 1.2. The table shows, for each month, the percent CPU utilization for each workload as well as the total CPU utilization. The utilization of any device is the fraction of time the device is busy.

Table 1.2 CPU Utilization (Percent) for the Last Six Months.

	CPU Utilization			Total CPU
Month	Workload A	Workload B	Workload C	Utilization
1	20	15	10	45
2	21	16	12	49
3	25	18	15	58
4	30	19	16	65
5	32	21	17	70
6	33	22	18	73

Monthly reports are sent to top management showing nicely drawn piecharts indicating CPU utilization by each of the three workloads. Needless to say, these reports are useless, since the top management is unconcerned about CPU utilization. One day, the capacity planning staff was asked by top management to answer the following question: When will the current machine have to be upgraded?

Since the planning staff had the CPU utilizations, they quickly ran a linear regression [2] model to predict CPU utilization in future months. (See Table 1.3 for this prediction.)

As seen from the predictions, the total percent CPU utilization would be 93% within three months. This observation leads the capacity planning staff to recommend a CPU upgrade by that time since "such a high CPU utilization would probably cause high response times."

There are several mistakes worth noting in the situation described above.

- The capacity planner did not take into account the predicted evolution of the workload. In other words, the capacity planner should have tried to figure out, from the strategic plans of the company and from some key indicators of the economy that might affect the business of the company, how the workload was supposed to evolve in the following months. In Chap. 2 we explore in further detail the issue of workload evolution forecasting.

- The capacity planner did not take into account the desired service levels of the three workloads under study.

- A linear regression prediction of CPU utilization is inadequate, although used by many people, since the CPU is a resource shared by workloads A, B, and C, and its utilization is a consequence of the execution of the workload on the computer system.[1] Thus, predicting CPU utilization requires a model—discussed at length in subsequent chapters—which reflects the behavior of a computer system. It will be seen that, just as response time is not linear with

Table 1.3 Future Predicted CPU Utilization (Percent).

Month	CPU Utilization			Total CPU Utilization
	Workload A	Workload B	Workload C	
7	37.1	23.6	20.3	81.0
8	40.0	25.0	21.9	86.9
9	43.0	26.5	23.5	93.0

[1]As will be seen in later chapters, the CPU utilization for a given workload is proportional to its throughput, which for certain types of workloads does not grow linearly with the workload intensity.

respect to the system load, CPU utilization is not a linear function of the load.

So, the question "When will the current machine have to be upgraded?" is rather vague. It should be replaced by a more precise question such as "Considering the expected evolution of the workload, when will the current machine not be able to deliver the desired service levels?"

Note that from the point of view of the user, it is not relevant to talk about CPU utilization, since what the user "feels" are performance metrics such as response time. Thus, saturation might very well happen with a lightly utilized CPU, either because the bottleneck is not the CPU or because the service levels are such that they are reached at low levels of CPU utilization. Obviously, a highly utilized CPU will probably cause high response times to be observed, but low CPU utilizations do not guarantee acceptable service.

In summary, capacity planning cannot be performed without considering service levels, workload evolution, and predictive models of computer system performance.

1.7 THE BANK PROBLEM REVISITED

Reconsider the bank problem discussed in Sec. 1.2. To answer the capacity planning questions that were posed at the onset of this chapter, the solution begins by analyzing workload evolution. Assume that all new branches will have 8 tellers and that the customer average arrival rate per branch during peak periods will be the same as in the already existing branches. Each branch generates 320 (8 tellers × 20 customers/hour/teller × 2 transactions/customer) transactions per hour. Since a new branch is opened every two months, this implies a 160 transaction/hour increase per month. Since the current arrival rate is 960 transactions/hour, the following is the relationship between the arrival rate, λ_{teller} (in transactions/hour), of teller on-line transactions, and the number of months in the future.

$$\lambda_{teller} = 960 + 160 \times \text{months} \qquad (1.1)$$

Now each ATM generates 18 transactions/hour. Since one new ATM will be installed at each of the 20 cities every two months, an increase of 180 (18 transactions/hour/city × 20 city ÷ 2) ATM transactions/hour per month is expected. Since the current average arrival rate of ATM transactions, λ_{ATM} (in transactions/hour), is 180, the following relationship holds:

$$\lambda_{ATM} = 180 + 180 \times \text{months} \qquad (1.2)$$

Figure 1.3 shows the response time of teller (solid curve) and ATM (dashed curve) transactions at peak time as a function of the months in the

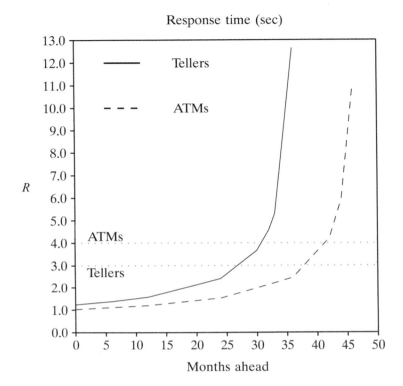

Figure 1.3 Teller and ATM transactions for the centralized environment.

future. These curves were obtained with the models and solution procedures discussed in later chapters. The dotted lines at 3 and 4 sec indicate, respectively, the service levels for teller and ATM transactions. As seen, the service level (3 sec) for the teller transactions will be violated in 27 months. The service level (4 sec) for ATM transactions will be violated before reaching 42 months from now.

Thus, the current IS facility will not support the full predicted expansion of the bank. Expansion scenarios have to be devised and analyzed in terms of cost–performance trade-offs. Cost aspects are not considered here since they depend on the given system configuration. The issue here is to compare, performance-wise, a set of possible alternatives for system expansion.

Consider, for example, the possibility of distributing the processing load of on-line transactions of the bank. That is, suppose that instead of using a single large centralized IS facility, as depicted in Fig. 1.4, the bank is considering the installation of three smaller regional IS facilities (see Fig. 1.5), interconnected by a communications network. It is expected that approximately 80% of the transactions will be able to be satisfied at their site of origin, while the remaining ones will require that some remote processing be done.

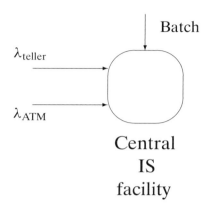

Figure 1.4 Centralized IS facility.

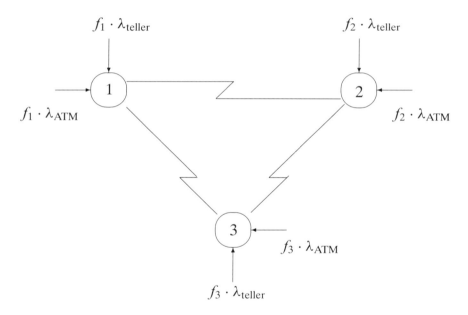

Figure 1.5 Distributed IS facility.

Let $\lambda^i_{\text{teller}}$ be the average arrival rate of teller transactions at regional IS facility i ($i = 1, \ldots, 3$) and let f_i be the fraction of the total teller traffic (λ_{teller}) that is originated at site i. The total teller traffic is the sum of the teller traffic originated at each regional site (i.e., $\lambda_{\text{teller}} = \sum_{i=1}^{3} \lambda^i_{\text{teller}}$). Assume that the nonlocal transactions are equally distributed among the two other sites. So each site i has to process its local transactions ($0.8 \times f_i \times \lambda_{\text{teller}}$) plus half of the nonlocal transactions of the remaining sites. Hence,

$$\lambda_{\text{teller}}^{i} = 0.8 \times f_i \times \lambda_{\text{teller}} + \sum_{j \neq i} \frac{1}{2} \times 0.2 \times f_j \times \lambda_{\text{teller}} \tag{1.3}$$

$$= \lambda_{\text{teller}}[0.8 f_i + 0.1(1 - f_i)] \tag{1.4}$$

$$= \lambda_{\text{teller}}(0.7 f_i + 0.1) \tag{1.5}$$

A similar relationship for the case of ATM transactions is given below, where λ_{ATM}^{i} is the average arrival rate of ATM transactions at center i, and $\lambda_{\text{ATM}} = \sum_{i=1}^{3} \lambda_{\text{ATM}}^{i}$.

$$\lambda_{\text{ATM}}^{i} = \lambda_{\text{ATM}}(0.7 f_i + 0.1) \tag{1.6}$$

Using prediction models discussed later in the book, the response time curves are found for teller and ATM transactions in the distributed environment as shown in Fig. 1.6. To derive the data for these curves, we assumed that the machine installed at each of the regional centers was 80% as fast as the original centralized machine. Also, for the sake of simplicity, it was

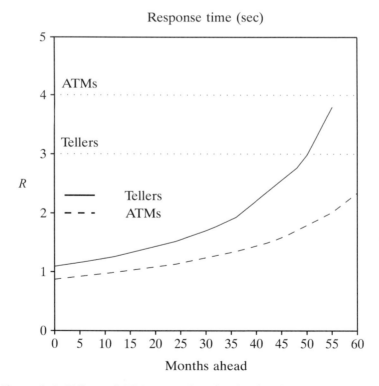

Figure 1.6 Teller and ATM transactions for the distributed environment.

considered that the total traffic was equally partitioned among the three sites (i.e., $f_1 = f_2 = f_3 = 1/3$).

As shown, the distributed solution saturates for the teller workload in the fiftieth month, which represents an improvement over the centralized solution which saturates in 27 months. The models indicate that, at saturation, the bottleneck will be the CPU, which will be 73% utilized. The distributed configuration will be able to support the predicted evolution of the ATM workload for the next five years (assuming that nothing else changes), as seen from the appropriate curve in Fig. 1.6.

Certainly, cost and operational factors must be taken into account when comparing several alternatives. But it is important to realize that the available alternatives cannot be compared adequately if their relative performance is not known. Of course, several other alternatives may be analyzed, using appropriate techniques and tools to be discussed at length in the following chapters.

1.8 CONCLUDING REMARKS

It should be clear by now that capacity planning of computer systems is a rather important activity that should not be overlooked. Since capacity planning requires being able to *predict* the performance of computer systems, adequate techniques (not just intuition or educated guessing) should be used. Since computer systems are not linear, neither intuition nor past experience can or should be used to predict the future behavior of a computer system as the workload characteristics change. In the next chapter we discuss a methodology that can be used for a complete capacity planning study.

1.9 EXERCISES

1. Consider an IS facility with which you are familiar. Describe the workloads of this installation. Are service levels specified for these workloads? What are they?

2. Your installation manager is conducting a capacity planning study using *only* software monitors as tools. Would you believe in the results of such a study? Why?

3. The average response time at an on-line reservation system was measured to be 2.5 sec and the CPU utilization was measured to be 60%. The established service level for the response time is 3.0 sec. Is the system saturated? Would it be saturated if the service level for the response time were 2.0 sec?

4. Consider Fig. 1.6. What is the service level for teller transactions that saturates the system in 40 months?

5. Consider Table 1.1. Which device is the bottleneck for query and for update transactions? What would your answer be if the service demand of disk 2 for query transactions were changed to 0.5 sec?

6. Take a look at several issues of the business section of your newspaper. Look for articles describing situations of business growth or company mergers. Try to imagine and describe some typical capacity planning situations that would typically arise in such scenarios.

BIBLIOGRAPHY

1. D. Ferrari, Considerations on the insularity of performance evaluation, *IEEE Transactions on Software Engineering*, Vol. SE-12, No. 6, June 1986, pp. 678–683.

2. T. H. Wonnacott and R. J. Wonnacott, *Introductory Statistics for Business and Economics*, Wiley International Edition, Wiley, New York, 1972.

Chapter 2

Capacity Planning Methodology

2.1 INTRODUCTION

Strategic information planning has been defined as the process of identifying a portfolio of information systems that will help an organization in executing its business plans and realizing its business goals [1]. Capacity planning is a process through which the information systems management attempts to specify the most cost-effective computing environment that meets the current and future corporate's information requirements, as specified by strategic planning. As in any other business, the activity of planning the capacity of a computing system involves obtaining answers to four basic questions:

- What is the current installed capacity?
- What services should be provided in the future?
- What quality goals are planned for the services?
- What is the most cost-effective system configuration to handle current and future services and still meet the planned quality goals?

Considering the corporate plans, the status of the current information system, and the hardware and software products offered in the marketplace, the capacity planning process generates several system configuration alternatives that satisfy the future information demands. Figure 2.1 illustrates the

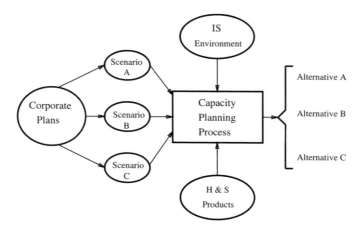

Figure 2.1 Capacity planning process.

input–output relationship existing in the capacity planning process. Corporate plans are the main source of information to capacity planning. Usually, alternative business scenarios develop from the corporate plans. Expanding automatic teller machines (ATMs) to gas stations is an example of a business scenario, as is acquiring another bank that has 60 branches. Each business scenario implies new applications or changes in the existing ones. These scenarios are inputs to the capacity planning process, and so are the information systems (IS) environment and available hardware and software products. Each scenario leads to an alternative system configuration capable of handling an expected workload under specific service levels.

Capacity planning applies to a business of any size. It can be used in a variety of situations, ranging from the problem of sizing a departmental minicomputer with 20 users to the problem of specifying the configuration of a computing system to support worldwide operations of a large credit card corporation.

After introducing a motivating example, we describe in this chapter the steps required for a capacity planning study. These steps include understanding the current system, characterizing its workload, calibration, workload forecasting, performance prediction, and validation.

2.2 THE RETAIL COMPANY PROBLEM

A large retail company owns a chain of 400 stores located across the country. Two classes of information systems support the retailer's operations: *mission-critical applications* and decision support systems (DSS). The former are those applications that are fundamental to running the business, and the latter represent the applications involved in producing information to support managerial decisions. In this example, the mission-critical applications include inventory, purchasing, accounting, payroll, and the point-of-sales (POS) system. Systems are updated in batch during the night and have their databases available to on-line queries. The exception is the point-of-sales application, which is a real-time on-line system that supports on-line credit authorization and runs the cash registers. The information systems run on two mainframe computers located at the corporate headquarters. The mainframes share a disk subsystem and support a network of 800 terminals and 1000 POS terminals located in 400 stores.

One of the goals of the corporate plan is to boost the company's sales in the next three years. This goal should be achieved by improving customer services and by cutting internal costs in order to become more competitive. As a member of the steering committee, the information system (IS) manager, helped by the planning staff, has developed a specific strategic information plan to meet the corporate goals. This plan involves: 1) the development and maintenance plans for the applications portfolio, 2) an equipment expansion strategy, 3) staffing plans, and 4) budget guidelines for the next three years. Specifically, the IS plan has the following goals:

- to have all point-of-sales automated.
- to establish quality goals for the mission-critical applications.
- to speedup the development process.
- to develop and implement (in a short period of time) a system to support the execution and management of telemarketing campaigns.

To achieve the specific goals, an equipment expansion is required. Thus, the IS manager faces the following problem: what is the best strategy, in terms of cost-benefit, to expand the company's computing system? The conventional approach would be to upgrade the current system to a larger mainframe. In this case, the capacity planning problem would be to size the new mainframe appropriately. Instead of taking the conventional approach, the IS manager may decide to take this opportunity to reshape the computing environment and to make use of new information technology. Figure 2.2 illustrates the proposed transformation of the computing environment. The current mainframe-centric environment is to be divided into three independent, but integrated, computing environments: an on-line transactions processing environment, a client-server distributed environment, and a mainframe environment.

- The *on-line transaction processing (OLTP) environment* consists of a multiprocessor system dedicated to process interactively a large number of relatively simple transactions, generated at the point-of-sale terminals. Transaction processing implies accessing a large database of customers

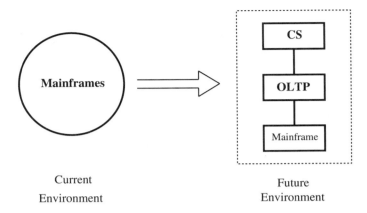

Current
Environment

Future
Environment

Figure 2.2 Computing environment transformation.

and products. This application was running originally on the mainframe and is to be ported to this special-purpose OLTP environment. Based on the current volume of transactions and taking into consideration the expected growth of the volume of transactions due to the increase in the number of POS terminals, the capacity planning problem refers to the specification of the number of processors and sizing of the I/O subsystem capable of supporting the expected transaction workload.

- The *distributed environment* consists of two local area networks (LANs), each with 20 workstations and one file server. One LAN is dedicated to DSS applications that will be ported from the mainframe. The other LAN supports the telemarketing application. The computing model adopted for this environment is the *client-server* (CS) model. This model is where application processing is shared between a workstation client and a server. The primary capacity planning problem focuses on the specification of the file server.

- The *mainframe environment* consists of a single computer system dedicated to mainframe-based applications, application development, and maintenance activities. The mainframe remains a general-purpose processing environment. Because the transaction processing application is to be moved to the OLTP system and the DSS applications are to be downsized to the distributed environment, it is necessary to size the new computer that is able to handle the remaining workload of the two original mainframes.

Before presenting, in the next sections, the steps required to solve a capacity planning problem, it is important to note some key issues. First, there is a strong relationship between corporate plans and capacity planning.

The former is the main source of information for the latter. Current and planned business activities identify the needs and opportunities of information systems, which become the external premises of the capacity planning process. If the organization does not have a clear plan, the capacity planning analyst should try to obtain, from users, business guidelines for the future. Second, capacity planning is not restricted to large problems. It also applies to small computing environments, such as the example of sizing a file server in a LAN system. Third, when faced with a large capacity planning project, it is always useful to break the problem down into smaller ones. This decomposition of the capacity planning problem leads to simpler tasks, whose solutions can be carried out separately, making them easier and faster to obtain.

2.3 METHODOLOGY OVERVIEW

How should one carry out a capacity planning project? The answer to this basic question lies in the use of a methodology composed of the following five major steps:

- Understanding the current environment
- Characterizing the workload
- Validating and calibrating the system model
- Forecasting the future workload
- Predicting future system performance

Two models are key components of the methodology: the workload model and the computing system performance model. Workload models are studied in detail in this chapter. Performance models are introduced in Chap. 3. Techniques for constructing models of different types of computing systems are developed in Chaps. 4 through 8.

Figure 2.3 shows a schematic diagram of the capacity planning methodology. The major steps are represented by rectangles. Viewing the corporation's business plans as the major guidelines, the methodology begins with obtaining a global understanding of the current computing environment. A global system model is constructed. This provides an overall description of the system and identifies key features (or, parameters) of the system workload. Using information collected by system monitors (e.g., the system accounting routines), the second step is to generate a workload model of the system. The workload model is used to parameterize the system model. The system model is "solved" (e.g., via simulation or analytical techniques). The model solution is compared against actual system measurements (i.e., baseline measurement data). Calibration may be necessary in constructing valid system and workload (i.e., performance) models which match observed system behavior. Several iterations

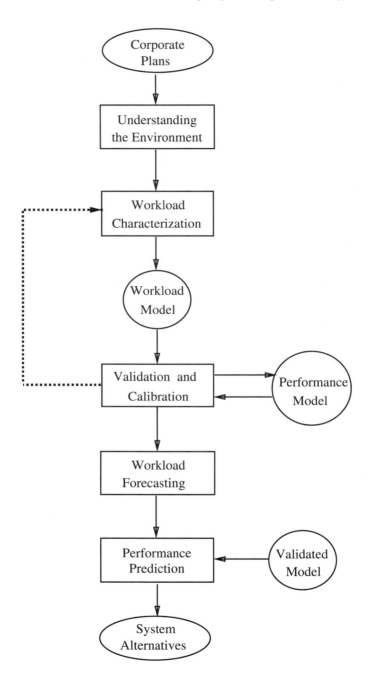

Figure 2.3 Model-based capacity planning methodology.

may be necessary to calibrate the model to achieve a valid model. Techniques to validate and calibrate performance models are presented in Chap. 10. The purpose of the forecasting step is to predict the future workload requirements. The validated performance models and the forecast workload model can then be used to predict the performance of the system under several different scenarios (e.g., upgraded devices, changes in the system workload). To help find the most cost-effective system configuration, different input scenarios are analyzed in this step. Basically, each scenario consists of a new future system feature and/or a new forecasted workload feature. Because every forecasted item carries a certain degree of uncertainty, several possible future scenarios are considered and different configurations of the system are analyzed. A selection of alternatives is generated so that IS management may choose the most appropriate option, in terms of cost/benefit.

2.4 UNDERSTANDING THE CURRENT ENVIRONMENT

As a preliminary step in any capacity planning effort, it is essential to have a global picture of the entire computing environment. A manager needs to understand thoroughly the current computing environment prior to assessing future reconfiguration options. A broad understanding of the environment also helps the analyst to narrow the scope of a capacity planning study and reduces time and cost involved in the project. The product of this initial step is an overall description of the computing environment. This is accomplished typically by constructing a global system model.

2.4.1 Computing Environment Structure

What are the key components of a computing environment? One answer relies on the view of a computing system as a series of layers, which together create an environment for the execution of user programs.

Figure 2.4 depicts a typical layered architecture of a computing system.

- The hardware configuration consists of one or more computers that may share common resources. Computers include single or multiple processors, memory, I/O processors, disk subsystems, tape units, printing facilities, and terminals. Networks are used to interconnect different computers.

- The operating system interacts directly with the hardware and provides services to support software and application programs. The operating system also isolates user programs from the hardware peculiarities. Commonly used operating systems include IBM/MVS, IBM/VM, DEC/VMS, UNIX, MS-NT, and MS-DOS.

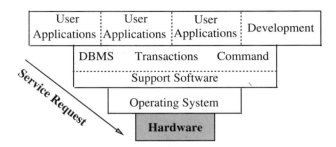

Figure 2.4 Architecture of a computing environment.

- The support software includes the command interpreter, editors, compilers, database management systems (DBMSs), and transaction monitors. DBMSs such as Oracle, Informix, Sybase, ADABAS, and DB2 and transaction monitors such as IBM/CICS, UNIX/Tuxedo, VAX/ACMS, Unisys TIP, and DECintact are examples of important components that constitute the environment for execution of transaction processing systems (OLTPs).
- The application programs solve user problems. The development of application programs involves creating, modifying, and testing programs for correctness and performance.

Each layer builds on the layers below but hides the internal details from layers above. Thus, each layer demands services from the layer immediately below and provides services to the layer immediately above. In the end, any *service request* involves using hardware resources. A key issue in capacity planning is the concept of *resource* and its associated *capacity* of providing service in response to a *demand* placed by a request. As an example, when a user initiates a transaction asking for the names of customers who have ordered blue pens, a series of requests begins. First, the transaction handled by the transaction monitor might generate a sequence of SQL-SELECT commands, which are analyzed and processed by the DBMS software, which, in turn, requests I/O operations from the operating system. All these activities are triggered by a user demand for service from the hardware resources. For instance, CPU time is consumed in the execution of instructions, and disk units remain busy performing I/O operations. Ultimately, these services result in requiring time from the system's resources.

2.4.2 What Is Capacity?

The *theoretical capacity* of a computing system has been defined as the maximum rate at which it can perform work. The rate at which requests are serviced is known as *throughput*. Thus, capacity is the upper limit of throughput. In our retail company example, the throughput of the OLTP system represents the number of transactions processed per second (tps), while the throughput of the batch applications executed on the mainframe corresponds to the number of jobs processed per second. File servers in a distributed environment have their performance measured by IOPS, which is the number of I/O operations per second processed by a server for network clients. In interactive environments, such as those used for program development activities, throughput refers to the number of commands processed per second.

From the user's viewpoint, the capacity of a system is measured by its ability to provide fast response to their requests. In other words, users are interested in response time. On the other hand, computer managers are interested in increasing throughput, to maximize resource utilization. It is useful to consider the combination of response time and throughput. Consider the banking example of Chap. 1 and the debit/credit transactions generated by ATM machines. The average response time of these transactions can be obtained by monitoring the system directly. The average response time can also be calculated using a model that represents the system behavior, as discussed in Chap. 4.

Figure 2.5 shows a typical curve of response time versus throughput for an on-line system. For a load of 3 transactions per second (tps), the average response time R is 0.14 sec. The service level agreed by users and the IS management determines that the average transaction response time should not exceed 0.2 sec. The dashed line in Fig. 2.5 indicates the acceptable

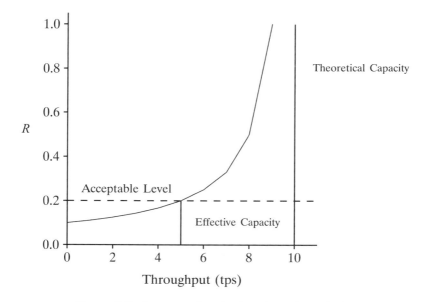

Figure 2.5 Response time (sec) × throughput (tps).

service level for response time. The vertical solid lines represent the effective and theoretical capacity of the system. Under heavy load, the system is able to process 9 tps, but the average response time approximates 1 sec, which is unacceptable for the current service level. Thus, the theoretical capacity of 10 tps is not useful to users because the corresponding response time far exceeds the acceptable level of service. A more realistic definition is that of the *effective capacity* of a system, defined as the largest throughput at which response time remains acceptable. In fact, responsiveness limits the amount of effective work processed by a system [2]. In Fig. 2.5, the effective capacity is 5 tps. Another important issue is that performance can only be discussed within the context of a defined workload. Performance by itself has no meaning; it must refer to a specific workload. In our example, throughput of 10 tps corresponds to the number of debit/credit transactions processed by the system. For instance, if the same system were to be used to process transactions generated by an inventory control application (which are more complex than debit/credit transactions), different performance figures would result.

Up to this point, the computing system has been viewed as a whole. System components have not been considered in isolation. Often, capacity planning studies require knowledge of the characteristics of the individual components of a system. For instance, Fig. 2.6 shows the main components of a typical file server configuration. Suppose that a file server in a LAN-based system is bogged down and request response times are too high. When analyzing the server, the performance analyst might find that the bottleneck is the processor. It might be interesting to predict the impact on performance if the processor were replaced by another processor three times faster. However, what does "three times faster" mean? The issue is that sometimes comparisons between system components are needed.

There are several performance measures that can be used to compare processors, I/O devices, and network components. Time and rate are the basic measures of a component's performance. Computer vendors refer to the speed of a processor by its cycle time, which can be expressed by its length [e.g., 20 nanoseconds (nsec)] or by its rate (e.g., 50 MHz). Another popular

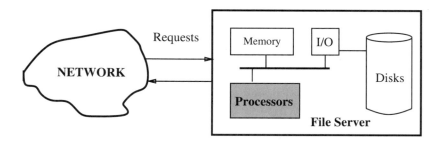

Figure 2.6 Configuration of a file server.

measure adopted to compare the performance of processors is MIPS (*millions of instructions per second*), which is defined as

$$\text{MIPS} = (\text{instructions/cycle}) \times (\text{cycles/second}) \times 10^{-6} \qquad (2.1)$$

The performance of a 20-nsec cycle time processor which executes an average of 0.8 instructions per cycle would be 40 MIPS. Although MIPS has been employed largely as a basis for comparisons of processors, it is important to warn the reader about the problems with its use. MIPS is dependent on the instruction set, which makes difficult the comparison of computers with different repertoires of instructions. For instance, using MIPS to compare the performance of a reduced instruction set computer (RISC) and a complex instruction set computer (CISC) has little meaning since an operation performed by one CISC instruction may require many instructions in a RISC machine. Thus, the MIPS of a VAX architecture and the MIPS of a SPARC architecture are not comparable. In the realm of multiprocessing, MIPS is also a meaningless metric. A multiprocessor with 32 processors of 10 MIPS is not equivalent to a 320 MIPS single processor. MIPS is not a scalable metric. Also, since MIPS is not defined in a domain of any specific application, its use may be misleading. Different programs running on the same computer can yield different MIPS ratings.

Because of the problems involved in the definition of MIPS, standard programs, known as *benchmarks*, have been used to evaluate the performance of processors. Benchmarking refers to running a set of standard programs on a machine to compare its performance with that of others. Several benchmarks have been proposed to measure hardware and basic software speed, including compilers and operating systems. The most often cited are Whetstone, Dhrystone, Linpack, Perfect Club, and SPEC [3].

Modern computer systems exhibit a large variation in the performance of different applications. No single number can represent the performance of a computer system on all applications. A consensus has evolved regarding the importance of domain-specific benchmarks. SPEC, for instance, is a benchmark suite intended to represent engineering and scientific applications that run on workstations [4]. The SPEC benchmark suite is composed of 10 programs implemented in C and Fortran, it is CPU intensive, and it performs little I/O. SPEC results are given as performance relative to a VAX 11/780. The overall performance for the suite is indicated by the "SPECmark", defined as the geometric mean of the SPECthruput of the 10 programs. SPECthruput measures the amount of work that a system under test can perform relative to a reference system (e.g., a VAX 11/780).

TPC (Transaction Processing Council) is a consortium of vendors that defines benchmarks for on-line transaction processing (OLTP) and database domains [5]. The TPC benchmarks evaluate the processor, the I/O subsystem, the operating system, and the database management system. The benchmarks assess the performance of an entire system processing debit/credit transactions.

TPC runs three benchmarks: A, B, and C. The focus of the TPC-B benchmark is on the performance of the database components of a transaction processing environment. The TPC-A benchmarks also measure the network performance of OLTP environments. TPC-C is also an OLTP benchmark that includes multiple transaction types. TPC-C runs a mix of five concurrent transactions of various types and complexities. The main metric reported by TPC is the system throughput, measured in transactions per second (tps), under the restriction that 90% of all transactions have a response time of 2 sec or less.

The performance of magnetic disks is usually characterized by the time required to carry out an operation of reading or writing a block of data. The disk access time consists of the following components:

- *Seek time*, which corresponds to the time to move the arm of the disk to the destination track
- *Rotational delay*, which is the time for the requested sector to rotate under the head
- *Transfer time*, which represents the time to transfer the bits of a sector
- *Controller time*, which corresponds to the overhead of the I/O controller

Most current disks rotate at 3600 rotations per minute, have an average seek time between 12 msec and 20 msec, and have typical transfer rates between 1 and 4 Mbytes/sec. The average time to read/write a disk block can be computed as

avg. access time

$$= \text{avg. seek} + \text{avg. rotational delay} + \frac{\text{block size}}{\text{transfer rate}} + \text{controller time}$$

Assuming an average seek time of 20 msec, a transfer rate of 2 Mbytes/sec, a rotational delay of 8.33 msec (half of the average rotation time) and 2 msec for the controller overhead, the average time to read or write a 512-byte sector is 30.58 msec. If a new disk with an average seek time 50% shorter than the old disk is considered, the new average access time becomes 20.58 msec, an improvement of 33%. Average access time is often used as a reference measure for performance comparisons of disks in capacity planning studies.

When considering networks, the capacity measure *bandwidth* specifies the amount of data that can be transmitted over the channel per time unit. The unit of measurement is typically bits-per-second. Ethernet and token-ring networks, for instance, offer bandwidths of 10 and 16 Mbits/sec, respectively.

2.4.3 Time Windows

Every business experiences cycles. It may be a weekly one, paydays for instance, or it may be seasonal. A study described in [6] about workload volumes in a retail store showed that peak loading occurs during the Christmas holiday season. Several days in that period, such as the Saturday before Christmas are the peak volume days. Additional workload studies for the busiest days indicated that volume varied from hour to hour and that the peak hourly volume was approximately twice the average hourly volume.

Suppose that an analyst is undertaking a capacity planning study for the retail store. The company management's orientation is to guarantee customer satisfaction. The response times at the point of sales should be fast enough to avoid customers waiting in line. Thus, the peak hours of the peak day should be used as a *time window* for the analysis and for planning the computing system capacity. The time interval during which the system, the workload, and the performance indexes are observed represents the time window.

Due to the diversity of work in a data processing (DP) shop, several time windows can be identified. Batch systems are driven by the *batch window*, which corresponds to the time period when on-line systems are shut down. During this time window, systems are heavily loaded with nightly batch jobs that must finish before on-line systems arise.

Most shops that run on-line work during the day find the period of 8:00 p.m. to 6:00 a.m.—the batch window—critical for the production work. Usually, database updates, reorganizations, and backups are carried out in that period. Suppose that the batch window of a data processing shop is overloaded. CPU utilization during the period approximates 100%. If it is known that the applications being executed in the batch window cannot be shifted to different times of the day, then for all practical purposes the computing system is running out of capacity, no matter what the level of system utilization during daytime. If management is planning new batch applications, the batch window is the interval to be used as a basis for capacity studies. In other words, determining the time windows is the first step to an evaluation of the installed capacity of a computing system.

Once we have understood the importance of the time window, a natural question arises: How can these periods be identified? Figure 2.7 shows CPU utilization of a computer system over a 24-hour period. This overall system activity graph can be used to gain understanding of system characteristics and to identify time windows. The utilization curve due to on-line work exhibits two periods of peak load: 10:00 a.m. to 12:00 a.m. and 2:00 p.m. to 4:00 p.m. By the same token, we can also point out the batch window: 11:00 p.m. to 6:00 a.m. Graphs displaying the variation of application response times from hour to hour also contribute to the identification of intervals that best represent the system activities. Continuous observations of system behavior for days or weeks, depending on the nature of the business, allow the capacity planner to pick the appropriate time windows on which to base capacity planning studies.

One should note the clear difference between average daily CPU utilization versus the utilization during the time window. In the example of Fig. 2.7, the average CPU utilization over a 24-hour period is 63%, as indicated by the horizontal dotted line. Although, at first sight this number may indicate

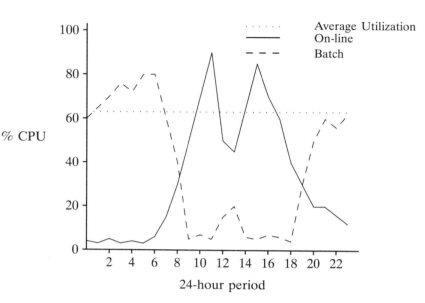

Figure 2.7 CPU utilization.

available capacity, examinations at the peak period, from 10:00 a.m. to 12:00 a.m., will lead to the conclusion that the system is almost saturated during this time window. Due to variations in the workload intensity over the day, average performance measures do not often describe the actual capacity. Most computer system installations have daily, weekly, or even monthly patterns of resource usage. Those patterns define peaks and valleys in system utilization, which clearly makes capacity a function of the time of day.

2.4.4 Service Levels

When one thinks about the quality of service provided by a telephone company to its customers, the following indicators naturally arise:

- 24-hour-a-day uninterruptible service
- Prompt dial tone
- Short repair-time in case of problems
- Very understandable bill

From the customer's point of view, the list of service characteristics above tailors the image of the company. Moreover, these indicators represent the level of service provided to customers at a given cost. The expected service levels rule the relationships between customers and the company. If the dial tone takes longer than usual or repair times exceed the acceptable limit, customers will certainly complain about the quality of service provided by the phone company. The source of the problems is immaterial to customers. They do not see the switching network, the trunks, and the links that constitute the telephone system. Resource utilization, blocking, and other measures of system capacity do not interest customers. What a customer sees is the level of service provided by the company.

Similarly, in a computing environment a user does not want to be involved with CPU utilization, memory contention, network bandwidth, and other indicators of system activities as well. A user looks for quality in the services provided by the computing environment, which is indicated by the service levels. Users perceive the computer services through performance metrics such as response time, *availability*, *reliability*, and cost.

When a system is working, performing user services, it is available. Availability is the metric used to represent the percentage of time a system is available during an observation period. UNIX systems, for example, have the command uptime, which displays the current time and the length of time the system has been up. The longer the uptime interval, the better the availability. When a system does not perform the user request correctly, an error has occurred in the processing of the request. Reliability measures the occurrence of failures during the processing of services. *Mean time to failure* (MTTF) is a measure of reliability.

During an observation period of one week (168 hours), a file server failed three times and had three periods of downtime (d1, d2, and d3), as indicated in Fig. 2.8. The intervals between the three failures were 48 and 72 hours, respectively. After the first failure (F1), the server remained down for 2 hours. The second and third failures implied in 4 and 1 hours out-of-service, respectively. The availability during the period was 95.8% [(168 − 7)/168 × 100] and the MTTF in the same interval was 60 [(48 + 72)/2] hours. Thus, the availability measure in a given interval is defined as follows.

$$\text{availability } (\%) = \frac{\text{interval length} - \text{total downtime}}{\text{interval length}} \times 100 \qquad (2.2)$$

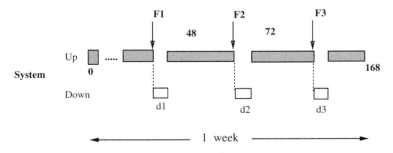

Figure 2.8 Intervals of operation of a file server.

Service level goals should be stated precisely. In the process of specifying them, one should avoid vague statements such as the following

- Response time satisfactory to the end users
- Availability better than before
- As reliable as possible

By contrast with the examples above, service levels should be stated through specific performance goals, as follows.

- Throughput of 30 debit/credit transactions per second, with at least 90% of the transactions responding in less than 2 sec.
- Average response time of 1 sec for *trivial transactions*, defined as a special class of transactions that place very little demand on system resources. For instance, trivial transactions could be characterized as demanding less than 5 msec of CPU and fewer than six I/O operations.
- File server availability of 98% during each one-month period.
- Average response time of 0.5 sec for commands from local terminals and 1.5 sec from remote ones.
- Mean time to failure (MTTF) of the disk subsystem should exceed 10,000 hours.

Before deciding on future service levels, the capacity planning analyst should assess the current level of service provided by the existing environment. This initial evaluation helps to identify problems as well as to detect services that are adequate to users. Many times, working procedures are associated with response time in on-line environments. An abrupt improvement in response time may cause negative impact to users. In a study reported in Ref. [7], in a group of terminal operators doing complex circuit layout, a 12-sec response time was considered optimal, because the group's error rate increased when response time varied from the 12-sec range. So it is important to be consistent in establishing new service levels.

After assessing the current level of service, management faces the following question: Do the service levels need to be changed? If they are unsatisfactory to the users or if they have to be changed as a function of business goals, new service levels should be determined. Following are some helpful criteria to establish new service levels.

- *Cost × benefit.* Service levels depend on both the workload and the system configuration. Improving service levels usually implies an expansion of system capacity. This means cost. A trade-off analysis between benefits and cost should be carried out. For instance, response time has repeatedly been reported to be inversely proportional to user productivity.

The shorter the response time, the higher the productivity. According to Ref. [8], a response time reduction from 1 sec to 0.3 sec in a conventional interactive work resulted in a 34% reduction in think time, which means an increase in the number of transactions submitted by users per time unit. Does the productivity increase compensate for the cost incurred to reduce response time in the system expansion? A popular saying in business, known by the acronym TINSTAAF (there is no such thing as a free lunch), perfectly applies to the problem of setting up service levels. The better the service level, the higher the system cost. For example, a transaction processed within a 3-sec response time may cost 50 cents, while a transaction executed with a 12-sec response time may cost only 5 cents [9]. Managers and users should discuss performance goals in light of the cost of providing the services.

- *Competition.* To stay in business, companies often have to catch up with customer services provided by competitors. As a matter of fact, these are the cases where the service levels are set outside the companies (i.e., by the competitors). For example, if the competition announces a new 24-hour nonstop on-line customer service, other companies in the same business might feel forced to provide the same kind of services to their customers, which means establishing new service levels for the computer systems.

- *Nature of the application.* To be acceptable to customers, customer service applications such as point-of-sale and airline reservation systems must provide fast response times. An airline reservation system decided to guarantee that 90% of the transactions should respond in 3 sec or less, with an average of 1.5 sec. According to Ref. [10] the airline company could not afford to leave a reservation agent or an airport agent, who has to deal with passengers, waiting much longer than 3 sec. Real-time applications that deal with customers or control manufacturing and other critical systems must respond to requests within specified time limits.

- *Past Performance goals.* Performance levels attained in the past can help IS management and users to reach an agreement for future service levels. Users have established expectations based on their past experience about the time required to complete a given task.

2.4.5 Overall Description

The first step in capacity planning methodology results in an overall description of current applications and the computing environment on which they are based. This high-level description gives the managers and capacity planners a definition of where the information systems are, before deciding where the company wants them to go. Identification of problems and critical concerns should also be part of this initial assessment of the information systems. The overall description should include the following information.

Major applications.   Major applications are those that have great impact on the definition of the capacity of future computing systems. Applications can be separated into two categories: production systems and user systems. The latter are characterized as being controlled and submitted by users. These applications consist of unstructured interactions, represented by activities such as decision support systems, adhoc queries to databases, editing, graphics, and test computations. This class of applications constitutes an *interactive* workload, characterized by the number of terminals and the average think time.

Production systems, also called mission-critical applications or control systems, represent those applications on which a company relies to operate. These applications keep track of inventory, checking accounts, finances, personnel, and related activities. Usually, they have centralized control and exhibit regularity in their patterns of hardware utilization. Production systems are referred to as batch systems or on-line transaction processing systems. A *batch workload* comprises the batch jobs submitted to the system. It is characterized by the average number of jobs executing simultaneously in the system. A *transaction workload* consists of on-line applications oriented to preplanned interactions that generate transactions, which often involve access to database systems; it is characterized by the transaction average arrival rate to the system.

Most IS shops exhibit a mix of workloads that combine the three classes: batch, transaction, and interactive. A key issue in this type of environment is determination of the percentage of each class as part of the overall workload in a given time window. The first part of the high-level description is aimed at specifying the company's major applications.

Computing environment.   The description of the computing environment has two parts: the mainframe-based systems and the distributed systems, composed of workstations, servers, and networks. Most companies combine these two types of systems into an integrated environment that supports the corporate information systems.

- Mainframe-based environment
  - CPU, specified by the number of processors and their capacity
  - Main memory, specified by the number of megabytes installed
  - I/O system, specified by the number of I/O processors or channels, capacity of the magnetic disk subsystem, and the number of tape drives

— Network system, specified by the number and capacity of front-end processors and the number of local and remote terminals connected to the system
— Operating systems
— Transaction monitors
— Database management systems

- Distributed Systems

  — Workstations, specified by their capacity
  — Servers, specified by their functions (e.g., file server, image processing server, printer server, etc.) and capacity of their processors and peripherals
  — Network, specified by the bandwidth and type of access protocol (e.g., Ethernet or token-ring)
  — Network operating systems

Time windows.   The identification of time windows allows the determination of measurement sessions, which are the intervals of time during which systems are monitored and performance data collected. The measurement data serve both as input to the workload characterization process and as reference to the model validation phase.

Service levels.   Once the major applications have been identified, the next step is assessment of the current service levels for these applications during the chosen time windows. According to the class of the application, the following measures should be reported in this phase:

- On-line response time
- Interactive user response time
- Batch turnaround time
- System throughput
- System availability

Batch turnaround time corresponds to the interval of time between the submission of a batch job and the completion of its output.

2.5 THE PROBLEM OF WORKLOAD CHARACTERIZATION

To help us understand the problem of workload characterization, consider a user working in a UNIX environment on his or her workstation, which is linked to a network system, as shown in Fig. 2.9.

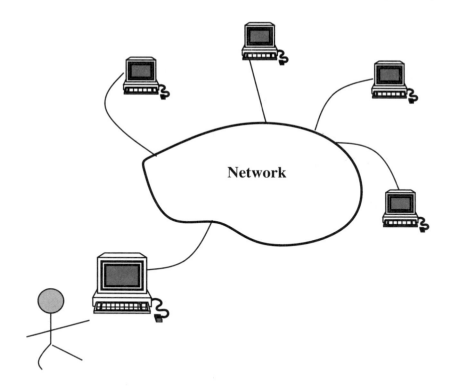

Figure 2.9 Network of workstations.

During the observed session, the user sent a message, previously stored in a file named text, to 12 chosen colleagues, also in the network. Thus, the user executed the command % mail colleague < text 12 times. What is the workload presented to the workstation in the period of time corresponding to the session?

According to the definition in Ref. [11], the term *workload* designates all the processing requests submitted to a system by the user community during any given period of time. Thus, the workload in question consists of the sequence of mail commands submitted by the single user of our example. How could this workload be characterized? In other words, how could the workload be described precisely?

2.5.1 First Approach to the Problem

The first step in the characterization process is identification of the basic components of the workload of a computer system. The *basic component* refers to a generic unit of work that arrives at a system from an external source. The nature of the service provided by the system determines the type of basic component. Common types are the job, the transaction, the command, and the request. In a mainframe environment, the most common basic components are both the job and the transaction. In an environment where users interact directly with the operating system, the command constitutes a basic component. In a UNIX workstation, for instance, users interact with the system through the shell commands, such as ls, cat, more, ..., etc., which comprise a workload. The basic component of the workload presented to a file server in a distributed environment is the request for service [12]. READ and WRITE operations to files are among the requests made by a diskless workstation to a file server. The file system requests received by a server from the workstations and other servers during any period of time make up the server's workload.

There are many forms of workload characterization. The one to be chosen depends on the purpose of the characterization. Basically, a characterization process yields a workload model that can be used in several activities, such as selection of computer systems, performance tuning, and capacity planning. Our interest concentrates on building workload models for capacity planning purposes, as illustrated by Fig. 2.10. The characterization process analyzes a workload and identifies its basic components and features that affect the system's performance. It also yields parameters that retain the characteristics capable of driving performance models used for capacity planning activities.

At the highest level, the *functional characterization* describes the programs or applications that make up the workload. In our example, the workload consists of a series of mail commands. This type of characterization does not depend on the underlying computer system, which makes the characterization system independent. For capacity planning purposes, a purely functional model presents a serious problem. It does not capture any quantitative information about the resource consumption behavior. This complicates the accomplishment of some basic capacity planning activities, such as sizing a system or evaluating the performance of a new machine. These activities typically

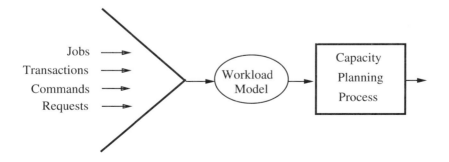

Figure 2.10 Workload characterization process.

require quantitative information about the workload as input. For example a `mail` command that sends a large text file to another user consumes much more CPU and I/O time than a `mail` command that contains just a short message. Thus, to make the characterization useful, it is necessary to include in the model some high-level information about resource requirements. For instance, a `mail` command could be described by the number of CPU instructions and I/O operations executed; a short `mail` command executes 50,000 CPU instructions and 20 I/O operations.

At the physical level, the *resource-oriented characterization* describes the consumption of the system resources by the workload. The resources to be included in the characterization are those whose consumptions have a significant impact on performance [11]. The `mail` command used for sending messages performs the following functions: read the file that contains the message, places it in an output file, and start up a process that will take care of sending the message through the network. Thus, the CPU and the I/O system (e.g., disks) are the main physical resources of the workstation employed in this execution. The network itself does not influence execution of the `mail` command, which is then characterized in terms of CPU and I/O time involved in its execution. The pair (CPU time, I/O time) characterizes the execution of a `mail` command in the workstation. All major operating systems provide facilities for determining how much CPU is being consumed by a particular process. Usually, the OSs include accounting logs that record the hardware resource usage by each process execution. CPU time, elapsed time, total I/O operations, core memory usage, and number of page faults are examples of the type of process execution information existing in a system accounting file.

2.5.2 Simple Example

Let us assume that the user of our preceding example sent exactly the same message to the 12 colleagues. This involves having about the same amount of CPU and I/O time for each of the 12 executions of the `mail` command. From data available in the system accounting files, we got the following characterization: 12 commands represented by the pair (CPU time, I/O time) = (0.01, 0.125). Now, let us consider that messages have different sizes, ranging from one to several pages. This results in variable-size input files, leading to variations in the values of the two parameters chosen for the characterization of this workload.

Table 2.1 shows the CPU, I/O, and execution times for each of the 12 `mail` commands with input files of different sizes. The execution time corresponds to the response time perceived by the user. The average response time equals 1.23 sec. Looking at Table 2.1, we note that each execution is represented by a different pair of values of CPU and I/O times. Which pair should be chosen as a representation for the 12 executions?

Table 2.1 Execution Time (in Seconds) of the `Mail` Command.

Command No.	CPU Time	I/O Time	Execution Time
1	0.02	0.12	0.24
2	0.03	0.14	0.31
3	0.05	0.18	0.36
4	0.09	0.25	0.43
5	0.60	1.00	2.00
6	0.72	1.12	2.10
7	0.08	0.20	0.38
8	0.11	0.30	0.48
9	0.91	1.50	3.00
10	0.81	1.20	2.20
11	0.08	0.25	0.41
12	0.96	1.50	2.90
Average	0.37	0.65	1.23

A key issue in workload characterization is *representativeness*, which indicates the accuracy in representing the real workload. Bearing this in mind, the next step is to determine a characterization for the workload described by Table 2.1. The first idea that comes to mind is that of a *typical mail command*, averaged over all the executions. Its characterizing parameters are the average CPU and I/O times. Table 2.2 shows the pair of parameters of a single command that now characterizes the workload displayed in Table 2.1. The real workload is now represented by a model composed of 12 commands characterized by the pair (0.37, 0.65), which places on the workstation the same CPU and I/O demands as those placed by the original commands. But how accurate is this representation?

One technique for assessing the accuracy of a workload model relies on an analysis of the effect caused on the system when a model replaces the actual workload. In a more general way, as proposed by Ferrari [11], the basic tenet of the workload characterization process can be stated as follows: A workload model $\mathcal{W}$ is a perfect representation of the real workload $\mathcal{R}$ if the performance measures (P) obtained when running $\mathcal{W}$ and $\mathcal{R}$ in the same system are identical, as shown in Fig. 2.11. Considering that the purpose of our workload characterization is to provide information to performance models, response time can be used to evaluate the accuracy of the workload model. Thus, the characterization is accurate if the response time of the workstation running the workload model is close to the average response time measured during execution of the real workload. If the response time of the execution

Table 2.2 Single-Class Characterization.

Type	CPU Time (sec)	I/O Time (sec)	Number of Components
Single	0.37	0.65	12
Total	4.46	7.76	12

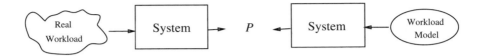

Figure 2.11   Representativeness of a workload model.

of the command characterized by (0.37, 0.65) approximates 1.23, the *typical command* turned out to be a good model.

Examination of the values displayed in Table 2.1 leads to a refinement in the characterization process. The average response time of 1.23 does not adequately reflect the behavior of the actual response times perceived by the user. Measured response times can be grouped into two distinct classes. The short response time class includes those values in the range 0.24 to 0.48 sec. The long response time group varies between 2.00 and 3.00 sec. Due to the heterogeneity of the components of a real workload, it is difficult to generate an accurate characterization if the workload is viewed as a single collection of commands. In the attempt to improve representativeness, the original workload is partitioned into two classes, based on resource usage.

A *class* comprises components that are similar to each other concerning resource usage. The first class, named *short messages*, includes those executions whose CPU and I/O times vary from 0.02 to 0.20 and 0.12 to 0.30, respectively. The response time of short messages ranges from 0.24 to 0.48. The other class, called *long messages*, consists of those executions whose CPU time range from 0.60 to 0.96 and I/O times vary from 1.00 to 1.50, respectively. Response times are in the interval 2.00 to 3.00. Table 2.3 presents two pairs of average parameters that now represent the original workload. Clustering the commands into two classes preserves some important features of the real workload and makes clear the distinction between commands that demand different amounts of resource time.

Let us take a look at the following example, which shows the importance of classes in the context of capacity planning. Suppose that the user of our example came to the conclusion that long files of text are too expensive to be sent through the command mail. A file transfer program (ftp) is to be used for long files. Before implementing the change, the user wants to evaluate its effect on response time. This kind of question could not be answered by a model with a single class, because the group of long messages is not explicitly represented. Breaking down the workload into classes increases the predictive power of a model.

Table 2.3   Two-Class Characterization.

Type	CPU Time (sec)	I/O Time (sec)	Number of Components
Short messages	0.07	0.21	7
Long messages	0.80	1.26	5
Total	4.46	7.76	12

Up to now, we have seen how to cluster a series of `mail` commands and represent them by one or more classes of commands. But one factor is missing to complete the characterization: the rate at which the `mail` commands are submitted to the workstation. When a user interacts with a system, as in our example, the average think time determines the intensity of the load. *Think time* is defined as the interval of time that elapses since the user receives the prompt (e.g., the % in UNIX) until he or she issues a new command. Figure 2.12 illustrates a user session that alternates between execution time (system response time) and think time.

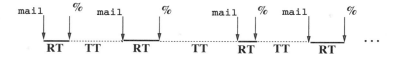

RT: response time   TT: think time

Figure 2.12 User session.

The workload of our previous example is simple and small: only 12 identical commands. In this case, if we wanted to test the performance of a faster workstation, it would be easier to run the real workload in the new machine, instead of building a workload model. *Real workloads* consist of all the original programs, transactions, and commands processed during a given period of time [11]. However, real systems exhibit very complex workloads, composed of thousands of different programs, transactions, and commands. It would be unrealistic, even impossible, to consider the use of real workloads in capacity planning studies, where several different scenarios of hardware and software are analyzed—hence the importance of building *workload models* that are compact and represent with accuracy the real workload.

2.5.3 Workload Model

A workload model is a representation that mimics the real workload under study. It would not be practical to have a model composed of thousands of basic components to mimic the real workload. This observation brings out another important issue: *compactness*. A compact model should place on the system a demand much smaller than that generated by the actual workload. Let us take as an example the characterization of the `mail` workload. The first model we built consists of a single typical `mail` command. The execution of a single command allows us to analyze the performance behavior of the execution of the real workload, which has 12 commands. Thus, a model should be representative and compact. Workload models can be classified into two categories, according to the way they are constructed:

- *Synthetic models* are constructed using basic components of the real workload and specially developed components (e.g., kernels and synthetic programs) as building blocks. When only subsets of the basic components are employed, the model is called natural synthetic or benchmark. A hybrid synthetic model consists of both subsets of the real workload and specially constructed components.
- *Artificial models* do not make use of any basic component of the real workload. Instead, these models are constructed out of special-purpose programs and descriptive parameters. We can also separate the artificial models into two classes: executable and non-executable models.

The executable artificial models consist of a suite of programs written especially to experiment with various aspects of a computer system. The class of executable models include workloads such as *instruction mixes, kernels*, and *synthetic programs*. Instruction mixes are hardware demonstration programs intended to test the speed of a computer on simple computational and I/O operations. Program kernels are pieces of code drawn out of the computationally intense parts of a real program. In general, kernels concentrate on measuring the performance of processors without considering the I/O system. Synthetic programs are specifically devised codes that place demands on different resources of a computing system. Unlike benchmarks, synthetic programs do not resemble the real workload. Benchmarks, synthetic programs, and other forms of executable models are not an adequate input for performance models.

When the performance of a system is analyzed through the use of analytical or simulation models, new representations for the workload are required. Because our approach to capacity planning relies on the use of analytical models for performance prediction, we focus on workload representations suitable for this kind of model. Due to their predictive power, analytical models form the core of capacity planning projects.

Nonexecutable workload models are described by a set of mean parameter values, that reproduce the resource usage of the real workload. Each parameter denotes an aspect of the execution behavior of the basic component on the system under study. The typical parameters used to describe a workload are the following:

- Program interarrival time
- Service demand
- Program size

- Execution mix (classes of programs and their corresponding levels of multiprogramming)

A study presented in Ref. [12] describes a parametric characterization of a workload on a distributed system file server. The study shows the factors that have a direct influence on the performance of a file server: system load, device capability, and locality of file references. From these factors, the following parameters are defined.

- Frequency distribution of the requests, which describes the participation of each request (e.g., read, write, create, rename, etc.) on the total workload.
- Request interarrival time distribution, which indicates the time between successive requests. It also indicates the intensity of the system load.
- File referencing behavior, which describes the percentage of accesses made to each file in the disk subsystem.
- Size of reads and writes, which have a strong influence on the time needed to service a request.

The parameters described above completely specify the workload model and are capable of driving synthetic programs that accurately represent real workloads. Could all of these parameters be represented in an analytical model?

Analytical models capture key aspects of a computer system and relate them to each other by mathematical formulas and/or computational algorithms. Basically, performance models require input information such as workload intensity (e.g., arrival rate, number of terminals, think time, etc.) and the service demand placed by the basic component of the workload on each resource of the system.

The representativeness of workload models for analytical models is limited. Very often, simplifying assumptions are introduced in the workload representation so that the solution of the analytical model can be kept simple and efficient. For instance, some of the analytical models developed throughout the book consider the assumption of homogeneous arrivals, which asserts that the arrival rate of the workload model is independent of the queue size of the system under study. To illustrate the problem, let us examine the case of modeling Ethernet environments. The workload of an Ethernet network consists of the packets transmitted by workstations on the network and can be characterized by packet length and interarrival time statistics. With the purpose of simplifying the model, many studies on workload characterization of Ethernet environments assume homogeneous arrivals of packets. However, measurement experiments described in Ref. [13] show that the packet arrival process in Ethernet environments is bursty. The packet arrival pattern follows a train model, where the network traffic consists of a collection of packet streams flowing between various pairs of workstations [14]. One of the sources of this arrival pattern stems from the fact that messages transmitted are often much larger than the maximum packet size on the Ethernet and must be partitioned into smaller units that are transmitted consecutively. This operational behavior of Ethernet networks clearly contrasts with the homogeneous arrival assumption. So, what is the impact of this assumption? On one hand, the use of a homogeneous arrivals assumption simplifies the model solution. On the other hand, this assumption oversimplifies the workload representation and contributes to reducing its accuracy. The loss of accuracy does not, however, invalidate the use of simple models; they are still capable of capturing some fundamental performance properties of computer systems. Simple performance models are valuable tools for practitioners.

2.6 WORKLOAD CHARACTERIZATION METHODOLOGY

Once we have seen the main issues associated with workload characterization, let us describe the steps required to construct a workload model to be used as input to analytical models. Our approach focuses on resource-oriented characterizations of workloads.

2.6.1 Identification of the Basic Component

In this step, we identify the basic components that form the workload. Job, transaction, command, and request are the most usual components. The choice of the component depends both on the nature of the system and the purpose of the characterization. The product of this step is a statement like this: The workload under study consists of transactions and commands.

2.6.2 Choice of the Characterizing Parameters

Once the basic components have been identified, the next step is choosing which parameters characterize each type of basic component. In fact, the nature of the characterizing parameters has already been defined by the input information required by analytical models. The parameters can be separated into two groups. One concerns the workload intensity. The other group refers to service demands of the basic components. What is missing here is the definition of which system resources are represented in the model. Usually, the resources chosen are those that most affect the performance of the target system when executing the workload under study. In summary, each component is represented by two groups of information.

- Workload intensity
  — Arrival rate

— Number of terminals and think time
— Number of programs in execution simultaneously

- Service demands, which are specified by the K-tuple $(D_{i1}, D_{i2}, \ldots, D_{iK})$, where K is the number of resources considered and D_{ij} is the service demand requested by basic component i at resource j

2.6.3 Data Collection

The data collection step assigns values to the parameters of each component of the model. It generates as many characterizing tuples as the number of components of the workload. Data collection includes the following tasks:

- Identify the time windows that define the measurement sessions.
- Monitor and measure the system activities during the defined sessions. Accounting tools available in the operating system and software monitors may be used to this end.
- From the data collected, assign values to each characterizing parameter of every component of the workload.

2.6.4 Partitioning the Workload

Real workloads can be viewed as a collection of heterogeneous components. Concerning the level of resource usage, for instance, a batch job that performs the backup of a large database differs notably from an on-line transaction that updates the checking account of a client. Because of this heterogeneity, the representation of a workload by a single class often lacks accuracy. The motivation for partitioning the workload is twofold: to improve representativeness of the characterization and to increase the predictive power of the model. The latter stems from the fact that most forecasting methodologies rely on key indicators that are closely associated with specific classes of the workload, as shown in Sec. 2.7.2. Partitioning techniques divide the workload into a series of classes such that their populations are grouped into homogeneous components. The aim is to group components that are somehow similar to each other. But, what attribute should be used as a basis for the measure of similarity? A description of some attributes [15] used for partitioning a workload into classes of similar components follows.

Resource usage.   The resource consumption per component can be used to break the workload into classes or clusters. Table 2.4 illustrates an example of classes of commands in an interactive environment.

In this example, processor and I/O are considered the critical elements of the system. The attributes that divide the workload are the maximum CPU

Table 2.4 Workload Partitioning Based on Resource Usage.

Type of Command	Frequency (%)	CPU Time (msec)	I/O Operations
Trivial	50	20	5
Light	25	60	15
Medium	18	160	100
Heavy	7	500	250

time and number of I/O operations required by a command. The *light* class, for example, comprises those commands that demand more than 20 msec and less than 60 msec of CPU time and a number of I/O operations that varies between 6 and 15.

Applications.   A workload can have its components grouped according to the application to which it belongs. As an example, Table 2.5 displays the classes of a partitioned workload and their corresponding CPU utilization. Some applications do not need a separate representation. Applications that are neither significant in terms of resource consumption nor critical to the business can be grouped into a single class. In the example, this class is called *others.* The problem with the choice of this attribute is the existence of very heterogeneous components within the same application. We can envision a very large batch job that updates a database and trivial transactions that perform a simple query to the same database. These two types of components are completely different in terms of resource usage.

Table 2.5 Partitioning Based on Applications.

Application	CPU Utilization (%)
Point of sales	25
Inventory	17
Purchasing	12
Shipping	11
Accounting	10
Others	10
CPU Idle	15

Geographical orientation.   A workload can be divided along lines of geography. The location from which the components are submitted defines the class. Let us consider as an example a system dedicated to on-line processing of transactions generated by point of sales. One class corresponds to transactions submitted in the northwest, another refers to northeast, and so forth. Table 2.6 summarizes the example and indicates the percentage of processed transactions corresponding to each geographic region.

Table 2.6 Workload Partitioning Based on Geographical Orientation.

Class	Percent of Total Transactions
Northwest	28
Northeast	30
Midwest	20
Southeast	17
Other regions	5

Functional classes.   The components of a workload may be grouped into classes according to the functions being serviced. For instance, a study of a VAX/VMS computer system in an academic environment may divide the workload into functional classes [16], as shown in Table 2.7.

Table 2.7 Workload Partitioning Based on Functional Attribute.

Class
Basic services
Compilers
Editors
File utilities
Communication
Scientific computation
Graphics
Text processing
All others

Basic services are characterized by small system services that are widely used and that require little computation. Examples of these services include commands such as `login`, `logout`, `directory`, `submit`, `delete`, and `rename`. As a rule of thumb, one should try to keep the number of classes to the minimum needed by the capacity planning study. If the initial number of classes is too large, aggregations of classes should be carried out. A helpful hint for aggregation is the following: Concentrate on those classes of interest to the organization; collapse the rest into a single class. Let us assume that our interest is to analyze the impact of predicted growth of graphics and scientific computation on the performance of the system. In light of this goal, the workload should be partitioned into three classes: scientific computation, graphics, and all other applications. The remaining six classes are represented by the class *all others*.

Organizational units.   A workload can be partitioned based on the organizational units of a company. This attribute may be useful for companies that have their strategic planning and growth forecasts generated on an organizational basis. Table 2.8 displays an example of a workload divided into classes, taking the organizational structure as an attribute of similarity.

Table 2.8 Workload Partitioning Based on Organizational Attribute.

Class
Marketing
Manufacturing
Retail
Research and development
Other applications

Type.   Three types of classes may be used to categorize the components of a workload (Table 2.9). The types are defined by their mode of processing (i.e., batch or on-line) and by the parameters chosen to describe them.

Table 2.9 Workload Partitioning Based on Component Type.

Class
Interactive
Transaction
Batch

- *Interactive* or *terminal*: on-line processing class with components generated by a given number of terminals or workstations with a given think time
- *Transaction*: on-line processing class that groups components that arrive at a computer system with a given arrival rate
- *Batch*: refers to components executed in batch mode, that can be described by the number of active jobs in the system

To be useful in performance evaluation, analytical models require classes of homogeneous components with respect to resource usage. It is clear that some attributes do not partition the workload into classes of homogeneous components. For instance, let us consider the case of a workload composed of transactions and batch jobs. Three classes of transactions are identified: trivial, medium, and complex. For instance, a transaction that accesses only a few records of a database demands much less CPU and I/O time than one that involves joining more than two database relations. Thus, the partitioning based only on the type of component would group into a single class called *transaction* components that are heterogeneous in the use of resources. Therefore, it is desirable to partition a workload using multiple attributes.

Table 2.10 illustrates a partitioning based on two attributes: type and resource usage. Within the *batch* class, two types of jobs are identified in terms

Table 2.10 Workload Partitioning Based on
Multiple Attributes.

Number	Type	Resource Usage
1	Batch	CPU bound
2	Batch	I/O bound
3	Transaction	Trivial
4	Transaction	Medium
5	Transaction	Complex

of amount and mix of resources considered. Transactions are also grouped as
a function of the level of resources demanded.

2.6.5 Calculating the Class Parameters

As we saw in the beginning of this methodology, each component (w_i) is
characterized by a k-tuple of parameters $w_i = (D_{i1}, D_{i2}, \ldots, D_{iK})$, where K is
the number of resources considered and D_{ij} is the service demand requested
by component i at resource j. After partitioning the workload into a number
of classes, the capacity planner faces the following problem: How should one
calculate the parameter values that represent a class of components? Two
techniques have been widely used for that matter: averaging and clustering.

Averaging

When a class consists of homogeneous components concerning service demand, an average of the parameter values of all components may be
used to represent the parameter values for the class. Thus, for a class composed of p components, the arithmetic mean of each parameter of the tuple
$(D_{i1}, D_{i2}, \ldots, D_{iK})$ is given by

$$\bar{D}_j = \frac{1}{p} \sum_{l=1}^{p} D_{lj}, \qquad j = 1, 2, \ldots, K \qquad (2.3)$$

where $\bar{D}_j$ is the mean service demand of this class at resource j. The K-tuple
$(\bar{D}_1, \bar{D}_2, \ldots, \bar{D}_K)$ then represents a given class. To evaluate the homogeneity
of a class, a capacity planner may use some statistical measures of variability
such as variance, coefficient of variation, and the relative difference between
the maximum and minimum values observed in the class.

Clustering

Figure 2.13 shows a graph for the two parameters that define a given
workload composed of transactions. Each point (x, y) in the graph corresponds to an execution of a transaction. The y-axis represents the CPU time
demanded by an execution whereas the x-axis displays the I/O time.

Suppose that we want to partition the workload of Fig. 2.13 into classes of similar transactions. The question is: How should one determine groups of components of similar resource requirements? The answer lies in *clustering analysis*. Basically, clustering of workloads is a process in which a large number of components are grouped into clusters of similar components. Although clustering analysis could be performed automatically by specific functions of software packages such as SPSS and SAS, the capacity planning analyst must be aware of the fundamentals of this technique.

Before discussing the technique in detail, let us state the problem more precisely. Let a workload W be represented by a set of p points $w_i = (D_{i1}, D_{i2}, \ldots, D_{iK})$ in a K-dimensional space, where each point w_i represents a component of W and K is the number of service demand parameters. A clustering algorithm attempts to find natural groups of components based on similar resource requirements. Let the *centroid* of a cluster be the point whose parameter values are the means of the parameter values of all points in the cluster. To determine cluster membership, most algorithms evaluate the distance between a point w_i and the cluster centroids in the K-dimensional space. The point is then included in the cluster that has the nearest centroid in the parameter space. As noted from Fig. 2.13, the components of the workload are naturally grouped into three clusters, C_1, C_2, and C_3, whose centroids are indicated by a bullet. The component

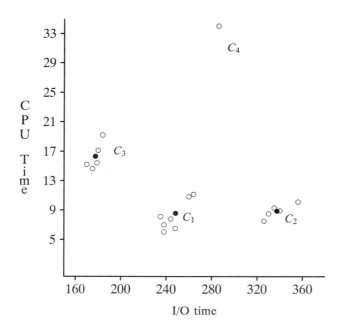

Figure 2.13 Resource demands of a simple workload.

represented by point C_4 is called an *outlier*, because it does not fit into any of the clusters within a reasonable distance.

The output from a cluster algorithm is basically a statistical description of the cluster centroids with the number of components in each cluster. For performance modeling purposes, each cluster defines a class of similar components. The characterization parameters of a class coincide with those of the cluster's centroid. The cluster analysis partitions a workload $\mathcal{W}$ into a set of R classes, as indicated by the following expression: $\mathcal{W} = \{w_1, w_2, \ldots, w_R\}$. Let us now describe the steps required to perform a clustering analysis of a given workload.

Data analysis. The first step prepares the raw data that characterize a workload. The input to this step consists of a set of K-tuples $(D_{i1}, D_{12}, \ldots, D_{iK})$ corresponding to the workload components. The input data analysis involves the following activities:

- Sampling drawing
- Parameter transformation
- Outlier removal

The number of components that make up a workload is a function of the length of measurement sessions. If this number is very large, a sample should be drawn from the measured workload. The purpose is to keep the processing time and amount of memory required to perform the clustering analysis within acceptable limits. Random sampling yields representative subsets of a workload. Special situations may, however, require other sampling criteria. For example, if the IS manager is interested in knowing the effect of large backup jobs on the response time of on-line transactions, the sample must include those backup jobs.

The distribution of each parameter of a tuple should undergo an analysis to eliminate values that may distort the mean parameter value. From the frequency distribution of a parameter, one may observe very few large values that correspond to a small percentage of the components (e.g., 1 or 2%). If a histogram is unable to exhibit useful information because of a highly skewed format of a distribution, a *logarithmic* or other transformation may be required to obtain a clearer representation of the data.

Parameter values that range over several orders of magnitude may lead to outliers. To prevent the extreme values of a parameter from distorting the distribution, one should use some kind of transformation or scaling. One technique consists of trimming the distribution and using the 95th or 98th percentile value as the maximum value in a linear transformation such as the following:

$$D_i{}^t = \frac{\text{measured } D_i - \text{minimum of } \{D_i\}}{\text{maximum of } \{D_i\} - \text{minimum of } \{D_i\}} \tag{2.4}$$

where D_i is the original service demand parameter i, D_i' is the transformed parameter, and $\{D_i\}$ represents the set of all measured values of D_i. The transformation above maps the parameter values onto the interval from 0 to 1. Outlier analysis should be done carefully to avoid the elimination of a very few components that have great impact on the system performance. As an example, jobs that reorganize large databases are among the heaviest resource consumers. Depending on how often they run, these jobs may be classified as outliers or they may form a special class in the workload characterization. For a complete treatment of this subject see Ref. [14].

Distance measures.   The distance between two points is the most common metric used by clustering techniques to assess similarity among components of a workload. A popular distance measure is the *Euclidean metric*, which defines the distance (d) between two points $w_i = (D_{i1}, D_{i2}, \ldots, D_{iK})$ and $w_j = (D_{j1}, D_{j2}, \ldots, D_{jK})$ as follows:

$$d = \sqrt{\sum_{n=1}^{K} (D_{in} - D_{jn})^2} \tag{2.5}$$

The use of raw data on the computation of Euclidean distances may lead to distorted results. For example, let us consider that the execution of a program in a diskless workstation is characterized by two variables: CPU time and physical memory usage. Table 2.11 presents the information concerning the execution of three programs, labeled A, B, and C. CPU time is measured in milliseconds and memory usage in kilobytes.

The Euclidean distances, calculated according to Eq. (2.5), are as follows:

$$d_{AB} = \sqrt{(2000 - 6600)^2 + (194 - 170)^2} = 4600.06$$

$$d_{AC} = \sqrt{(2000 - 10,000)^2 + (194 - 80)^2} = 8000.81$$

$$d_{BC} = \sqrt{(6600 - 10,000)^2 + (170 - 80)^2} = 3401.19$$

We can note from the results above that point B is closer to C than to A. Let us now change the unit of the parameter that represents CPU time,

Table 2.11   Execution Profile.

Program	CPU Time (msec)	Memory Usage (Kbytes)
A	2000	194
B	6600	170
C	10,000	80
Mean	6200	148
Standard deviation	4014.97	60.10

from milliseconds to seconds. The new values of CPU time for programs A, B, and C are 2, 6.6, and 10 sec, respectively. Thus, the Euclidean distances among the same points become

$$d_{AB} = \sqrt{(2 - 6.6)^2 + (194 - 170)^2} = 24.44$$

$$d_{AC} = \sqrt{(2 - 10)^2 + (194 - 80)^2} = 114.28$$

$$d_{BC} = \sqrt{(6.6 - 10)^2 + (170 - 80)^2} = 90.06$$

A change of parameter unit resulted in the modification of the relative distances among points A, B, and C. Now point B is closer to A than to C. When the CPU time was specified in milliseconds and memory usage in kilobytes, the first parameter dominated computation of the Euclidean distance, making the effect of the second parameter on the results negligible. Scaling techniques should be used to minimize problems that arise from the choice of units and from the different ranges of values of the parameters [17].

Scaling techniques.   Scaling is used to avoid problems arising from parameters with very different relative values and ranges. As we saw in the example of the computation of Euclidean distances, there are cases where it is desirable to work with unit-free parameters. Thus, a transformation is needed. The *z score* is a transformation that makes use of the mean and standard deviation of each parameter over the values measured. The *z* score of a given parameter is calculated as follows:

$$z \text{ score} = \frac{\text{measured value} - \text{mean value}}{\text{standard deviation}} \qquad (2.6)$$

Let us now calculate the *z* score of the CPU time parameter of Table 2.11. Both units (msec and sec) are used to show that the *z* score is unit-free. The mean and standard deviation for the CPU time in milliseconds are 62 and 40.15, respectively.

$$z_{CPU_A} = \frac{2000 - 6200}{4014.97} = \frac{2 - 6.2}{4.015} = -1.046$$

$$z_{CPU_B} = \frac{6600 - 6200}{4014.97} = \frac{6.6 - 6.2}{4.015} = 0.099$$

$$z_{CPU_C} = \frac{10,000 - 6200}{4014.97} = \frac{10 - 6.2}{4.015} = 0.946$$

scores for the parameter that represents memory use are as fol-

$$z_{memory_A} = \frac{194 - 148}{60.1} = 0.765$$

$$z_{memory_B} = \frac{170 - 148}{60.1} = 0.366$$

$$z_{memory_C} = \frac{80 - 148}{60.1} = -1.131$$

Clustering algorithms.   The goal of a clustering algorithm is to identify natural groups of components, based on similar resource requirements.
Various clustering algorithms are available in the literature. References [18]
and [19] present a thorough review of clustering techniques. They can be
grouped into two broad categories: hierarchical and nonhierarchical. The former includes those techniques where the input data are not partitioned into
the desired number of classes in a single step. Instead, a series of successive
fusions of data are performed until the final number of clusters is obtained.
Nonhierarchical techniques start from an initial partition corresponding to
the desired number of clusters. Points are reallocated among clusters so that
a particular clustering criterion is optimized. A possible criterion is the min-
imization of the variability within clusters, as measured by the sum of the
variance of each parameter that characterizes a point. Two widely known
clustering algorithms are discussed in detail.

The *minimal spanning tree* (MST) method is a hierarchical algorithm that
starts by considering each component of a workload to be a cluster. Next, the
two clusters with the minimum distance are fused to form a single cluster.
The process continues until either all jobs are grouped into a single cluster
or the final number of clusters desired is reached. The definition of the desired number of clusters may be obtained with the help of a measure called
linkage distance, which represents the greatest distance between a component
in one cluster and a component in another cluster [20]. The linkage distance
increases as a function of how different the components being combined are.
If it exceeds a given limit, the algorithm stops with the current number of
clusters. Considering a workload represented by p tuples $(D_{i1}, D_{i2}, \ldots, D_{iK})$,
the steps required by the MST algorithm [14] are shown in Fig. 2.14.

A *k-means algorithm* is a nonhierarchical clustering technique that begins by finding k points in the workload, which act as initial estimates of
the k cluster's centroids. The remaining points are then allocated to the
cluster with the nearest centroid. The allocation procedure iterates several
times over the input points until no point switch cluster assignment or a maximum number of iterations is performed. Having as input data the p points
$w_i = (D_{i1}, D_{i2}, \ldots, D_{iK})$, the steps required by the k-means algorithm are
shown in Fig. 2.15.

---

1. Set the initial number of clusters equal to the number of components of the workload (i.e., $j = p$).
2. Repeat the following steps until the final number of clusters is obtained.
3. Determine the parameter values of centroid C_j of each of the j clusters. Their parameter values are the means of the parameter values of all points in the cluster.
4. Calculate the $j \times j$ intercluster distance matrix, where each element (m, n) represents the distance between the centroids of clusters m and n.
5. Determine the minimum nonzero element (q, r) of the distance matrix. It indicates that clusters q and r are to be merged. Then decrease the number of clusters ($j \leftarrow j - 1$).

Figure 2.14   Minimal spanning tree algorithm.

---

1. Set the number of clusters to k.
2. Choose k starting points, to be used as initial estimates of cluster centroids. For example, one can select either the first k points of the sample or the k points mutually farthest apart. In this case, the distance matrix is required.
3. Examine each point of the workload and allocate it to the cluster whose centroid is nearest. The centroid's position is recalculated each time a new point is added to the cluster.
4. Repeat step 3 until no point changes its cluster assignment during a complete pass or a maximum number of passes is performed.

Figure 2.15 k-Means algorithm.

A common problem found in clustering analysis is the difficulty of deciding about the number of clusters present in a workload. For practical purposes in capacity planning studies, it is desirable to keep this number small. The value depends on factors such as the goals of the study, the number of critical applications and the modes of processing (e.g., transaction, interactive, or batch).

Example

To illustrate the use of clustering techniques, let us consider the example of a server composed of a fast processor and a large disk subsystem. The server is dedicated to on-line transaction processing. During a specific time window, the accounting logs of the operating system recorded the execution behavior of all transactions. With the purpose of keeping the example small, a random sample of the workload was drawn and six transactions selected. Table 2.12 shows the parameters that characterize execution of a transaction: CPU and I/O demands.

Table 2.12   Workload Sample.

Transaction	Service Demand (msec)	
	CPU	I/O
1	4	240
2	12	400
3	200	880
4	6	280
5	5	240
6	13	440

As can be noted from Table 2.12, the components of this workload are not homogeneous. A step-by-step description of the clustering process is now presented.

1. Because of the difference in magnitude in the values of CPU and I/O demands, a change of scale is required. Table 2.13 shows the parameter values transformed by a $\log_{10}$ function; that is, each value y in Table 2.13 is equal to $\log_{10} x$, where x is the value in Table 2.12 corresponding to y.

Table 2.13   Logarithmic Transformation of Parameters.

Transaction	Service Demand ($\log_{10}$)	
	CPU	I/O
1	0.60	2.38
2	1.08	2.60
3	2.30	2.94
4	0.78	2.45
5	0.70	2.38
6	1.11	2.64

2. Let us consider that our goal is to obtain three clusters. We use the Euclidean distance as the metric to evaluate distances between clusters. The MST algorithm is the one selected.

3. The initial number of clusters is set to 6, which is the number of components.

4. The parameter values of the centroids of each cluster coincide with the parameter values of the components, as shown in Table 2.14. In this case, each cluster has a single component.

5. Let us now calculate the intercluster distance matrix, using expression (2.5). For instance, we note from Table 2.15 that the distance between clusters C2 and C5 is 0.43.

6. The minimum distance among the clusters of Table 2.15 is that between C2 and C6 (i.e., 0.05). These clusters are merged to form a larger cluster C26 with centroid $[1.10 = (1.08 + 1.11)/2, \ 2.62 = (2.60 + 2.64)/2]$.

7. Now we have five clusters. Let us recompute the distance matrix for the new number of clusters (see Table 2.16).

Table 2.14 Centroids of the Initial Clusters.

Cluster	Parameters	
C1	0.60	2.38
C2	1.08	2.60
C3	2.30	2.94
C4	0.78	2.45
C5	0.70	2.38
C6	1.11	2.64

Table 2.15 Intercluster Distance Matrix.

Cluster	C1	C2	C3	C4	C5	C6
C1	0	0.53	1.79	0.19	0.10	0.57
C2		0	1.27	0.33	0.44	**0.05**
C3			0	1.60	1.70	1.23
C4				0	0.11	0.38
C5					0	0.48
C6						0

Table 2.16 Intercluster Distance Matrix.

Cluster	C1	C26	C3	C4	C5
C1	0	0.53	1.79	0.19	0.57
C26		0	1.24	0.36	0.47
C3			0	1.60	1.70
C4				0	**0.11**
C5					0

8. The smallest element of Table 2.16 corresponds to the distance between clusters C4 and C5, which are therefore merged. The parameter values of the centroid of C45 are $[0.74 = (0.78 + 0.70)/2,\ 2.42 = (2.45 + 2.38)/2]$.

9. The number of clusters is now 4, and the distance matrix for the new cluster configuration is given in Table 2.17.

Table 2.17 Intercluster Distance Matrix.

Cluster	C1	C26	C3	C45
C1	0	0.53	1.79	**0.15**
C26		0	1.24	0.41
C3			0	1.64
C45				0

10. In Table 2.17 the minimum distance is between clusters C1 and C45 (i.e., 0.15). These two clusters are merged and the centroid has the following parameters: $[0.69 = (0.60 + 0.70 + 0.78)/3,\ 2.41 = (2.38 + 2.45 + 2.40)/3]$. Now that we have obtained three clusters, the termination condition is true and the clustering process stops.

11. The original workload given in Table 2.12 has been partitioned into three classes of similar transactions. Each class is represented by parameter values that are equal to the average of the parameter values of all components of the class. Table 2.18 presents the output of the clustering process. It contains the description of the centroids that represent each cluster and its number of components. Each cluster corresponds to one class in the workload. In the example, classes are named according to their resource usage. For instance, the class of trivial transactions indicates that resource consumption is small: on the average 5.0 msec of CPU and 253 msec of I/O time. Note that the values in Table 2.18 were scaled back to the original millisecond scale. □

Table 2.18 Output of the Clustering Process.

Type	Class	CPU Demand (msec)	I/O Demand (msec)	Number of Components
Trivial	C145	5.0	253	3
Medium	C26	12.5	420	2
Complex	C3	200.0	880	1

2.7 WORKLOAD FORECASTING

What is the expected workload for next year? This a typical question that comes up often during the course of a capacity planning project. Before discussing the techniques available to answer this kind of question, let us first examine why workload changes must be predicted. Workloads change; they may grow or shrink, depending on the business prospective. A company that closes out a business line and eliminates the applications associated with that business provides an example of workload shrinking. However, the most common situation is that of workload increase. The workload growth comes primarily from the following sources: new applications, increase in the volume processed by existing applications, and enhancements of the application environment. Many installations run old applications that need to be upgraded to new technologies. New database management systems, new security software systems, and fourth-generation languages are examples of software resources usually incorporated in old systems. These software systems demand additional resources from the computer system and increase the workload.

Three problems are commonly faced by a capacity planner during the forecasting phase. First, it is difficult to obtain reliable information from users when they have to deal with terms whose exact meaning they do not quite understand. For the purpose of performance modeling, workload characterization has been defined as a set of parameters that specify the service demands and load intensity. Those parameters are too vague for the user community. It is also hard to obtain resource usage information for new systems that have not yet been developed completely. This problem is addressed in detail in Chap. 11. The third problem refers to the *latent demand*, which is a portion of the workload that is not submitted to the system, for several reasons. For example, a user may refrain from submitting transactions to a system when it is saturated and the response times are too long. Systems with poor turnaround times may discourage a programmer from submitting a large number of test cases. When capacity is upgraded and response times improve, users feel motivated to make more use of the system. Improvements in the service level create conditions for unexpected growth of workloads. In this section we discuss aspects and techniques for workload forecasting.

2.7.1 From Business Plans to Computer Demands

As specified in Sec. 2.6, the information required to characterize a workload can be divided into two groups: component and load intensity. The former describes the service demands required by a component of a class (e.g., program, job, transaction, or command). The second group indicates the load placed on the system by a class of programs. Table 2.19 summarizes the parameters that characterize each type of workload.

The ultimate goal of a forecasting process is to determine the parameters of the workload estimated for the planning horizon. Therefore, a capacity planning analyst should determine both the variations in the parameters of the existing workload and the parameters for new classes of workload. In other words, the forecasting process involves answering questions such as the following:

- What will be the demand made by the inventory application next year?
- What will be the arrival rate of trivial transactions of the checking account application?
- What will be the number of interactive users of a spreadsheet application?
- What will be the average number of production batch jobs running at night?

Answers to the questions above should come primarily from the users. Hence, the first step in the workload forecasting process is to consult the user community to determine the estimated growth in workload. Questionnaires and interviews are useful tools for getting forecasting information. In general,

Table 2.19   Class Parameters.

Type	Component	Load Intensity
Transaction	Service demands	Arrival rate
Interactive	Service demands	Number of terminals, think time
Batch	Service demands	Number of jobs

questionnaires and interviews help to identify problems in the computing services as well as to develop future plans concerning information systems. For instance, interviews can be an efficient way to locate users with latent demand due to poor service levels.

The major problem in contacting users relates to the nature of the information required by the workload forecasting process. The kind of information shown in Table 2.19 has nothing to do with the user world. One can easily imagine the perplexity of a user trying to answer a question about the amount of CPU time that his/her trivial transaction will demand next year. It is clear that alternative ways should be used to obtain quantitative information regarding future workload. Let us examine one approach that makes use of business-related information to predict workload growth.

In most companies, the business critical applications account for the major fraction of system resource usage. With direct relation to the business of a company, these applications perform such functions as inventory control, customer services, checking accounts, finances, and so on. The amount of computer resource required by these applications can be associated with some kind of quantifiable business variable, called a *key value indicator* (KVI), *natural business unit* (NBU), or *forecasting business unit* (FBU) [21, 22]. They provide a good indication of the volume of activity of a business or administrative function. Some examples of business units and their associated applications are shown in Table 2.20

Methodologies based on business units assume that the volume of business activity in a company may be related to demands for computer resources. Users estimate their computing needs in terms of business units, which are then converted to some form of computer requirements (e.g., CPU utilization, service demands, number of I/O operations, etc). The basic steps involved in workload forecasting using business units are as follows.

1. Select the applications to be forecasted. Look for the few major applications that account for most of the utilization of the computing resources. All other applications should be lumped together for forecasting purposes.
2. Identify the business units associated with the applications whose growth will be forecasted. For example, the number of orders placed by customers is a good business unit for an order-entry application.

Table 2.20 Natural Business Units.

Application	Business Unit
Checking account	Number of customers
Payroll	Number of employees
Inventory	Number of stock lines
Rental car	Number of vehicles
Accounts receivable	Number of invoices

3. Summarize the statistics (e.g., resource usage, number of transactions, etc.) of the applications selected. The frequency of execution of an application and the time window chosen determine the periodicity of the summarization. For instance, an order-entry transaction processing system should be analyzed on a daily basis.

4. Collect statistics concerning the business units chosen. In the example, obtain from the users the daily number of orders placed by customers.

5. Translate business units into computer demands. For example, divide the resource use in the time window selected by the number of orders processed in the same period. The result is an estimate of the amount of computing resources required by the system to handle a customer order.

6. Forecast the future resource demand as a function of the business units. In the example of an order-entry system, one should estimate the growth in the number of customer orders, which represent the business unit. Using some kind of forecasting technique, the capacity planner should be able to relate the future number of orders to the future workload demand.

2.7.2 Forecasting Techniques

The literature [7, 14, 22] describes several forecasting techniques. In selecting one of them, some factors need to be considered. The first is the availability and reliability of historical data. The accuracy degree and the planning horizon are also factors that determine the forecasting technique. The pattern found in historical data has a strong influence on the choice of the technique. The nature of historical data may be determined through visual inspection of a plot of the data as a function of time. As displayed in Fig. 2.16, four patterns of historical data can be identified: trend, cyclical, seasonal, and stationary. While the trend pattern reflects a workload that tends to increase (or decrease, in some cases), the stationary pattern does not show any sign of systematic increase or decrease. Seasonal and cyclical patterns are similar with respect to the presence of fluctuations. The difference is the periodicity of the fluctuations exhibited by the seasonal pattern. The underlying hypothesis of forecasting techniques is that the information to be forecasted is somehow directly related to historical data; this emphasizes the importance of knowing the pattern of historical data. Let us now examine in detail some forecasting methods. The techniques applied most often to workload forecasting are moving averages, exponential smoothing, and linear regression [23].

Moving average.   This is a simple forecasting technique that makes the value to be forecasted for the next period equal to the average of a number of previous observations. When applied to nearly stationary data, the accuracy achieved by the technique is usually high [22]. A major disadvantage of simple moving averages is that only one forecast value into the future can be calculated at a time. This technique is appropriate for short-term forecasting. The forecast value is given by the following expression:

$$f_{t+1} = \frac{y_t + y_{t-1} + \cdots + y_{t-n+1}}{n} \qquad (2.7)$$

where f_{t+1} is the forecast value for period $t + 1$, y_t the actual value (observation) at time t, and n the number of observations used to calculate f_{t+1}. As can be noted from expression (2.7), a forecast for time $t + 2$ cannot be made until the actual value for time $t + 1$ becomes known. One problem with this technique is the determination of n, the number of periods included in the averaging. One should try to select a value for n that minimizes the forecasting error, which is defined by the square of the difference between the forecast and actual values. The mean squared error (MSE) is given by

$$\text{MSE} = \frac{\sum_{t=1}^{n}(y_t - f_t)^2}{n} \qquad (2.8)$$

Different values of n may be tested to find the one that gives the smallest MSE.

    Example.   A capacity planning analyst is interested in analyzing the growth pattern of an inventory application that runs on a mainframe. Consumption of CPU time is the metric chosen by the analyst to indicate the activity level of the application. Thus, CPU hours were measured on a monthly

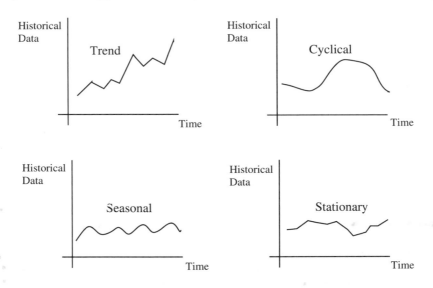

Figure 2.16 Historical data patterns.

Table 2.21 CPU Hours Consumed by the Inventory Application.

	CPU Hours	
Month	Observed	Forecast
April	38.0	-
May	35.0	-
June	41.0	-
July	44.0	38.0
August	39.0	40.0
September	46.0	41.3
October	42.0	43.0
November	40.0	42.3

basis for the inventory application. Table 2.21 exhibits the data observed for a period of eight months, ranging from April to November. The manager wants to know in advance what will be the CPU hours consumed by the application in December.

When applying the moving averages, three values of n were tried (3, 5, and 7) on the existing data. The use of three observations gives the smallest MSE. Thus, the CPU hours for December is given by $f = (40 + 42 + 46)/3 = 42.7$. □

Exponential smoothing. Exponential smoothing is similar to moving averages with respect to the way that both techniques calculate the forecast value. They both make the average of known observations equal to the forecast value. The difference is that exponential smoothing places more weights on the most recent historical data. The motivation for using different weights stems from the hypothesis that the latest observations give a better indication of the future. As with the moving averages, this technique is appropriate to data that present little variation and for short-term prediction. The forecast value is calculated as follows:

$$f_{t+1} = f_t + \alpha(y_t - f_t) \qquad (2.9)$$

where f_{t+1} is the forecast value for period $t + 1$, y_t the actual value (observation) at time t, and α the smoothing weight $(0 < \alpha < 1)$.

Example. Let us apply the exponential smoothing technique to the data shown in Table 2.21. The problem is to calculate the estimated CPU hours for December, given that we have historical data composed of eight observations. Table 2.22 displays the results using two values of α (0.25 and 0.6) for calculating the forecast value. The smallest MSE is provided by $\alpha = 0.25$. The estimated for December CPU hours is $f = 41.33 + 0.25(40 - 41.33) = 40.99$. Figure 2.17 displays a plot of the observed CPU hours

Table 2.22 CPU Hours Consumed by the Inventory
Application.

Month	CPU Hours		
	Observed	$\alpha = 0.25$	$\alpha = 0.6$
April	38	-	-
May	35	38.00	38.00
June	41	37.25	36.20
July	44	38.19	39.08
August	39	39.64	42.02
September	46	39.48	40.21
October	42	41.58	43.68
November	40	41.33	42.67

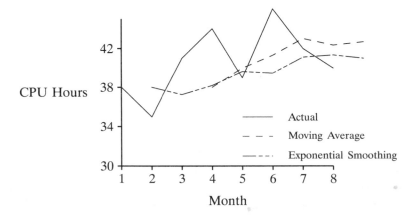

Figure 2.17 Monthly consumption of CPU hours.

consumed per month by the inventory application, as well as the forecast
values obtained with the moving averages and the exponential smoothing
techniques. □

Regression methods.   Regression models are used to estimate the value
of a variable as a function of several other variables. The predicted variable is
called the *dependent variable*, and those used to forecast the value are known
as *independent variables*. The mathematical relationship established between
the variables can take many forms. The most commonly used relationship
assumes that the dependent variable is a linear function of the independent
variables.

In this section we present simple linear regression analysis used to determine the linear relationship between two variables. The general equation
for the regression line is

$$y = a + bx \tag{2.10}$$

where y is the dependent variable, x the independent variable, a the y-intercept, and b is called the slope of the line that represents the linear relationship between the two variables. The *method of least squares* determines the values of a and b that minimize the sum of the squares of the error of forecasting. Thus,

$$b = \frac{\sum_{i=1}^{n} x_i y_i - n \bar{x} \bar{y}}{\sum_{i=1}^{n} x_i^2 - n(\bar{x}^2)} \tag{2.11}$$

$$a = \bar{y} - b\bar{x} \tag{2.12}$$

where $\bar{y} = \frac{1}{n} \sum_{i=1}^{n} y_i$, $\bar{x} = \frac{1}{n} \sum_{i=1}^{n} x_i$, and n is the number of observations.

Example.   Consider a client-server environment, where a number of workstations are connected via a LAN to shared resources, such as a file server and its disks [12, 24]. When focusing on the file server, one can view its workload as a series of requests for file services, made by the workstations. For characterization purposes, each request can be described by the service demands (e.g., CPU and disk times) that it places on the server. For instance, a client program writes Kx bytes to a remote file server through a sequence of K requests for writing x bytes. Table 2.23 displays the observed CPU time required by the server to execute a write request, for several values of x.

Let us examine the development of a simple linear regression model to forecast the server CPU time. The number of bytes to be written represents the independent variable (x) and the CPU time is the dependent variable (y). From the data of Table 2.23, we have $n = 10$, $\bar{x} = 2388.8$, $\bar{y} = 991.7$, $\sum x_i^2 = 85,632,384$, $\sum x_i y_i = 35,196,016$, $n\bar{x}^2 = 57,063,654$, $n\bar{x}\bar{y} = 23,689,729.6$, $b = 0.40276$, and $a = 29.587$. The expression for the linear relationship between the number of bytes (x) and the server CPU time (y) is $y = 29.587 + 0.40276x$. Thus, we can forecast the server CPU time for new values of x. For example, for $x = 7168$, the forecast CPU time is equal to 2916.57. □

Table 2.23 Server CPU Time per Write Request.

Bytes	CPU Time (μsec)	
	Observed	Forecast
128	82	81.10
512	200	235.80
1024	440	442.01
1400	610	593.54
1600	705	674.00
2000	860	835.10
3400	1360	1398.97
4096	1650	1679.29
4608	1920	1885.50
5120	2090	2091.71
7168	—	2916.57

Applying forecasting techniques.   Before performing the forecasting, the techniques selected should be validated on the available data. This can be done using only part of the historical data to exercise the model. The remaining data, which correspond to actual values, can then be compared to the forecasted values to assess the accuracy of the method. Tests can be made to assess the mean squared error (MSE) of each method under study, so that the one that gives the smallest MSE is selected.

For example, one of the major on-line applications of an equipment vendor is customer service tracking. The capacity planner wants to forecast the growth of this application for the next two years. As we saw earlier, an on-line workload is characterized by the transaction arrival rate and the service demands of a typical transaction. If the application forecasting process considers only the arrival rate growth, an important aspect will be ignored: the service demand variations. Let us focus on the customer database that supports the application. The size of this database is related directly to the number of customers. The larger the number of customers, the larger the database. As the database increases, the time required by a transaction to query or update information may also increase, because more I/O operations may be needed to access the desired information. As a consequence, the service demands may vary with the number of customers. The important issue here is that the process of workload forecasting should not be restricted to a specific parameter; it should cover all parameters that characterize the workload.

Future workloads can be forecasted in two different modes [22]: causal and trend. The causal mode uses business units as the independent variable and workload parameters as the dependent variable. For instance, a regression model can be used to estimate the future CPU demand of a payroll application as a function of the number of employees. The trend mode performs the forecast of a workload descriptor as a function of time, based only on historical data on the descriptor. In the same example, the future CPU demand could be calculated by a forecasting technique using as input data the past application CPU time recorded by the accounting logs.

2.8 PERFORMANCE PREDICTION

The heart of a capacity planning process is its ability to predict adequately the performance of a particular computer system configuration executing a given workload. Using this ability, the capacity planner may have to analyze several configurations, because so many options are available to construct a system solution. Workstations, servers, mainframes, special-purpose systems (e.g., OLTP systems), and networks may be combined into many different configurations. Because forecasts always carry a degree of uncertainty, various future workload scenarios should also be considered.

What is needed at this point in a capacity planning process is a technique that predicts performance. Having configuration alternatives and workload forecasts as input, a prediction technique should be able to calculate perform- ance measures for the systems considered. There is no need of very accurate predictions for use in capacity planning. What really counts in a planning process is the ability to obtain correct trends.

Figure 2.18 shows the typical output of a prediction technique. This graph plots response time of a transaction processing system as a function of workload intensity for various system configurations. Each scenario cor- responds to a specific forecast. Let us assume that scenario 2 is the most likely. For instance, assume that scenario 2 corresponds to an expected work- load of 15 tps for the next year. Two alternatives to the expected workload are also considered. Scenario 1 refers to a pessimistic growth estimate. A likely low growth would be, for example, 60% of the most probable value. Thus, scenario 1 projects 9 tps for next year. Scenario 3 considers an op- timistic business forecast, which would involve more transactions arriving at the system. We could view the optimistic forecast as being 160% of the most probable value. The dotted horizontal line indicates the acceptable limit for transaction response time, which is part of the service level agreement. As we can see, configuration C has the best performance among the three alterna- tives. It provides transaction response times within the acceptable limit. But, could we conclude that C is the best option? Clearly, configuration A is out

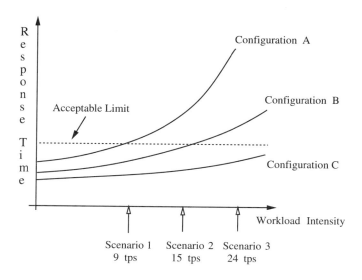

Figure 2.18 On-line transaction processing scenarios.

of the question, because it does not satisfy the service level requirement for any of the future scenarios. A cost comparison between B and C is missing in reaching the final decision. When considering various future scenarios, the capacity planner creates different alternatives for the system, with different service levels and costs. This kind of analysis encourages users to make better forecasts to obtain better cost-performance relations for their services.

What techniques are used for performance prediction? Various techniques have been described in the literature [7, 11, 14]. Basically, they differ in three aspects: complexity, accuracy, and cost. Figure 2.19 illustrates the spectrum of the most used prediction techniques [21], ranked in order from least to most complex and costly. It is expected that as complexity and cost increase, the technique becomes more accurate. At the low end of the figure, we see rules of thumb as a simple, easy-to-use technique, but without any guarantee of accuracy. At the high end, we have benchmarks that are accurate but are also costly and complex. Performance models based on analytical techniques or simulations are a middleground between benchmarks and rules of thumb. They have been widely used in performance prediction, because of their relative low cost, general applicability, and flexibility of use. Performance prediction is treated in detail throughout the rest of the book. Let us now review each of the other techniques noted in Fig. 2.19, pointing out their strengths and weaknesses.

2.8.1 Rules of Thumb

Rules of thumb are used to determine the overall system capacity as a function of the utilization of key individual components. By focusing on key resources, rules of thumb attempt to prevent excessive queuing delays that may degrade the responsiveness of a system as a whole. In general, rules of thumb define limits that should be used as guidelines. Usually, rules of thumb are extracted from manufacturers' information, production experience, benchmarks, and people's experience. Examples of some popular rules are as follows [7, 25].

- I/O channel utilization should be inferior to 35%.

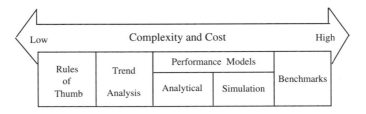

Figure 2.19 Performance prediction techniques.

- 80% of CPU utilization is a limit for good service.
- Peak utilization should not exceed 90%. If we assume a peak-to-average ratio of 2.25:1, average utilization should be inferior to 40%. The peak-to-average ratio is calculated assuming that a peak hour-to-average hour ratio is 1.5:1 and a peak day-to-average day ratio is also 1.5:1.

It is worth noting that rules are general in nature; specific DP shops may demonstrate large deviations. So be cautious in the use of rules of thumb! Usually, the CPU has been considered to be the key component of a system and performance limits are estimated based on it. Rules of thumb offer the advantage of simplicity, low cost, and ease of use. Although they may be useful in some cases, there are many hidden problems in the use of this simple technique, as pointed out in Chap. 1. First, it does not address the important issue of service levels; even though the utilization of the key resource is below the limit, there is no guarantee that performance measures satisfy the service level requirements. For instance, the response time of a transaction depends on the time it spends on each component of the system. If the bottleneck does not coincide with the key resource, it is useless to conduct an analysis based solely on this resource. In fact, this is a serious limitation on rules of thumb; they do not take into account the interactions among components of a system. The applicability of this technique to modern distributed systems is also limited, because of the difficulty of finding a single key resource. Therefore, we do not recommend its use in performance prediction.

2.8.2 Trend Analysis

Trend analysis can be viewed as a technique that predicts what will happen in a system, based on historical data regarding past behavior. In the case of capacity planning, historical data recorded by accounting logs are used to analyze the relationship between performance and workload. From these data one attempts to identify a trend in performance behavior. The prediction process consists of extrapolating the trend to the expected workload level.

Often, prediction is performed using linear extrapolation of recent trends, as shown in Fig. 2.20. From the expected workload intensity, one obtains the point corresponding to the performance value predicted.

There are problems with this kind of prediction technique. First, it assumes a linear relationship between performance and workload intensity. This assumption may be a valid approximation for lightly loaded systems, where the contention for resources is minimum. As the workload intensity rises, bottlenecks appear, congestion increases, and performance degrades at a very fast rate. Linear approximations do not maintain any resemblance to the real behavior. As we saw in several previous examples, real computer systems execute different classes of workload. Usually, trend analysis predicts performance for

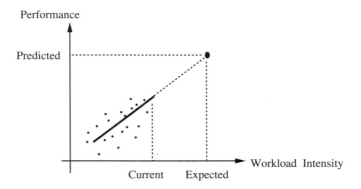

Figure 2.20 Performance prediction using trend analysis.

each class separately. In doing so, the negative effects on performance that stem from the interaction among classes that share common resources are ignored. Predictions become excessively optimistic.

2.8.3 Benchmarks

Computer system benchmarking has been regarded as a useful approach for predicting the capacity of new computer systems. A study aimed at predicting the performance of a system is viewed as being done correctly if both the workload and the system resources are adequately represented in the benchmark. In performance prediction, the key question is how a particular system configuration will perform when processing a given workload. To answer this question using the benchmark approach, one simply runs the workload on the system and measures the resulting performance. This direct measurement approach is only applicable to operational systems. Thus, an analysis of various configuration alternatives is not feasible in practice because of the high cost involved in setting up and running representative benchmark experiments. Distributed environments composed of multiple vendors make the problem even more critical. Another drawback in the direct measurement process is the impossibility of evaluating the impact of new applications not yet completely developed.

When conducted properly, benchmarks yield accurate results, for they deal with real systems and real workloads. Their results are very reliable and have wide acceptance. Benchmarks have frequently been viewed as a technique to compare systems. Usually, computer systems procurement studies and comparative analysis of products rely on benchmarks. However, their use in practical capacity planning studies has been limited.

2.9 CONCLUDING REMARKS

We started the chapter by describing an example of information systems planning in a retail company. Let us go back to the example and re-examine it. A retail company decides to reshape its computing environment, moving from a mainframe-centric architecture to distributed systems. The new architecture consists of three basic components: a LAN-based system, an OLTP multiprocessor, and a downsized mainframe. The main problem is to define the systems that will process the current and expected workloads within the service levels specified. Capacity planning appears as a means to specify and size the new systems. The steps required to carry out a capacity planning effort are described at length in this chapter. A key issue in the methodology is the model needed to predict performance of future systems. In our example, three different models are needed, one for each type of component. In the next chapter we introduce performance models. In Chap. 7 we study in detail the construction of models of LAN-based systems. Multiprocessor models are treated in Chap. 8. The downsized mainframe, which serves as a general-purpose system, requires a multiclass model, which is the subject of Chap. 6. In conclusion, we summarize the basic steps of a practical capacity planning methodology.

- Understand the current environment.
- Specify the service levels.
- Perform a workload characterization and generate a workload model.
- Develop a performance model.
- Validate and calibrate the system model, which is composed of the workload and performance models.
- Forecast workload growth.
- Using the system model, analyze the performance of different system configurations and various workload scenarios.
- From the performance results obtained with the model, select the alternative that presents the best cost-performance relation while satisfying the service levels specified.

2.10 EXERCISES

1. For the workload of Table 2.12, apply the k-means algorithm described in Fig. 2.15 to obtain three clusters. Compare the results obtained with those shown in Table 2.18.

2. What kind of natural forecasting units would you associate with the major applications of the following: insurance company, airline company, and college?

3. Construct a synthetic workload program to run on a SUN system to which you have access. This program *may* (but it's your choice) be constructed as follows. It goes through phase I, which is computation intensive and spends time burning CPU cycles for a couple of minutes. Then the program goes through phase II, which is I/O intensive and spends a couple of minutes using the disk or doing screen I/O or some other I/O operations. Finally, the program goes through phase III, which balances CPU and I/O activity. Learn about the "perfmeter" (a SunView utility that displays performance values for a given host name) by reading through the *man* pages. There are roughly 10 features that can be monitored (e.g., CPU, packets, interrupts, disk, etc.), the monitoring time interval can be modified, and the data collected using the perfmeter can be sent to a file. Run your synthetic workload program with the perfmeter turned on. (You may even want to have your program running in different windows at the same time.) Collect the perfmeter data and perform a workload characterization study on it. Do not make the dataset too large (e.g., a few hundred points will probably be plenty). In your characterization, you may want to find, say, the two features that explain the most total variance, plot those two features, and do a clustering analysis (even just visually would be acceptable). Try to relate the quantitative characterization that you perform back to the qualitative behavior of your workload program. Be creative.

4. Consider a computing environment with which you are familiar (e.g., at the university or at your company). Describe this computing environment using the guidelines of Sec. 2.4.5.

BIBLIOGRAPHY

1. A. Lederer and V. Gardiner, Strategic information systems planning, *Information Systems Management*, Summer 1992.

2. C. Smith, *Performance Engineering of Software Systems*, Addison-Wesley, Reading, Mass., 1990.

3. R. Weicker, An overview of common benchmarks, *IEEE Computer*, December 1990.

4. J. Hennessy and D. Patterson, *Computer Architecture: A Quantitative Approach*, Morgan Kaufmann, San Mateo, Calif., 1990.

5. J. Gray, *The Benchmark Handbook for Database and Transaction Processing Systems*, Morgan Kaufmann, San Mateo, Calif., 1991.

6. G. Anderson, The coordinated use of five performance evaluation methodologies, *Communications of the ACM*, Vol. 4, No. 2, 1984.

7. S. Lam, S. and K. Chan, *Computer Capacity Planning: Theory and Practice*, Academic Press, London, 1987.

8. J. Brady, A theory of productivity in the creative process, *IEEE CG & A*, May 1986.

9. K. Chandy, Planning information systems, *Journal of Capacity Management*, Vol. 1, No. 1, 1982.

10. D. Gifford and A. Spector, The TWA reservation System, *Communications of the ACM*, Vol. 27, No. 7, July 1984.

11. D. Ferrari, G. Serazzi, and A. Zeigner, *Measurement and Tuning of Computer Systems*, Prentice Hall, Englewood Cliffs, N.J., 1983.

12. R. Bodnarchuk, Characterizing and modeling the workload of a distributed system file server, M.Sc. thesis, Department of Computational Science, University of Saskatchewan, Saskatoon, Saskatchewan, Canada, 1990.

13. S. Ling, R. Bunt, and D. Eager, Characterizing client-server workload on an Ethernet, *Proceedings of CMG '91, International Conference on Management and Performance of Computer Systems*, The Computer Measurement Group, Nashville, Tenn., December, 1991.

14. R. Jain, *The Art of Computer System Performance: Analysis, Techniques for Experimental Design, Measurement, Simulation, and Modeling*, Wiley, New York, 1991.

15. J. Mohr and S. Penansky, A forecasting oriented workload characterization methodology, *CMG Transactions*, No. 36, June 1982.

16. K. Raatikainen, Experiences of hierarchical workload modeling in capacity planning, *Proceedings of CMG'89, International Conference on Management and Performance Evaluation of Computer Systems*, The Computer Measurement Group, Reno, Nevada, December 1989.

17. C. Elms, Clustering - one method for workload characterization, *Proceedings of the International Conference on Computer Capacity Management*, San Francisco, Calif., 1980.

18. M. Anderberg, *Cluster Analysis for Applications*, Academic Press, New York, 1973.

19. B. Everitt, *Cluster Analysis*, 2nd. ed., Halsted Press, New York, 1980.

20. J. Cady and B. Howarth, *Computer System Performance Management and Capacity Planning*, Prentice Hall, Brookvale, New South Wales, Australia, 1990.

21. L. Bronner, Overview of the capacity planning process for production data processing, *IBM Systems Journal*, Vol. 18, No. 1, 1980.

22. H. Letmanyi, *Guide on Workload Forecasting*, Special Publication 500-123, Computer Science and Technology, National Bureau of Standards, Washington, D.C., 1985.

23. T. Lo, Computer workload forecasting techniques: a tutorial, *Proceedings of the International Conference on Computer Capacity Management*, San Francisco, 1980.

24. E. Drakopoulos, Study of the performance impact of NFS workload on large mainframe UNIX systems, *Proceedings of CMG'91, International Conference on Management and Performance Evaluation of Computer Systems*, The Computer Measurement Group, Nashville, Tenn., December 1991.

25. H. Limmer, Rules of thumb '90, *CMG Transactions*, Spring 90.

Chapter 3

Performance Models

3.1 INTRODUCTION

A *model* is a representation of a system. In the case of computer systems, models may be used for at least two purposes: to represent the operation of the system—functional models—or to represent the behavior of the system in terms of its performance—performance models. Functional models are employed when one is interested in studying certain properties of the behavior of a system. An example is the use of Petri nets [1] in order to prove the absence of deadlocks or starvation in concurrent systems, such as multiprogrammed operating systems or network protocols. On the other hand, performance models are useful for predicting the values of performance measures of a system from a set of values of workload, operating system, and hardware parameters. Examples of performance measures are response times, throughputs, and utilizations.

Figure 3.1 shows a pictorial representation of a performance model. The input parameters to such a model fall into one of three categories: workload, basic software, and hardware parameters. The workload parameters describe the load imposed on the computer system of interest by the jobs or transactions submitted to it. Examples of such parameters are transaction average arrival times, number of terminals in an interactive system, and the service demands placed on each of the system's resources by each type of job or

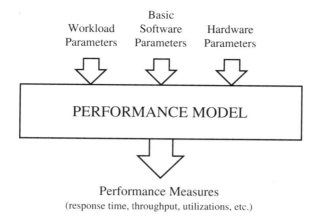

Figure 3.1 Pictorial representation of a performance model.

transaction. The basic software parameters describe features of the basic soft-ware, such as the operating system, that affect performance. Examples of such parameters are the maximum degree of multiprogramming and the CPU dispatching priority. Examples of hardware performance parameters include processor speeds, disk latencies and transfer rates, and local area network speed, to name a few. The output of a performance model is a set of perform-ance measures. Examples include response times, throughput, and resource utilizations.

As seen in Chaps. 1 and 2, a key issue in capacity planning is performance prediction. In this chapter we guide the reader through the nature of models commonly used in analyzing computer systems. We also discuss what kind of parameters are needed to use these models. However, the issue of how to solve performance models is left for the remaining chapters of the book. The emphasis here is on how to build a model from a description of the system being studied.

3.2 BUILDING A PERFORMANCE MODEL OF A SIMPLE COMPUTER SYSTEM

Consider that you are responsible for conducting a capacity planning study of the following computer system. *A database server, which is composed of a CPU and two disks, is devoted to the processing of on-line DB query transactions which arrive from a large community of users at a rate of 0.5 tps. The operating system of the server is multiprogrammed and its main memory is divided into areas called partitions. To execute, a transaction must be loaded into one of the memory partitions. The system in question has five memory partitions, which implies that at most five transactions may be using or waiting to use an active resource.*

Several capacity planning questions are to be evaluated. For instance, what is the impact on response time if the transaction arrival rate is increased by 100%? Or if the CPU is upgraded to the next model, as suggested by the manufacturer? Or if more memory is installed, so that more transactions may run simultaneously? The answer to all these questions, and many others of a similar nature, requires the use of a predictive performance model. The first step in building the model is understanding the nature of the basic operation of such a transaction processing system in order to reflect in the model the aspects that influence performance.

Let us start by examining one transaction at a time. The execution of a transaction requires use of the CPU for a certain amount of time and the use of both disks for executing the I/O operations needed to answer the query. The following steps describe the behavior of a typical transaction T from its arrival at the system until its departure.

1. Transaction T has to acquire a memory partition to run on. If five trans-actions are already in execution, T has to *queue for memory*.

2. Once memory is obtained, transaction T will try to use the CPU to start its execution. But if the CPU is already in use by another transaction, T will have to *queue for the CPU*.

3. Once at the CPU, the transaction will use it until either:

   (a) *It requires an I/O operation.* In this case, it will have to *queue for the disk* if the device is busy. After completing the I/O, T returns to the CPU queue.
   (b) *Its timeslice expires.* In this case, transaction T is suspended and again placed in the CPU ready queue.
   (c) *It completes execution.* In this case, T releases the memory partition it was holding and departs from the system.

Therefore, during its execution, a transaction will cycle between CPU and I/O a certain number of times until it completes execution. In the ex-ample above, a transaction may be found in one of the five following states: queuing for memory, queuing for the CPU, using the CPU, queuing for a disk, or using a disk. From the above description, we may identify two classes of resources: *active* and *passive*. *Active resources*, also called *servers* or *de-vices*, are those which deliver a certain service to the transaction at a finite rate or speed. In our case, the CPU and disks are examples of active re-sources. The CPU, for instance, is capable of executing a certain number of instructions per unit time. The more accurate way to gauge the speed of a CPU in order to compare it with other CPUs is by measuring the time it takes to execute a certain program. Some simpler measures, such as MIPS, have also been proposed and used by many manufacturers. As discussed in Chap. 2 and pointed out by Hennessy and Patterson [2], MIPS ratings are not very reliable. Other units for rating CPUs, such as MFLOPS (millions of floating-point operations) for scientific computations, SPEC marks, and TPC (for transaction processing systems), may also be used. The disk speed depends on its physical characteristics, such as seek time, rotational speed, and transfer rate. These figures, along with the characteristics of the records to be retrieved, determine the number of I/O operations that can be performed per second.

The speed of active resources directly influences the execution time of a transaction. Consider the CPU, for instance. The number of instructions needed to execute a transaction type may vary from transaction execution to transaction execution and is called the transaction *path length*. Thus, the total CPU service demand needed to execute all instructions of a transaction may roughly be estimated as the following ratio

$$\frac{\text{path length}}{\text{CPU speed}}$$

On the other hand, passive resources are not characterized by a speed of service delivery to transactions or jobs. Memory partitions are an example of such resources. Once a transaction is in possession of a memory partition, its execution progresses at a rate that is independent of any characteristic of the passive resource. Passive resources are generally limited in quantity, and therefore queues may form for the acquisition of an instance of such resources. In our case there are only five memory partitions. An arriving transaction that finds all memory partitions seized will have to wait.

To help us visualize the system being modeled, let us introduce the standard pictorial representation for servers and queues shown in Fig. 3.2. Servers are represented by circles and their associated waiting lines as rectangles. The arrows indicate the flow of incoming and outgoing transactions. The term *queue* will be used hereafter to denote the server and its associated waiting line. The term *waiting queue* will also be used as a synonym of *waiting line*.

Passive resources are represented in a somewhat different manner, as indicated in Fig. 3.3. The upward-pointing triangle represents an allocation of an instance of a passive resource, while the downward-pointing triangle stands for the release of a previously allocated instance of the passive resource. The rectangle at the top of the figure stands for the pool of passive resources, and the number n inside it indicates the total number of instances of the passive resource.

Sometimes, for the sake of simplicity, we will use an alternative graphical representation for passive resources, indicated in Fig. 3.4, when it is clear from the system description when the passive resources have been allocated and released. In this notation, the maximum number of instances of the passive resource is shown in parentheses near the associated queue.

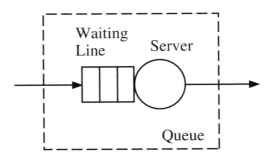

Figure 3.2 Graphic notation for single-server queue.

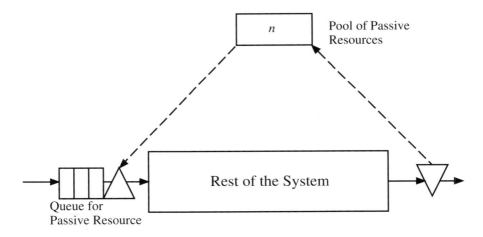

Figure 3.3 Graphic notation for a passive resource.

We can now draw the complete pictorial representation of our transaction processing system, as depicted in Fig. 3.5. So, as we can see, a computer system may be modeled as a network of queues, or a *queueing network* (QN). In a QN, when completing service at a given queue, transactions may either leave the system or move into another queue to receive additional service. The term *transaction* is very specific to this example. We are going to use a more general term—*customer*—to indicate the entities that flow through the system receiving service from its various servers. The identification of customers in each case depends on the kinds of performance measures in which one is interested. In the examples that follow, we will have the opportunity to see several examples of customers in performance models.

Since we are interested in obtaining performance metrics from our model, we must complete the model description with sufficient numerical data, so that we will be able to derive the performance metrics of interest. As

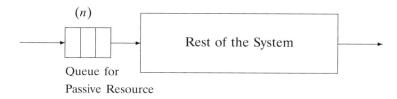

Figure 3.4 Simplified graphical notation for passive resource.

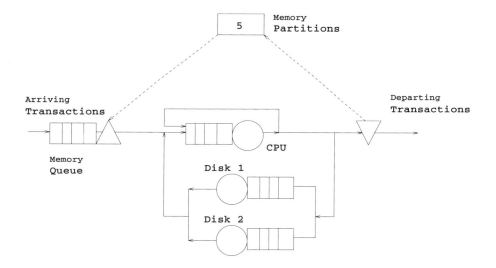

Figure 3.5 Graphic notation for the transaction processing system.

indicated in Chaps. 1 and 2, the workload can be characterized by two types of parameters: service demands and workload intensity. In our example, one would have to indicate the service demands at the CPU and at disks 1 and 2. As you may recall, the service demand at a server is the total average time spent by a transaction at this particular server. This time does not include the time spent waiting in the queue for this server. Since the service demand does not include waiting time, the effect of replacing the server by a faster or slower one is easily reflected in the value of the service demand. For instance, if we decided to replace the CPU by one twice as fast, the service demand at the CPU would be halved. In other words, a faster CPU performs the same amount of work in less time. We will use the notation D_i to denote the service demand at device i.

Although the issue of obtaining the values of the parameters of a performance model is treated in Chap. 9, it is instructive at this point to investigate how the service demand for a given device may be obtained. Let us consider that you monitored your system for 1 hour. Your software monitor tells you that in this period, the CPU was 80% utilized. In other words, during 80% of the time the CPU was busy executing transactions. During the same period, 1000 transactions were executed. If the CPU was 80% utilized for a period of 1 hour (3600 sec), it was busy delivering service to transactions during 2880 sec (0.8 × 3600). If 1000 transactions were executed during this period, then, on the average, each of them demanded 2.88 (2880/1000) sec of service from the CPU. In general, we may write that

$$D_i = \frac{U_i \times T}{C_0} \qquad (3.1)$$

where U_i is the utilization of device i, T is the monitoring interval, and C_0 is the total number of completed transactions during the monitoring interval. Note that the ratio C_0/T is simply equal to the average number of completed transactions per unit time, or the average throughput as defined previously. So if we denote the average throughput as X_0, we may rewrite Eq. (3.1) as

$$D_i = \frac{U_i}{X_0} \qquad (3.2)$$

Let the service demands for our transaction processing system have the values indicated in Table 3.1.

Table 3.1 Service Demands for the Transaction Processing System.

Server	Service Demand (sec)
CPU	0.80
Disk 1	0.75
Disk 2	0.25
Total (T_0)	1.80

If we sum the values of the average service demands for all devices, we obtain the average response time, T_0, experienced by a transaction under no-load conditions. This is the response time of a transaction that does not spend any time waiting for any device or for memory. This happens when the transaction runs by itself, with no other transaction running concurrently. In our example, T_0 is equal to 1.80 sec. In general,

$$T_0 = \sum_{i=1}^{K} D_i \qquad (3.3)$$

where K is the total number of devices.

The workload intensity reflects the degree of congestion in the system and directly affects the time spent by the transactions in the several queues.

In our example, the workload intensity would be given by the following two parameters:

- The *average transaction arrival* rate, λ, which is equal to 0.5 tps.
- The *maximum degree of multiprogramming*, N^{max}, that is, the maximum number of transactions that can be in execution at a given time. In our case this is equal to the number of memory partitions, since each transaction requires a memory partition to execute. Thus, the maximum degree of multiprogramming is 5 in this example.

It is worthwhile at this point to analyze, in a qualitative manner, the behavior of the several system queues as a function of the values of the workload intensity parameters. Quantitative analyses will be the subject of future chapters.

The average response time, T, can be expressed as the following sum:

$$T = T_0 + W_{mem} + W_{cpu} + W_{disk1} + W_{disk2} \tag{3.4}$$

where $W_{mem}, W_{cpu}, W_{disk1}$, and W_{disk2} stand for the average total waiting time at the memory queue, CPU, disk 1, and disk 2, respectively. When the transaction arrival rate, λ, is very low, the congestion on the system is very low. In this case, the average number of transactions waiting in the queue for memory will be very close to zero, and the average number of transactions in the system internal waiting queues (CPU and disks) is also close to zero. Thus, the average transaction response time will be very close to the minimum average response time (1.8 sec in our case).

Now let us consider the effect of the increase in arrival rate. Up to a certain value of λ, say λ_1, an arriving transaction will probably find ≤ 4 transactions in the system. So it will not have to queue for memory ($W_{mem} \cong 0$). Therefore, an increase of λ in the range $[0, \lambda_1]$ causes an increase in the time spent in the system internal waiting queues, and therefore results in an increase in T.

When λ is greater than λ_1, arriving transactions will tend to queue for memory as they arrive and find five transactions already in the system. An increase in λ in this range implies an increase in W_{mem} but no longer influences the values of W_{cpu}, W_{disk1}, and W_{disk2}, since the number of transactions inside the computer system contending for the same system resources does not continue to grow any more since it is limited by the maximum degree of multiprogramming. So in this range, T also increases with λ because of the increase in W_{mem}. The preceding analysis is summarized in Table 3.2.

Let us return to some of the capacity planning questions posed at the beginning of this section. To answer these questions, we need to solve the performance model we have just built. Although we have not yet shown the reader how to do this, we are going to advance the answers. A more elaborate analysis of these questions will be carried out later in the book. The numerical

Table 3.2 Qualitative Analysis as a Function of Load.

Range of λ	Trends
$\lambda \cong 0$	$W_{mem} \cong 0$, $W_{cpu} \cong 0$, $W_{disk1} \cong 0$, $W_{disk2} \cong 0$, and $T \cong T_0$
$\lambda \leq \lambda_1$	$W_{mem} \cong 0$; W_{cpu}, W_{disk1}, W_{disk2}, and T grow with λ
$\lambda > \lambda_1$	W_{mem} grows with λ; W_{cpu}, W_{disk1}, and W_{disk2} do not grow with λ; and T grows with λ

solution of the performance model described above would give us as a result an average response time of 2.87 sec. If the arrival rate were increased to 1.00 tps (i.e., a 100% increase), the new value of the response time would jump to 21.70 sec. In other words, a 100% increase in the average arrival rate would result in a 656% increase in the response time. This nonlinear behavior of computer systems is due to the nonlinearity of queuing systems. If we doubled the CPU speed, at a load of 1.00 tps, the response time would go down to 4.77 sec. Doubling the CPU speed can be reflected in the performance model by halving the service demand at the CPU.

It is interesting to note at this point that our performance model did not consider all the details of the I/O subsystem. In general, modern mainframe computers have I/O subsystems that are composed of several interconnected components, such as I/O channels, head of strings, device controllers, disk caches, and the devices themselves. Instead of modeling all those intricate details, we built a simpler model in which much of this complexity was abstracted by a single server representing each disk. In this simplified model, the average service demand at any disk incorporates not only the time spent by a transaction at a disk, but also all other delays associated with it, such as I/O channel contention and device controller delays. This *abstraction* is valid as long as we are not interested in evaluating the impact on performance of several I/O subsystem architecture features, in which case the I/O subsystem would have to be modeled explicitly. Chapter 8 deals with models of complex I/O subsystems.

The previous discussion points out an important principle to be followed in modeling—the principle of minimal complexity—which establishes that the complexity of a model should be kept at the minimum degree of complexity required to obtain the desired performance metrics.

3.3 PERFORMANCE MODEL OF AN INTERACTIVE SYSTEM

Let us consider again the computer system described in the preceding section. However, instead of using it to process a database query processing workload, it will be used to support an interactive computer system composed of 20 terminals. Each terminal is running the same data-entry application, where several fields of a screen must be filled out and the entire screen submitted to the computer system for appropriate processing and database update. Each user spends an average of 30 sec to key in all data of a screen. Figure 3.6 gives a pictorial representation of the interactive system. The internal part of the computer system, composed of the CPU and the disks, is not represented explicitly.

Suppose that you are responsible for analyzing the performance of this system. In particular, you must answer the following capacity planning questions:

- What is the impact on response time if the number, M, of terminals is increased from 20 to 50?
- What is the impact on response time if the layout of the data-entry form is changed so that instead of spending 30 sec, each user spends an average of 20 sec typing the data in the form?

Again, to answer these and other related questions, let us review the flow of execution of a command (unit of processing in an interactive system— customers in this case), including its preparation at the terminal and its execution by the system. Initially, right after receiving a prompt from the

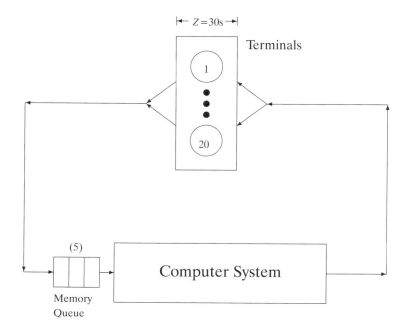

Figure 3.6 Graphic notation for the interactive system.

previous command, the user spends some time preparing and typing the next screen. This time interval is the think time defined in Chap. 2. Its average value is denoted by Z. Notice that, in general, Z is a characteristic of the application. In our case, Z depends on the time needed by a user to fill out all the fields of the data entry screen. In other words, Z does not change with response time. This statement may not hold in extreme cases where the response time increases so much that user behavior is influenced by it (e.g., users may get distracted, involved in conversations, leave the room for a cup of coffee).

So user commands alternate between two states: the think state, when they are at the terminal, and the submitted state, when they have already been submitted for execution by the computer system. Figure 3.7 shows the two possible states of a command and their relationship to think time and response time.

In an interactive system, each user in the think state generates a new command at an average rate that is inversely proportional to the think time Z. Thus, each user generates commands at a rate equal to $1/Z$ commands per second. In our example, each user in the think state generates commands at a rate of $1/30$ command per second.

Let us examine in this case what kind of parameters would be necessary to solve the performance model of the interactive system. The service demand parameters for this case are given in Table 3.3.

The workload intensity parameters must reflect the load in the system. If the number of terminals is increased, there will be an increase in the load submitted to the system. Also, if the average think time is de-

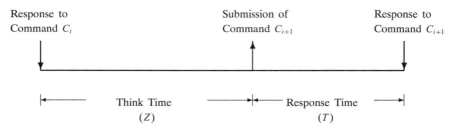

Figure 3.7   Think time–response time cycle.

Table 3.3   Service Demands for the Interactive System.

Server	Service Demand (sec)
CPU	0.30
Disk 1	0.45
Disk 2	0.30
Total (T_0)	1.05

creased, users will submit commands at a higher rate, increasing the load submitted to the system. As in the previous case, the maximum degree of multiprogramming is a parameter that affects the load in the system. So, in summary, the workload intensity parameters for our interactive system are:

- The *average think time*, Z, which in our case is 30 sec
- The *number of terminals*, M, which is 20 in this case
- The *maximum degree of multiprogramming*, N^{max}, which is 5 in our case

Let us develop a qualitative analysis of the performance behavior of the interactive system. In particular, let us examine the variation of the response time as a function of the number of terminals. When the number of terminals is very small ($M \cong 1$), each command submitted will not encounter any other command, neither in the memory queue nor in any system internal queue. So the response time will be T_0. When the number of terminals increases up to a certain number M_1, such that arriving transactions will never meet more than four commands in execution, the congestion in the system internal queues increases and so does the response time. After M_1 terminals, arriving transactions will tend to find five commands in execution, and will have to queue for memory. An increase in the number of terminals in this range causes the response time to increase due to an increase in the memory queuing time. However, the time spent within the computer system will not vary with M since the number of commands inside the computer system will tend to be close to the maximum. The preceding analysis is summarized in Table 3.4.

A quantitative analysis of this interactive system can be done using the solution methods described in the remaining chapters of this book. This analysis yields a response time of 1.35 sec. If the number of terminals were increased from 20 to 50, the response time would increase to 2.69 sec. Now if we maintain the number of terminals at 20 and decrease the average think time to 20 sec, the response time would go up to 1.56 sec as a function of the increased load.

Table 3.4   Qualitative Analysis as a Function of M.

Range of M	Trends
$M \cong 1$	$W_{mem} \cong 0$, $W_{cpu} \cong 0$, $W_{disk1} \cong 0$, $W_{disk2} \cong 0$, and $T \cong T_0$
$M \leq M_1$	$W_{mem} \cong 0$; W_{cpu}, W_{disk1}, W_{disk2}, and T grow with M
$M > M_1$	W_{mem} grows with M; W_{cpu}, W_{disk1}, and W_{disk2} do not grow with M; T grows with M

3.4 PERFORMANCE MODEL OF A BATCH SYSTEM

Let us assume that the computer system described above is used by a company to process the payroll system. This kind of application generally runs in batch mode (i.e., without user interaction). The payroll job scans, in sequential order, all records of the EMPLOYEE file. For each record, the program performs the necessary salary and benefit calculations and prints the employee paycheck. Other batch jobs may also be in execution. Some examples are:

- A job for printing mailing labels for all suppliers of a list of products
- A job for generating the Internal Revenue Service forms for the annual income tax return
- A job to increase by 5% the salary of all employees of the company

A batch system may be visualized as indicated in Fig. 3.8. As can be seen in this figure, a batch job that completes execution is replaced almost immediately by another equivalent job. The term *equivalent* is used here to indicate similar service demand values. When we characterize the workload in this manner, one is usually interested in the *residence time* (i.e., the time spent by the job once it is loaded into memory).

As you may have noticed, in this example batch jobs are the customers of our performance model. Let us now consider the numerical parameters needed to characterize the batch system described above. As in the transaction and interactive systems, the model parameters are divided into service demands and workload intensity parameters. Table 3.5 contains the values of the service demands for the batch system.

When analyzing batch systems, we are generally interested in the following performance measures:

- *Elapsed time*, which is the total time spent by a job from its submission to its completion.

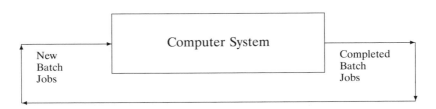

Figure 3.8 Graphical representation of a batch system.

Table 3.5 Service Demands for
the Batch System.

Server	Service Demand (sec)
CPU	5.00
Disk 1	0.55
Disk 2	0.60
Total (T_0)	6.15

- *Throughput*, which is the number of jobs that can be completed per unit time.

In batch systems, the elapsed time may be of less concern than throughput, since in many situations batch applications run during periods (usually at night) when on-line processing is almost nonexistent. This is called the *batch window*. A common service level requirement of most installations is that all batch jobs be processed during the batch window. Consider, for example, a situation where a period of 6 hours during the night shift is devoted to the processing of parts shipment orders. Suppose that on the average, 12,000 orders have to be processed every day. Therefore, the throughput of the system must allow for the processing of at least $12,000/6 = 2000$ shipment orders per hour.

In the case of a batch workload, the measure of load is given by the average number of batch jobs that are concurrently in execution. This number is called the *average degree of multiprogramming* and is denoted by $\overline{N}$. Let us assume that in our case this value is 5 jobs. Solving an appropriate performance model, one would find the average elapsed time to be 25.26 sec and the average throughput to be 0.20 job/sec.

3.5 MULTIPLE-CLASS PERFORMANCE MODELS

In most real-life situations, a computer system is used by applications of different nature. For instance, one could easily envision a system that runs an on-line database query application and which has a certain number of terminals dedicated to users who are developing a new application supported by an interactive system. Simultaneously, some batch jobs could also be sharing the same computing facility. Suppose, for instance, that the computer system considered in previous sections is now going to be used simultaneously by the three workloads described earlier.

To analyze the performance behavior of the system, we need a multiple-workload model. The term *workload* will be reserved for the physical set of jobs or transactions submitted to the system. In our performance models, workloads will be abstracted by the concept of transaction or job *class*.

The attributes or parameters of the class represent the features of the work-load that are relevant to performance. So there is a one-to-one correspondence between classes and workloads. The maximum number of customers of a class is called the *class population*.

For each transaction or job class, one has to indicate the service demands per device as well as the workload intensity parameters that are appropriate for the class. So the service demands for a multiple-class model are given by a $K \times R$ matrix, where K is, as defined previously, the number of devices and R is the number of classes. The element $D_{i,r}$ of the matrix stands for the service demand of transactions of class r at device i. Hereafter we will use the letter i to indicate a generic device and the letter r to denote a generic class. Thus, the service demand matrix for our three-class example is as given in Table 3.6.

Table 3.6 Service Demands (in Seconds) for the
Three-Class Example.

Server	Class		
	Transaction	Interactive	Batch
CPU	0.80	0.30	5.00
Disk 1	0.75	0.45	0.55
Disk 2	0.25	0.30	0.60

3.5.1 Aggregation of Classes

In the example above, a three-class model was built because the three classes were different in nature (i.e., transaction, interactive, and batch). How-ever, the need to build a multiple-class performance model may arise even when all workloads are of the same nature. Consider the following example.

Let the same computer system considered in all previous examples be subject to an on-line database transaction processing workload. The transactions fall into the following four categories:

- *Trivial transactions (TT):* the query transactions that need to access only a few database records, from a single database relation,[1] in order to give a response to the user
- *Medium transactions (MT):* the query transactions that involve joining two database relations
- *Complex transactions (CT):* the query transactions that involve joining more than two database relations
- *Update transactions (UT):* the transactions that modify the contents of the database

[1]A *database relation* can be thought as being a table where each line corresponds to a database record.

Consider the following capacity planning questions:

- What is the effect on response time of trivial transactions if their arrival rate increases by 50%?
- What is the effect on response time of update transactions if their arrival rate is increased by 25%?
- What is the effect on the response time of TT transactions if update transactions are run on a different machine?

As we can see from the foregoing questions, in the current capacity planning study, one is only interested in specific performance measures on transactions of type TT and UT. Thus, although a four-class performance model would allow us to answer these questions, a three-class model would suffice. The three classes in our simplified model would be TT, UT, and other transactions (OT), which are those that are either MT or CT. So, as pointed out in Chap. 1, *the degree into which one should refine or aggregate the class definition must be guided by the goals of the capacity planning study.* The advantage of using simpler models whenever possible is that the computational effort to solve them is reduced substantially when the number of classes and or devices is reduced. A simple rule to be followed when building performance models for capacity planning is: *Classes for which no performance measures are desired as the output of the capacity planning study should be aggregated into a single class.*

If you are considering using the simplified three-class model and you have not started to collect the data for your model, you may do so according to the needs of your model (i.e., collect data at the level of aggregation of your model). However, suppose that you had already collected data for a previous study, in which the four transaction categories were explicitly considered. The question is: How should one aggregate the performance parameters for our simplified model? Let us use our current example to answer this question. Table 3.7 contains the original data for a four-class model. The table contains the arrival rate per class as well as the service demands for the CPU and the disks.

Table 3.7 Parameters for a Four-Class Performance Model.

	Class			
	TT	MT	CT	UT
Arrival rate (tps)	0.20	0.30	0.20	0.10
Service demand (sec)				
CPU	0.15	0.30	0.45	0.70
Disk 1	0.20	0.35	0.55	0.30
Disk 2	0.10	0.30	0.60	0.20

We want to aggregate classes MT and CT into a single class called OT (other transactions). So we need to determine the arrival rate λ_{OT} for this class, as well as the service demands $D_{i,OT}$ for every device i for transactions of class OT. If the system receives 0.3 tps from class MT and 0.2 tps from class CT, the arrival rate of class OT will be simply the sum of the arrival rates of the classes being aggregated (i.e., 0.5 tps). Now, let us consider the aggregation of service demands. When we aggregate MT and CT transactions into a single class, we have that the fraction of MT transactions in the new class OT is given by

$$\frac{\lambda_{MT}}{\lambda_{MT} + \lambda_{CT}} = \frac{0.3}{0.3 + 0.2} = \frac{3}{5} \tag{3.5}$$

and the fraction of CT transactions in the new class is given by

$$\frac{\lambda_{CT}}{\lambda_{MT} + \lambda_{CT}} = \frac{0.2}{0.3 + 0.2} = \frac{2}{5} \tag{3.6}$$

Therefore, the average service demand at any device i of transactions of class OT are obtained from the service demand values of the original classes CT and MT, weighted by the appropriate influence of the original class in the new one. A proof of this is left as an exercise. So, for instance, the service demand at the CPU for OT transactions is given by

$$D_{\text{cpu,OT}} = \frac{3}{5} \times 0.30 + \frac{2}{5} \times 0.45 = 0.36 \tag{3.7}$$

Table 3.8 summarizes the results of this procedure for all devices.

In general, the algorithm to aggregate transaction-type classes is given in Fig. 3.9.

Suppose now the problem of aggregating two or more classes of type interactive. We will assume that the nonaggregated model was solved once before one proceeds to aggregating classes in order to conduct other capacity planning studies. Let $X_{0,r}$ be the throughput of class r commands obtained by solving the complete model. The new aggregated class will have a number of terminals equal to the sum of the number of terminals of each class being aggregated. The average aggregated think time must be obtained as the weighted sum of the individual think times. The weights in this case are the

Table 3.8 Parameters for the Aggregated Three-Class Performance Model.

	Class		
	TT	OT	UT
Arrival rate (tps)	0.20	0.50	0.10
Service Demand (sec)			
CPU	0.15	0.36	0.70
Disk 1	0.20	0.43	0.30
Disk 2	0.10	0.42	0.20

Let $1, \ldots, p$ be the transaction-type classes to be aggregated into a single class ag. Let λ_r be the average arrival rate of class r ($r = 1, \ldots, p$) transactions, and $N_r^{\max}$ be the maximum degree of multiprogramming of class r ($r = 1, \ldots, p$) transactions. So the average arrival rate for the aggregated class, λ_{ag}, is given by

$$\lambda_{ag} = \sum_{r=1}^{p} \lambda_r \tag{3.8}$$

The maximum multiprogramming level, $N_{ag}^{\max}$, of the aggregated class is given by

$$N_{ag}^{\max} = \sum_{r=1}^{p} N_r^{\max} \tag{3.9}$$

and the service demand at every device i for class ag is given by

$$D_{i,ag} = \frac{\sum_{r=1}^{p} \lambda_r \times D_{i,r}}{\lambda_{ag}} \tag{3.10}$$

Figure 3.9   Algorithm for aggregating transaction classes.

proportion of terminals of each class with respect to the total. Finally, the service demands are weighted by the fraction of the class throughput over the total throughput of all classes being aggregated. Figure 3.10 summarizes the aggregation procedure for interactive classes described above.

Finally, when aggregating batch-type classes, one has to sum the average degree of multiprogramming of each component class in order to obtain the average degree of multiprogramming of the aggregated class. The service demand of the aggregated class at any device is obtained as the weighted average of the service demands of the component classes at this device. As with the interactive class, the weights in this case are the fractions of the class throughput over the total throughput of the classes being aggregated. See Fig. 3.11 for the aggregation algorithm for batch-type classes.

3.5.2 Priorities

Consider a computer system consisting of a CPU and a disk. Assume that the following two workloads share the computer facility: an interactive workload with 20 terminals and an average think time of 15 sec, and a batch workload. The maximum degree of multiprogramming for interactive commands is 6. The average degree of multiprogramming for batch jobs is 4.8. The matrix of service demands for this two-class performance model is given in Table 3.9.

Let $1, \ldots, p$ be the interactive-type classes to be aggregated into a single class ag. Let Z_r be the average think time of class r $(r = 1, \ldots, p)$, $X_{0,r}$ $(r = 1, \ldots, p)$ be the throughput of class r commands, and M_r be the number of terminals in class r $(r = 1, \ldots, p)$. So, the number of terminals of the aggregated class, M_{ag}, is given by

$$M_{ag} = \sum_{r=1}^{p} M_r \qquad (3.11)$$

The average think time, Z_{ag}, of the aggregated class is given by

$$Z_{ag} = \frac{\sum_{r=1}^{p} Z_r \times M_r}{M_{ag}} \qquad (3.12)$$

The service demand at every device i for class ag is given by

$$D_{i,ag} = \frac{\sum_{r=1}^{p} X_{0,r} \times D_{i,r}}{\sum_{r=1}^{p} X_{0,r}} \qquad (3.13)$$

Figure 3.10 Algorithm for aggregating interactive classes.

Let $1, \ldots, p$ be the batch-type classes to be aggregated into a single class ag. Let $\overline{N}_r$ be the average degree of multiprogramming of class r $(r = 1, \ldots, p)$, and $X_{0,r}$ $(r = 1, \ldots, p)$ be the throughput of class r jobs. So, the average degree of multiprogramming of the aggregated class, $\overline{N}_{ag}$, is given by

$$\overline{N}_{ag} = \sum_{r=1}^{p} \overline{N}_r \qquad (3.14)$$

The service demand at every device i for class ag is given by

$$D_{i,ag} = \frac{\sum_{r=1}^{p} X_{0,r} \times D_{i,r}}{\sum_{r=1}^{p} X_{0,r}} \qquad (3.15)$$

Figure 3.11 Algorithm for aggregating batch classes.

If we solve the performance model above, we find that the average response time for interactive commands is 5.27 sec and that the average elapsed time for batch jobs is 90 sec. In most situations, response time for the interactive subsystem is of utmost importance and 5.27 sec may be too high. On the other hand, the elapsed time of batch jobs is generally of less importance when evaluating system performance. So, if one is willing to trade performance between batch and interactive, one can tell the operating system that interactive commands should have priority, with respect to batch jobs, in ob-

Table 3.9 Service Demands (in Seconds) for an Interactive and a Batch Model.

Server	Class	
	Interactive	Batch
CPU	0.45	10.0
Disk	0.25	0.3

taining the CPU. Most operating systems allow for priorities to be considered at the scheduler level. A priority scheduling discipline is said to be *preemptive* when lower-priority jobs or transactions immediately relinquish control of the server if there are higher-priority jobs waiting to use it. In the previous example, if we gave preemptive priority at the CPU to interactive commands, they would exhibit an average response time of 1.29 sec, while batch jobs would have their elapsed time increased to 206.4 sec. So, as we see, the CPU dispatching priority is an important parameter when specifying a performance model.

In a multiclass performance model, one may have P priority groups. Many classes may have the same relative priority. The priority of a class is a number in the range $[1, \ldots, P]$. We will use the notation Prior(r) to denote the priority of class r transactions. We will also assume that the highest priority is numbered 1, and that the priority number increases as the priority decreases. So, in our previous example one would have that Prior(interactive) $= 1$ and Prior(batch) $= 2$. Chapter 8 shows how priority based CPU schedulers may be modeled.

3.5.3 Shared Domains

In our previous examples we introduced the concept of maximum degree of multiprogramming as being the maximum number of transactions of a certain class that can be concurrently in execution. There are two reasons for imposing such limits:

- *Memory constraints.* In this case, there is no more main memory available to load the code of additional transactions.
- *Performance goals.* In this case, no more additional transactions are allowed to enter the multiprogramming set because this would increase congestion in the system internal queues and would, consequently, degrade performance.

In our previous examples we considered that such a limit existed separately for each class. For instance, consider a transaction processing system with two classes of transactions, and maximum multiprogramming degrees equal to $N_1^{\max} = 3$ and $N_2^{\max} = 4$. The number of class 1 transactions in the system varies from 0 to 3, and the number of class 2 transactions varies from 0 to 4. In some cases, one is interested in establishing a limit that is shared by more than one class of transactions. Suppose that we wanted to limit to 7 the total number of transactions in the system, irrespective of their class being 1 or 2. In this case, the number of class 1 and class 2 transactions would vary from 0 to 7, provided that the sum of the number of class 1 transactions plus the number of class 2 transactions does not exceed 7. This concept is called *shared domain* and refers to a domain where several classes of transactions share the same maximum degree of multiprogramming. Figure 3.12 shows the difference between single and shared domains. The horizontal axis represents the number of class 1 transactions, and the vertical axis stands for the number of class 2 transactions. Each black circle represents a possible combination of class 1 and class 2 transactions in the system.

In the IBM MVS [3] operating system, the concept of shared domain is directly implemented by the operating system, and receives the same name. In other environments, similar situations may be found. For instance,

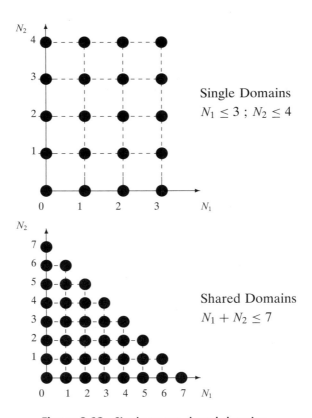

Figure 3.12 Single versus shared domains.

VAX/VMS [4], Digital Equipment's operating system, implements the notion of a *process* as the entity that has to be activated for an execution to take place. In VAX/VMS there is an operating system parameter that specifies the maximum number of processes to be created. This number limits the maximum number of concurrently executing transactions of any kind. In other words, a shared domain is implemented in this way. We will use the notation $\text{Dom}(r)$ to indicate the domain associated to class r.

3.5.4 Summary of Parameter Types for Multiclass Performance Models

We may now summarize in Table 3.10 the parameters that must be specified for performance models of centralized computer systems.

Table 3.10   Parameters per Class Type.

Parameter	Type of Class		
	Batch	Interactive	Transaction
Service demands	√	√	√
Priority	√	√	√
Domain	√	√	√
Max. multiprogramming degree		√	√
Avg. multiprogramming degree	√		
Average arrival rate			√
Number of terminals		√	
Think time		√	

3.6 BASELINE MODEL AND MODIFICATION ANALYSIS

Performance models may be used in, at least, two different situations: to model existing computer systems, or to model computer systems being developed or to be developed. In the former case the parameters must be obtained through measurements made in the existing system, while in the latter case, the values of the parameters must be guessed or estimated. The purpose of building a performance model is to be able to carry out an analysis of the effect on the performance measures of the variation of the values of the various model parameters. This is called a *modification analysis*. But before the modification analysis can be executed, one must build a performance model— called a *baseline model*—which reflects the action of the current workload on the actual system. The baseline model must be validated and calibrated to guarantee that it reflects with reasonable accuracy the system being modeled. Baseline model validation and calibration are done by comparing model predicted values of performance metrics with their actual values obtained through measurements done in the actual system. The techniques used to validate and calibrate performance models are discussed in Chap. 10. We show in this section some examples of modification analysis. Again, the emphasis here is on how to modify the model parameters to conduct the modification analysis of interest.

3.6.1 Baseline Model

Consider the following baseline model, which will be used to illustrate several situations of modification analysis. *A computer system composed of a CPU and two disks is used to support a transaction processing system. Two classes of transactions are considered: trivial transactions and complex transactions.* Table 3.11 shows the values of the input parameters for the baseline model as well as the values of the average response times for each transaction class.

Table 3.11 Baseline Model Parameters and Response Time.

	Class	
	Trivial	Complex
Arrival rate (tps)	0.50	0.30
Max. multiprog. degree	3	2
Service demand (sec)		
CPU	0.20	0.45
Disk 1	0.30	0.55
Disk 2	0.45	0.60
Response time	1.39	2.50

Assume that the transaction processing software was developed using conventional access method primitives invoked directly from the application programs to access the several files managed by the system.

3.6.2 Using a Database Management System

Let us assume that one is interested in rewriting the software of the system using a database management system (DBMS) to support all file accesses. Using a DBMS would allow for easier expansion and evolution of the system, due to the quite strong data independence provided by a DBMS to application programs. Since many upgrades are planned for the system, the first step would be to convert the existing version of the software to a DBMS based version. One question that arises is: How will performance change after the conversion is done?

Let us consider that it is known from published benchmarks that use of the selected DBMS implies an average increase in CPU usage of 25% and an average increase of 10% in I/O activity due to the fact that a DBMS has to translate DB access commands into sequences of file access commands. In the original version of the software, file access commands are directly wired in the code. So, to answer our capacity planning question, we have to change the values of the service demands at the CPU and at both disks accordingly. Let $D'_{i,r}$ denote the new value of the service demand of class r transactions at device i. So

$$D'_{cpu,r} = 1.25 \times D_{cpu,r} \tag{3.16}$$

$$D'_{disk_1,r} = 1.10 \times D_{disk_1,r} \tag{3.17}$$

$$D'_{disk_2,r} = 1.10 \times D_{disk_2,r} \tag{3.18}$$

Table 3.12 shows the new values of the service demands as well as the new values of the response times.

Table 3.12 Using a DBMS.

	Class	
	Trivial	Complex
Service demand (sec)		
CPU	0.25	0.56
Disk 1	0.33	0.61
Disk 2	0.50	0.66
Response time (sec)	1.79	3.36

So using a DBMS would result in a 28.7% increase in the response time of trivial transactions, and a 34.4% increase in the response time of complex ones.

3.6.3 Using a DBMS and an Optimizing Compiler

Let us assume that access to DBMS commands is done via calls to subroutines from the application code, which is written in a high-level language such as C or COBOL. Let us investigate the impact on response time of the use of an optimizing version of the compiler, which is known to generate a 50% more efficient (in terms of execution time) code. The compiler is going to be used only to optimize the application program code. Measurements made on the system revealed that 40% of the CPU consumption is due to the application code and 60% due to the data base management system.

Let $D_{cpu,r}^{appl}$ and $D_{cpu,r}^{dbms}$ be the portion of the service demand of class r transactions at the CPU due to the application code, and the portion of the service demand of class r transactions at the CPU due to the DBMS, respectively. So we can write the relationships

$$D_{cpu,r} = D_{cpu,r}^{appl} + D_{cpu,r}^{dbms} \tag{3.19}$$

$$D_{cpu,r}^{appl} = 0.40 \times D_{cpu,r} \tag{3.20}$$

$$D_{cpu,r}^{dbms} = 0.60 \times D_{cpu,r} \tag{3.21}$$

The application code and DBMS service demands at the CPU using the optimizing compiler will be indicated by an "opt" as a superscript and are given by the expressions

$$D_{\text{cpu},r}^{\text{opt,appl}} = 0.50 \times D_{\text{cpu},r}^{\text{appl}} = 0.5 \times 0.4 \times D_{\text{cpu},r} = 0.2 \times D_{\text{cpu},r} \qquad (3.22)$$

$$D_{\text{cpu},r}^{\text{opt,dbms}} = D_{\text{cpu},r}^{\text{dbms}} = 0.6 \times D_{\text{cpu},r} \qquad (3.23)$$

Thus, using Eqs. (3.22) and (3.23), we get that

$$D_{\text{cpu},r}^{\text{opt}} = 0.2 \times D_{\text{cpu},r} + 0.6 \times D_{\text{cpu},r} = 0.8 \times D_{\text{cpu},r} \qquad (3.24)$$

Therefore, the service demand matrix for this example is obtained from the previous one by multiplying the CPU line by 0.8. The response time values obtained are 1.77 sec and 3.09 sec for trivial and complex transactions, respectively. If we compare these values with those shown in Table 3.12, we see that use of an optimizing compiler represents a negligible improvement (on the order of 1%) for trivial transactions and a small improvement (on the order of 8%) for complex transactions.

3.6.4 Increasing Buffer Pool Size

Many database management systems use an area of main memory called the buffer pool to keep copies of the most recently accessed records. Therefore, at every access, the DBMS checks for the presence of the record in the buffer pool. If the record is present, we say that a *hit* occurred, and a physical I/O operation is not necessary. Otherwise, we say that a *miss* occurred and the record must be read from the disk into the buffer pool. If the buffer pool is full, another record must be flushed out of the pool according to any replacement policy. One of the most popular replacement policies is LRU, which replaces the least recently used record.

Let us now investigate the effect of adding more main memory to the computer system so that the buffer pool size can be increased. According to the performance tuning manual of the database management system in use, the amount of main memory devoted to the buffer pool will provide an estimated *hit ratio (h)* of 30%. In other words, 30% of the record references will be satisfied by the presence of the record in the buffer pool. Let $D_{\text{disk}_i,r}^{\text{bpool}}$ be the service demand of class r transactions at disk$_i$ in the expanded buffer pool situation and $D_{\text{disk}_i,r}$ be the original service demand of class r transactions at disk$_i$. Therefore, we may write that

$$D_{\text{disk}_i,r}^{\text{bpool}} = (1 - h) \times D_{\text{disk}_i,r} = 0.7 \times D_{\text{disk}_i,r} \qquad (3.25)$$

Table 3.13 shows the matrix of service demands for this case as well as the response time values for both classes. These values represent a significant improvement over the values indicated previously for the case of using a

Table 3.13   Using an Expanded Buffer Pool.

	Class	
	Trivial	Complex
Service demand (sec)		
CPU	0.250	0.563
Disk 1	0.231	0.424
Disk 2	0.347	0.462
Response time (sec)	1.17	2.18

DBMS with limited buffer pool (see Table 3.12). In fact, the improvement is on the order of 34% for trivial transactions and 35% for complex ones.

3.6.5 Using the Log Option for Crash Recovery

The DBMS being used has an option, which can be enabled selectively, which logs into disk all update transactions, to allow for crash recovery in case of system failures. Let us investigate the effect on response time of the use of the log option. Assume that we are using the expanded buffer pool of the preceding subsection. Consider that all complex transactions are update transactions, and consider that each update transaction generates a 2048-byte record in the LOG file. Let the LOG file be placed on disk 1.

We need to estimate the additional service demand on disk 1 due to the activity on the LOG file. For this purpose, we will neglect I/O channel or other disk controller contention effects. Let disk 1 have an average "seek + latency" time of 36 msec and a transfer rate of 750 Kbytes/sec. Thus the average time to write a log record in this disk is approximately equal to the average "seek + latency" time plus the average time needed to write a LOG file record. Hence, the additional service demand on disk 1 is equal to

$$36 \text{ msec} + \frac{2.048 \text{ Kbyte}}{0.750 \text{ Kbyte/msec}} = 38.7 \text{ msec}$$

Therefore, to reflect the use of the log option in our performance model we need to add 0.0387 sec to the service demand value of complex transactions at disk 1. Solving the performance model we obtain the new values of the response times, which are 1.17 and 2.26 sec for trivial and complex transactions, respectively. As we can see, the use of the log option increased the response time of complex transactions by only 4%.

3.6.6 Summary of Modification Analysis Results

Table 3.14 presents a summary of all the results of the previous modification analysis. The two rightmost columns show the percent variation of

Table 3.14 Summary of Results of the Modification Analysis.

Scenario	Response Time (sec)		Percent Variation with Respect to the BLM	
	Trivial	Complex	Trivial	Complex
Baseline model (BLM)	1.39	2.50		
Using a DBMS	1.79	3.36	28.8	34.4
DBMS + optimizing comp.	1.77	3.09	27.3	23.6
DBMS + buffer pool	1.17	2.18	-15.8	-12.8
DBMS + buffer pool + log	1.17	2.26	-15.8	-9.6

response time for all modification analysis scenarios with respect to the baseline model (BLM). Positive values indicate an increase in the response time and negative values indicate a decrease.

3.7 PERFORMANCE MODEL OF A CLIENT-SERVER SYSTEM

In previous sections we discussed performance models of centralized multiprogrammed computer systems. In this section we give an example of a performance model of a distributed system. This issue is treated extensively in Chap. 7.

Downsizing, replacing large mainframes with local area networks of workstations, has been the trend in many organizations. One popular structure for this type of arrangement is the *client-server paradigm* [5]. In this paradigm, some workstations—called server workstations or simply *servers*—provide services to user workstations—called client workstations or simply *clients*. Examples of servers include file servers, printer servers, disk servers, and database servers.

Consider the following capacity planning problem. A local area network (LAN) is composed of 20 diskless single-user client workstations and a *database server (DS)* which contains a database stored on a single disk. The workstations and database server are all connected by a 10-Mbps local area network as indicated in Fig. 3.13.

Users' think time at the client workstation is 10 sec. Commands are preprocessed at the station for syntactic and semantic checking. If correct, the command is inserted in a message that is sent to the database server. The SQL server receives commands from all workstations, submits them to the database management system, which runs at the server, and sends the result back to the workstation.

Assume that the SQL server is implemented in a 25-MIPS CPU computer and that each workstation is a 1-MIPS CPU computer. Consider that, on the average, database commands are 110 bytes long and that their results are 960 bytes long. Let us assume that, the preprocessing of commands at the workstation takes approximately 10,000 machine instructions, and that

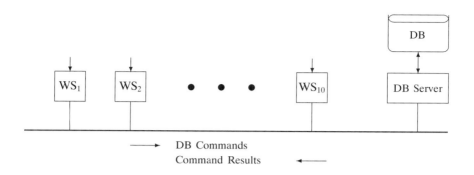

Figure 3.13 LAN based database system.

the execution of the command at the database server takes on the order of 100,000 instructions.

Assume that the disk has the following physical characteristics: 16 msec of revolution time, 20 msec of average seek time, and a 5 Mbyte/sec transfer rate. Each disk access reads or writes a 4-Kbyte data page. Each database command issues an average of 15 I/O operations.

Some examples of capacity planning problems are:

- What is the impact on the response time of commands if the number of user workstations is doubled?

- What is the impact on performance if the server CPU power is increased by 50%?

- What is the impact on response time if an additional disk is installed in the database server?

To answer these and similar questions we need a performance model. To build such a model, let us examine the types of delays suffered by a database command since it is submitted at a workstation until its result is received back at the workstation.

1. The message containing the command is transmitted to the server. This message suffers a *transmission delay*, which is the time needed to transmit the message through the network, and a *network access delay*, which is the time needed to get access to the network. The former delay is constant and equal to the command size divided by the network speed. For instance, in our case, this delay is equal to $110 \times 8/10,000,000 = 0.000088$ sec. The network access delay depends on the protocol being used (e.g., CSMA/CD, token ring, etc.) and on the load of the network.

2. The command is received by the server and cycles between the CPU and the disk in order to complete its execution.

3. The result has to be transmitted back to the workstation. Again, the command will be delayed by a transmission time and a network access delay. The transmission time in this case is equal to $960 \times 8/10,000,000 = 0.000768$ sec.

Figure 3.14 illustrates the performance model of our LAN-based database management system. The server denoted by WS represents the activity at a workstation. In particular, the service demand at this server is equal to the sum of the user think time and the processing time of an SQL command at the client CPU. There is no queuing in this server since each command returns to its own workstation and workstations are dedicated to a single user. Servers of this type are called *delay servers*. The server crossed with an arrow, labeled as Net, represents the total network delay incurred by a command in its way to and from the server. The arrow indicates that the delay in the server depends on the load of the server (i.e., in this case on the number of stations trying to access the network). Servers of this type are called *load-dependent servers*.

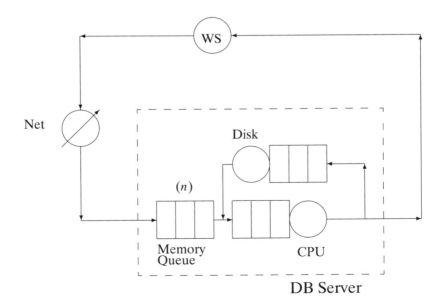

Figure 3.14 Performance model of the LAN-based database system.

We are now in a position to calculate the values of the numerical parameters of the performance model of our LAN-based database server. Let D_{sta}, D_{serv}, D_{disk}, and D_{net} be the service demands of a database command at the client CPU, at the server CPU, at the server disk, and at the network, respectively. The service demand at a client CPU can be computed as the average number of instructions executed at that workstation divided by the rate at which the CPU at that workstation executes instructions. So,

$$D_{sta} = \text{think time}$$

$$+ \frac{\text{no. instructions executed at client CPU}}{\text{client CPU speed}}$$

$$= 10 + \frac{10,000}{1,000,000} = 10.01 \text{ sec} \tag{3.26}$$

Similar reasoning can be used to obtain the service demand at the server CPU:

$$D_{serv} = \frac{\text{no. instructions executed at server CPU}}{\text{server CPU speed}} = \frac{100,000}{25,000,000} = 0.004 \text{ sec} \tag{3.27}$$

The average service demand per DB command at the server disk can be estimated by multiplying the average number of I/O operations per DB command by the average time to execute an I/O operation. Hence

$$D_{disk} = \text{no. I/O ops. per DB command} \times \text{avg. time per I/O operation}$$

$$= \text{no. I/O ops. per DB command}$$

$$\times (\text{rotational delay} + \text{seek} + \text{transfer time})$$

$$= 15 \times \left(\frac{0.016}{2} + 0.020 + \frac{4}{5000} \right) \text{ sec}$$

$$= 0.432 \text{ sec} \tag{3.28}$$

The service demand at the network server can be computed as the average time spent to transmit a DB command to the server plus the time required to transmit the result back to the user station plus twice (one for the DB command and one for the result) the average delay (in seconds), Δ, to get access to the network. As mentioned before, Δ depends on the network load, on the network access protocol, and on the network physical characteristics. Thus,

$$D_{net} = (\text{network delay of message with DB command})$$

$$+ (\text{network delay of message with command result})$$

$$= (0.000088 + 0.000768) + 2 \times \Delta \text{ sec}$$

$$= (0.000856 + 2 \times \Delta) \text{ sec} \tag{3.29}$$

Since each of the 20 clients does not submit a new DB command until it receives the answer to the previous one, there will only be one DB command from every station, cycling from the station to the server and back to the station. So our model can be characterized as a single class model with a customer population of 20 customers, one corresponding to each client.

As we can see from the parameters above, the disk is the bottleneck. Performance models can be used, for instance, to evaluate the impact of using a disk cache at the server in order to reduce the number of physical I/O operations, in a manner similar to the buffer pool example.

Notice that we chose to use DB commands as the customers in our example since all capacity planning questions of interest were posed in terms of DB commands. Consequently, all parameters were related to these entities. If we had considered that workstations submitted DB transactions which may be composed of one or more DB commands, we could use DB transactions as our customer definition. In this case, all performance measures and parameters should relate to transactions rather than commands.

3.8 MULTIPROCESSING

Many modern high-performance computer systems have more than one processor sharing a common global memory. Each processor may also have its own private memory. Main memory is made up of several independently accessible modules, interconnected to the processors through a processor-memory interconnection network, such as a multistage interconnection network (MIN), a crossbar switch, or global multiple buses, as indicated in Fig. 3.15. Cooperating processes run at different processors, sharing common pieces of data, in order to execute a single parallel application. A single operating system coordinates the operation of the entire multiprocessor.

Let us try to understand the points of possible contention in a multiprocessor such as the one depicted in Fig. 3.15. A process $\mathcal{P}$ running at a given processor P_i alternates between periods, in which it makes references to its own local memory (typically, where most of the code and local data reside) and references to an address at one of the global memory modules. Since local memory is addressable only by a single processor, no contention arises when a local memory access is performed. On the other hand, if a word of global memory module M_j is referenced by processor P_i, it must not only acquire the memory module, but also of one of the buses in order to transfer the desired word from the memory module into the processor. Therefore, queues may arise in two points: for bus access and for memory access. Another

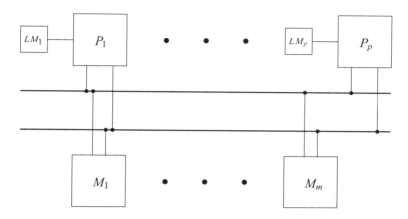

P_i = Processor i

M_j = Memory Module j

LM_i = Local Memory i

Figure 3.15 Multiprocessor with a double common bus.

interesting issue to be discussed here is that a processor must get hold of two resources at the same time: the bus and the desired memory module. This situation is generally called *simultaneous resource possession*.

Some typical performance metrics of a multiprocessor are:

- The speedup, $S(p)$, defined as the ratio between the execution time of a parallel application in a single processor, $T(1)$, over the execution time, $T(p)$, of the same application when executed in a p-processor multiprocessor:

$$S(p) = \frac{T(1)}{T(p)} \tag{3.30}$$

- The average number of busy processors, $\overline{p}$.
- The average total utilization, $\overline{U}$, defined as

$$\overline{U} = \frac{\sum_{i=1}^{p} U_i}{p} \tag{3.31}$$

where U_i is the utilization of processor P_i.

Performance models of multiprocessors and their solution are discussed in Chap. 8.

3.9 TYPES OF MODELS

The emphasis in this chapter has been on performance model construction rather than on their solution. There are basically two different approaches to the solution of performance models: simulation and analytical solution.

Simulation models are based on computer programs that emulate the different dynamic aspects of a system as well as their static structure. Customers (transactions, jobs, commands, etc.) are generated through a probabilistic process, using random number generators, and their flow through the system generates events such as arrival of a customer at the waiting queue of a server, beginning of service at any given server, end of service, and so on. The events are processed according to their order of occurrence in time. Counters accumulate statistics that are used at the end of a simulation run to estimate the values of several performance measures. For instance, the average response time at a single-server queue, T, can be estimated as

$$T = \frac{\sum_{i=1}^{n_t} T_i}{n_t} \tag{3.32}$$

where T_i is the response time experienced by the ith transaction and n_t is the total number of transactions that visited the server during the simulation. The values of T obtained in a single simulation run must be viewed as single points in a sample space. Thus, several simulation runs are required to generate a sample of adequate size to allow for a statistical analysis to be carried out on the sample.

Because of the level of detail generally necessary in simulation models, they are often too expensive to run, develop, and validate. On the other hand, they allow for the investigation of phenomena at any desired level of detail provided that one is ready to pay for it. For this reason, simulation programs are typically run on powerful workstations or even mainframes. Good references to simulation techniques are Refs. [6] to [8].

Analytical models are composed of a set of formulas and/or computational algorithms that provide the values of desired performance measures as a function of the set of values of the performance parameters. For analytical models to be mathematically tractable, they are generally less detailed than simulation models. Therefore, they are generally less accurate but more efficient to run. Hence, it is quite common to run analytical models on a personal computer. So, for example, in a single-server queue and under certain assumptions, to be discussed in later chapters, the average response time can be computed as

$$T = \frac{S}{1 - \lambda S} \tag{3.33}$$

where S is the average time spent at the server (service time) and λ is the average arrival rate of customers to the queue.

We summarize the advantages and disadvantages of simulation and analytical models.

- Analytical models tend to be computationally more efficient to run than simulation models.
- Because of their higher level of abstraction, obtaining the values of the input parameters in analytical models is simpler than in simulation models.
- Simulation models can be made as detailed as needed and can be more accurate than analytical models.

In some situations, exact analytical models are not available or are computationally inefficient. In these cases we can resort to approximations that may render the model easier to solve or solvable in a more efficient manner. One question that arises is how to gauge the accuracy of the approximation. Simulation models are quite useful in this regard, since we can always compare the results obtained from a detailed simulation model with those obtained by approximate analytic models. Once we are convinced that the approximation is reasonably accurate, we can abandon the simulation model and use the simpler and more efficient analytical one.

In capacity planning we are generally interested in being able quickly to compare and evaluate different scenarios. Accuracies at the 10 to 30% level are acceptable for this purpose. So, because of their efficiency and flexibility, analytic models—exact or approximate—are generally preferable for capacity planning purposes. This is the approach taken in this book.

3.10 CONCLUDING REMARKS

In this chapter we described, through various examples, the construction of performance models from a system description. We summarize below the steps that should be followed to construct a performance model of a computer system.

1. Identify the performance metrics of interest.
2. Identify the customers (transactions, jobs, commands, etc.) of the system.
3. Determine the various customer classes.
4. Determine the system components that result in delays and queuing, and specify the servers and their types (delay servers, queuing servers, load-dependent servers). The system components should be described at the minimum level of detail needed to obtain the performance measures specified in step 1.
5. Determine whether there are any passive resources.

6. Determine whether there are any instances of simultaneous resource possession.

7. For each server, determine the service demands per customer class.

8. For each class, determine the appropriate parameters that measure the workload intensity and obtain their values.

3.11 EXERCISES

1. Conduct a qualitative analysis of the impact of the variation of the think time on the response time of an interactive system.

2. Refer to the algorithm for aggregating transaction classes shown in Fig. 3.9. Assume that the average arrival rate for each class, λ_r, can be thought of as being approximately equal to the system throughput for each class, $X_{0,r}$. In other words, the number of arriving transactions during an observation period is approximately equal to the number of completing transactions during the same period. This assumption is called *flow-equilibrium assumption*. Demonstrate Eq. (3.10), which is repeated below. [*Hint:* Use Eq. (3.2) and its generalized version for multiple classes $D_{i,r} = U_{i,r}/X_{0,r}$.]

$$D_{i,\text{ag}} = \frac{\sum_{r=1}^{P} \lambda_r \times D_{i,r}}{\lambda_{\text{ag}}}$$

3. Which of the following factors may affect the value of the service demand at the CPU: (a) increase in the transaction arrival rate, (b) recoding of the transaction, (c) change of the CPU, (d) use of a different compiler?

4. Think of the operating systems and transaction monitor systems with which you are familiar and make a correspondence between the performance parameters defined in this chapter and presented in Table 3.10 with the terms and concepts used by the manufacturers to describe their systems.

5. A transaction processing system was monitored for 1 hour. During this period 7200 transactions were processed. A software monitor measured the following values for the utilizations of the CPU and the two disks: 30% for the CPU, 35% for disk 1 and 40% for disk 2.

   (a) Calculate the service demands at the CPU and at the two disks.
   (b) What is the minimum value for the response time?
   (c) What would be the new value of the CPU service demand if it were replaced by another four times faster?

6. Let λ be the average transaction arrival rate and D_i $(i = 1, \ldots, K)$ be the service demands at device i. Show that

$$\lambda \leq \frac{1}{\max_{i=1}^{K} D_i} \tag{3.34}$$

[*Hint:* The utilization of any device must be ≤ 1.]

7. Prove that the device that saturates first (utilization reaches 100%) is the one with the largest service demand.

8. The performance model built for the LAN-based database server example of Sec. 3.7 is a single class model with a population of 20 customers. Under what circumstances would one need to use a multiple-class model instead?

9. Consider a computer system composed of M terminals connected to an interactive system. The maximum number of concurrent interactive users is 5. The same system is also used simultaneously to process a transaction processing application. Due to memory constraints, there may be at most 6 transactions being executed simultaneously. Draw a graph that shows the qualitative behavior of the average response time of interactive users and of transactions as a function of the number of interactive terminals.

10. Table 3.15 shows the values of service demands and arrival rates for a transaction processing system composed of a CPU and one disk. Transactions were classified in five categories: T1, T2, T3, T4, and T5. The following capacity planning question has to be answered: *What is the impact on the response time of T1 and T3 transactions due to an increase in the average arrival rate of T1 transactions?* Show a table containing the parameters for a model with the minimum number of classes that should be used to answer this question.

Table 3.15 **Five Class Model Parameters.**

	Class				
	T1	T2	T3	T4	T5
Arrival rate (tps)	0.2	0.1	0.3	0.6	0.1
N^{max}	3	4	3	2	5
Service Demand (sec)					
CPU	0.20	0.15	0.35	0.10	0.30
Disk	0.30	0.10	0.20	0.30	0.10

11. Many modern I/O subsystems are composed of various elements, such as channels, disk controllers, and the devices themselves. Study the operation of several commercial I/O subsystems and determine which are the contention points as well as the instances of possible simultaneous resource possession.

12. Read Appendix D and learn how to use the capacity planning package *QSolver/1* provided with the book. Use the software to solve the 3-class performance model described in Sec. 3.5. The service demands for this example are given in Table 3.6. The other parameters needed are given in Table 3.16. Use *QSolver/1* to examine the effect on response time of increasing the transaction average arrival rate from its initial value to 0.4 tps. Using *QSolver/1*, determine possible alternatives (e.g., upgrading the CPU, using faster disks, changing the multiprogramming levels, changing priorities, etc.) that would make the average response time at an arrival rate of 0.4 tps to be only 10% higher than its original value. Try also combinations of alternatives.

13. You just hired Sue as a member of your performance management staff. You asked her to take some measurements of the OLTP system. She provides you with the following data: "each transaction requires, on the average, 0.12 sec

Table 3.16 Input Parameters for Exercise 12.

	Class		
	Transaction	Interactive	Batch
Arrival rate (tps)	0.05	NA	NA
N^{max}	3	4	NA
$\overline{N}$	NA	NA	1.50
No. terminals	NA	20	NA
Think time (sec)	NA	30	NA

of service from disk 1 and 0.15 sec of service from disk 2. The measured throughput is equal to 8 transactions per second." Would you believe in her measurements?

BIBLIOGRAPHY

1. J. L. Peterson, *Petri Net Theory and the Modeling of Systems*, Prentice Hall, Englewood Cliffs, N.J., 1981.

2. J. L. Hennessy and D. A. Patterson, *Computer Architecture: A Quantitative Approach*, Morgan Kaufmann, San Mateo, Calif., 1990.

3. S. L. Samson, *MVS Performance Management: Mechanisms and Methods*, McGraw-Hill, New York, 1990.

4. H. M. Deitel, *An Introduction to Operating Systems*, Addison-Wesley, Reading, Mass., 1984.

5. A. Sinha, Client-server computing, *Communications of the ACM*, Vol. 35, No. 7, July 1992, pp. 77–98.

6. A. M. Law and W. D. Kelton, *Simulation Modeling and Techniques*, 2nd ed., McGraw-Hill, New York, 1990.

7. M. H. MacDougall, *Simulating Computer Systems: Techniques and Tools*, MIT Press, Cambridge, Mass., 1987.

8. S. M. Ross, *A Course in Simulation*, Macmillan, New York, 1990.

Chapter 4

Intuitive Solutions for a Single-Processor Computer System Performance Model

4.1 INTRODUCTION

The goal of Chap. 3 was to introduce and motivate the use of performance models. The goal of this chapter is to provide insight and intuition regarding how these models are constructed and solved. The emphasis here is developing a complete understanding of simple models. More complex models and more clever solution techniques can then be understood at least conceptually if not completely.

4.2 ALTERNATIVE VIEW OF THE MODELING PARADIGM

It is useful to view the modeling process from different perspectives. One such alternative perspective is illustrated in Fig. 4.1. The initial step is to construct a suitable performance model. Two primary types of models were introduced briefly in Chap. 3: analytical models and simulation models. Analytical models specify the interactions between the various components of a computer system via formulas. [For instance, the formula $T = S/(1 - \lambda S)$ given in Chap. 3 states a relationship between the average response time T, the average service time S, and the arrival rate of customers to a queue, λ.] Simulation models mimic the behavior of the actual system by

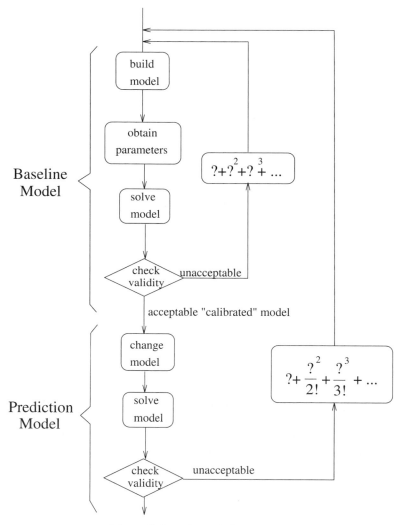

Figure 4.1 Baseline/prediction modeling paradigm.

running a simulation program. For instance, if the average service time of a customer at the CPU is 5 msec, the simulation program may randomly pick a number between 0 and 10, "play" as if the CPU were busy for that amount of time, advance the simulation clock by that amount, record that the CPU was busy for that amount of time, and continue. Other suitable performance models are possible. These include prototype models (e.g., actual hardware running actual code), numerical/statistical models (e.g., a plot of the utilization of the system as a function of time with a least-squares curve fit), or various hybrid models (e.g., a simulation model of the I/O behavior and an analytical model of the CPU behavior).

Once a suitable model has been chosen, the necessary parameters must be obtained and the necessary assumptions stated. The assumptions will vary depending on the type of model chosen. For example, if an analytical model is chosen, the average service time of a device may be needed and it may be assumed that the service times are exponentially distributed. If a simulation model is chosen, trace data may be required to simulate a specific assumed instruction mix. If a prototype model is used, the required hardware must be obtained and it may be assumed that the speed of the prototype hardware is a certain fraction of the speed of the modeled hardware. If a numerical/statistical model is selected, system log data may be needed and it may require the assumption that the system behaves in a continuous manner (so that smooth curves can be fit through the observed data). In every model, the parameters must be obtained and the assumptions must be stated.

After model construction and parameterization, the model is "solved." That is, the model parameters are manipulated in some fashion to yield performance measures (e.g., throughput, utilization, response time). This model solution step has traditionally received the most attention, since without a solution, the model is useless. Many solution techniques have been suggested. These solution techniques can loosely be grouped into either exact solutions of more approximate models (e.g., the exact solution of an analytical formula based on the inaccurate assumption that all variables are exponentially distributed) or approximate solutions of more accurate models (e.g., a simulation based upon confidence intervals but which models the variable distributions more closely). The other two possibilities are approximate solutions of approximate models (e.g., intuition-based guesstimates) and exact solutions of exact models (i.e., experimentally executing the desired workload on the desired system—since the only truly accurate model of a system is the system itself). The exact solution of simple analytical (approximate) models is the topic of this chapter.

Once the model has been constructed, parameterized, and solved, it should be "validated." That is, the performance measures found by solving the model should be compared against actual measurement data of the system being modeled. For instance, the actual device utilizations should be compared against the device utilizations found by solving the model. This comparison check will be judged to be either acceptable or unacceptable. The choice of what determines "acceptable" versus "unacceptable" is left to the modeler (or to the modeler's boss). As a rule of thumb, device utilizations within 10%, system throughput within 10%, and response time within 20% are considered acceptable. If the comparison is unacceptable, a "series of questions" must be addressed to determine the source of the errors.

Errors are possible within each modeling step. Ignored system components, inaccurately measured parameters, or incorrect assumptions are just a
few of the types of errors that may cause the comparison check to be unacceptable. Even though it is easy to hypothesize the source of possible errors in hindsight, it is often *quite* difficult to isolate them and correct them.
Therefore, it is normal to iterate among the steps above until an "acceptable"
model is found. Critics may term this iteration procedure "cheating": Because the model has so many free variables (e.g., model parameters, model
assumptions), it is always possible to adjust the model in any of several ways
to force the model to fit the behavior actually observed. There is some truth
to this criticism. Instead of referring to this as an acceptable "valid" model,
we choose to refer to it as a *calibrated* model. Calibration and validation are
the subject of Chap. 10.

The calibrated model forms the baseline model. It is a model that
matches the observed system behavior. Even though the baseline model is
somewhat useful by itself for descriptive purposes, the real power of modeling
is for predictive purposes. We wish to be able to ask "what if" questions and
to have the model be able to provide such performance predictions. What if a
certain device were upgraded? What if the workload changes and additional
users login? Therefore, once an acceptable baseline model has been developed, the first step in building a prediction model is to change the baseline
model to reflect the prediction task at hand. For instance, if we wish to predict the effect of upgrading a particular device, the appropriate model change
would be to replace the device in the baseline model. Often, a simple parameter change (e.g., changing the service time parameter S) in the baseline
model is sufficient. However, the interactions and interdependencies among
the various parameters must be considered. For instance, by upgrading one
device, the workload on another device may be influenced and must also be
reflected by changing its parameters. To construct good prediction models,
these primary and secondary effects must be both understood and modeled.
As a specific example, if the CPU is being upgraded by a factor of 2, the
primary effect on the prediction model would be to change the service rate
parameter of the CPU by a factor of 2. However with a faster CPU, one might
expect that average degree of multiprogramming might decrease (since customers exit the system quicker). This multiprogramming level decrease may
reduce the amount of paging activity since fewer customers are contending
for memory simultaneously. This may lead to a change in the paging device's
parameters since its workload changes. A single primary modification of the
model may need to be accompanied by secondary and tertiary modifications.
Therefore, while the model solution step has received the most attention, the
most important and challenging step is the change model step. Once the modifications have been made, the resulting prediction model is then re-solved.
The output of the model represents the model's predicted performance if the
corresponding modifications were actually implemented.

The final step in the modeling paradigm is the validity check step of the prediction model. This step is the one that is most often ignored. A typical modeling scenario is as follows. Company X is dissatisfied with its current computer service level—the system is too slow. The company decides to upgrade its current facility and has allocated a certain amount of funds for the upgrade. An analyst, Joe, is hired to recommend the best alternative. Joe (after having read this book and liking it!) follows the modeling paradigm steps in Fig. 4.1. A baseline model is constructed, parameterized, solved, and calibrated to match X's current system. Joe then constructs several prediction models, one for each of the alternative upgrades. Each of these prediction models is solved and the one that gives the highest performance prediction is the alternative that is recommended to X's board of directors. The board thanks Joe, accepts his recommendation, pays him well, sends him on his way, and places the order for the new upgrade. After a few months, the upgrade is installed. Joe is gone and is working on other projects. The company now has new fires to fight and nobody thinks about going back and seeing if Joe's prediction/recommendation was, in retrospect, correct. Thus, this validation step is often ignored. Idealistically, each of the upgrade alternatives would be installed, their performance measured, and the results compared against the model's predictions. If the model accurately predicted the results (or, at least, correctly ranked the relative performance of the various alternatives), the model is dubbed truly *valid* and not simply calibrated. However, if this final comparison check is unacceptable, it is necessary to determine the cause, by addressing a "more difficult series of questions" and returning to an earlier modeling step.

Viewing this modeling paradigm in perspective, we now concentrate on the model solution step. The remainder of this chapter provides an intuitive approach, based on simple state diagrams. In succeeding chapters we develop more clever and more generally applicable solution techniques.

4.3 SIMPLE SERVER SYSTEM I

Motivating problem: *Suppose that an average of 30 tps arrive at a computer system. Each transaction requires an average of 20 msec of processing from the central processor. What is the current performance of the system (e.g., the processor's utilization, the system response time, the system throughput, the average queue length)? What is the predicted performance if the workload increases by 50% more transactions per second? What is the predicted performance if the workload increases by 50% but the processor is upgraded by 50%?*

By following the modeling paradigm, a model of this system is initially constructed. Pictorially, the representation of an analytical model might be as simple as that shown in Fig. 4.2. Here transactions (customers, jobs) enter

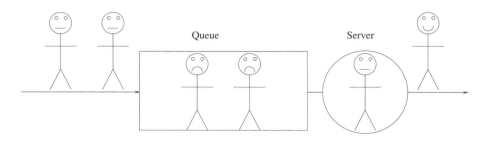

Figure 4.2 Simple server system.

the system, possibly queue up while waiting for the single server to become available, obtain service, and then exit the system.

The model parameterization step consists of obtaining workload (i.e., software) parameters and system (i.e., hardware) parameters. The primary workload parameter is the arrival rate of transactions, denoted by λ. The primary system parameter is the service rate of the server, denoted by μ. In this example, $\lambda = 30$ tps, and

$$\mu = \frac{1 \text{ transaction}}{20 \text{ milliseconds}} = 50 \text{ tps}$$

(*Note:* The service rate μ is actually dependent on both the workload and the system. It is a bit of a lie to say that the service rate is a system parameter only.)

4.3.1 Model Solution

To "solve" this system, the first step is to construct the state-space diagram. This implies that an appropriate state description is necessary. That is, if one were to take a snapshot of the system, what information would be necessary to capture the system's current state, so that if the system were interrupted and later reset to the state, the system would resume execution as if the interruption had not occurred? To be complete, the state description would need to record which customers were at each device, how long each executing customer has been in execution, how much remaining service time is required by each executing customer, and several additional parameters that may influence the system's behavior. That is, to recreate a system state at a later time, a complete state description would require a complete trace file (i.e., history) of all previous events leading up to the current time. This is clearly too much information to be useful. Therefore, some appropriate approximation/simplification of the complete state description is needed. The state description chosen is a *single* parameter, the number of customers currently in the system. Using such a state description implies that two important assumptions are made.

- All customers are statistically indistinguishable. Which customers are present is not important, only the number of present customers. This is the single-class, or homogeneous workload, assumption.
- Old history is irrelevant. It does not matter how the system arrived in a state, just that it is currently in the state. This subtly implies that the length of time that a customer has been executing at a server is also irrelevant. If two snapshots were taken, one just after a customer's arrival to the system and one just before the customer's departure, the two states (i.e., the number of customers currently in the system) are indistinguishable. This is the memoryless, or Markov, assumption.

We will return to these assumptions and relax them at a later time. (After all, this is supposed to be a *simple* example.)

With this state description, it is possible to construct the appropriate (Markov) state-space diagram, as shown in Fig. 4.3. In this diagram the system "flows" from state to state depending on the workload and system parameters, λ and μ. Suppose that the system is in state k. That is, there is one customer in execution, executing at rate μ and there are $k - 1$ customers in the queue, awaiting service. The state will change if either a new customer arrives (with rate λ) or the executing customer completes service (with rate μ). (*Note:* It is assumed that at most one event, a customer arrival or a customer completion, happens at any point in time. That is, it is not possible to go directly from state k to any state other than to state $k - 1$ or to state $k + 1$.) This system is often termed a *birth–death system*.

Once the state-space diagram has been constructed, the flow balance equations can be derived easily. *Flow balance* means that over a long period of time (i.e., in *steady-state*), the total flow arriving into any system state must equal the total flow departing from that state. Consider state 0 in Fig. 4.3. The total flow coming into this state is μ *if* the system is currently in state 1. Let P_k denote the (long-term or steady-state) probability of being in state k. Therefore, the total flow coming into state 0 is μP_1. Likewise, the total flow going out of state 0 is λP_0. These two flows must equal each other. Similarly, from the state diagram, the total flow coming into state 1 is the sum of two

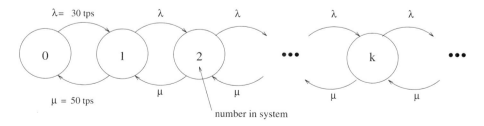

Figure 4.3 State-space diagram—system I.

flows, λP_0 coming from state 0 and μP_2 coming from state 2. The total flow out of state 1 is also the sum of two flows, λP_1 flowing toward state 2 and μP_1 flowing toward state 0. Thus, the system of flow balance equations for this system is

$$\text{flow in} = \text{flow out}$$

$$\mu P_1 = \lambda P_0$$

$$\lambda P_0 + \mu P_2 = \lambda P_1 + \mu P_1$$

$$\vdots$$

$$\lambda P_{k-1} + \mu P_{k+1} = \lambda P_k + \mu P_k$$

$$\vdots$$

The next step is to solve this system of linear equations to find P_0, P_1, $P_2, \ldots, P_k, \ldots$, which represent the steady-state probabilities of no one being in the system, one customer being in the system, two customers being in the system, ..., k customers being in the system, ..., respectively. When solving systems of equations that result from Markov diagrams of this type, it is often easiest (and relatively straightforward) to represent all unknowns (i.e., the P_i's) in terms of a single unknown, usually P_0. That is, from the first balance equation, $\mu P_1 = \lambda P_0$, the unknown P_1 can be represented in terms of P_0:

$$P_1 = \frac{\lambda}{\mu} P_0$$

Knowing this, from the second balance equation, $\lambda P_0 + \mu P_2 = \lambda P_1 + \mu P_1$, the unknown P_2 can also be represented in terms of P_0. (*Note:* Actually, the second balance equation can be reduced immediately to $\mu P_2 = \lambda P_1$ by canceling the λP_0 term on the left-hand side against the μP_1 term on the right-hand side, due to the first balance equation.) Thus,

$$P_2 = \frac{\lambda}{\mu} P_1 = \left(\frac{\lambda}{\mu}\right)^2 P_0$$

In general,

$$P_k = \frac{\lambda}{\mu} P_{k-1} = \frac{\lambda}{\mu} \frac{\lambda}{\mu} P_{k-2} = \cdots = \left(\frac{\lambda}{\mu}\right)^k P_0$$

Thus, since now all unknowns are in terms of the single unknown P_0, to complete the solution it is necessary to find an expression for P_0. To do this, an extra "given" equation is needed. Since the unknown quantities are probabilities, it must be that the sum of all probabilities is 1. That is, at any given time, the system must be in exactly one of the states 0, 1, 2, ... This is known as the *conservation of total probability*. The equation is:

$$P_0 + P_1 + P_2 + \cdots = 1$$

After substitution and a bit of simplification, the steady-state solution for being in state 0 is derived.

$$P_0 + P_1 + P_2 + \cdots = 1$$

$$P_0 + \left(\frac{\lambda}{\mu}\right) P_0 + \left(\frac{\lambda}{\mu}\right)^2 P_0 + \cdots = 1$$

$$P_0 = \left[1 + \left(\frac{\lambda}{\mu}\right) + \left(\frac{\lambda}{\mu}\right)^2 + \cdots\right]^{-1} = \left[\sum_{i=0}^{\infty} \left(\frac{\lambda}{\mu}\right)^i\right]^{-1}$$

$$= [1/(1 - \lambda/\mu)]^{-1} = 1 - \frac{\lambda}{\mu}$$

Therefore, the final steady-state probability for being in any particular state k is:

$$P_k = \left(\frac{\lambda}{\mu}\right)^k \left(1 - \frac{\lambda}{\mu}\right)$$

[*Note:* A bit of caution is needed here. The sum $\sum_{i=0}^{\infty} (\lambda/\mu)^i$ is finite *only* if $\lambda < \mu$. Otherwise, if $\lambda \geq \mu$, the sum is infinite and P_0 would reduce to 0. (Actually, in this case, all P_k would reduce to 0.) This makes sense because if the arrival rate were larger than the service rate, the system would not be able to service the customers as fast as they arrived. The queue would become increasingly longer as a function of time. This system would not be in "steady-state." Thus, the condition for steady-state in this system is $\lambda < \mu$.]

In the original problem, $\lambda = 30$ and $\mu = 50$. Therefore, the probability that no one is in the system (i.e., that the system is idle) is $P_0 = 1 - \lambda/\mu = 1 - 30/50 = 2/5 = 40\%$. Similarly, the probability that exactly one, two, or three customers are in the system (i.e., P_1, P_2, or P_3) is 24%, 14%, and 9%, respectively.

From these basic steady-state probabilities, it is possible to find expressions of more useful performance measures. For example, the system is busy (i.e., being utilized) when one or more customers are in the system. Thus, the utilization of the system is

$$\text{utilization} = P_1 + P_2 + \cdots = 1 - P_0 = \frac{\lambda}{\mu} = \frac{30}{50} = 60\%$$

The total system throughput is the rate at which customers leave the system after being served. Total throughput is the sum of the individual state throughputs, weighted by the probability of being in the individual states. For example, in state 0 the system is idle and there is no system throughput. Thus, with probability P_0, the throughput is 0. In state 1, the system is busy working and is putting out customers at rate μ (i.e., the service rate *not* the arrival rate). Thus, with probability P_1, the throughput is μ. Similarly, with probability P_2, the throughput is μ. In general,

$$
\begin{aligned}
\text{throughput} &= 0P_0 + \mu P_1 + \mu P_2 + \cdots \\
&= \mu(P_1 + P_2 + \cdots) \\
&= \mu \times \text{utilization} \\
&= \mu \times \frac{\lambda}{\mu} \\
&= \lambda \\
&= 30 \text{ customer transactions per second}
\end{aligned}
$$

This is hardly surprising. The throughput of the system is equal to the arrival rate. Flow out equals flow in.

Another useful performance measure is the average number of customers in the system. This is referred to as the mean queue length and includes both the number of customers in the queue and the number being served. Again, a state-by-state enumeration is done. In state 0, no one is in the system. Thus, with probability P_0 the queue length is 0. In state 1, one customer is in the system. Thus, with probability P_1 the queue length is 1. In general, with probability P_k the queue length is k. Thus,

$$
\begin{aligned}
\text{queue length} &= 0P_0 + 1P_1 + 2P_2 + \cdots \\
&= \sum_{k=1}^{\infty} k P_k \\
&= \sum_{k=1}^{\infty} k \left(\frac{\lambda}{\mu}\right)^k \left(1 - \frac{\lambda}{\mu}\right) \\
&= \left(1 - \frac{\lambda}{\mu}\right) \frac{(\lambda/\mu)}{(1 - \lambda/\mu)^2} \\
&= \frac{\lambda/\mu}{1 - \lambda/\mu} \\
&= \frac{\lambda}{\mu - \lambda} \\
&= \frac{30}{50 - 30} \\
&= 1.5 \text{ customers}
\end{aligned}
$$

Another useful performance measure is the average response time. This is the average time that a customer spends in the system, from arrival time until completion time. There are two components to a customer's response time, the time spent waiting in the queue and the time spent in service. The time that a customer spends waiting in the queue is equal to the time required to clear out the customers who are currently in the system when the customer arrives. Upon arrival, a customer "sees" steady-state. (*Note:* This is a consequence of the *arrival theorem* [1] which states that an arriving customer sees steady-state of the system with itself removed. Since, in this system there is a infinite customer population, an arriving customer sees the overall steady-state.) Therefore, an arriving customer sees $\lambda/(\mu - \lambda)$ other customers ahead of itself (i.e., the mean queue length). It requires $1/\mu$ time units to flush each one of these earlier arrived customers out of the system. Thus, the time that a tagged customer spends waiting in the queue is equal to $(1/\mu)[\lambda/(\mu - \lambda)]$ time units. Then, once the tagged customer gets to the head of the queue, it requires an additional $1/\mu$ time units to complete its own service. Therefore, the average response time is

$$\text{response time} = \underbrace{\frac{1}{\mu} \times \underbrace{\frac{\lambda}{\mu - \lambda}}_{\text{no. I see at arrival time}}}_{} + \underbrace{\frac{1}{\mu}}_{\text{my service time}} = \frac{1}{\mu - \lambda} = \frac{1}{20} \text{ sec}$$

time to finish those ahead of me

Alternatively, the average response time can be found using Little's result. However, because of the importance and general applicability of Little's result, a separate subsection is devoted to it.

4.3.2 Little's Result

Conceptually, Little's result [2] is quite simple and intuitively appealing. We describe the result by way of an analogy. Consider a pub. Customers arrive at the pub, stay for a while, and leave. Little's result states that the average number of folk in the pub (i.e., the queue length) is equal to the arrival rate of customers at the pub times the average time each customer stays in the pub (see Fig. 4.4).

This result applies across a wide range of assumptions. For instance, consider a deterministic situation where a new customer walks into the pub every hour on the hour. Upon entering the pub, suppose that there are three other customers in the pub. Suppose that the bartender regularly kicks out the customer who has been there the longest, every hour at the half hour. Thus, a new customer will enter at 9:00, 10:00, 11:00, ..., and the oldest remaining customer will be booted out at 9:30, 10:30, 11:30, ... It is clear that the

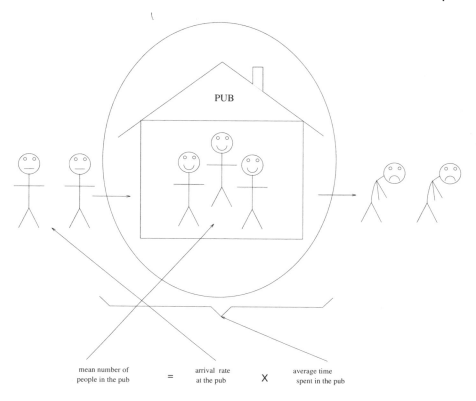

mean number of   =   arrival rate   ×   average time
people in the pub   at the pub   spent in the pub

Figure 4.4 Little's result.

average number of persons in the pub will be $3\frac{1}{2}$, since 4 customers will be in
the pub for the first half hour of every hour and only 3 customers will be in the
pub for the second half hour of every hour. The arrival rate of customers at
the pub is one customer per hour. The time spent in the pub by any customer
is $3\frac{1}{2}$ hours. Thus, Little's result holds:

number in pub $=$ arrival rate at pub $\times$ time spent in pub

$$3\frac{1}{2} = 1 \times 3\frac{1}{2}$$

Also, it does not matter which customer the bartender kicks out. For
instance, suppose that the bartender chooses a customer at random to kick
out. Thus, the average time a customer spends in the pub is one half hour
with probability 0.25, one and a half hours with probability $(0.75)(0.25) =$
0.1875 (i.e., the customer avoided the bartender the first time around, but was
chosen the second), two and a half hours with probability $(0.75)(0.75)(0.25)$,

and so on. That is,

average time spent in pub

$$
= \left(\frac{1}{2}\right)\left(\frac{1}{4}\right) + \left(\frac{3}{2}\right)\left(\frac{3}{4}\right)\left(\frac{1}{4}\right) + \left(\frac{5}{2}\right)\left(\frac{3}{4}\right)\left(\frac{3}{4}\right)\left(\frac{1}{2}\right) + \cdots
$$

$$
= \frac{1}{8} \sum_{i=0}^{\infty} (2i + 1) \left(\frac{3}{4}\right)^i
$$

$$
= \frac{1}{4} \sum_{i=0}^{\infty} i \left(\frac{3}{4}\right)^i + \frac{1}{8} \sum_{i=0}^{\infty} \left(\frac{3}{4}\right)^i
$$

$$
= 3 + \frac{1}{2} = 3\frac{1}{2}
$$

Therefore, it does not matter which customer the bartender kicks out. Little's result is quite general and requires few assumptions.

Restating Little's result as

$$
\begin{array}{ccc}
\text{average number of} & = & \text{arrival rate} \\
\text{customers in a system} & & \text{at the system}
\end{array} \times \begin{array}{c}
\text{average time spent} \\
\text{in the system}
\end{array} \tag{4.1}
$$

the term *system* can refer to virtually any group of objects. For example, reconsider Fig. 4.2. Let the designated system be the server only, excluding the queue. Applying Little's result, the average number of customers in the system is interpreted as the average number of customers in the server. The server will either have a single customer who is utilizing the server, or the server will have no customer present. The probability that a single customer is utilizing the server is equal to the server utilization. The probability that no customer is present is equal to the server idle time. Thus, the *average* number of customers in the server equals $1 \times$ Prob[single customer present] $+ 0 \times$ Prob[no customer present]. This simply equals the server's utilization. Therefore, the average number of customers in the server equals the server's utilization. The arrival rate at the server (i.e., the arrival rate at the system) equals the external arrival rate, which equals the external departure rate, since flow in equals flow out. This is system throughput. Therefore, the arrival rate at the server equals throughput. The average time spent by a customer at the server is simply the mean service time of the server. Thus, with this interpretation of Little's result:

$$
\begin{array}{ccc}
\text{average number of} & = & \text{arrival rate} \\
\text{customers in a system} & & \text{at the system}
\end{array} \times \begin{array}{c}
\text{average time spent} \\
\text{in the system}
\end{array}
$$

$$
\text{server utilization} = \text{throughput} \times \text{mean service time}
$$

$$
\text{utilization} = \lambda \times \frac{1}{\mu}
$$

In the preceding subsection, for the simple server example it was shown that

$$\text{response time} = \frac{1}{\mu - \lambda} = \frac{1}{20} \text{ sec}$$

By interpreting Little's result applied to the simple server system, we obtain

$$\begin{array}{ccc}
\text{average number of} & = & \text{arrival rate} \\
\text{customers in a system} & & \text{at the system}
\end{array} \times \begin{array}{c}
\text{average time spent} \\
\text{in the system}
\end{array}$$

$$\text{queue length} = \text{throughput} \times \text{response time}$$

$$\text{response time} = \frac{\text{queue length}}{\text{throughput}} = \frac{\lambda/(\mu - \lambda)}{\lambda} = \frac{1.5}{30} = \frac{1}{20} \text{ sec}$$

Thus, once knowing the queue length and throughput of a system, the response time can be calculated immediately using Little's result.

4.3.3 Model Predictions

Recall the motivating problem at the beginning of this section, the transaction system. *Suppose that an average of 30 tps arrive at a computer system. Each transaction requires an average of 20 msec of processing from the central processor. What is the current performance of the system (e.g., the processor's utilization, the system response time, the system throughput, the average queue length)?* The modeling paradigm (Fig. 4.1) was applied. A model was constructed (Fig. 4.2). The model was parameterized using an arrival rate $\lambda = 30$ tps and using a service rate $\mu = 50$ tps. The model was then solved by constructing the underlying state-space diagram (Fig. 4.3) and by forming and solving the flow balance equations. It was found that

$$\text{utilization} = \frac{\lambda}{\mu} = 60\%$$

$$\text{throughput} = \lambda = 30 \text{ tps}$$

$$\text{queue length} = \frac{\lambda}{\mu - \lambda} = 1.5 \text{ customers}$$

$$\text{response time} = \frac{1}{\mu - \lambda} = \frac{1}{20} \text{ sec}$$

Recall the prediction aspect of the motivation problem. *What is the predicted performance if the workload increases by 50% more transactions per second? What is the predicted performance if the workload increases by 50% but the processor is upgraded by 50%?* By following the modeling paradigm, the necessary steps are to change the model and re-solve the model.

Consider the effect of increasing the workload by 50% more transactions per second. The appropriate primary change to the model is to increase the transaction arrival rate parameter, λ, from 30 tps to 45 tps. Let λ' represent the predicted new transaction arrival rate. Thus, letting $\lambda' = 45$ (and assuming that there are no secondary effects, so the μ remains at 50 tps), the above equations can be re-solved to obtain the desired predicted performance measures:

$$\text{utilization} = \frac{\lambda'}{\mu} = 90\%$$

$$\text{throughput} = \lambda' = 45 \text{ tps}$$

$$\text{queue length} = \frac{\lambda'}{\mu - \lambda'} = 9 \text{ customers}$$

$$\text{response time} = \frac{1}{\mu - \lambda'} = \frac{1}{5} \text{ sec}$$

Thus, by increasing the workload by 50%, the utilization of the system and the throughput of the system also increase by 50%. However, the mean queue length increases from 1.5 to 9, a 500% increase, and the mean response time increases from 0.05 sec to 0.2 sec, a 300% increase. This indicates that queue lengths and response times are much more sensitive to changes in the system parameters. As a result, it is more difficult to predict queue lengths and response times accurately, since a relatively small error in the predicted parameters (e.g., λ and μ) can lead to relatively large errors in the predicted values of queue lengths and response times. These general rules of thumb have been observed repeatedly in practice.

Now consider the effect of increasing the workload by 50% more transactions per second, but at the same time, upgrading the processor by 50%. As before, the effect of modeling the 50% workload increase is captured by letting $\lambda' = 45$ tps. To capture the effect of upgrading the processor by 50%, the new processor would be able to handle 75 tps instead of the old rate of 50 transactions per second. Let μ' represent the new predicted processor service rate. Thus, let $\mu' = 75$ tps. By re-solving the equations, the desired performance predictions are found to be

$$\text{utilization} = \frac{\lambda'}{\mu'} = 60\%$$

$$\text{throughput} = \lambda' = 45 \text{ tps}$$

$$\text{queue length} = \frac{\lambda'}{\mu' - \lambda'} = 1.5 \text{ customers}$$

$$\text{response time} = \frac{1}{\mu' - \lambda'} = \frac{1}{30} \text{ sec}$$

Thus, by increasing both the workload (λ) and the processing capacity (μ) by 50%, utilization of the system and the mean number of customers in the system (i.e., queue length) remain unchanged. The system throughput improves by 50%, as one would hope and expect. However, one might originally expect that the system response time would remain basically unaffected since the two competing effects would tend to cancel each other (i.e., an increased workload which would drive response times up, against a faster processor, which would drive response times down). In actuality, the processor speed is a more dominating factor and increasing the processor speed by 50% more than offsets a 50% increase in the workload. In this example, when both λ and μ are increased by 50%, the response time drops from $\frac{1}{20}$ sec to $\frac{1}{30}$ sec, a 33% improvement. Thus, to maintain a given response time level as the workload increases by $p\%$, a less than $p\%$ faster processor is required.

4.4 SIMPLE SERVER SYSTEM II

Motivating problem: *Suppose that there are three users of a transaction system. Assume that each user submits a new transaction to the system an average of 0.5 sec after the response to the previous request. Assume that when there is only one request in the system, the system responds to the request in an average of 1.5 sec. However, because of pipelining and overlapping effects, when there are two requests in the system, the system can complete a transaction in an average of 1 sec. For similar reasons, when there are three requests in the system, the system can complete a transaction in an average of 0.75 sec. What is the current performance of the system (e.g., the processor's utilization, the system response time, the system throughput, the average queue length)? What is the predicted performance if the users went to a training session and their mean time between transaction requests drops to 0.4 sec? What is the predicted performance if an improved pipeline were installed which is advertised to be 50% faster than the original pipeline?*

An illustration of this system is shown in Fig. 4.5. This setup represents a *closed system*, where there is a fixed maximum number of users in the system (three in this case). Closed systems are depicted by a feedback loop from the system to the users. Users iterate between "thinking" and receiving service. This is in contrast to the *open system* in the preceding section, where an unlimited number of customers could be present in the system simultaneously and where users arrive, receive service, and exit. As shown below, closed systems lead to finite state-space diagrams, and open systems lead to infinite state-space diagrams.

This problem, although seemingly much more complex than the original problem, requires only slight modifications for its solution. The issue here is *state-dependent* arrival and service rates, as opposed to *state-independent* arrival (i.e., $\lambda = 30$) and service (i.e., $\mu = 50$) rates in the preceding problem. Here,

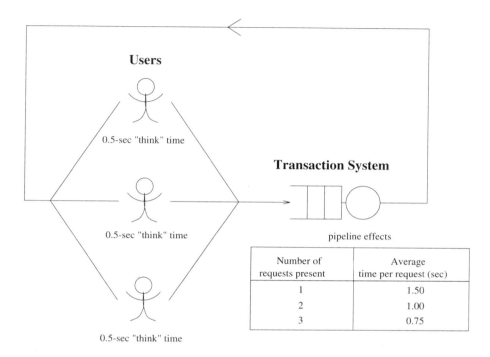

Figure 4.5 Three-user transaction system—system II.

if there is no one in the system, the arrival rate per user is 2 tps (i.e., an average of 0.5 sec between transaction submissions). Because there are three users each in the process of submitting requests, the total arrival rate, when there is no one in the system, is 6 tps. If there is one user in the system, then only the other two users are submitting requests, making a total arrival rate of 4 tps. Similarly, if two users are in the system, the remaining user is submitting new requests at a rate of 2 tps. If all three users are in the system, no new arrivals will be seen.

Now consider the state-dependent service rate. If there is a single request in the system, that request is serviced at rate $\frac{2}{3}$ tps (i.e., the inverse of 1.5 sec per transaction request). If there are two requests in the system, the service rate is 1 tps. If all three requests are in the system, the service rate is $\frac{4}{3}$ tps.

Therefore, the appropriate state-space diagram is shown in Fig. 4.6. The corresponding flow balance equations are

$$\text{flow in} = \text{flow out}$$

$$\frac{2}{3}P_1 = 6P_0$$

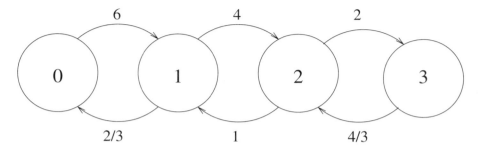

Figure 4.6   State-space diagram—system II.

$$6P_0 + 1P_2 = \frac{2}{3}P_1 + 4P_1$$

$$4P_1 + \frac{4}{3}P_3 = 1P_2 + 2P_2$$

$$2P_2 = \frac{4}{3}P_3$$

There are four equations and four unknowns. However, one of the equations is redundant and can be deleted. (Check it out. You won't be able to solve the above set of equations for a unique solution.) Thus, as done in the previous motivating problem, one of the equations is replaced by

$$P_0 + P_1 + P_2 + P_3 = 1$$

The solution to this set of equations is

$$P_0 = \frac{1}{100}$$

$$P_1 = \frac{9}{100}$$

$$P_2 = \frac{36}{100}$$

$$P_3 = \frac{54}{100}$$

From these steady-state probabilities, the desired performance measures can be obtained:

$$\text{utilization} = 1 - P_0 = 99\%$$

$$\text{throughput} = \frac{2}{3}P_1 + 1P_2 + \frac{4}{3}P_3 = \frac{114}{100} \text{ tps}$$

$$\text{queue length} = 1P_1 + 2P_2 + 3P_3 = \frac{243}{100} \text{ customers}$$

$$\text{response time} = \frac{\text{queue length}}{\text{throughput}} = \frac{243}{114} \text{ sec}$$

The predicted performance measures when the users attend a training session and when the pipeline is upgraded are left as exercises.

4.5 GENERALIZED BIRTH–DEATH MODELS

The previous models have been examples of *birth–death systems*. Given that the system is in a particular state k, indicating k customers in the system, one of two events can occur that can cause the system to leave state k. Either a *birth* occurs, where the arrival of another customer causes the system to enter state $k + 1$, or a *death* occurs, where the departure of a customer causes the system to enter state $k - 1$. In the Markov state-space diagram represented by Fig. 4.3, the corresponding model is open (indicated by an infinite number of possible states), the arrival rate λ is independent of the current state, and the departure rate μ is also independent of the current state. In the Markov state-space diagram represented by Fig. 4.6, the corresponding model is closed (indicated by a finite number of possible states), the arrival rates (i.e., the arrows going to the right) are dependent on the current state, and the departure rates (i.e., the arrows going to the left) are also dependent on the current state.

The generalization of these models is straightforward. Given that the current state is state k, assume that the arrival rate (i.e., the birth rate) of new customers is λ_k and that the completion rate (i.e., the death rate) of customers is μ_k. That is, the birth and death rates are state-dependent. Using this notation, the example shown in Fig. 4.3 would have $\lambda_i = 30$ tps for $i = 0, 1, 2, \ldots,$ $k - 1, k, \ldots$ and would have $\mu_i = 50$ tps for $i = 1, 2, 3, \ldots, k, k + 1, \ldots.$ Using this notation, the example shown in Fig. 4.6 would have $\lambda_0 = 6, \lambda_1 = 4, \lambda_2 = 2,$ and $\lambda_i = 0$ for $i = 3, 4, \ldots$ and would have $\mu_1 = \frac{2}{3}, \mu_2 = 1, \mu_3 = \frac{4}{3}$, and $\mu_i = 0$ for $i = 4, 5, \ldots.$ This generalization is indicated by Fig. 4.7.

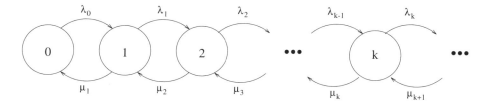

Figure 4.7 Generalized birth–death state-space diagram.

Following the solution approach given in Sec. 4.3.1, the system of flow balance equations is

$$\text{flow in} = \text{flow out}$$

$$\mu_1 P_1 = \lambda_0 P_0$$

$$\lambda_0 P_0 + \mu_2 P_2 = \lambda_1 P_1 + \mu_1 P_1$$

$$\vdots$$

$$\lambda_{k-1} P_{k-1} + \mu_{k+1} P_{k+1} = \lambda_k P_k + \mu_k P_k$$

$$\vdots$$

By substituting and rewriting appropriately, we have

$$P_k = \frac{\lambda_{k-1}}{\mu_k} P_{k-1} = \frac{\lambda_{k-1}}{\mu_k} \frac{\lambda_{k-2}}{\mu_{k-1}} P_{k-2} = \cdots = \frac{\lambda_{k-1}}{\mu_k} \frac{\lambda_{k-2}}{\mu_{k-1}} \frac{\lambda_{k-3}}{\mu_{k-2}} \cdots \frac{\lambda_0}{\mu_1} P_0$$

$$= P_0 \prod_{i=0}^{k-1} \frac{\lambda_i}{\mu_{i+1}}$$

Using the conservation of total probability, $P_0 + P_1 + P_2 + \cdots = 1$, substitution, and some simplification yields

$$P_0 = \left[\sum_{k=0}^{\infty} \prod_{i=0}^{k-1} \lambda_i / \mu_{i+1} \right]^{-1}$$

where the first term in the summation is defined to be 1. Therefore, the generalized steady-state solution, for any birth–death system, for being in any particular state k is:

$$P_k = \left[\sum_{k=0}^{\infty} \prod_{i=0}^{k-1} \lambda_i / \mu_{i+1} \right]^{-1} \prod_{i=0}^{k-1} \lambda_i / \mu_{i+1} \qquad \text{for } k = 0, 1, 2, \ldots \quad (4.2)$$

From this generalized steady-state solution, obtaining expressions for other performance measures is straightforward:

$$\text{utilization} = P_1 + P_2 + \cdots = 1 - P_0 \qquad\qquad (4.3)$$

$$\text{throughput} = \mu_1 P_1 + \mu_2 P_2 + \cdots = \sum_{k=1}^{\infty} \mu_k P_k \qquad\qquad (4.4)$$

$$\text{queue length} = 0P_0 + 1P_1 + 2P_2 + \cdots = \sum_{k=1}^{\infty} kP_k \qquad (4.5)$$

$$\text{response time} = \frac{\text{queue length}}{\text{throughput}} = \frac{\sum_{k=1}^{\infty} kP_k}{\sum_{k=1}^{\infty} \mu_k P_k} \qquad (4.6)$$

4.6 ALTERNATIVE APPROACH: OPERATIONAL ANALYSIS

The approach followed until now is termed the *stochastic analysis* approach. This is because all parameters (e.g., the interarrival time of customers, the service time of customers) are random variables with certain mean values (e.g., $1/\lambda$, $1/\mu$) characterized by given distributions (e.g., exponential). An alternative approach is known as the *operational analysis* approach [3]. The key point is that all quantities are based on measured or known data.

To see how the operational approach might be applied, reconsider an open system and a variation of the motivating problem from Sec. 4.3.

Motivating problem: *Suppose that during an observation period of 1 minute, a single device is observed to be busy for 36 sec. A total of 1800 transactions were observed to arrive to the system. The total number of observed completions is 1800 transactions. What is the performance of the system (e.g., the mean service time per transaction, the utilization of the device, the system throughput)?*

Prior to solving this problem, some commonly accepted operational analysis notation is required for the measured or known data. The following is a partial list of such measured or known quantities.

T = length of time in the observation period

K = number of devices in the system

M = number of terminals in the system

Z = average measured think time at a terminal

B_i = total busy time of device i in the observation period T

A_i = total number of service requests (i.e., arrivals) to device i in the observation period T

$A_{i,j}$ = number of service requests from device i that next request service at device j

$A_{0,i}$ = number of service requests (i.e., arrivals) to device i that arrived directly from the outside world and not from another device

A_0 = total number of jobs submitted to the system in the observation period T

C_i = total number of service completions from device i in the observation period T

$C_{i,j}$ = number of times a job completing service at device i requests service next at device j

$C_{i,0}$ = number of service completions (i.e., job completions) at device i that "exit" the system to the outside world and do not visit any further devices

C_0 = total number of jobs completed by the system in the observation period T

From these known measurable quantities, a set of derived quantities can be obtained. A partial list includes the following.

S_i = mean service time between completions at device i; $S_i = B_i/C_i$

U_i = utilization of device i; $U_i = B_i/T$

X_i = throughput of device i; $X_i = C_i/T = (C_i/B_i)/(T/B_i) = (1/S_i)/(1/U_i) = U_i/S_i$ (this result, $U_i = S_i X_i$, is known as the *utilization law* of operational analysis).

X_0 = system throughput; $X_0 = C_0/T$

V_i = average number of visits (i.e., the visit count) per job to device i; $V_i = C_i/C_0$

Using the notation above, the motivating problem can be formally stated and solved in a straightforward manner using operational analysis. The measured quantities are:

$$T = 60 \text{ sec}$$

$$K = 1 \text{ device}$$

$$B_1 = 36 \text{ sec}$$

$$A_1 = A_0 = 1800 \text{ transactions}$$

$$C_1 = C_0 = 1800 \text{ transactions}$$

Thus the derived quantities are

$$S_1 = \frac{B_1}{C_1} = \frac{36}{1800} = \frac{1}{50} \text{ second per transaction}$$

$$U_1 = \frac{B_1}{T} = \frac{36}{60} = 60\%$$

$$X_0 = \frac{C_0}{T} = \frac{1800}{60} = 30 \text{ tps}$$

Additional useful relationships between operational quantities can easily be derived. One of them is the *interactive response time law*. Consider an interactive system composed of M terminals with an average think time equal to Z seconds. Let $\overline{M}$ and $\overline{N}$ be the average number of users in the think state (in the terminals) and the average number of commands being processed at the computer system, respectively. Clearly, $\overline{M} + \overline{N} = M$ since a user is either at the think state or waiting for a reply for his/her submitted command. If we apply Little's result to the set of M terminals, we get

$$\overline{M} = X_0 Z \tag{4.7}$$

since the average number of commands submitted per unit time (throughput of the set of terminals) must equal the number of completed commands per unit time (system throughput) since we are assuming equilibrium. Applying Little's result to the computer system, we get

$$\overline{N} = X_0 R \tag{4.8}$$

where R is the average response time. If we add Eqs. (4.7) and (4.8) we get that

$$\overline{M} + \overline{N} = M = X_0(Z + R) \tag{4.9}$$

Thus, the interactive response time is given by

$$R = \frac{M}{X_0} - Z \tag{4.10}$$

Example

If 7200 commands were processed for 1 hour by an interactive computer system with 40 terminals and an average think time of 15 sec, the average response time would be

$$R = \frac{40}{7200/3600} - 15 = 5 \text{ sec} \qquad \square$$

Another powerful relationship is the *forced flow law*. It relates the system throughput X_0 with the throughput X_i of a particular device i. Since the average number of visits V_i is equal to C_i/C_0, we get the desired relationship by dividing both C_i and C_0 by the observation period T. So

$$V_i = \frac{C_i}{C_0} = \frac{C_i/T}{C_0/T} = \frac{X_i}{X_0} \tag{4.11}$$

Example

An interactive system was monitored for 1 hour. During this time, the utilization of a certain disk was measured to be 50%. Each command makes an average of two accesses to this disk, which has an average service time equal to 25 msec. Considering that the system has 150 terminals and that the average think time is 20 sec, what is the average response time?

The known quantities are: $U_{\text{disk}} = 0.5$, $V_{\text{disk}} = 2$, $S_{\text{disk}} = 0.025$ sec, $M = 150$, and $Z = 10$ sec. From the utilization law,

$$U_{\text{disk}} = S_{\text{disk}} X_{\text{disk}}$$

So $X_{\text{disk}} = 0.5/0.025 = 20$ commands/sec. From the forced flow law,

$$X_0 = \frac{X_{\text{disk}}}{V_{\text{disk}}} = \frac{20}{2} = 10 \text{ commands/sec}$$

Finally, from the interactive response time law,

$$R = \frac{M}{X_0} - Z = \frac{150}{10} - 10 = 5 \text{ sec} \qquad \square$$

4.7 CONCLUDING REMARKS

In this chapter an alternative modeling paradigm is presented. The basic steps of this paradigm include model construction, parameterization, model solution, calibration, model alteration, model prediction, and validation. Emphasis is placed on the model solution step using the stochastic analysis approach. Simple motivating examples illustrate the intuitive nature of model solution. The technique is based on constructing intuitive state-space diagrams. Once an appropriate diagram is constructed, a corresponding system of flow balance equations can be formed and solved. The solution of these equations gives the steady-state probabilities of being in any particular system state. The steady-state probabilities can then be used to derive more useful performance measures (e.g., system utilization, system throughput, queue lengths, response times). The model can then be used in a (relatively) straightforward fashion to answer "what if?" performance prediction questions. Examples are given to illustrate the entire technique. Little's result is important and is introduced. The operational analysis approach is also introduced. Related readings include Refs. [4] and [5].

4.8 EXERCISES

1. Consider the transaction system motivation problem. What would be the effect on the performance measures (i.e., utilization, throughput, queue length, and response time) under the following changes:
   (a) The workload changes by -200%, -100%, -50%, -10%, $+10\%$, $+50\%$, $+100\%$, and $+200\%$. Draw the appropriate curves.
   (b) The processor speed changes by -200%, -100%, -50%, -10%, $+10\%$, $+50\%$, $+100\%$, and $+200\%$. Draw the appropriate curves.

2. Consider the transaction system motivation problem. If the workload were to increase by $p\%$, by what amount would the processor need to be speeded up to maintain the original response time of $\frac{1}{20}$? Draw the appropriate curve as a function of p.

3. Consider the transaction system motivation problem. If the processor were speeded up by $q\%$, what percentage increase in workload could be accommodated to maintain the original response time of $\frac{1}{20}$? Draw the appropriate curve as a function of q.

4. The original motivation problem allowed for any number of customers to be in the system. Now suppose that the number of buffers in the transaction system

is limited to 3. Thus, if a transaction arrives and there are already 3 other transactions in the system, the newly arriving transaction is lost. Redraw the appropriate state-space diagram, form the corresponding flow balance equations, solve them, and derive the appropriate performance measures (i.e., utilization, throughput, queue length, and response time).

5. Consider Exercise 4 on a limited buffer system. Show that the general expression for P_k, the steady-state probability of finding k transactions in the system is given by

$$P_k = \frac{1 - \lambda/\mu}{1 - (\lambda/\mu)^{K+1}} \left(\frac{\lambda}{\mu}\right)^k \qquad k = 0, \dots, K$$

where K is the number of buffers (maximum number of transactions in the system). Proceed as follows:

(a) Draw the state-space diagram and give an expression for λ_i and μ_i.
(b) Use the general birth–death result given in Eq. (4.2).

6. In the original motivation problem, the transaction server always processed requests at a rate of 50 tps, regardless of the number of transactions in the system. Now suppose that the transaction server is "smart" and works faster when there are more waiting transactions in the system. Specifically, suppose that the server processes transactions at a rate of $50k$ transactions per second when there are k transactions in the system. Thus, the server speed is a function of the number of customers in the system. Redraw the appropriate state-space diagram, form the corresponding flow balance equations, solve them, and derive the appropriate performance measures (i.e., utilization, throughput, queue length, and response time) for this new system.

7. Now suppose that the arrival rate changes as a function of the system state. In the original motivation problem, the transaction arrival rate was constant at 30 tps, regardless of the number of transactions in the system. Now suppose that the arrival rate decreases as a function of the number in the system. Specifically, suppose that the transactions arrive to the system at a rate of $50(3 - k)$ transactions per second when there are k transactions in the system. (*Note:* This implicitly assumes that no more than 3 transactions will ever be present in the system, because when there are 3 transactions in the system, the arrival rate at that time would be 0 and no new transactions would arrive.) Draw the appropriate state-space diagram, form the corresponding flow balance equations, solve them, and derive the appropriate performance measures (i.e., utilization, throughput, queue length, and response time) for this new system.

8. Find the predicted performance measures in the second motivation problem when the users go to a training session and their mean time between transaction requests drops to 0.4 sec.

9. Find the predicted performance measures in the second motivation problem if an improved pipeline were installed which is advertised to be 50% faster than the original pipeline. That is, the new pipeline could process one transaction in 0.75 sec if it is the sole request, could complete a request in 0.50 sec if there

are two requests in the system, and could complete a request in 0.375 sec when there are three requests in the system.

10. System administrators tend to be concerned with making sure that the system exhibits a high throughput. Users, on the other hand, are concerned with their response time. Unfortunately, as the throughput increases, so does response time in most cases. A compromise performance measure, called *power* and denoted Φ, is defined as the ratio of the throughput X and the response time R. So, the power increases as the throughput increases and as the response time decreases. Give an expression for the power of the single-server system of the first motivating problem as a function of the system utilization U. Draw a graph of Φ versus U. For which value of the utilization is the power maximum?

11. A computer system was monitored for 1 hour. During this period 7200 transactions were executed and the average multiprogramming level was measured to be equal to 5 jobs. What is the average time spent by a job in the system once it is in the multiprogramming mix (i.e., the average time spent by the job once it is memory resident)?

12. A computer system was measured during 30 minutes. During this time, 5400 transactions were completed and 18,900 I/O operations were executed on a certain disk which had a utilization equal to 40%. What is the average number of I/O operations per transaction on this disk? What is the average service time per transaction on this disk?

13. A transaction processing system was monitored for 1 hour. During this period, 5400 transactions were processed. What was the utilization of a disk that has an average service time equal to 30 msec and that is visited three times on the average by every transaction?

14. The average delay experienced by a packet when traversing a computer network is 100 msec. The average number of packets that cross the network per second is 128 packets/sec. What is the average number of packets in transit in the network?

15. Verify the interactive response time law by applying it to the motivating problem of Sec. 4.4.

16. A file server was monitored for 60 minutes, during which time, 7200 requests were completed. The disk utilization was measured to be 30%. The average service time at this disk is 30 msec per file operation request. What is the average number of accesses to this disk per file request?

BIBLIOGRAPHY

1. K. C. Sevcik and I. Mitrani, The distribution of queueing network states at input and output instants, *Journal of the ACM*, Vol. 28, No. 2, April 1981, pp. 358–371.

2. J. D. C. Little, A proof of the queueing formula $L = \lambda W$, *Operations Research*, Vol. 9, 1961, pp. 383–387.

3. P. J. Denning and J. P. Buzen, The operational analysis of queueing network models, *Computing Surveys*, Vol. 10, No. 3, September 1978, pp. 225–261.

4. E. D. Lazowska, J. Zahorjan, G. S. Graham, and K. C. Sevcik, *Quantitative System Performance: Computer System Analysis Using Queueing Network Models*, Prentice Hall, Englewood Cliffs, N.J., 1984.

5. L. Kleinrock, *Queueing Systems*, Volume I: *Theory*, Wiley-Interscience, New York, 1975.

Chapter 5

Efficient Solutions for
Computer System Models

5.1 INTRODUCTION

In Chap. 4 we illustrated the basic analytic modeling steps: model construction, parameterization, solution, calibration, alteration, prediction, and validation. The motivation was to construct and solve simple models for performance prediction purposes. The focus was on the model solution step. This step was developed from first principles. That is, given a motivating problem, a corresponding state-space (Markov) diagram was constructed. The underlying flow balance equations were formulated from the state-space diagram. This set of linear equations was solved to obtain the steady-state probabilities of being in each possible system state. Once these steady-state probabilities were known, the calculation of more useful performance measures (e.g., throughput, response time, utilization, queue length) was possible. Making performance predictions, by changing and resolving the model, were then possible.

This simple solution technique is relatively straightforward and intuitive. However, there is a fundamental problem. As the number of servers increases, as the number of customers increases, as the number of different types of customers increases, as the complexity of the servers increases (e.g., pipelining, parallelism, multiprocessing), as the interaction between customers increases (e.g., message passing, synchronization, forking and joining), or as several other subtleties are introduced, the computational effort required to construct and solve the underlying flow balance equations can quickly become overwhelming. Better solution techniques are required. Fortunately, some rather clever solution algorithms have been developed. The goal of this chapter is to "discover" these algorithms built up from the simple first principles introduced in Chap. 4.

5.2 FIRST-PRINCIPLES APPROACH REVIEW

Although not stated explicitly, the model solution approach introduced in Chap. 4 followed an ordered, well-defined (and hopefully intuitive) set of first-principle steps.

1. *State description specification.* The first step is to specify explicitly what information is necessary to capture the "state" of the system. That is, if a snapshot of the system were taken, what information is necessary to adequately describe the current state of the system? In the examples presented in Chap. 4, the state description was a single number, indicating the number of customers currently present in the system. This decision of an appropriate state description is nontrivial, for several assumptions can be implicitly introduced. For example, with a single number representing the number of customers present, it is implicitly assumed that there is no distinction between the customers (i.e., the model is *single-class*). If such a *multiclass* distinction were important, say, if there were batch jobs and interactive jobs that behaved quite differently and if separate performance measures were desired on each, then it would be necessary to distinguish between the two types of customers in the state description. In a multiclass model with R distinct customer classes, an appropriate state description could be as simple as an R-tuple, $(n_1, n_2, \ldots, n_R)$, where n_r represents the number of class r customers in the system. Also, with a single number representing the number of customers present in the system, it is assumed implicitly that the customer location is unimportant (e.g., when there is only one device). If customer location were important, say, if there were distinct processors and disk queues and if separate performance measures were desired on each, it would be necessary to distinguish customer location. In a multiple-device model with K distinct devices, but where the customers are indistinguishable, an appropriate state description could be as simple as a K-tuple, $(n_1, n_2, \ldots, n_K)$, where n_k represents the number of customers present at device k. Finally, with a single number representing the number of customers present in the system, it is assumed implicitly that the length of time that each customer has been in the system is unimportant. This is the memoryless (i.e., Markov) assumption. If the length of time in the system were important, say, if the execution

time of a customer were two-phased, an initialization phase and a computation phase, then it would be necessary to distinguish which phase of execution each customer is in. The state could be described by a tuple composed of the number of customers in their first execution phase and the number of customers in their second execution phase. Thus, depending on the level of detail (e.g., multiple classes, multiple devices, multiple execution phases), the state description specification may become complex and it may incorporate several implicit assumptions.

2. *State enumeration.* Once an appropriate state description has been established, the entire state-space can be enumerated. This corresponds to drawing the complete state transition diagram. Often, the explicit listing of all states is not required, and, in some cases, listing all states is not possible. For instance, if the model is open, where customers arrive, receive service, and exit, the number of theoretically possible system states is infinite. What is required is to be able to specify clearly which states are possible (i.e., those states in which the system may be found). Being able to indicate the entire state-space is sufficient, as was done in the birth–death systems in Chap. 4 (e.g., see Fig. 4.3).

3. *Transition rate specification.* For each possible state, it is necessary to determine those system events that can cause the system to change from one system state to another. Such events include the arrival of a new customer to the system, the departure of a customer from the system, the transfer of a customer from one device to another, or the change of execution phase. For each state and for each possible state transition, an arc in the state diagram is drawn from the prior state to the later state and labeled with the transition rate. The transition rate depends on the transition type. For example, if the transition is caused by the arrival of a new customer to the system, the transition rate is just the arrival rate of new customers. Similarly, if the transition is caused by a customer departure, then the transition rate is the service rate of the device that completes the job. That is, the transition rate is equal to the rate at which the corresponding event occurs in the actual system.

4. *Balance equation formulation.* For each system state, there is a corresponding linear balance equation, often referred to as the state's global balance equation. It is formed by equating the total flow into the state (i.e., the sum of the flows coming into the state along each arc) to the total flow going out of the state (i.e., the sum of the flows going out of the state along each arc). The flow rate along an arc is a simple product of the steady-state probability of being in the prior state (i.e., one of the unknown quantities that is being solved for) times the arc's transition rate (i.e., a known input parameter). Given that the system has n states, the resulting system of equations is comprised of n equations, one formed from each state, and n unknowns, the steady state probabilities

of being in each state. Once all of the balance equations are written, one of them (and it does not matter which) is discarded, since it is redundant and can be inferred from the remaining equations. The conservation of total probability equation, where the sum of all the unknown steady-state probabilities must sum to 1, is included in the system of equations.

5. *Balance equation solution.* The resulting system of n simultaneous linear equations in n unknowns has a unique solution. This solution can be found by any of a set of standard means. In the worst case, where no particular structure exists within the equations, they can be solved numerically to any desired accuracy. This solution gives the steady-state probability of being in any specified system state.

6. *Performance metric derivation.* From the steady-state probabilities and from certain known relationships (e.g., Little's result), any of a number of useful performance metrics can be derived. For instance, the utilization of a device is a simple sum of all those steady-state probabilities of the states in which the state description indicates that the device is active. The throughput of the system is a simple weighted sum of all the steady-state probabilities, each weighted by the rate at which customers complete their service and exit the system from that state. The mean queue length of a device is a simple weighted sum of all of the steady-state probabilities, weighted by the number of customers resident at the device in that state. The mean waiting (i.e., the residence or response) time at a device, including both queuing and service time, can be derived using Little's result by forming the ratio of the device's mean queue length to the system throughput.

These first-principle steps are applied to a *slightly* more complex motivating example. From the solution of this example, the clever solution techniques promised earlier will be discovered.

5.3 BASIC CENTRAL SERVER SYSTEM

Motivating problem: *Consider a database workstation server that is composed of a single CPU and two disks, a fast disk and a slow disk. Users remotely login to the server, perform some database transactions, and logout. Because of the limited power of the workstation, at most two users are allowed to be logged onto the system at any one time. However, the demand for the system is sufficiently high so that it may be assumed that exactly two users are logged onto the system at all times. That is, as soon as one user completes the requested transactions and exits the system, another eager user logs on and effectively picks up where the departed user left off and initiates further database transactions. Each transaction alternates between using the CPU and using a disk. The particular disk used depends on the transaction, since different transactions access different files, and*

*different files are resident on different disks. Suppose that the "typical" transaction
(1) requires an average of 10 sec of CPU time, (2) is equally likely to access files
on the fast disk as the slow disk, (3) requires an average of 20 sec of fast disk time
if a file on the fast disk is accessed, and (4) requires an average of 30 sec of slow
disk time if a file on the slow disk is accessed. What is the current performance of
the system? How much would performance be improved if code for transaction
handling by the CPU were rewritten to execute 33% faster? How much would
performance be improved if the slow disk were replaced by a second fast disk?
What is the optimal file placement across the two disks?*

The six steps presented in Sec. 5.2 are applied to solve this example.
As the solution is developed, generalizations are made, and techniques are
derived that are applicable to a relatively broad class of systems.

It is always useful to visualize the system model. The appropriate model
is illustrated in Fig. 5.1. This model is referred to as a *central server model* with
the CPU acting as the central server since every database transaction must be
served by (i.e., pass through) the CPU. To make the model more general,
the device service rates and the disk routing probabilities (or, visit ratios) are
represented by variables. The service rates of the CPU, the fast disk, and the
slow disk are denoted by μ_c, μ_f, and μ_s, respectively. In the example above,
$\mu_c = 6$ transactions per minute (i.e., the mean transaction service time at
the CPU is $1/\mu_c = 10$ sec per transaction), $\mu_f = 3$ transactions per minute
(i.e., the mean transaction service time at the fast disk is $1/\mu_f = 20$ sec per
transaction), and $\mu_s = 2$ transactions per minute (i.e., the mean transaction

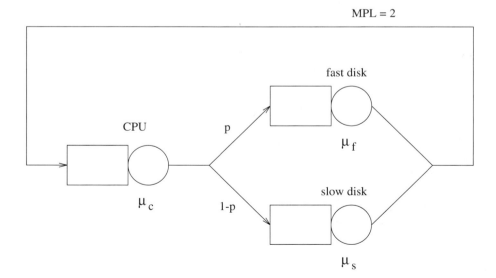

Figure 5.1 Central server model example.

service time at the slow disk is $1/\mu_s = 30$ sec per transaction). The disk routing probabilities, p and $1 - p$, represent the relative frequencies that the fast disk and the slow disk are accessed, respectively. These probabilities are dependent on the file placement. If all files are accessed equally often, then p represents the fraction of the files that are resident on the fast disk. In the example above, $p = 1 - p = 1/2$. The average multiprogramming level, MPL, represents the average number of active transactions (i.e., customers or jobs) in the system. In this example, MPL $= 2$.

5.3.1 State Description Specification

The first step in the solution is the state description specification. An appropriate state description in this example is a 3-tuple (n_c, n_f, n_s), where n_c represents the number of transactions currently being serviced or enqueued at the CPU. Likewise, n_f and n_s represent the number of transactions at the fast disk and slow disk, respectively. By definition, $n_c + n_f + n_s = $ MPL, since every active customer (i.e., transaction) must be at some device.

This state description can easily be generalized, to any number of devices and any number of customers. Given K devices and MPL customers, the state description would generalize to $(n_1, n_2, \ldots, n_K)$ where n_k represents the number of customers at device k. For internal consistency, $0 \leq n_k \leq$ MPL for all devices k and $\sum_{k=1}^{K} n_k = $ MPL.

This state description implicitly makes certain assumptions. One assumption is that all transactions are indistinguishable. If one customer is at the CPU and the other at the fast disk, the state is represented by $(1, 1, 0)$, and the distinction of which customer is at which device is lost. Thus, the model is termed a single-class model, where each customer is statistically identical. Also, it is not possible to determine from the state description how long the system has been in a particular state. That is, given that the system is in state $(2, 0, 0)$, it is known only that both customers are currently at the CPU, one being serviced and one waiting in the queue. It is not known whether or not the customer in service has been in service for a long time and is nearly finished, or if the customer in service just started service. This is the "memoryless" property, which implicitly assumes that all of the service time distributions (i.e., the times spent in service at each of the three devices) are exponentially distributed.

5.3.2 State Enumeration

The next step is to enumerate all possible system states. In the present example, this is an easy task since there are only a limited number of customers and devices. There are only six ways to distribute two customers among three devices. That is, there are only six ways to specify (n_c, n_f, n_s) such that $0 \leq n_c, n_f, n_s \leq 2$, where $n_c + n_f + n_s = 2$. The possible states in this example are $(2, 0, 0), (1, 1, 0), (1, 0, 1), (0, 2, 0), (0, 1, 1),$ and $(0, 0, 2)$.

In general, given a closed system with K devices and MPL single-class customers, it is possible to enumerate the state-space completely. The total number of ways to distribute MPL customers among K devices [i.e., the number of ways to specify $(n_1, n_2, \ldots, n_K)$, where $0 \leq n_k \leq$ MPL for all k and $\sum_{k=1}^{K} n_k =$ MPL] is given by the expression

$$\binom{\text{MPL} + K - 1}{K - 1}$$

To understand this formula, a new but equivalent state description is introduced. In this new state description, each customer is viewed as the number "0." Given MPL 0's, it must be determined how many are assigned to each of the K devices. This partitioning can be determined by a set of $K - 1$ *fences*. Each fence is represented by the number "1." The 1's (i.e., the fences) are interspersed among the 0's (i.e., the customers). All customers to the left of the initial fence are assigned to the first device, customers between the first and second fences are assigned to the second device, $\ldots$, and all customers to the right of the $(K - 1)$st fence are assigned to device K. As an example, given 4 devices and 5 customers, the bitstring 11000100 represents the state where no customers are at the first device (because there are no 0's to the left of the initial fence, the first 1), no customers are at the second device (because there are no 0's between the first two fences), 3 customers are at the third device (because there are three 0's between the second and third fences), and the remaining 2 customers are at the fourth device (because there are two 0's to the right of the third fence). Using this new state description, there is a one-to-one mapping with the state description [i.e., $(n_1, n_2, \ldots, n_K)$] introduced earlier. In the example above with 3 devices and 2 customers, where $K = 3$ and MPL $= 2$, the original set of states $\{(2, 0, 0), (1, 1, 0), (1, 0, 1), (0, 2, 0), (0, 1, 1), (0, 0, 2)\}$ would, in the new state description, map directly to the bitstrings $\{0011, 0101, 0110, 1001, 1010, 1100\}$, respectively. With the new state description, each bitstring composed of $(K - 1)$ 1's and MPL 0's represents a valid system state, and vice versa. Determining the total number of such bitstrings (i.e., the total number of system states) is equivalent to determining the number of ways the $K - 1$ fence positions can be chosen in a bitstring whose total length is MPL $+ K - 1$ bit positions. This leads to the simple combinatorial expression

$$\binom{\text{MPL} + K - 1}{K - 1}$$

In the motivating example above, where MPL $= 2$ and $K = 3$, the total number of possible system states is

$$\binom{\text{MPL} + K - 1}{K - 1} = \binom{4}{2} = \frac{4!}{(4 - 2)! \, 2!} = 6$$

5.3.3 Transition Rate Specification

After the states have been enumerated, it is necessary to specify the possible state transitions from each state and the corresponding transition rates. For instance, consider state $(2, 0, 0)$ where both customers are at the CPU. The next "event" (i.e., action that will cause the system state to change) is that the customer at the CPU will complete service and will access a disk file. This event will happen in an average of 10 sec, or, equivalently, will happen with rate $\mu_c = 6$ transactions per minute. With probability $p = 0.5$, the accessed file will be on the fast disk and with probability $1 - p = 0.5$, the accessed file will be on the slow disk. Therefore, from state $(2, 0, 0)$, the system will make a transition either to state $(1, 1, 0)$ or state $(1, 0, 1)$. The rate at which these transitions take place are $\mu_c \times p$ and $\mu_c \times (1 - p)$, respectively. That is, the total flow rate out of state $(2, 0, 0)$, which is equivalent to the flow rate out of the CPU, is μ_c, p of which goes to the fast disk [i.e., to state $(1, 1, 0)$] and $1 - p$ of which goes to the slow disk [i.e., to state $(1, 0, 1)$].

As another example, consider state $(1, 1, 0)$. In this state, one of the customers is active using the CPU and the other customer is active using a file on the fast disk. From this state, one of two events could occur that would cause the system state to change: either the customer at the CPU could complete its service, or the customer at the fast disk could complete its service. The transition rates of these two events are μ_c and μ_f, respectively. From the first event (i.e., a customer completing at the CPU), two succeeding states are possible. The customer leaving the CPU could next visit (i.e., request service from) the fast disk. This causes a transition from state $(1, 1, 0)$ to state $(0, 2, 0)$ with a transition rate of $\mu_c \times p$. Similarly, the customer leaving the CPU could next visit the slow disk, causing a transition from state $(1, 1, 0)$ to state $(0, 1, 1)$ with a rate of $\mu_c \times (1 - p)$. From the second event (i.e., a customer completing at the fast disk), only one succeeding state is possible. The customer leaving the fast disk next visits the CPU. This causes a transition from state $(1, 1, 0)$ to state $(2, 0, 0)$ with a transition rate of μ_f. Using similar reasoning, it is relatively straightforward to specify all possible state transitions from every system state. The complete Markov state-space diagram is shown in Fig. 5.2.

5.3.4 Balance Equation Formulation

After the transition rate specification (i.e., the state-space diagram), the next step is to form the balance equations. In general, there is one balance equation for each system state. The flow into each state must equal the flow out of every state. (*Note:* If this were not true, there would exist states with more flow in than flow out. Such states become absorbing states, where the system gravitates to these states and, after some period of time, the system remains in these states with probability 1—not an interesting system to analyze. Similarly, if a state exists with more flow out than flow in, this state is termed

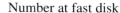

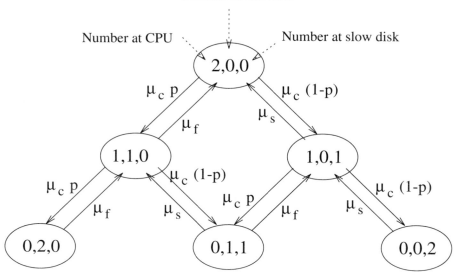

Figure 5.2 State space diagram.

a *transient state* and, after some period of time, the system would never be in such a state.) Consider state $(2, 0, 0)$. The flow into this state comes from two sources, from state $(1, 1, 0)$ and from state $(1, 0, 1)$. If the system is in state $(1, 1, 0)$, the flow into state $(2, 0, 0)$ is μ_f. If the system is in state $(1, 0, 1)$, the flow into state $(2, 0, 0)$ is μ_s. Thus, the total flow into state $(2, 0, 0)$ is

$$\mu_f P_{110} + \mu_s P_{101}$$

where P_{xyz} is the (steady-state) probability that the system is in state (x, y, z). Similarly, the flow out of state $(2, 0, 0)$ comes from one source, a customer completion at the CPU. Thus, the total flow out of state $(2, 0, 0)$ is

$$\mu_c P_{200}$$

Therefore, the balance equation associated with state $(2, 0, 0)$ is

$$\mu_f P_{110} + \mu_s P_{101} = \mu_c P_{200}$$

By proceeding in this fashion, the balance equations for the six system states $(2, 0, 0)$, $(1, 1, 0)$, $(1, 0, 1)$, $(0, 2, 0)$, $(0, 1, 1)$, and $(0, 0, 2)$ are, respectively,

$$\mu_f P_{110} + \mu_s P_{101} = \mu_c P_{200}$$

$$\mu_c p P_{200} + \mu_f P_{020} + \mu_s P_{011} = (\mu_f + \mu_c) P_{110}$$

$$\mu_c(1 - p) P_{200} + \mu_f P_{011} + \mu_s P_{002} = (\mu_s + \mu_c) P_{101}$$

$$\mu_c p P_{110} = \mu_f P_{020}$$

$$\mu_c(1 - p) P_{110} + \mu_c p P_{101} = (\mu_s + \mu_f) P_{011}$$

$$\mu_c(1 - p) P_{101} = \mu_s P_{002}$$

This constitutes a system of six equations in six unknowns, P_{200}, P_{110}, P_{101}, P_{020}, P_{011}, and P_{002}. As in Chap. 4, since this is a system of stochastic equations, one of the equations is redundant. To solve this system of equations uniquely, one of the equations must be deleted and replaced by the conservation of total probability equation, $P_{200} + P_{110} + P_{101} + P_{020} + P_{011} + P_{002} = 1$.

5.3.5 Balance Equation Solution

The next step is to solve the foregoing system of balance equations. This can be done in a straightforward manner, typically using one of several standard software packages designed for solving systems of linear equations. This "brute force" solution technique is referred to as *solving the global balance equations*. It works. However, there is a slight problem using this approach. As the modeled system grows (e.g., as the number of disks increases, as the number of customers increases), the number of system states grows exponentially, thus implying that the number of equations grows exponentially, implying that the solution technique of solving the set of simultaneous equations quickly becomes intractable. There is often a simpler way, referred to as *solving the local balance equations*.

The concept of *local balance* (LB) states that the flow into a state due to an arrival at a queue is equated to the flow out of that state due to a departure from that queue. To understand this concept intuitively, consider the portion of Fig. 5.2 shown in Fig. 5.3.

Let's now interpret the local balance statement above when the state considered is $(0, 1, 1)$ and the considered queue is the slow disk. Local balance states that the flow into state $(0, 1, 1)$ due to an arrival at the slow disk is equated to the flow out of state $(0, 1, 1)$ due to a departure from the slow

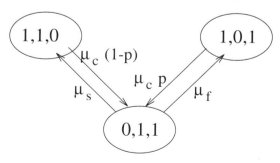

Figure 5.3 Local balance illustration.

disk. This states that

$$\mu_c(1 - p)P_{101} = \mu_s P_{011}$$

Similarly, by interpreting local balance in the context of state $(0, 1, 1)$ when the queue considered is the fast disk, we have

$$\mu_c p P_{101} = \mu_f P_{011}$$

Practically speaking, we have just taken the global balance equation associated with state $(0, 1, 1)$,

$$\mu_c(1 - p)P_{110} + \mu_c p P_{101} = (\mu_s + \mu_f)P_{011}$$

and reduced it to

$$\mu_c(1 - p)P_{101} = \mu_s P_{011}$$

$$\mu_c p P_{101} = \mu_f P_{011}$$

by pairing up the left-hand side against the right-hand side in a term-by-term basis. That is, the single global balance (GB) equation has been replaced by two local balance (LB) equations. In general, local balance replaces a single global balance equation for each state by a set of local balance equations, the number of which is equal to the number of nonempty queues in the state description. (A full listing of the local balance equations for this example is left as an exercise.) Only $n - 1$ of the local balance equations are required to find a solution of the system, where n is the number of system states.

The solution to the set of LB equations implies the solution of the GB equations. This is because local balance simply equates certain terms on each side of the global balance equations. In this sense, local balance can be viewed as a solution technique for the global balance equations.

Another intuitive interpretation of local balance is that of *pairing of the arcs* (PA). That is, equate the flow from state A to state B to the flow from state B to state A. From Fig. 5.2, this leads to six (simpler) PA equations:

$$\mu_f P_{110} = \mu_c p P_{200}$$

$$\mu_s P_{101} = \mu_c(1 - p)P_{200}$$

$$\mu_f P_{020} = \mu_c p P_{110}$$

$$\mu_s P_{011} = \mu_c(1 - p)P_{110}$$

$$\mu_f P_{011} = \mu_c p P_{101}$$

$$\mu_s P_{002} = \mu_c(1 - p)P_{101}$$

By viewing Fig. 5.2 and by applying the local balance definition given above, it is not difficult to transform the set of LB equations into the set of PA equations in this example. (The proof of this is left as an exercise.)

At this point, it may be tempting to think the following: This point about local balance and pairing of the arcs is all well and good, but to what point? So what if the individual LB or PA equations are a bit simpler than the GB equations? There are still just as many, if not more, LB or PA equations to solve. The complexity of solving the set of linear equations has not been reduced.

However, solving the PA (or LB) equations *really* helps. To see this, a bit of notation is introduced. Define $\mathcal{U}_f = \mu_c p / \mu_f$ and define $\mathcal{U}_s = \mu_c (1 - p) / \mu_s$. The PA equations above can now be rewritten as

$$P_{110} = \mathcal{U}_f P_{200}$$
$$P_{101} = \mathcal{U}_s P_{200}$$
$$P_{020} = \mathcal{U}_f P_{110} = \mathcal{U}_f^2 P_{200}$$
$$P_{011} = \mathcal{U}_s P_{110} = \mathcal{U}_s \mathcal{U}_f P_{200}$$
$$P_{011} = \mathcal{U}_f P_{101} = \mathcal{U}_f \mathcal{U}_s P_{200}$$
$$P_{002} = \mathcal{U}_s P_{101} = \mathcal{U}_s^2 P_{200}$$

Since the two equations for P_{011} are redundant, one can be deleted and replaced with the conservation of total probability equation. Therefore, substituting into

$$P_{200} + P_{110} + P_{101} + P_{020} + P_{011} + P_{002} = 1$$

yields

$$P_{200} + \mathcal{U}_f P_{200} + \mathcal{U}_s P_{200} + \mathcal{U}_f^2 P_{200} + \mathcal{U}_f \mathcal{U}_s P_{200} + \mathcal{U}_s^2 P_{200} = 1$$

Thus,

$$P_{200} = \frac{1}{1 + \mathcal{U}_f + \mathcal{U}_s + \mathcal{U}_f^2 + \mathcal{U}_f \mathcal{U}_s + \mathcal{U}_s^2}$$

By defining $\mathcal{U}_c = 1$, this can be rewritten as

$$P_{200} = \mathcal{U}_c^2 \mathcal{U}_f^0 \mathcal{U}_s^0$$
$$\times (\mathcal{U}_c^2 \mathcal{U}_f^0 \mathcal{U}_s^0 + \mathcal{U}_c^1 \mathcal{U}_f^1 \mathcal{U}_s^0 + \mathcal{U}_c^1 \mathcal{U}_f^0 \mathcal{U}_s^1$$
$$+ \mathcal{U}_c^0 \mathcal{U}_f^2 \mathcal{U}_s^0 + \mathcal{U}_c^0 \mathcal{U}_f^1 \mathcal{U}_s^1 + \mathcal{U}_c^0 \mathcal{U}_f^0 \mathcal{U}_s^2)^{-1}$$

By defining $G(2)$ to be equal to the denominator,

$$P_{200} = \frac{\mathcal{U}_c^2 \mathcal{U}_f^0 \mathcal{U}_s^0}{G(2)}$$

By knowing P_{200}, expressions for the remaining steady-state probabilities are

$$P_{110} = \frac{\mathcal{U}_c^{\ 1}\mathcal{U}_f^{\ 1}\mathcal{U}_s^{\ 0}}{G(2)}$$

$$P_{101} = \frac{\mathcal{U}_c^{\ 1}\mathcal{U}_f^{\ 0}\mathcal{U}_s^{\ 1}}{G(2)}$$

$$P_{020} = \frac{\mathcal{U}_c^{\ 0}\mathcal{U}_f^{\ 2}\mathcal{U}_s^{\ 0}}{G(2)}$$

$$P_{011} = \frac{\mathcal{U}_c^{\ 0}\mathcal{U}_f^{\ 1}\mathcal{U}_s^{\ 1}}{G(2)}$$

$$P_{002} = \frac{\mathcal{U}_c^{\ 0}\mathcal{U}_f^{\ 0}\mathcal{U}_s^{\ 2}}{G(2)}$$

Interpretations and generalizations are now appropriate. The interpretation of $\mathcal{U}_k$ is that of the *relative* utilization of device k. To see this, *suppose that the utilization of the CPU were 100%.* That is, suppose that $\mathcal{U}_c = 1$. Since it is fully utilized, the CPU would act as a steady source of customers with rate μ_c. That is, customers would flow out of the CPU with rate μ_c. Due to the probabilistic splitting, the arrival rate of customers to the fast disk would be $\mu_c p$. The fast disk would act as a standard simple server (see Chap. 4) with an arrival rate of $\mu_c p$ and a service rate of μ_f. Thus, from Chap. 4, the utilization of the fast disk would be $\mu_c p/\mu_f$, which is $\mathcal{U}_f$. Similarly, the slow disk would act as a standard simple server with an arrival rate of $\mu_c(1 - p)$ and a service rate of μ_s and its utilization would be $\mu_c(1 - p)/\mu_s$, which is $\mathcal{U}_s$. Thus, the $\mathcal{U}_k$'s are simply the relative utilizations of the devices.

The interpretation of $G(\ )$ is that of a normalization constant. Each steady-state probability has $G(\ )$ in the denominator. Thus, $1/G(\ )$ is the factor by which each steady-state probability is multiplied, so that the sum of the state probabilities is 1. The number of terms in $G(\ )$ is equal to the number of states in the underlying Markov state-space diagram. Therefore, it is dependent on the number of devices in the system and the multiprogramming level. [*Note:* Historically speaking, however, $G(\ )$ is usually denoted as simply a function of the multiprogramming level, $G(\text{MPL})$. This explains the use of $G(2)$ above.]

In general, suppose that a system has K devices and has a multiprogramming level MPL. Let $(n_1, n_2, \ldots, n_K)$ represent the system state where n_1 customers are at device 1, n_2 customers are at device 2, $\ldots$, and n_K customers are at device K. As above, $\mathcal{U}_k$ represents the relative utilization of device k. The generalization of the steady-state probability of being in state $(n_1, n_2, \ldots, n_K)$ is

$$P_{n_1 n_2 \cdots n_K} = \frac{\mathcal{U}_1{}^{n_1} \mathcal{U}_2{}^{n_2} \cdots \mathcal{U}_K{}^{n_K}}{\sum_{\text{all states}} \prod_{k=1}^{K} \mathcal{U}_k^{\text{no. customers at } k \text{ in the state}}}$$

The generalization of $G(\text{MPL})$ is dependent on the number of ways MPL customers can be distributed among the K devices. The generalization is

$$G(0) = \mathcal{U}_1^0 \mathcal{U}_2^0 \cdots \mathcal{U}_K^0 = 1$$

$$G(1) = \mathcal{U}_1^1 \mathcal{U}_2^0 \cdots \mathcal{U}_K^0 + \mathcal{U}_1^0 \mathcal{U}_2^1 \cdots \mathcal{U}_K^0 + \cdots + \mathcal{U}_1^0 \mathcal{U}_2^0 \cdots \mathcal{U}_K^1$$

$$\vdots$$

$$G(\text{MPL}) = \sum_{\text{all states}} \prod_{k=1}^{K} \mathcal{U}_k^{\text{no. customers at } k \text{ in the state}}$$

Therefore,

$$P_{n_1 n_2 \cdots n_K} = \frac{1}{G(\text{MPL})} \prod_{k=1}^{K} \mathcal{U}_k^{n_k}$$

represents the solution to the balance equations. This steady-state solution is termed *product form* due to the property that the steady-state probability of being in a given state is a simple (normalized) product of the relative device utilizations. Alternatively, the term *separable* is often applied to these networks since the states of the individual servers can be separated.

5.3.6 Performance Metric Derivation

Given the steady-state solution, the final step is to derive expressions for more useful performance metrics. Returning to the motivating example, suppose that one wanted to find the utilization of the fast disk. Let $U_i(\text{MPL})$ denote the utilization of device i when the multiprogramming level in the system is MPL. From looking at the state-space diagram (Fig. 5.2), the fast disk is busy when there is at least one customer at the fast disk [i.e., if the system is in state $(1, 1, 0)$, $(0, 2, 0)$, or $(0, 1, 1)$]. Thus,

$$U_f(2) = P_{110} + P_{020} + P_{011}$$

$$= \frac{1}{G(2)} \mathcal{U}_c^1 \mathcal{U}_f^1 \mathcal{U}_s^0 + \frac{1}{G(2)} \mathcal{U}_c^0 \mathcal{U}_f^2 \mathcal{U}_s^0 + \frac{1}{G(2)} \mathcal{U}_c^0 \mathcal{U}_f^1 \mathcal{U}_s^1$$

$$= \mathcal{U}_f \frac{1}{G(2)} \left(\mathcal{U}_c^1 \mathcal{U}_f^0 \mathcal{U}_s^0 + \mathcal{U}_c^0 \mathcal{U}_f^1 \mathcal{U}_s^0 + \mathcal{U}_c^0 \mathcal{U}_f^0 \mathcal{U}_s^1 \right)$$

$$= \mathcal{U}_f \frac{G(1)}{G(2)}$$

In general,

$$U_i(\text{MPL}) = \mathcal{U}_i \frac{G(\text{MPL}-1)}{G(\text{MPL})} \tag{5.1}$$

That is, the actual utilization of device i is its relative utilization $\mathcal{U}_i$ "normalized" by $G(\text{MPL}-1)/G(\text{MPL})$. This is a general result of all closed product-form networks.

Let $X_i(\text{MPL})$ denote the throughput of device i when the multiprogramming level in the system is MPL. Recall from Chap. 4, via Little's result, that the utilization of a server is equal to the product of its throughput and its mean service time.

$$U_i(\text{MPL}) = X_i(\text{MPL}) \times \frac{1}{\mu_i}$$

Therefore, the throughput of, say, the fast disk is given by

$$X_f(2) = \mu_f U_f(2) = \mu_f \mathcal{U}_f \frac{G(1)}{G(2)}$$

However, $\mu_f \mathcal{U}_f$ is the *relative* throughput of the fast disk. [Recall that if the (relative) utilization of the CPU were 1, its flow out (i.e., the relative throughput of the CPU) would be μ_c. After the probabilistic split to the fast disk, this implies that the relative arrival rate to the fast disk would be $\mu_c p$. Since flow in must equal flow out, the relative throughput of the fast disk is also $\mu_c p$. By simple algebra, $\mu_c p = \mu_f(\mu_c p/\mu_f) = \mu_f \mathcal{U}_f$.] Therefore, the actual throughput of device i is its relative throughput $\mu_i \mathcal{U}_i$ normalized by $G(\text{MPL}-1)/G(\text{MPL})$. In general,

$$X_i(\text{MPL}) = \mu_i \mathcal{U}_i \frac{G(\text{MPL}-1)}{G(\text{MPL})} \tag{5.2}$$

An expression for the mean queue length at a device, say the fast disk, can also be derived easily. From referring to Fig. 5.2 and from going through the diagram in a state-by-state fashion, the queue length of the fast disk when the system state is $(2,0,0)$ is 0. The queue length of the fast disk when the system state is $(1,1,0)$ is 1. The queue length of the fast disk when the system state is $(1,0,1)$ is 0. The queue length of the fast disk when the system state is $(0,2,0)$ is 2. The queue length of the fast disk when the system state is $(0,1,1)$ is 1. The queue length of the fast disk when the system state is $(0,0,2)$ is 0. Let $\bar{n}_i(\text{MPL})$ denote the mean queue length of device i when the multiprogramming level in the system is MPL. Therefore,

$$\bar{n}_f(2) = 1P_{110} + 2P_{020} + 1P_{011}$$

$$= \frac{1}{G(2)}\mathcal{U}_c^1\mathcal{U}_f^1\mathcal{U}_s^0 + \frac{2}{G(2)}\mathcal{U}_c^0\mathcal{U}_f^2\mathcal{U}_s^0 + \frac{1}{G(2)}\mathcal{U}_c^0\mathcal{U}_f^1\mathcal{U}_s^1$$

$$= \frac{\mathcal{U}_f}{G(2)}(\mathcal{U}_c^1\mathcal{U}_f^0\mathcal{U}_s^0 + \mathcal{U}_c^0\mathcal{U}_f^1\mathcal{U}_s^0 + \mathcal{U}_c^0\mathcal{U}_f^0\mathcal{U}_s^1) + \frac{\mathcal{U}_f^2}{G(2)}$$

$$= \mathcal{U}_f \frac{G(1)}{G(2)} + \mathcal{U}_f^2 \frac{G(0)}{G(2)}$$

$$= \sum_{i=1}^{\text{MPL}} \mathcal{U}_f^i \frac{G(\text{MPL} - i)}{G(\text{MPL})}$$

In general,

$$\bar{n}_i(\text{MPL}) = \sum_{m=1}^{\text{MPL}} \mathcal{U}_i^m \frac{G(\text{MPL} - m)}{G(\text{MPL})} \tag{5.3}$$

The final performance metric derived is the response time of a device. This represents the time from the arrival of a customer at a server until its departure from the server. It includes the queuing time and the service time. Often this metric is referred to as the wait time of a device. Let $R_i(\text{MPL})$ denote the mean response time (waiting time in the queue plus service time) of a customer at device i when the multiprogramming level in the system is MPL. Therefore, from Little's result,

$$R_f(2) = \frac{\bar{n}_f(2)}{X_f(2)} = \frac{\mathcal{U}_f \frac{G(1)}{G(2)} + \mathcal{U}_f^2 \frac{G(0)}{G(2)}}{\mu_f \mathcal{U}_f \frac{G(1)}{G(2)}} = \frac{G(1) + \mathcal{U}_f G(0)}{\mu_f G(1)}$$

In general,

$$R_i(\text{MPL}) = \frac{\sum_{m=1}^{\text{MPL}} \mathcal{U}_i^{m-1} G(\text{MPL} - m)}{\mu_i G(\text{MPL} - 1)} \tag{5.4}$$

Using the expressions above, it is now possible to address the questions posed in the original motivating example. That is, what is the current performance of the original system? (This is found by a straightforward substitution into the utilization, throughput, queue length, and wait-time formulas.) How much would performance be improved if code for transaction handling by the CPU were rewritten to execute 33% faster? (This implies changing μ_c from 6 to 8 and resolving the performance metric formulas.) How much would performance be improved if the slow disk were replaced by a second fast disk? (This implies changing μ_s from 2 to 3 and resolving the performance metric formulas.) What is the optimal file placement across the two disks? (This implies varying the value of p, observing the effect upon performance, and selecting the optimal value of p.) Specific answers to these questions are left as exercises.

5.4 SIMPLE CONVOLUTION

The expressions for the various performance metrics, including $U_i(\text{MPL})$, $X_i(\text{MPL})$, $\bar{n}_i(\text{MPL})$, and $R_i(\text{MPL})$ [i.e., Eqs. (5.1) to (5.4)], are all functions of the device μ_i's, $\mathcal{U}_i$'s, and the $G(\ )$'s. The $G(\ )$'s are functions of the $\mathcal{U}_i$'s,

which are functions of the device speeds μ_i's and the device branching probabilities $p_{i,j}$'s. The parameter $p_{i,j}$ represents the probability of next requesting
service from device j as soon as service from device i is completed. A key
issue then is the determination of the $G(\ )$'s and the $\mathcal{U}_i$'s, given the μ_i's and
the $p_{i,j}$'s. As it turns out, the determination of the $\mathcal{U}_i$'s is not *too* difficult and
can easily be automated.

   In general, the $\mathcal{U}_i$'s can be found by solving the set of simultaneous linear
equations represented by

$$\vec{\mathcal{X}} \times \mathcal{P} = \vec{\mathcal{X}}$$

where $\vec{\mathcal{X}}$ is a vector of the device *relative throughputs* $\mathcal{X}_i$'s and $\mathcal{P}$ is a matrix
of device routing probabilities $p_{i,j}$'s. The $\mathcal{P}$ matrix is known and the relative
throughputs are to be found. Once the relative throughputs are calculated,
the relative utilizations (i.e., the $\mathcal{U}_i$'s) are easily derived.

   Reconsider the example with a CPU, a fast disk, and a slow disk.
The relative throughput vector $\vec{\mathcal{X}}$ is represented by

$$\vec{\mathcal{X}} = \begin{bmatrix} \mathcal{X}_c & \mathcal{X}_f & \mathcal{X}_s \end{bmatrix}$$

and the device routing probability matrix $\mathcal{P}$ is represented by

$$\mathcal{P} = \begin{bmatrix} p_{c,c} & p_{c,f} & p_{c,s} \\ p_{f,c} & p_{f,f} & p_{f,s} \\ p_{s,c} & p_{s,f} & p_{s,s} \end{bmatrix} = \begin{bmatrix} 0 & p & 1-p \\ 1 & 0 & 0 \\ 1 & 0 & 0 \end{bmatrix}$$

That is, each element in the $\mathcal{P}$ matrix, $p_{i,j}$, is the routing probability of going
directly from device i to device j. By (arbitrarily) ordering the devices (CPU,
fast disk, slow disk), for example, $p_{1,3}$ represents the probability of going to
device 3 as soon as service is completed at device 1. This represents the probability of going from the CPU to the slow disk. From Fig. 5.1, this branching
probability is $p_{c,s} = 1 - p$. Similarly, $p_{c,f} = p$, $p_{f,c} = 1$, and $p_{s,c} = 1$.

   Particularized to our example, the system of linear equations represented
by $\vec{\mathcal{X}} \times \mathcal{P} = \vec{\mathcal{X}}$ becomes

$$\begin{bmatrix} \mathcal{X}_c & \mathcal{X}_f & \mathcal{X}_s \end{bmatrix} \begin{bmatrix} 0 & p & 1-p \\ 1 & 0 & 0 \\ 1 & 0 & 0 \end{bmatrix} = \begin{bmatrix} \mathcal{X}_c & \mathcal{X}_f & \mathcal{X}_s \end{bmatrix}$$

Or, represented equivalently by doing the vector matrix multiplication, this set
of equations is

$$\mathcal{X}_f + \mathcal{X}_s = \mathcal{X}_c$$
$$p\mathcal{X}_c = \mathcal{X}_f$$
$$(1 - p)\mathcal{X}_c = \mathcal{X}_s$$

These equations can be solved using standard techniques. (*Note:* In numerical analysis terminology, the solution to $\vec{X} \times \mathcal{P} = \vec{X}$ is an eigenvector problem, where the goal is to find the left eigenvector $\vec{X}$ of the stochastic matrix $\mathcal{P}$ associated with eigenvalue 1. Every stochastic matrix, where each of the rows sum to 1, has an eigenvalue of 1. The solution to this problem is unique only up to a constant. This is why the terminology *relative* throughputs and utilizations are used.)

One of the (relative) solutions to this set of equations is

$$X_c = \mu_c$$

$$X_f = \mu_c p$$

$$X_s = \mu_c(1 - p)$$

This now explains the "relative throughput" terminology. *If* the throughput of the CPU were μ_c, then, due to the probability split upon leaving the CPU, the flow into the fast disk would be $\mu_c p$. Since flow in equals flow out, this also equals the throughput of the fast disk. The situation with the slow disk is analogous.

Once the relative throughputs have been found, the relative utilizations follow immediately. The (relative) throughput of a device is the simple product of the (relative) utilization of the device and the device's service rate, $X_i = U_i \mu_i$. Thus,

$$U_c = 1$$

$$U_f = \frac{\mu_c p}{\mu_f}$$

$$U_s = \frac{\mu_c(1 - p)}{\mu_s}$$

Therefore, from the device service times and the device routing probability matrix, the device relative utilizations can be calculated by solving a system of linear equations, one equation per device. This is not a difficult computation.

The remaining problem is to solve for the $G(\ )$'s. From before,

$$G(\text{MPL}) = \sum_{\text{all states}} \prod_{k=1}^{K} U_k^{\text{no. customers at } k \text{ in the state}}$$

It appears that the calculation of the $G(\ )$'s is quite complex, since the number of possible system states grows exponentially as the number of devices and/or customers increases. However, due to an observation by Buzen [1], a simple recursive technique for calculating the $G(\ )$'s is possible.

To illustrate Buzen's technique, also referred to as *convolution*, a slight change in notation is necessary. Until now, the notation has been $G(\text{MPL})$, which is a function of a single parameter, the number of customers in the network. In actuality, two parameters are necessary, both the number of customers and the number of devices. Thus, let $g(m, k)$ denote the normalization constant for a network with m customers and k devices. Therefore, using earlier notation, $G(\text{MPL}) \equiv g(\text{MPL}, K)$.

The recursive technique is illustrated via the CPU/fast disk/slow disk example. From before,

$$G(2) \equiv g(2, 3)$$
$$= \mathcal{U}_c^2 \mathcal{U}_f^0 \mathcal{U}_s^0 + \mathcal{U}_c^1 \mathcal{U}_f^1 \mathcal{U}_s^0 + \mathcal{U}_c^1 \mathcal{U}_f^0 \mathcal{U}_s^1$$
$$+ \mathcal{U}_c^0 \mathcal{U}_f^2 \mathcal{U}_s^0 + \mathcal{U}_c^0 \mathcal{U}_f^1 \mathcal{U}_s^1 + \mathcal{U}_c^0 \mathcal{U}_f^0 \mathcal{U}_s^2$$

By rearranging terms, we obtain

$$G(2) \equiv g(2, 3)$$
$$= \mathcal{U}_c^2 \mathcal{U}_f^0 + \mathcal{U}_c^1 \mathcal{U}_f^1 + \mathcal{U}_c^0 \mathcal{U}_f^2$$
$$+ \mathcal{U}_s \left(\mathcal{U}_c^1 \mathcal{U}_f^0 \mathcal{U}_s^0 + \mathcal{U}_c^0 \mathcal{U}_f^1 \mathcal{U}_s^0 + \mathcal{U}_c^0 \mathcal{U}_f^0 \mathcal{U}_s^1 \right)$$
$$= g(2, 2) + \mathcal{U}_s g(1, 3)$$

Therefore, the general recursive definition of $G(\ )$ is

$$G(\text{MPL}) \equiv g(\text{MPL}, K) = g(\text{MPL}, K - 1) + \mathcal{U}_K g(\text{MPL} - 1, K)$$

where the base of the recursion is $G(0) = g(0, k) = 1$ for all values of k and where $g(m, 1) = \mathcal{U}_1^m$ when there is a single device in the network. (The proof that this is the correct base for the recursion is left as an exercise.) The recursive definition above is termed *convolution* since devices are "convolved" into the solution of $G(\ )$ one device at a time.

The implementation of the calculation of the $G(\ )$'s is easy. An MPL $\times K$ matrix given the $g(\ ,\ )$'s can be found by initializing the first row to 1 and the first column to the appropriate power of $\mathcal{U}_1$. The remainder of the matrix can then be filled in either on a row-by-row basis or on a column-by-column basis. A missing entry can be found by forming the sum of (1) the matrix entry to the left, and (2) the product of the matrix entry above times the appropriate $\mathcal{U}$. This is illustrated in Fig. 5.4. Note that the final column contains *all* the necessary $G(\ )$'s required for the calculation of the performance metrics $U_i(\text{MPL})$, $X_i(\text{MPL})$, $\bar{n}_i(\text{MPL})$, and $R_i(\text{MPL})$ [i.e., Eqs. (5.1) to (5.4)].

To summarize the convolution technique: Given a model with input parameters being the device speeds μ_i's, the interdevice branching probabilities $\mathcal{P}$, and the multiprogramming level MPL:

1. Find the relative throughputs X_i's by solving the eigenvector problem, $\vec{X} \times \mathcal{P} = \vec{X}$.

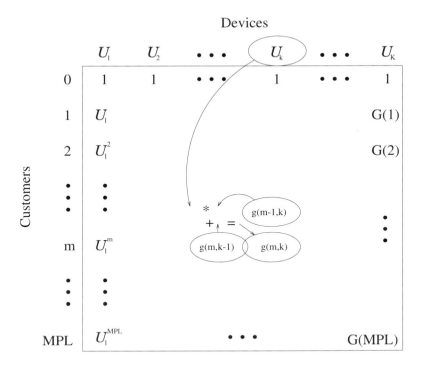

Figure 5.4   G( ) Table calculation.

2. Find the relative utilizations $\mathcal{U}_i = \mathcal{X}_i/\mu_i$.
3. Find the normalization constants $G(\ )$'s by the technique shown in Fig. 5.4.
4. Solve Eqs. (5.1) to (5.4) to obtain the performance metrics $U_i(\text{MPL})$, $X_i(\text{MPL})$, $\bar{n}_i(\text{MPL})$, and $R_i(\text{MPL})$.

5.5 SIMPLE MEAN VALUE ANALYSIS

Although the convolution algorithm is useful and simple to implement, it is susceptible to numerical instabilities. At high multiprogramming levels, the value of $G(\ )$ can overflow (or underflow) the accuracy of floating-point arithmetic. This is due to the fact that in the calculation of $G(\ )$, the relative utilizations $\mathcal{U}_i$'s are raised to powers, whose magnitudes are based on the multiprogramming level. Thus, the value of $G(\text{MPL})$ can be quite large (or very nearly zero). The reason that the performance metrics do not attain unreasonable values is that the performance metrics are based on *ratios* of the $G(\ )$'s, not their absolute values.

A technique that avoids numerical instabilities, while maintaining the ease of implementation, is the *mean value analysis* (MVA) technique [2]. Like convolution, MVA is an iterative technique, but where convolution iterates on the number of devices, MVA iterates on the number of customers. The development of the MVA technique is intuitive and elegant.

Returning briefly to the CPU/fast disk/slow disk example, the formula for the response time of a customer at the fast disk was

$$R_f(2) = \frac{G(1) + \mathcal{U}_f G(0)}{\mu_f G(1)}$$

Therefore,

$$R_f(2) = \frac{1}{\mu_f} \left[1 + \mathcal{U}_f \frac{G(0)}{G(1)} \right]$$

However, $\mathcal{U}_f G(0)/G(1)$ is simply $\bar{n}_f(1)$. Thus,

$$R_f(2) = \frac{1}{\mu_f} \left[1 + \bar{n}_f(1) \right]$$

In general, an alternative expression for the response time equation, Eq. (5.4), is

$$R_i(\text{MPL}) = \frac{1}{\mu_i} \left[1 + \bar{n}_i(\text{MPL} - 1) \right] \tag{5.5}$$

Another interpretation of this formula is that the wait time experienced by an arriving customer is the sum of the arriving customer's required service time (i.e., $1/\mu_i$) plus the time that it takes to empty the queue that the arriving customer "sees" upon arrival. The number of customers seen upon arrival turns out to be $\bar{n}_i(\text{MPL} - 1)$, which is the steady-state queue length with one customer (i.e., the arriving customer) removed from the system. This is an instance of the *arrival theorem* result [3], which states that an arriving customer sees $\bar{n}_i(\text{MPL} - 1)$ customers ahead of itself. The time required to empty the queue is, thus, $(1/\mu_i)\bar{n}_i(\text{MPL} - 1)$.

An alternative expression for $X_i(\text{MPL})$ is now derived. From Little's result (see Chap. 4),

$$\begin{array}{ccc} \text{average number of} \\ \text{customers in a system} \end{array} = \begin{array}{c} \text{arrival rate} \\ \text{at the system} \end{array} \times \begin{array}{c} \text{average time spent} \\ \text{in the system} \end{array}$$

and viewing the "system" as the cloud illustrated in Fig. 5.5, Little's result can be viewed with the following interpretation. The average number of customers in the system (i.e., in the cloud) equals the multiprogramming level, MPL. The average arrival rate at the system equals the average departure rate from a selected device, $X_i(\text{MPL})$. (The device selected in Fig. 5.5 happens to be the slow disk.) The average time spent in the system equals the time it takes to

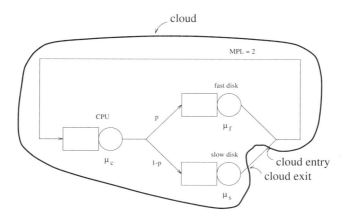

Figure 5.5 Cycle time via Little's result.

cycle through the system to return to the selected device. Define this cycle time as $CT_i(MPL)$. Therefore,

$$MPL = X_i\ (MPL) \times CT_i\ (MPL)$$

or, equivalently,

$$X_i\ (MPL) = \frac{MPL}{CT_i\ (MPL)}$$

The cycle time, measured at a device, can be expressed as a sum of component parts. To see this, consider the CPU/fast disk/slow disk example. Consider a customer just as it arrives at the CPU. The time that it will take for the customer to make a complete cycle back to its position is either $R_c(2) + R_f(2)$ or $R_c(2) + R_s(2)$, depending on whether the customer goes to the fast disk or to the slow disk after visiting the CPU. This depends on the branching probability. That is, $CT_c(2) = R_c(2) + pR_f(2) + (1 - p)R_s(2)$. The situation for expressing the cycle time measured at one of the disks is complicated by the fact that a customer could visit the CPU and the other disk multiple times before returning to the selected disk. Consider the fast disk. For every visit to the CPU, p visits are made to the fast disk. Or, alternatively, for every visit to the fast disk, $1/p$ visits are made to the CPU, and thus $(1-p)/p$ visits are made to the slow disk. Thus, $CT_f(2) = R_f(2) + (1/p)R_c(2) + [(1 - p)/p]R_s(2)$. Similarly, for the slow disk, $CT_s(2) = R_s(2) + [1/(1 - p)]R_c(2) + [p/(1 - p)]R_s(2)$. For notational convenience, let $\mathcal{V}_i$ represent the number of relative visits a typical customer makes to device i. Thus, $\mathcal{V}_c = 1$, $\mathcal{V}_f = p$, and $\mathcal{V}_s = (1 - p)$. [*Note:* Recall from Sec. 5.4 that the relative throughputs were calculated to be $\mathcal{X}_c = \mu_c$, $\mathcal{X}_f = \mu_c p$, and $\mathcal{X}_s = \mu_c(1 - p)$. Since these are *relative* values, by dividing each by μ_c, it is observed that $\mathcal{X}_c = 1$, $\mathcal{X}_f = p$, and $\mathcal{X}_s = (1 - p)$. That is, $\mathcal{X}_i = \mathcal{V}_i$. Thus, in general, the $\mathcal{V}_i$'s can be calculated in the exact same fashion as the $\mathcal{X}_i$'s, by solving the eigenvector problem in Sec. 5.4. To reduce the notation, we did not need to introduce the $\mathcal{V}_i$'s. The $\mathcal{X}_i$'s are sufficient. However, for historical reasons and for the notation used in succeeding chapters, the $\mathcal{V}_i$'s are introduced. They are referred to as "relative visit counts" or "visit ratios" and denote the number of visits a typical customer makes to each device. They are relative throughputs.] Note that the ratio $\mathcal{V}_k/\mathcal{V}_i$ between any two relative visit counts is identical to the ratio V_k/V_i between the corresponding actual visit counts. Therefore, in general,

$$ CT_i(MPL) = \sum_{k=1}^{K} \left[R_k(MPL) \frac{V_k}{V_i} \right] $$

and the desired alternative expression for $X_i(MPL)$ is

$$ X_i(MPL) = \frac{MPL}{\sum_{k=1}^{K} [R_k(MPL)V_k/V_i]} \tag{5.6} $$

The final equation needed to specify the MVA technique completely is the simple application of Little's result to an individual server.

$$ \bar{n}_i(MPL) = X_i(MPL) \times R_i(MPL) \tag{5.7} $$

Therefore, the complete MVA technique is to solve iteratively the three MVA equations [i.e., Eqs. (5.5), (5.6), and (5.7)],

$$ R_i(n) = \frac{1}{\mu_i} [1 + \bar{n}_i(n-1)] $$

$$ X_i(n) = \frac{n}{\sum_{k=1}^{K} [R_k(n)V_k/V_i]} \tag{5.8} $$

$$ \bar{n}_i(n) = X_i(n) \times R_i(n) $$

for $m = 1, 2, \ldots, MPL$, where the initialization of the iteration is $\bar{n}_i(0) = 0$ for all devices i. MVA derives the same performance metrics as found using convolution except for $U_i(MPL)$. [Adding a fourth MVA equation to find $U_i(MPL)$ is left as an exercise.] Extensions to MVA to multiple-class networks and to load-dependent networks will be made in succeeding chapters.

MVA is a simple, yet general solution technique. To summarize the MVA technique: Given a model with input parameters being the device speeds μ_i's, the interdevice branching probabilities $\mathcal{P}$, and the multiprogramming level MPL:

1. Find the relative visit counts V_i's by solving the eigenvector problem, $V \times \mathcal{P} = V$ (or, the V_i's may be specified directly as input parameters), and

2. Perform the MVA iteration to solve Eq. (5.8) to obtain the performance metrics $U_i(\text{MPL})$, $X_i(\text{MPL})$, $\bar{n}_i(\text{MPL})$, and $R_i(\text{MPL})$.

Clever!

In many cases, the given input parameters are the service demands D_i's. As you recall, $D_i = V_i (1/\mu_i) = V_i S_i$. Fortunately, the MVA equations may be rewritten as a function of the service demands D_i's rather than as a function of the individual values of μ_i's and V_i's. The proof of this is left as an exercise. The resulting equations are given below. Note that instead of using the average response time $R_i(n)$, we use the average residence time $R_i'(n)$, defined as the average time spent by a job at device i in all its visits to that device. So $R_i'(n) = V_i R_i(n)$.

$$R_i'(n) = V_i R_i(n) = D_i[1 + \bar{n}_i(n-1)]$$

$$X_0(n) = \frac{n}{\sum_{k=1}^{K} R_k'(n)} \tag{5.9}$$

$$\bar{n}_i(n) = X_0(n) R_i'(n)$$

A useful performance metric is defined as the factor by which the service time at device i is stretched due to queuing at the device. This factor, called *stretch factor* (SF), is given by the following ratio

$$\text{SF}_i(n) = \frac{R_i(n)}{S_i} = \frac{R_i'(n)}{D_i} \tag{5.10}$$

Note that if $\text{SF}_i(n) = 1$, the response time is equal to the service time, which indicates that there is no queuing at the device. The larger the stretch factor the larger the effect of queuing at the device.

5.6 SIMPLE DECOMPOSITION/AGGREGATION

When analyzing large systems, it is often useful to partition the system into various component parts, model the internal behavior within each part separately, and then model the higher-level interactions between the component parts. For instance, the system may be partitioned into a processor part and an I/O part. One person (or a team of people) may be responsible for constructing and analyzing each part. Upon completion, the two parts may be integrated into one composite system and analyzed together. This is the basic idea of decomposition and aggregation. The system is decomposed into its parts, analyzed separately, and then aggregated back into its composite whole. Decomposition/aggregation represents a basic divide-and-conquer solution technique.

A technique based on the construction of *flow-equivalent service centers* (FESC) is described here [4, 5]. This is an example of a simple decomposition/aggregation technique. The system is decomposed into parts. Each part is analyzed separately and replaced by a single server (i.e., its FESC). The collection of FESCs can then be analyzed to produce a model of the entire aggregated system.

The technique is illustrated on the CPU/fast disk/slow disk example. Suppose that the input parameters are changed such that the MPL $= 3$, $\mu_c = 10$, $\mu_f = 8$, $\mu_s = 6$, and $p = 0.7$. Assuming that $V_c = 1$, we get that $V_f = p = 0.7$ and $V_s = 1 - p = 0.3$. By solving the system using either convolution or MVA, the performance metrics shown in Table 5.1 are found.

Now suppose that the system is decomposed into two subsystems, the CPU subsystem and the I/O subsystem (see Fig. 5.6). Because the CPU sub-

Table 5.1   Performance Metrics for FESC.

	$X(3)$	$\bar{n}(3)$	$U(3)$	$R'(3)$
CPU	7.33	1.38	73%	0.19
fast disk	5.13	1.12	64%	0.15
slow disk	2.20	0.50	37%	0.07

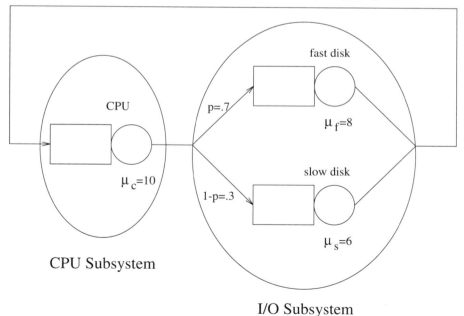

Figure 5.6   Decomposition/aggregation example.

system consists of a single server, its flow-equivalent service center, FESC$_{cpu}$, consists of the original CPU server with service rate $\mu_c = 10$.

To find the flow-equivalent service center for the I/O subsystem, the I/O subsystem is analyzed in isolation. That is, the CPU is removed from the subsystem model (i.e., "shorted" out) (see Fig. 5.7). This model is solved to find the throughput of the model, measured at the place where the CPU has been removed, for all multiprogramming levels MPL $= 1, 2$, and 3. Denote these three metrics as $X_{i/o}(1)$, $X_{i/o}(2)$, and $X_{i/o}(3)$. These throughputs can be derived by solving one model using convolution or MVA with MPL $= 3$ and summing the throughputs of the two disks. The throughputs at lower MPL values are computed as by-products when the model is solved with MPL $= 3$. The solution yields $X_{i/o}(1) = 7.27$, $X_{i/o}(2) = 9.46$, and $X_{i/o}(3) = 10.40$.

Having found $X_{i/o}(1)$, $X_{i/o}(2)$, and $X_{i/o}(3)$, the flow-equivalent service center for the I/O subsystem, FESC$_{i/o}$, is parameterized as a single load-dependent server, whose service rates are the $X_{i/o}$'s. That is, when a single customer is at the FESC$_{i/o}$, its service rate $\mu_{i/o}(1) = X_{i/o}(1) = 7.27$. Similarly, when two customers are at the FESC$_{i/o}$, its service rate $\mu_{i/o}(2) = X_{i/o}(2) = 9.46$, and when three customers are at the FESC$_{i/o}$, its service rate $\mu_{i/o}(3) = X_{i/o}(3) = 10.40$ (see Fig. 5.8).

This aggregate model can be solved using a load-dependent MVA algorithm (to be given in Chap. 7) or the model can be solved from first principles by constructing and solving the underlying Markov diagram, shown in Fig. 5.9. The state description is (i, j), where i customers are at the CPU and j customers are at the FESC$_{i/o}$. The solution yields the results shown in Table 5.2.

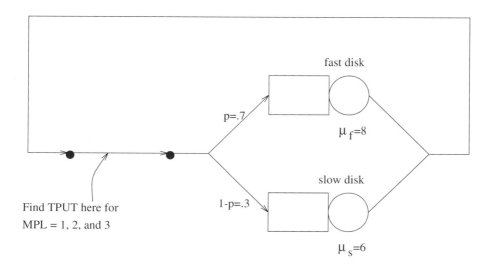

Figure 5.7 I/O subsystem model.

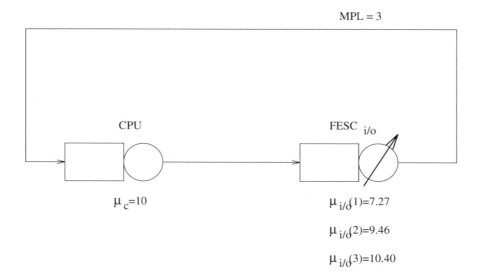

Figure 5.8 Aggregate model.

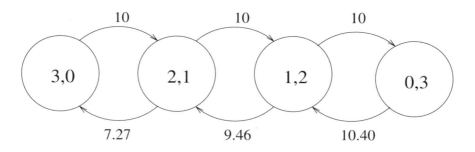

Figure 5.9 Markov diagram of the aggregate model.

Table 5.2 Performance Metrics for $\text{FESC}_{i/o}$.

	$X(3)$	$\bar{n}(3)$	$U(3)$	$R(3)$
CPU	7.33	1.38	73%	0.19
$\text{FESC}_{i/o}$	7.33	1.62	81%	0.22

In this example, the decomposition/aggregation technique is exact. That is, the performance measures can be computed by either solving the entire network directly using convolution or MVA, or the network can be decomposed into subsystems, each solved independently, with the results being used to parameterize an aggregate model. Decomposition/aggregation is exact when applied to product-form networks [6].

To summarize the decomposition/aggregation technique: Given a model, partition (i.e., decompose) the model into various subsystems:

1. Solve each subsystem independently to obtain the subsystem throughputs, as a function of the multiprogramming level.

2. Form the load-dependent flow-equivalent service centers (FESCs) for each subsystem.

3. Aggregate the FESCs together and solve the resulting load-dependent aggregate model.

5.7 SIMPLE BOUNDING TECHNIQUES

Although the solution techniques based on convolution, MVA, and decomposition/aggregation are efficient and exact when applied to single-class product-form networks, there are instances when even these techniques are too computationally expensive. For example, suppose that a user creates a file and the operating system must decide in which disk to store the file. Or, suppose that a message is to be routed through a communications network and the system must decide, based on the current load of the links, which route will result in the minimum delay. In situations such as these, it would be reasonable for the system to construct automatically a model of each of the alternatives, solve each, and select the alternative that is predicted to have the best performance. Even though convolution, MVA, and decomposition/aggregation might be able to solve each model in a matter of a few seconds, the operating system needs to be able to make a decision within a few microseconds. Also, relative or approximate performance (and not absolute or exact performance) is often all that is required. That is, knowing that $X = 9.87654321$ for a particular model is overkill. Simply knowing that $X \approx 10$ for one alternative and that $X \approx 14$ for another alternative is sufficient information to select one option over another (e.g., file placement on disk D_1 as opposed to disk D_2, message routing along path P_1 as opposed to path P_2). Situations such as these provide the motivation for the development of simple bounding techniques, sometimes referred to as *quick bounds* or *back-of-the-envelope* techniques. These techniques provide extremely fast solutions to models, requiring only a few arithmetic operations. The price paid is a (hopefully modest and acceptable) loss of accuracy.

Two of the most simple bounding techniques are "rediscovered" here. The first technique is known as asymptotic bound analysis (ABA) [7]. To illustrate the technique, reconsider the CPU/fast disk/slow disk example (see

Fig. 5.1). From the first MVA formula, Eq. (5.5),

$$R_i(\text{MPL}) = \frac{1}{\mu_i}[1 + \bar{n}_i(\text{MPL} - 1)]$$

Since $\bar{n}_i(\text{MPL} - 1) \geq 0$, $R_i(\text{MPL}) \geq 1/\mu_i$. This makes sense since the waiting time experienced by an arriving customer at a service station is at least the customer's service time.

From the second MVA formula, Eq. (5.6),

$$X_i(\text{MPL}) = \frac{\text{MPL}}{\sum_{k=1}^{K}[R_k(\text{MPL})V_k/V_i]}$$

By defining $X_{\text{system}}(\text{MPL})$ to be the throughput measured at a designated point, say at device i^*, and letting the relative visit ratios be such that $V_{i^*} = 1$, then

$$X_{\text{system}}(\text{MPL}) = X_{i^*}(\text{MPL}) = \frac{\text{MPL}}{\sum_{k=1}^{K}[R_k(\text{MPL})V_k]}$$

(*Note:* When the relative visit count at the point where the throughput is measured is set to 1, all other relative visit counts become equal to the absolute visit counts.) In the CPU/fast disk/slow disk example, it is natural to let the designated device be the CPU. Thus, $X_{\text{system}}(\text{MPL}) = X_c(\text{MPL})$ and continue to let $V_c = 1$, $V_f = p$, and $V_s = (1 - p)$.

By slipping into operational analysis terminology (see Chap. 4), $S_i = 1/\mu_i$ is the mean service time experienced by a customer at device i. Since $R_i(\text{MPL}) \geq 1/\mu_i = S_i$,

$$X_{\text{system}}(\text{MPL}) \leq \frac{\text{MPL}}{\sum_{k=1}^{K}V_kS_k}$$

This is sometimes called the "no queuing" case upper bound for system throughput, since this is the best that throughput can be, and it occurs only if there were no queuing in the system. It is a good bound when the system load is light [i.e., when the MPL is small and, thus, $R_k(\text{MPL}) \approx S_k$].

From the forced flow law and the utilization law (see Chap. 4), it follows that

$$X_{\text{system}}(\text{MPL}) = \frac{1}{V_j}X_j(\text{MPL})$$

$$= \frac{1}{V_j}U_j(\text{MPL})\mu_j$$

for any device j. Under heavy-loading conditions (i.e., when the MPL is large) the device utilizations tend to be high, but cannot exceed 100%. This leads to other upper bounds on throughput, one for each device, which are good bounds under heavy-loading conditions as the device utilizations approach 100%.

$$X_{\text{system}}(\text{MPL}) = \frac{1}{V_j}U_j(\text{MPL})\mu_j$$

$$\leq \frac{\mu_j}{V_j}$$

$$= \frac{1}{V_j S_j}$$

Putting these bounds together, the ABA bounds are

$$X_{\text{system}}(\text{MPL}) \leq \min\left[\frac{\text{MPL}}{\sum_{k=1}^{K} V_k S_k}, \frac{1}{V_j S_j}\right] \tag{5.11}$$

Clearly, the tightest bound in the heavy-loading case is the device b such that $V_b S_b \geq V_j S_j$ for any device j. This device b with the largest $V_b S_b$ is called the *bottleneck* device. Thus, we can write that

$$X_{\text{system}}(\text{MPL}) \leq \min\left[\frac{\text{MPL}}{\sum_{k=1}^{K} V_k S_k}, \frac{1}{V_b S_b}\right] \tag{5.12}$$

Since the V_i's are equivalent to the relative throughputs, dividing by the μ_i's (i.e., multiplying by the S_i's) yields relative utilizations. Therefore, $V_i S_i$ is the relative utilization of device i. The bottleneck device is simply the device with the highest relative (and, therefore, also the highest absolute) utilization.

To visualize the ABA bounds of Eq. (5.11), consider the CPU/fast disk/slow disk example with $\mu_c = 6$, $\mu_f = 3$, $\mu_s = 2$, $V_c = 1$, $V_f = p = 0.5$, and $V_s = (1 - p) = 0.5$. Therefore, the relative utilizations are $V_c S_c = 1/6$, $V_f S_f = 1/6$, and $V_s S_s = 1/4$. Because of its largest relative utilization, the bottleneck device is the slow disk, with $V_b S_b = 1/4$. This leads to the following ABA bounds:

$$X_{\text{system}}(\text{MPL}) \leq \min\left[\frac{12}{7}\text{MPL}, 4\right]$$

These bounds are illustrated in Fig. 5.10.

Two of the problems with ABA bounds is that they are quite loose and that no good lower performance bound is given. It is often this lower bound that is important since one would like to know that system throughput will be at least some known amount. This motivates a second bounding technique, known as *balanced job bound analysis* (BJB) [8]. Consider the CPU/fast disk/slow disk example again with $V_c S_c = 1/6$, $V_f S_f = 1/6$, and $V_s S_s = 1/4$. Suppose that the nonbottleneck devices (i.e., the CPU and the fast disk) are slowed down to where all the $V_i S_i$'s are equal. That is, slow down the CPU

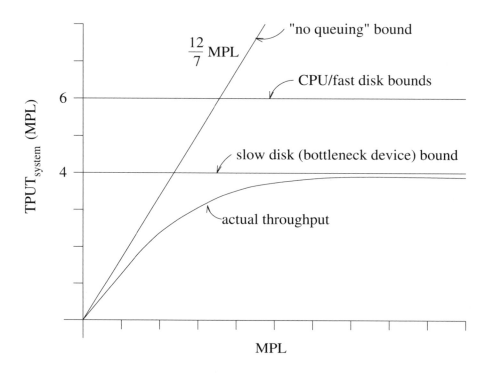

Figure 5.10 Asymptotic bounds analysis (ABA) example.

from $\mu_c = 6$ to $\mu_c = 4$. This would make $V_c S_c = 1/4$. Similarly, slow down
the fast disk from $\mu_f = 3$ to $\mu_f = 2$. This would make $V_f S_f = 1/4$. The effect
of making these changes is that all of the devices would now have the same
relative (and actual) utilizations. Effectively, all the devices have been slowed
down to the bottleneck device's speed. This represents a pessimistic bound
on performance. Actual throughput will be better. Because the devices are
now all (effectively) the same, all devices will have the same queue lengths,
regardless of the multiprogramming level. (If you do not believe this, check it
out.) This means that if the multiprogramming level is MPL, and if there are
K devices, then $\bar{n}_i(\text{MPL}) = \text{MPL}/K$ for each device i. From the first MVA
formula, Eq. (5.5),

$$R_i(\text{MPL}) = \frac{1}{\mu_i}[1 + \bar{n}_i(\text{MPL} - 1)]$$

$$= \frac{1}{\mu_i}\left(1 + \frac{\text{MPL} - 1}{K}\right)$$

$$= S_i\left(\frac{K + \text{MPL} - 1}{K}\right)$$

and from the second MVA formula, Eq. (5.6),

$$X_{\text{system}}(\text{MPL}) = \frac{\text{MPL}}{\sum_{k=1}^{K} V_k R_k(\text{MPL})}$$

$$= \frac{\text{MPL}}{\sum_{k=1}^{K} V_k S_k \, (K + \text{MPL} - 1) \, / \, K}$$

But if all devices are slowed down to the bottleneck's $V_b S_b$,

$$X_{\text{system}}(\text{MPL}) \geq \frac{\text{MPL}}{\sum_{k=1}^{K} V_b S_b \, (K + \text{MPL} - 1) \, / \, K}$$

$$= \frac{\text{MPL}}{K V_b S_b \, (K + \text{MPL} - 1) \, / \, K}$$

$$= \frac{\text{MPL}}{V_b S_b \, (K + \text{MPL} - 1)}$$

This represents the lower BJB bound.

To construct the upper BJB bound for $X_{\text{system}}(\text{MPL})$, and without going through all the details of a formal proof, it is known that $X_{\text{system}}(\text{MPL})$ is less than if all the devices had the same "average" $V_i S_i$. (See Ref. [8] for the formal proof.) In the example where $V_c S_c = 1/6$, $V_f S_f = 1/6$, and $V_s S_s = 1/4$, the sum of the $V_i S_i$'s is 7/12. Thus, the average $V_a S_a = 7/36$. Since system throughput is worse than a system with all devices have the average $V_a S_a$, by following the same steps as given above,

$$X_{\text{system}}(\text{MPL}) \leq \frac{\text{MPL}}{V_a S_a \, (K + \text{MPL} - 1)}$$

Putting these bounds together, the BJB bounds are

$$\frac{\text{MPL}}{V_b S_b \, (K + \text{MPL} - 1)} \leq X_{\text{system}}(\text{MPL}) \leq \frac{\text{MPL}}{V_a S_a \, (K + \text{MPL} - 1)} \quad (5.13)$$

Particularized to the CPU/fast disk/slow disk example,

$$\frac{\text{MPL}}{\frac{1}{4} \, (2 + \text{MPL})} \leq X_{\text{system}}(\text{MPL}) \leq \frac{\text{MPL}}{\frac{7}{36} \, (2 + \text{MPL})}$$

These bounds are illustrated in Fig. 5.11.

5.8 CONCLUDING REMARKS

In this chapter, several solution techniques have been developed from first principles. It is always possible to construct the underlying Markov model, form the global balance equations, one per system state, and solve them to

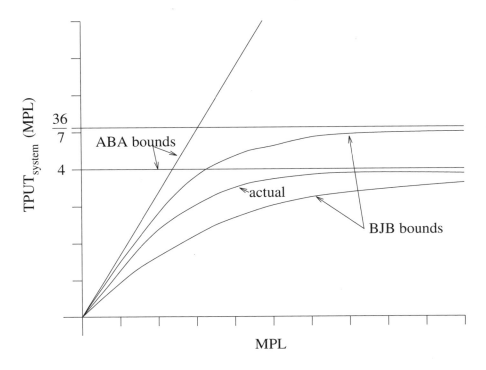

Figure 5.11   Balanced job bounds (BJB) example.

obtain the desired performance metrics. This is often inefficient since the number of system states grows exponentially. Efficient alternative solution techniques exist. These include convolution and MVA. Simple versions of these techniques have been developed in this chapter. Each of these can be extended to include multiple classes of customers, load-dependent servers, and other extensions. Simple decomposition and aggregation has been presented as a way in which to analyze smaller components of a system independently and then combine the smaller components back into the composite whole. Decomposition/aggregation forms the basis for many approximation techniques. Finally, two simple bounding techniques, ABA and BJB, have been developed. These are useful when trying to get quick estimates and bounds of a system model.

As indicated, each of the techniques presented has several extensions. Indeed, entire papers and texts could (and have) been written on each (albeit the mathematics gets a bit more complex). The motivation here has been to introduce these techniques and have them understood completely and intuitively.

5.9 EXERCISES

1. Give a full listing of the local balance equations for the example illustrated in Fig. 5.2.

2. Prove that the set of local balance (LB) equations is equivalent to the set of equations found by pairing of the arcs (PA) for the example illustrated in Fig. 5.2.

3. What is the performance (utilizations, throughputs, queue lengths, and wait times of each device) of the original system proposed by the motivating example in Sec. 5.3?

4. Referring to the motivating example in Sec. 5.3, by how much would performance be improved if code for transaction handling by the CPU were rewritten to execute 33% faster?

5. Referring to the motivating example in Sec. 5.3, by how much would performance be improved if the slow disk were replaced by a second fast disk?

6. Referring to the motivating example in Sec. 5.3, by how much is CPU throughput improved if 10% of the files are moved from the slow disk to the fast disk? What about 50%? (This implies changing the value of p.)

7. Referring to the motivating example in Sec. 5.3, what is the optimal file placement across the two disks? (This implies varying the value of p, observing the effect upon performance, and selecting the optimal value of p.)

8. Referring to the motivating example in Sec. 5.3, by how much is CPU throughput improved by increasing the MPL from 2 to 3?

9. Consider the normalization constant $G(\ )$ and its recursive definition, $G(\text{MPL}) = g(\text{MPL}, K) = g(\text{MPL}, K-1) + \mathcal{U}_K g(\text{MPL}-1, K)$. Show that the appropriate base for the recursion is $G(0) = g(0, k) = 1$ for all values of k and $g(m, 1) = \mathcal{U}_1{}^m$ when there is a single device in the network.

10. Write a convolution-based program. The program should input the number of devices, the device service rates, the multiprogramming level, and the interdevice routing probability matrix. The program should output the device utilizations, throughputs, queue lengths, and wait times. Use it to verify the answers to Exercise 3.

11. The vanilla MVA technique does not find the utilizations of the devices. Derive a fourth equation to add to the MVA technique to find $U_i(\text{MPL})$.

12. Derive the MVA formulas given in Eq. (5.9) from those given by Eq. (5.8). (Hint: Use the forced flow law.)

13. Write a mean value analysis program. Use it to verify the answers to Exercises 3 through 8.

14. Compare the computational complexity of convolution versus MVA. That is, how many arithmetic operations are needed for convolution and MVA? Are there situations where one solution technique is more efficient than the other?

15. A computer system has one CPU and two disks, disk 1 and disk 2. The system was monitored for 1 hour and the utilization of the CPU and of disk 1 were measured to be 32% and 60%, respectively. Each transaction makes 5 I/O requests to disk 1 and 8 to disk 2. The average service time at disk 1 is 30 msec and at disk 2 is 25 msec.

(a) Find the system throughput.
(b) Find the utilization of disk 2.
(c) Find the average service demands at the CPU, disk 1, and disk 2.
(d) Use MVA to find the system throughput, response time, and average queue length at the CPU and the disks when the degree of multiprogramming is n, for $n = 0, \ldots, 4$.
(e) Based on your results for item (d), what would be a good approximation for the average degree of multiprogramming during the measurement interval?

16. Consider the CPU/fast disk/slow disk example, with $\mu_c = 6$, $\mu_f = 3$, $\mu_s = 2$, $p = 0.5$, and MPL $= 2$. Solve this system using the decomposition/aggregation technique and compare the answers by solving the same system using convolution.

17. Perform simple bounding analysis using ABA and BJB on the example shown in Fig. 5.6. Graph the ABA bounds, the BJB bounds, and the actual performance curves. Show all work.

BIBLIOGRAPHY

1. J. P. Buzen, Computational algorithms for closed queuing networks with exponential servers, *Communications of the ACM*, Vol. 16, No. 9, September 1973, pp. 527–531.

2. M. Reiser and S. S. Lavenberg, Mean value analysis of closed multichain queuing networks, *Journal of the ACM*, Vol. 27, No. 2, April 1980, pp. 313–322.

3. K. C. Sevcik and I. Mitrani, The distribution of queuing network states at input and output instants, *Journal of the ACM*, Vol. 28, No. 2, April 1981, pp. 358–371.

4. K. K. Chandy, U. Herzog, and L. S. Woo, Parametric analysis of queuing networks, *IBM Journal of Research and Development*, Vol. 19, No. 1, January 1975, pp. 966–975.

5. E. D. Lazowska, J. Zahorjan, G. S. Graham, and K. C. Sevcik, *Quantitative System Performance: Computer System Analysis Using Queuing Network Models*, Prentice Hall, Englewood Cliffs, N.J., 1984.

6. F. Baskett, K. M. Chandy, R. R. Muntz, and F. G. Palacios, Open, closed, and mixed networks of queues with different classes of customers, *Journal of the ACM*, Vol. 22, No. 2, April 1975, pp. 248–260.

7. R. R. Muntz and J. W. Wong, Asymptotic properties of closed queuing network models, *Proceedings of the 8th Princeton Conference on Information Sciences and Systems*, 1974.

8. J. Zahorjan, K. C. Sevcik, D. L. Eager, and B. I. Galler, Balanced job bound analysis of queuing networks, *Communications of the ACM*, Vol. 25, No. 2, February 1982, pp. 134–141.

Chapter 6

Multiple-Class Models

6.1 INTRODUCTION

The real power of performance models becomes evident when they are applied to predictive purposes. In capacity planning, models are essential because of their ability to predict adequately the performance of a particular computer system under different workloads. Real-life systems experience a wide variety of customers (jobs, transactions, commands, and requests) with different resource usage profiles. Thus, actual workloads can hardly be considered as a single class of homogeneous customers. Typically, each customer differs from every other customer. Because it is impractical to represent each individual customer in a model, they are grouped into classes of somehow similar components. Usually, *"what if"* questions that appear in capacity planning are associated with individual classes of customers. As an example, one could ask what the performance of a given system will be if the arrival rate of query transactions increases by 60% or if the number of update batch jobs doubles. Single-class models are unable to answer most of the capacity planning questions related to specific classes of the workload; they are limited in their predictive capability. Therefore, techniques are needed that solve multiclass performance models. This chapter provides MVA-based algorithms for solving open and closed product-form queuing network models with multiple classes. The techniques include exact and approximate solutions.

Although multiple-class models are more useful and natural for describing workloads of real systems, they present problems to the modeler. For instance, it is difficult to obtain parameters (e.g., multiclass service demands, multiclass visit ratios, multiclass multiprogramming levels) for models with multiple classes. Usually, monitoring tools do not provide measurements on a per-class basis. Inferences (sometimes wild guesses) have to be made to parameterize each workload class and to apportion the system overhead among the classes. As a result, it is more difficult to obtain accurate parameters for multiple-class models than for single-class ones. As will be seen in Chap. 10, the process of validation and calibration of multiple-class models is also difficult.

6.2 SIMPLE TWO-CLASS MODEL

Consider a transaction processing system with a processor (CPU) and two disks. The load on the system consists of two types of transactions: queries and updates. During the peak hours, the system is under heavy load, such that four transactions are in memory almost all the time. In an attempt to optimize the average response time, the support analyst might specify that the best execution mix is a combination of three query transactions and one update transaction. The capacity planner wishes to investigate the system performance that would result from possible modifications of the system. Because of the type of workload (i.e., transactions), it would be natural to represent the system as an open model with a maximum multiprogramming level of four. In this case, if a transaction arrives at the system and finds four other transactions already in memory, it has to queue up for memory. Thus, it is necessary to represent the effects of memory constraints, which makes the model non product-form. An alternative view is that of a closed model with a constant number of four transactions in execution. This view is both a good representation for the system during peak hours and does not violate product-form assumptions. The drawback is that the model represents only the time a transaction spends in execution. Memory contention is not captured.

The two types of transactions differ in both the functions they perform and their patterns of resource usage. Update transactions demand more resources than query transactions. It is natural for the analyst to decide to represent the system as a two-class model, as illustrated in Fig. 6.1; one class for query transactions and another class for update transactions. Suppose that the measurement data of Table 6.1 have been collected for the transaction processing system. From Table 6.1 note that the two classes are characterized by different sets of service demands. For example, while update transactions divide their I/O load among the two disks, query transactions do not make use of disk 2 (i.e., service demand at disk 2 is equal to 0). Since the transactions of

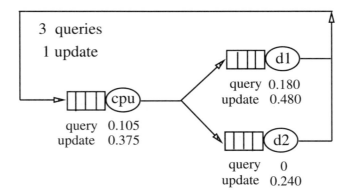

Figure 6.1 Two-class model.

Table 6.1 Measurement Data for the Transaction Processing System.

| Class | Service Demand (sec) | | | Multiprogram-ming Level | Transactions Completed | Monitoring Period (sec) |
	Processor	Disk 1	Disk 2			
Query	0.105	0.180	0	3	7368	1800
Update	0.375	0.480	0.240	1	736	1800

both classes share the same devices, it is reasonable to assume that the service times are roughly the same across the two classes. Thus, the differences in service demands at a given device stem from the number of visits that a transaction makes to the device. In this example, the service demands show that an update transaction performs many more I/O operations than does a query transaction, (i.e., updates require more visits to the disks).

In a single-class model, customers are assumed to be statistically identical in terms of their resource requirements. As a result, customers are undistinguishable in single-class models and the order in which transactions are serviced at a device is irrelevant. This observation, however, is not valid for multiclass models, because customers of different classes are distinct. Therefore, the issue of scheduling is relevant in models of multiple classes. Suppose that at a given instant of time, the four transactions of the example are contending for processor time (i.e., all transactions are at the CPU). A natural question is: Which transaction (query or update) will be serviced next? The goal of a *scheduling policy* is to assign customers to be executed by a server to optimize some system objective, such as minimizing average response time or maximizing throughput. For instance, by specifying a priority scheduling policy, one could force a processor to spend most of its time on classes of customers that are considered critical. In the same way, one could define a scheduling discipline that gives priority to short transactions over large batch jobs, in the attempt of minimizing average response time of short requests.

Actual operating systems implement versions of well-known scheduling disciplines such as *first come first served (FCFS)*, *round robin (RR)*, *shortest job first*, and *shortest remaining time*. In short, multiclass models must specify their assumed scheduling disciplines.

Once the usefulness for multiclass models is recognized, an appropriate solution technique is needed. That is, a solution technique is required that calculates performance measures for each workload class in the model. Making use of methods learned so far, a first approach to solving a multiclass model is to construct an equivalent single-class model. To do that, it is necessary to aggregate the performance parameters of the multiple classes into a single class. The service demand of the aggregate class at any device is the average of the individual classes weighted by the relative class throughputs, as shown in Chap. 3. The degree of multiprogramming of the aggregate class corresponds to the sum of the multiprogramming levels of each component. If the measured throughput of the two classes are $7368/1800 = 4.093$ tps and $736/1800 = 0.409$ tps, respectively, then the processor service demand of the aggregate class is calculated as follows:

$$D_{\text{processor,aggr}} = \frac{0.105 \times 4.093 + 0.375 \times 0.409}{4.502} = 0.1295 \text{ sec}$$

Table 6.2 summarizes the parameters obtained for the aggregate class. The single-class model defined by the parameters of Table 6.2 can then be solved by the techniques introduced in Chap. 5. The calculated throughput for the single-class model equals 4.49, which is worse than its multiclass counterpart, 4.502. Dowdy et al. [1] have shown that a single-class model of an actual multiclass system pessimistically bounds the performance of the multiclass system. These bounds can help the analyst to identify errors that come from an incorrect workload characterization of a multiclass system. Using operational relationships ($U_i = X_0 \times D_i$ and $R = n/X_0$), the following are results for the single-class model: $R = 4/4.49 = 0.891$, $U_{\text{cpu}} = 0.130 \times 4.49 = 58.37\%$, $U_{\text{disk 1}} = 0.207 \times 4.49 = 92.94\%$, and $U_{\text{disk 2}} = 0.022 \times 4.49 = 9.87\%$.

Once the equivalent single-class model has been built and solved, the analyst often wants to use it to investigate the effects of possible future modifications to the system. For example,

- What is the predicted increase in the throughput of query transactions if the load of the update class is moved to off-peak hours?

Table 6.2 Parameters for the Aggregate Class.

Class	Service Demand (sec)			Multiprogramming Level
	Processor	Disk 1	Disk 2	
Aggregate	0.130	0.207	0.022	4

- Realizing that disk 1 is the bottleneck (i.e., the device with the highest utilization) and disk 2 is lightly loaded, what is the predicted response time if the total I/O load of query transactions is moved to disk 2?

Clearly, the equivalent single-class model is not able to answer these questions, because it does not provide performance results on an individual class basis. Therefore, techniques to calculate the performance of models with multiple classes are needed.

6.3 NOTATION AND ASSUMPTIONS

When customers in a queuing network model exhibit different routing patterns and different service time requirements, the model is said to have multiple classes of customers. Consider, for instance, a local area network with P workstations and Q file servers. Each workstation may have its own local storage, but it also requires storage services from the servers. After executing in the workstation, a job goes through the network to require service from the file servers. Each workstation places one job request at a time on the network. A queuing model of this system is proposed by Woodside and Tripathi [2]. If all the workstations have identical workload requirements and assign their services to all file servers, the system can be modeled by a single-class workload with P jobs. However, since each job has a different routing probability (i.e., each job visits a different set of servers), a separate workload class is required for each workstation. Thus, the system is modeled with P classes, each with exactly one job.

The queuing networks considered here consist of K devices (or service centers) and R different classes of customers. A central concept in the analysis and solution of queuing networks is the state of the network. The state represents a distribution of customers over classes and devices. The network state is denoted by a vector $\vec{n} = (\vec{n}_1, \vec{n}_2, \ldots, \vec{n}_K)$, where component $\vec{n}_i$ ($i = 1, \ldots, K$) is a vector that represents the number of customers of each class at server i. That is, $\vec{n}_i = (n_{i,1}, n_{i,2}, \ldots, n_{i,R})$. For instance, the state of the transaction system example is defined as $(\vec{n}_1, \vec{n}_2, \vec{n}_3)$, where $\vec{n}_i =$ (update, query) specifies the number of update and query transactions at device i. Possible states of the transaction system example include $((1, 3), (0, 0), (0, 0))$ and $((0, 1), (0, 2), (1, 0))$. Whereas the former indicates that all transactions are at the processor, the latter represents the situation where one query transaction is executing at the processor, two queries are at disk 1, and the update transaction is being serviced at disk 2.

The BCMP theorem [3], developed by Baskett, Chandy, Muntz, and Palacios, specifies the combination of service time distributions and scheduling disciplines that yield multiclass product-form queuing networks. Open, closed, or mixed networks are allowed. A closed class is one in which a constant number of customers remain in the network at all times. In contrast, in an open class, customers are allowed to enter or leave the network. A mixed network is closed with respect to some classes and open with respect to other classes. Basically, the set of assumptions required by the BCMP theorem for a product-form solution is as follows.

- *Service centers with a FCFS discipline.* In this case, customers are serviced in the order in which they arrive. The service time distributions are required to be exponential with the same mean for all classes. Although all classes must have the same mean service time at a given device, they may have different visit ratios, which means the possibility of different service demands for each class at a given device. The service rate is allowed to be load dependent, but it can be dependent only on the total number of customers at the server and not on the number of customers of any particular class. For instance, service requests from workstations to a file server can be adequately modeled by the FCFS discipline. Disks are usually modeled as FCFS service centers.

- *Service centers with a PS discipline.* When there are n customers at a server with a processor sharing discipline, each customer receives service at a rate of $1/n$ of their normal service rate. Each class may have a distinct service time distribution. The *round robin* (RR) scheduling discipline allows customers to receive a fixed quantum of service. If the customer does not finish execution within its allocated quantum, it returns to the end of the queue, awaiting further service. In the limiting case, when the quantum approaches zero, the RR discipline becomes the PS discipline. Time-sharing operating systems such as UNIX employ the RR discipline to processor scheduling. Thus, PS is a reasonable approximation to represent processor scheduling disciplines of actual operating systems.

- *Service centers with infinite servers (IS).* When there is an infinite supply of servers in a service center, there is never any waiting for a server. This situation is known as IS, delay server, or no queuing. For instance, think time at terminals in an interactive system is usually modeled by delay servers. In a lightly loaded LAN, the time needed to send a request from a workstation to a server can also be approximated by a delay server.

- *Service centers with a LCFS-PR discipline.* Under last come first served preemptive resume, whenever a new customer arrives, the server ceases (i.e., preempts) servicing the previous customer (if any) and proceeds to serve the new arrival. When a customer completes, the server resumes executing its previously preempted job. Each class may have a distinct service time distribution.

In open networks, the time between successive arrivals is assumed to be exponentially distributed. Bulk arrivals are not allowed. Multiclass product-form networks have efficient computational algorithms for their solution. The two major algorithms are convolution and MVA. Because of their simplicity and intuitive appeal, in this chapter we concentrate on MVA-based algorithms for exact and approximate solutions of models with multiple classes (see also Ref. [4] for MVA-based algorithms of QNs and Ref. [5] for solution algorithms based on decomposition and aggregation techniques). The following notation is used for multiclass models.

K = number of devices or service centers of the model
R = number of classes of customers
M_r = number of terminals of class r
N_r = class r population
λ_r = arrival rate of class r
$S_{i,r}$ = average service time of class r customers at device i
$V_{i,r}$ = average visit ratio of class r customers at device i
$D_{i,r}$ = average service demand of class r customers at device i; $D_{i,r} = V_{i,r} S_{i,r}$
$R_{i,r}$ = average response time per visit of class r customers to device i
$R'_{i,r}$ = average residence time of class r customers at device i (i.e., the total time spent by class r customers at device i over all visits to the device); $R'_{i,r} = V_{i,r} R_{i,r}$
$\bar{n}_{i,r}$ = average number of class r customers at device i
$\bar{n}_i$ = average number of customers at device i
$X_{i,r}$ = class r throughput at device i
$X_{0,r}$ = class r system throughput
R_r = class r response time

6.4 CLOSED MODELS

The load intensity of a multiclass model with R classes and K devices is represented by the vector $\vec{N} = (N_1, N_2, \ldots, N_R)$, where N_r indicates the number of class r customers in the system. The goal of multiclass algorithms is to calculate the performance measures of the network as a function of $\vec{N}$. In the transaction system example, the performance measures are calculated for each class (update and query) for the population $\vec{N} = (1, 3)$ (i.e., for one update and three query transactions in the model).

The two types of processing that are usually modeled as closed classes are batch and interactive. The key feature is that the total load placed by these classes on a system is constant; no job leaves the system, as depicted in Fig. 6.2. In the case of batch processing, it is assumed that the system operates under backlog, which means that whenever a job leaves the system

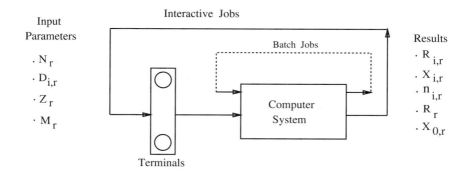

Figure 6.2   Multiclass closed model.

it is replaced by a new job. Thus, the number of jobs in the system remains constant. In an interactive system, each terminal is associated with a user, who alternates between thinking and waiting. The thinking state corresponds to the period of time that elapses since a user receives a reply from the system due to the previous request until a new request (i.e., job) is issued. After submitting a new job, the user enters the waiting state while the system executes the job. With M_r terminals associated with class r, we can say that there exist M_r jobs in the system, where each job can be viewed as spending R_r units of time executing and Z_r time units thinking at a terminal. For an interactive class r, the number of jobs in the system is equal to the number of active terminals (i.e., $N_r = M_r$). A closed model is a combination of interactive and batch classes. The closed system analysis begins with the load intensity vector $\vec{N}$ and the class descriptor parameters $(D_{i,r}, M_r, Z_r)$. The analysis completes when the throughputs, response times, and queue lengths of each class are determined.

As with the single-class model, the MVA-based solution of a multiclass system relies on three basic equations applied to each class.

$$X_{0,r}(\vec{N}) = \frac{N_r}{Z_r + \sum_{i=1}^{K} R'_{i,r}(\vec{N})} \tag{6.1}$$

Equation (6.1) is found by applying Little's result separately to each class of customers. If r is a batch class, then Z_r is zero. The residence time $(R'_{i,r})$ corresponds to the total time a class r customer spends at server i during its execution. It includes the service demand $(D_{i,r})$ plus the total waiting time at the device. The average response time of class r customers can then be written as $R_r(\vec{N}) = \sum_{i=1}^{K} R'_{i,r}(\vec{N})$.

The application of Little's result and the forced flow law to each service center yields Eq. (6.2).

$$\bar{n}_{i,r}(\vec{N}) = X_{i,r}(\vec{N}) R_{i,r}(\vec{N})$$

$$= X_{0,r}(\vec{N}) V_{i,r} R_{i,r}(\vec{N})$$

$$= X_{0,r}(\vec{N}) R'_{i,r}(\vec{N}) \tag{6.2}$$

Summing up customers of all classes at device i gives the total number of customers at that device, $\bar{n}_i(\vec{N})$.

$$\bar{n}_i(\vec{N}) = \sum_{r=1}^{R} \bar{n}_{i,r}(\vec{N})$$

$$= \sum_{r=1}^{R} X_{0,r}(\vec{N}) R'_{i,r}(\vec{N}) \tag{6.3}$$

The key equation of the MVA technique can be derived from the observation that the mean response time of a class r customer at service center i equals its own mean service time at that device plus the time to complete the mean backlog seen upon its arrival (i.e., the average number of customers *seen* upon arrival multiplied by each customer's mean service time). Therefore,

$$R_{i,r}(\vec{N}) = S_{i,r}[1 + \bar{n}_{i,r}^{A}(\vec{N})]$$

$$V_{i,r} \, R_{i,r}(\vec{N}) = V_{i,r} S_{i,r}[1 + \bar{n}_{i,r}^{A}(\vec{N})]$$

$$R'_{i,r}(\vec{N}) = D_{i,r}[1 + \bar{n}_{i,r}^{A}(\vec{N})] \tag{6.4}$$

where $\bar{n}_{i,r}^{A}$ is the average queue length at device i *seen* by an arriving class r customer. As seen in Eq. (6.4), the average residence time is a function of the service demand and not of the individual values of the service times and visit ratios.

In the case of a delay server, it follows directly by definition that the backlog is zero, $[\bar{n}_{i,r}^{A}(\vec{N}) = 0]$, which makes $R'_{i,r}(\vec{N}) = D_{i,r}$. When the scheduling discipline of center i is PS or LCFS-PR, the expression $1 + \bar{n}_{i,r}^{A}(\vec{N})$ can be viewed as an inflation factor of the service demand, due to the congestion by other customers. For FCFS service centers, Eq. (6.4) represents the customer's own service demand plus the time to complete the service of all customers in front of it. For practical purposes, scheduling disciplines can be grouped into two categories: delay and queuing. The latter encompasses load-independent servers with the following disciplines: PS, LSFC-PR, and FCFS.

Having as a starting point the fact that queue length is zero when there are no customers in the network ($\bar{n}_i(\vec{0}) = 0$), Eqs. (6.1), (6.2), and (6.4) can be used iteratively to calculate the performance measures of the model. However, there is a minor problem; no expression for $\bar{n}_{i,r}^{A}(\vec{N})$ has yet been given. Given that expression it would be easy to solve a multiclass model. Multiclass model solution techniques are grouped into either exact or approximate solutions, depending on the way the backlog *seen* upon arrival [i.e., $\bar{n}_{i,r}^A(\vec{N})$] is calculated.

6.4.1 Exact Solution Algorithm

As pointed out in Chap. 4, an exact solution technique means the exact solution of analytic formulas of approximate models of actual systems. The key to the exact solution of multiclass closed queuing networks is the arrival theorem [6, 7], which states that a class r customer arriving at service center i in a system with population $\vec{N}$ *sees* the distribution of the number of customers in that center as being equal to the steady-state distribution for a network with population $(\vec{N} - \vec{1}_r)$. The vector $\vec{1}_r$ consists of a 1 in the rth position and zeros in the rest of the vector [i.e., $(0, 0, \ldots, 1, \ldots, 0)$]. In other words, it states simply that the arriving customer sees the system in equilibrium with itself removed. In the transaction system example with population $\vec{N} = (1, 3)$, a query transaction that arrives at the CPU sees a queuing distribution equal to that of the system with population $\vec{N} = (1, 2)$. From the arrival theorem, it follows that

$$\bar{n}_{i,r}^A(\vec{N}) = \bar{n}_i(\vec{N} - \vec{1}_r). \tag{6.5}$$

Combining Eqs.(6.1), (6.2), (6.3), (6.4), and (6.5), the algorithm for the exact solution of closed multiclass models is described in Fig. 6.3.

Recall the motivating problem of Sec. 6.2. The algorithm of Fig. 6.3 can be used to obtain the performance measures for each class. The first step is to apply the exact algorithm to the baseline model described in Table 6.1 [i.e., to calculate the results for the population of one update and three query transactions, $\vec{N} = (1, 3)$]. From the arrival theorem, to calculate the residence time at the devices (processor and two disks) for population $(1, 3)$, the device queue lengths are required for populations $(0, 3)$ and $(1, 2)$. These correspond to one less update transaction and one less query transaction, respectively. By continually removing one customer from each class, eventually the performance measures for population $(0, 0)$ are calculated, which is the starting point of the algorithm. Fig. 6.4 shows the precedence relationships required to calculate the results of a system with population $(1, 3)$ using exact MVA.

Table 6.3 shows for each population of the sequence of Fig. 6.4 the results calculated by the exact MVA algorithm for the baseline model of the transaction system example. It is worth noting that each class can be calculated separately, as indicated in Table 6.3. However, the interaction among the multiple classes is explicitly represented by the term $\bar{n}_i(\vec{N} - \vec{1}_r)$ in the equation $R_{i,r}(\vec{N}) = D_{i,r}[1 + \bar{n}_i(\vec{N} - \vec{1}_r)]$. The average number of customers at device i reflects the contention for common shared resources among the distinct classes of the workload.

Input Parameters
$D_{i,r}$ and N_r
Initialization
For $i := 1$ to K do $\bar{n}_i(\vec{0}) := 0$
Iteration Loops:
For $j_1 := 0$ to N_1 do
  For $j_2 := 0$ to N_2 do
  . . .
      For $j_R := 0$ to N_R do
        Begin
          $\vec{N} := (j_1, j_2, \ldots, j_R)$
          If $\vec{N} \neq \vec{0}$
        Then Begin
            For $r := 1$ to R do
              Begin
              If $j_r > 0$
                Then For $i := 1$ to K do
                  $R'_{i,r}(\vec{N}) = \begin{cases} D_{i,r} & \text{delay} \\ D_{i,r}[1 + \bar{n}_i(\vec{N} - \vec{1}_r)] & \text{queuing} \end{cases}$
                Else $R'_{i,r}(\vec{N}) = 0$;
                $X_{0,r}(\vec{N}) = \dfrac{j_r}{Z_r + \sum\limits_{i=1}^{K} R'_{i,r}(\vec{N})}$
              End;
            For $i := 1$ to K do
              $\bar{n}_i(\vec{N}) = \sum\limits_{r=1}^{R} X_{0,r}(\vec{N}) R'_{i,r}(\vec{N})$
          End
      End
  End

Figure 6.3 Exact MVA algorithm for multiple classes.

From Table 6.3 it is noted that the calculated throughputs for the query and update classes are 4.093 tps and 0.409 tps, respectively, which match the measurement results of Table 6.1. Either using Little's result, or summing the average device residence times, the average response times are obtained for the two classes: 0.733 sec for queries and 2.444 sec for updates. Once the baseline model has been solved and validated, attention is directed to the prediction phase. To construct a predictive model, the parameters of the predicted system need to be specified. The two questions proposed in Sec. 6.2 are analyzed.

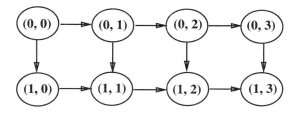

Figure 6.4 Sequence of calculations of MVA.

Table 6.3 Step-by-Step Results of the Two-Class Model Solution.

Class	Variable	Population (Update, Query)							
		(0,0)	(0,1)	(0,2)	(0,3)	(1,0)	(1,1)	(1,2)	(1,3)
Query	$R_{1,q}$	-	0.105	0.144	0.174	-	0.141	0.177	0.204
	$R_{2,q}$	-	0.180	0.294	0.422	-	0.259	0.388	0.529
	$R_{3,q}$	-	0.000	0.000	0.000	-	0.000	0.000	0.000
	$X_{0,q}$	-	3.509	4.566	5.034	-	2.500	3.540	4.093
	$n_{1,q}$	0	0.368	0.658	0.876	-	0.352	0.627	0.835
	$n_{2,q}$	0	0.632	1.342	2.124	-	0.648	1.373	2.165
	$n_{3,q}$	0	0.000	0.000	0.000	-	0.000	0.000	0.000
Update	$R_{1,u}$	-	-	-	-	0.375	0.513	0.622	0.704
	$R_{2,u}$	-	-	-	-	0.480	0.783	1.124	1.500
	$R_{3,u}$	-	-	-	-	0.240	0.240	0.240	0.240
	$X_{0,u}$	-	-	-	-	0.913	0.651	0.504	0.409
	$n_{1,u}$	0	-	-	-	0.343	0.334	0.313	0.288
	$n_{2,u}$	0	-	-	-	0.438	0.510	0.566	0.614
	$n_{3,u}$	0	-	-	-	0.219	0.156	0.121	0.098

1. What is the predicted increase in the throughput of query transactions if the load of the update class is moved to off-peak hours?

   Answer: Since the update class will be removed, it is reasonable to assume that the multiprogramming level will remain the same and the system will have a population of 4 query transactions. Solving a single-class model with 4 queries, a throughput of 5.275 tps is obtained. This new value indicates that the removal of the update class increases throughput by 28.87%.

2. Realizing that disk 1 is the bottleneck (i.e., the device with the highest utilization) and disk 2 is lightly loaded, what is the predicted response time if the total I/O load of query transactions is moved to disk 2?

   Answer: To construct the predictive model, it is only necessary to shift the value of $D_{2,q}$ to $D_{3,q}$, to indicate that the I/O load of query transactions will be moved from disk 1 to disk 2. With the new parameters, the model is resolved to give the following results: $X_{0,q} = 4.335$ tps, $X_{0,u} = 0.517$ tps, $R_q = 0.692$ sec, and $R_u = 1.934$ sec. These results indicate a reduction of 5.6% in the average response time of queries and 20.9% in the mean response time of update transactions. Why does the proposed modification favor the update class? First, consider the system performance measures obtained by the baseline and predictive models, respectively. From Table 6.4, note that the proposed modification changes the bottleneck from disk 1 to disk 2 and, at the same time, provides a better balance of disk utilization. Now, consider where the two types of transactions spend their time. Let the residence time percentage be the time a transaction spends at device i, expressed as a percentage of the average response time for the transaction [i.e., $(R'_{i,r} / \sum_{i=1}^{K} R'_{i,r}) \times 100$]. From Table 6.5 note that in the baseline model, query transactions spend 72.2% of their average response time at the bottleneck device, whereas update transactions spend 61.4%. When the I/O load of query transactions is moved to disk 2, it becomes the bottleneck. Update transactions benefit more from the modification because they get better disk utilization balance. To confirm this, the results in Table 6.5 show that update transactions spend 24.8% and 38.8% of their time at disk 1 and disk 2, respectively. Moreover, disk 1 has no contention, since it is dedicated to the update transaction class. In contrast, query transactions concentrate their I/O on disk 2, which is also used by updates.

Table 6.3 provides a good idea regarding the number of operations required to compute the results of the simple transaction system example that consists of only 2 classes, 4 customers, and 3 devices. Not surprising, the computational effort required to compute performance measures of models

Table 6.4   Device Utilization.

		Utilization (%)		
Model	Class	Processor	Disk 1	Disk 2
Baseline	Query	42.98	73.67	0
	Update	15.33	19.63	9.81
	Total	58.31	**93.3**	9.81
Modified	Query	45.51	0	78.03
	Update	19.38	24.81	12.40
	Total	64.89	24.81	**90.43**

Table 6.5   Residence Time Percentage.

		Residence Time (%)		
Model	Class	Processor	Disk 1	Disk 2
Baseline	Query	27.8	72.2	0
	Update	28.8	61.4	9.8
Modified	Query	31.5	0	68.5
	Update	36.4	24.8	38.8

of practical systems with many classes, many jobs in execution, and hundreds of I/O devices is "significant."

Looking at Fig. 6.4, note that to compute the results of the model with population $(1, 2)$, the results of populations $(1, 1)$ and $(0, 2)$ are needed. Each of these populations requires, as input, queue lengths from two related populations. In the general case, when a system has R classes, each calculation of metrics for a given population demands inputs from R other populations. Due to the precedence relationships in the calculation of performance measures of a multiclass model, the computational complexity of MVA algorithms grows exponentially with the number of classes. The number of multiplications and the number of additions required to solve a multiclass model is proportional to

$$KR \prod_{r=1}^{R}(1 + N_r) \tag{6.6}$$

Modeling distributed systems often involve large queuing networks. For example, client-server systems may be modeled as multiclass models [8]. The workload may be viewed as processes running at the workstations, which during their execution require access to a number of files that can be either local or remote. Assume that each process visits three other workstations for file services. Suppose that we have a LAN-based system with 20 workstations (processor and disk) and 1 process per workstation. To represent the different routings and service requests, a separate class is used for each workstation. Thus, a closed model is constructed with 20 classes, 5 devices (processor, disk, and 3 file servers), and 1 customer in each class. Substituting these numbers into Eq. (6.6), the solution of this hypothetical model would require approximately 104 million operations. So how can one avoid the high computational cost of exact MVA algorithms?

6.4.2 Approximate Solution Algorithms

The source of the large number of operations required to compute the exact MVA algorithm is the recursion expressed in the equation

$$\bar{n}_{i,r}^{A}(\vec{N}) = \bar{n}_{i,r}(\vec{N} - \vec{1}_r) \tag{6.7}$$

With the goal of reducing the complexity of the MVA algorithm, several approximations have been proposed to break up the recursion [9]. A very simple approximation, due to Bard [10], is as follows:

$$\bar{n}_{i,r}(\vec{N}) \approx \bar{n}_{i,r}(\vec{N} - \vec{1}_r)$$
$$\bar{n}_{i,r}^{A}(\vec{N}) = \bar{n}_{i,r}(\vec{N}) \tag{6.8}$$

This approximation is attractive when the number of customers becomes large.

The most commonly used approximation is one proposed by Schweitzer [11] for BCMP models. It is based on the assumption that the number of class *r* customers at each service center increases proportionally to the number of class *r* customers in the network. From this observation, it follows that

$$\frac{\bar{n}_{i,r}(\vec{N} - \vec{1}_r)}{\bar{n}_{i,r}(\vec{N})} = \frac{N_r - 1}{N_r} \tag{6.9}$$

$$\bar{n}_{i,r}(\vec{N} - \vec{1}_r) = \frac{N_r - 1}{N_r} \, \bar{n}_{i,r}(\vec{N}) \tag{6.10}$$

Equation (6.10) is the basis of an iterative method for calculating performance measures of a closed model, described by the algorithm of Fig. 6.5. The basic idea is to substitute estimates for queue lengths $[\bar{n}_{i,r}(\vec{N})]$ into Eq. (6.10) and use the MVA equations to compute the next estimates for $\bar{n}_{i,r}(\vec{N})$. The iterative process starts with an estimate $\bar{n}_{i,r}^e(\vec{N})$ which assumes that class *r* customers are equally distributed among the *K* devices of the network. Iteration stops when successive values of $\bar{n}_{i,r}(\vec{N})$ are sufficiently close [i.e., $|[\bar{n}_{i,r}^e(\vec{N}) - \bar{n}_{i,r}(\vec{N})]/\bar{n}_{i,r}^e(\vec{N})| < \epsilon$, where ϵ is a tolerance bound]. Note that in the algorithm, the notation K_r is used to indicate the number of devices for which $D_{i,r} > 0$.

The computational cost of solving the iterative method is proportional to the product ($K \times R$) and typical errors are less than 20% [12]. For example, the iterative solution of the model of the hypothetical distributed system discussed in Sec. 6.4.1 would require a number of operations proportional to ($5 \times 20 = 100$), as opposed to 104 million operations for the exact solution. Although approximate methods provide a cheaper solution for product-form multiclass models, they have a serious drawback. The commonly used approximate methods for solving multiclass models do not provide bounds on the errors introduced by the approximations. Therefore, to assess the approximation's reliability, one has to validate the results against the exact MVA results, which may be impossible in the case of large systems.

To exemplify the accuracy of Schweitzer's approximation, compare the exact results of the transaction system example with those calculated by the iterative process, given that the maximum tolerance for the absolute difference between successive values of the queue lengths is 0.01. Table 6.6 shows the throughput and response time computed under both methods. As seen, the maximum observed relative error is 2.25%.

Now, consider a closed model that represents a packet switching store and forward communication network with flow control mechanism [12].

Table 6.6 Exact and Approximate Results.

Method	Throughput		Response Time	
	Query	Update	Query	Update
Exact MVA	4.093	0.409	0.733	2.445
Approximate	4.001	0.407	0.749	2.456
Relative error ($|\%|$)	2.25	0.49	0.22	0.45

Input Parameters
$D_{i,r}$, N_r, and ϵ
Initialization
$\vec{N} = (N_1, N_2, \ldots, N_R)$
For $r := 1$ to R do
    For $i := 1$ to K do
        If $D_{i,r} > 0$ then $\bar{n}^e_{i,r}(\vec{N}) = N_r/K_r$
Iteration Loop
Repeat
    For $r := 1$ to R do
        For $i := 1$ to K do $\bar{n}_{i,r}(\vec{N}) = \bar{n}^e_{i,r}(\vec{N})$
    For $r := 1$ to R do
        For $i := 1$ to K do
            For $t := 1$ to R do

$$\bar{n}_{i,r}(\vec{N} - \vec{1}_t) = \begin{cases} \bar{n}_{i,r}(\vec{N}) & t \neq r \\ \dfrac{N_r - 1}{N_r}\, \bar{n}_{i,r}(\vec{N}) & t = r \end{cases}$$

    For $r := 1$ to R do
        Begin
            For $i := 1$ to K do

$$R'_{i,r}(\vec{N}) = \begin{cases} D_{i,r} & \text{delay} \\ D_{i,r}\left[1 + \displaystyle\sum_{t=1}^{R} n_{i,t}(\vec{N} - \vec{1}_r)\right] & \text{queuing} \end{cases}$$

$$X_{0,r}(\vec{N}) = \frac{N_r}{Z_r + \displaystyle\sum_{i=1}^{K} R'_{i,r}(\vec{N})}$$

        End;
    For $r := 1$ to R do
        For $i := 1$ to K do
            $\bar{n}^e_{i,r}(\vec{N}) = X_{0,r}(\vec{N}) R'_{i,r}(\vec{N})$

Until $\max_{i,r}\{ |[\bar{n}^e_{i,r}(\vec{N}) - \bar{n}_{i,r}(\vec{N})] / \bar{n}^e_{i,r}(\vec{N})| \} < \epsilon$

Figure 6.5 Approximate MVA algorithm for multiple classes.

Consider that each virtual channel is represented by one class. Thus, the number of customers in each class represents the window size (i.e., the maximum number of messages allowed on the virtual channel). To keep the example simple, assume that the devices of the model represent the sink node, the source node, and the virtual channel. All devices are assumed to meet the BCMP requirements. The model to be solved has the following parameters: 2 classes (i.e., 2 virtual channels), $N_1 = 20$, $N_2 = 25$ (window sizes), $\vec{D}_1 = (0.0030, 0.0009, 0.0123)$, and $\vec{D}_2 = (0.0035, 0.0215, 0.0011)$. Table 6.7 shows the iterations required by Schweitzer's approximation to solve this model. The termination criterion is to have 0.01 as the maximum difference between successive values of $N_{i,r}$. Within 9 iterations, the approximate method obtains results whose maximum error compared to the exact results is 1.59%. Notice that the exact solution requires the computation of queue lengths for 500 (25×20) different populations.

Table 6.7 Approximate MVA Computation.

	Class 1				Class 2			
	Queue Length				Queue Length			
Iteration	Channel	Source	Sink	TPUT	Channel	Source	Sink	TPUT
1	8.333	8.333	8.333	78.80	6.667	6.667	6.667	61.13
2	3.704	1.111	15.185	81.07	3.352	20.593	1.054	48.34
3	1.914	1.652	16.433	79.73	1.341	22.745	0.915	44.53
4	0.995	1.817	17.189	78.26	0.655	23.448	0.897	43.50
5	0.610	1.843	17.545	77.43	0.399	23.688	0.911	43.22
6	0.459	1.842	17.697	77.05	0.301	23.775	0.923	43.14
7	0.401	1.839	17.758	76.90	0.264	23.806	0.929	43.11
8	0.379	1.837	17.782	76.83	0.249	23.818	0.932	43.10
9	0.371	1.837	17.791	76.83	0.244	23.822	0.933	43.10
Exact	0.377	1.863	17.760	77.43	0.246	23.813	0.942	43.27
Relative error ($|\%|$)	1.59	1.39	0.17	0.77	0.81	0.03	0.98	0.39

6.5 OPEN MODELS

Consider a distributed system environment, made up of a collection of workstations and servers connected via a local area network (LAN). Servers are placed in the system to provide service upon request. A file server is a key component of this kind of environment. Its purpose is to provide file services for the workstations on the network. Basically, a file server is composed of processors, memory, and a disk subsystem. The workload of a file server can be viewed as a series of file service requests such as read, write, create, and remove, which arrive from the workstations via the LAN. The operation of a file server can be viewed as follows. Requests arrive to the server. A typical request enters the server, possibly queues up while waiting for some resource (processor, memory, disks) to become available, obtains service from the resources, and exits the server. The number of requests being handled concurrently by the server varies over time depending on factors such as the load placed by the workstations (i.e., the request arrival rate), the file system capacity, the available memory, and the processor speed.

A file server is a good example of a system suitable to be modeled as an open model. It exhibits the key characteristic of open systems: the variation of the number of customers over time. In practice, the number of customers (transactions, processes, requests) varies dynamically, due to such factors as program termination, program initiation, and process spawning. An open class is able to represent this variation, because it has a potentially unlimited number of customers. Chapter 4 introduced and analyzed the birth-death system, which gives the underlying theory for the single-class open model. This analysis is extended here to multiclass models.

The load intensity of a multiclass model with R open classes and K devices is represented by the vector $\vec{\lambda} = (\lambda_1, \lambda_2, \ldots, \lambda_R)$, where λ_r indicates the arrival rate of class r customers. As illustrated in Fig. 6.6, the goal of the analysis of multiclass open models is to determine, for each class, performance measures such as average response time, $R_r(\vec{\lambda})$, and queue lengths, $\bar{n}_i(\vec{\lambda})$, as a function of the load intensity, $\vec{\lambda}$.

6.5.1 Analysis of Multiclass Open Models

In steady state, the throughput of class r equals its arrival rate:

$$X_{0,r} = \lambda_r \tag{6.11}$$

The application of Little's result to each device gives

$$\bar{n}_{i,r}(\vec{\lambda}) = X_{i,r}(\vec{\lambda})R_{i,r}(\vec{\lambda}) \tag{6.12}$$

where $R_{i,r}(\vec{\lambda})$ is the average class r customer response time per visit to device i.

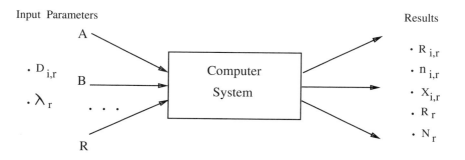

Figure 6.6 Multiclass open models.

The average residence time for the entire execution is $R'_{i,r} = V_{i,r} R_{i,r}$. Using the forced flow law and Eq. (6.11), the throughput of class r is

$$X_{i,r}(\vec{\lambda}) = X_{0,r}(\vec{\lambda}) V_{i,r} = \lambda_r V_{i,r} \tag{6.13}$$

Using Eq. (6.13) in Eq. (6.12) the average queue length per device for each class becomes

$$\bar{n}_{i,r}(\vec{\lambda}) = \lambda_r R'_{i,r}(\vec{\lambda}) \tag{6.14}$$

Combining the utilization law and the forced flow law, the utilization of device i by class r customers can be written as

$$U_{i,r}(\vec{\lambda}) = X_{i,r}(\vec{\lambda}) S_{i,r} = \lambda_r V_{i,r} S_{i,r} = \lambda_r D_{i,r} \tag{6.15}$$

Thus, to compute the average number of class r customers in service center i, $R'_{i,r}$ is needed as a function of the input parameters (i.e., $\vec{\lambda}$ and the service demands $D_{i,r}$'s). The average time a class r customer spends at a device, from arrival until completion, has two components: the time for receiving service and the time spent in queue. The latter is equal to the time required to service customers that are currently in the device when the customer arrives. Thus,

$$R_{i,r}(\vec{\lambda}) = S_{i,r}[1 + \bar{n}^A_{i,r}(\vec{\lambda})]$$

$$V_{i,r} R_{i,r}(\vec{\lambda}) = V_{i,r} S_{i,r}[1 + \bar{n}^A_{i,r}(\vec{\lambda})]$$

$$R'_{i,r}(\vec{\lambda}) = D_{i,r}[1 + \bar{n}^A_{i,r}(\vec{\lambda})] \tag{6.16}$$

where $\bar{n}^A_{i,r}(\vec{\lambda})$ is the average queue length at device i seen by an arriving class r customer when the load on the system is $\vec{\lambda}$. For delay servers, $R'_{i,r}(\vec{\lambda}) = D_{i,r}$.

The arrival theorem [7] states that in an open product-form queuing network, a class r arriving customer at service center i *sees* the steady-state distribution of the device state, which is given by the queue length. (*Note:* This is consistent with the arrival theorem result concerning closed systems. In closed systems, an arriving customer sees the steady-state distribution with itself removed. In an open system, since there is an infinite customer population, removing oneself from the network has no effect. Thus, the steady-state distribution seen by an arriving customer is equal to the overall steady-state distribution.) Thus,

$$\bar{n}^A_{i,r}(\vec{\lambda}) = \bar{n}_i(\vec{\lambda}) \tag{6.17}$$

From Eqs. (6.16) and (6.17), we get

$$R'_{i,r}(\vec{\lambda}) = D_{i,r}[1 + \bar{n}_i(\vec{\lambda})] \tag{6.18}$$

Substituting Eq. (6.18) into Eq. (6.14), yields

$$\bar{n}_{i,r}(\vec{\lambda}) = \lambda_r D_{i,r}[1 + \bar{n}_i(\vec{\lambda})] = U_{i,r}(\vec{\lambda})[1 + \bar{n}_i(\vec{\lambda})] \tag{6.19}$$

Notice that expression $[1 + \bar{n}_i(\vec{\lambda})]$ in Eq. (6.19) does not depend on class r. As a consequence, for any two classes r and s, we have

$$\frac{\bar{n}_{i,r}(\vec{\lambda})}{\bar{n}_{i,s}(\vec{\lambda})} = \frac{U_{i,r}(\vec{\lambda})}{U_{i,s}(\vec{\lambda})} \tag{6.20}$$

Using Eq. (6.20) and considering the fact that $\bar{n}_i(\vec{\lambda}) = \sum_{s=1}^{R} \bar{n}_{i,s}(\vec{\lambda})$, Eq. (6.19) can be rewritten as

$$\bar{n}_{i,r}(\vec{\lambda}) = \frac{U_{i,r}(\vec{\lambda})}{1 - U_i(\vec{\lambda})} \tag{6.21}$$

Applying Little's result to Eq. (6.21), the average residence time for class r customers at device i is

$$R'_{i,r}(\vec{\lambda}) = \frac{D_{i,r}}{1 - U_i(\vec{\lambda})} \tag{6.22}$$

The interaction among the open classes of a multiclass model is explicitly represented by the term $U_i(\vec{\lambda})$ of Eq. (6.22), which corresponds to the total utilization of device i by all the classes in the model.

The analysis of a product-form model with multiple open classes begins with the constraint that $U_i(\vec{\lambda}) \leq 1$ for all devices of the network and proceeds with the formulas summarized in Fig. 6.7. From Eq. (6.15), the stability condition for an open model is

$$U_i \leq 1 \; \forall \; i \qquad \text{or} \tag{6.23}$$

$$\sum_{r=1}^{R} \lambda_r D_{i,r} \leq 1 \; \forall \; i, r \tag{6.24}$$

6.5.2 Open Model Example

Consider a distributed environment made up of a number of diskless workstations connected via a LAN to a file server, composed of a single processor and one large disk. The company is planning to double the number of workstations. Because the system performance is critically dependent on the file server, management wishes to assess the impact of the expansion before it is implemented. So, the first question to be answered is: What is the predicted performance of the file server if the number of diskless workstations doubles?

Following the modeling paradigm of Fig. 4.1, the initial step is constructing the baseline model, which begins with the workload characterization. The workload to the file server consists of file service requests, which can be grouped into three classes: *read*, *write*, and *all others*. The latter comprises control requests of the network file system and other file service requests less used. During a period of 1 hour, the file server was monitored and the following measurement data were collected:

Input Parameters
$D_{i,r}$ and λ_r

Formulas

$$U_{i,r}(\vec{\lambda}) = \lambda_r V_{i,r} S_{i,r} = \lambda_r D_{i,r}$$

$$U_i(\vec{\lambda}) = \sum_{r=1}^{R} U_{i,r}(\vec{\lambda})$$

$$\bar{n}_{i,r}(\vec{\lambda}) = \frac{U_{i,r}(\vec{\lambda})}{1 - U_i(\vec{\lambda})}$$

$$R_{i,r}(\vec{\lambda}) = \begin{cases} D_{i,r} & \text{delay} \\ \dfrac{D_{i,r}}{1 - U_i(\vec{\lambda})} & \text{queuing} \end{cases}$$

$$R_r(\vec{\lambda}) = \sum_{i=1}^{K} R_{i,r}(\vec{\lambda})$$

$$n_i(\vec{\lambda}) = \sum_{r=1}^{R} n_{i,r}(\vec{\lambda})$$

Figure 6.7 Formulas for models with multiple open classes.

- Measurement period: 3600 sec.
- Number of reads: 18,000
- Number of writes: 7200
- Number of other file service requests: 3600
- Total processor utilization: 32%
- Total disk utilization: 48%

The measurement data also provide resource utilization on a per-class basis, as shown in Table 6.8. Using the measurement data and the operational relationship $(D_{i,r} = U_{i,r} / X_{0,r})$, each request is characterized in terms of its service demands. Once $D_{i,r}$ has been calculated, it is possible to compute $V_{i,r}$ using the disk service time provided by the manufacturer. For the processor, the parameter $V_{\text{proc},r}$ is calculated using the following expression that relates the visit ratio at the processor to the visit ratios at the I/O devices in a central server model

$$V_{\text{proc},r} = 1 + \sum_{i=2}^{K} V_{i,r} \tag{6.25}$$

Table 6.8 File Server Workload Characteristics.

Class	Arrival Rate (req./sec)	Processor				Disk			
		U (%)	V	S	D (sec)	U (%)	V	S	D (sec)
Read	5	9	3	0.006	0.018	20	2	0.020	0.040
Write	2	18	6	0.015	0.090	20	5	0.020	0.100
All-others	1	5	5	0.100	0.050	8	4	0.020	0.080

where devices 2 through K are the I/O devices. Table 6.8 summarizes the parameters that characterize the file server workload.

Motivated by simplicity, the analyst in charge of the capacity planning project decided to construct a single-class model of the file server. The model constructed is an open model where only the file service components (processor and disk) are directly represented. It is assumed that the file server has enough memory so that no request queues for memory. The workstations are implicitly represented in the workload model by the file service requests generated by them. The larger the number of workstations, the larger the request arrival rate. The single-class model equivalent to the three-class model is obtained by calculating the aggregate demands.

$$D_{\text{aggr,proc}} = \frac{0.018 \times 5 + 0.09 \times 2 + 0.05 \times 1}{8} = 0.04$$

$$D_{\text{aggr,disk}} = \frac{0.04 \times 5 + 0.10 \times 2 + 0.08 \times 1}{8} = 0.06$$

By solving the model, the following residence times are obtained: $R'_{\text{proc}} = 0.04/(1 - 0.32) = 0.059$ and $R'_{\text{disk}} = 0.06/(1 - 0.48) = 0.115$. The sum gives an average request response time of 0.174 seconds.

To answer the *"what if"* question, it is necessary to change the baseline model to reflect the effects of doubling the number of workstations. Since this number is not directly specified in the input parameters, some assumptions are necessary. It is assumed that the new workstations will have the same usage as the installed ones. This means they will run the same group of applications and will generate file service requests that follow the current pattern of requests. Thus, by increasing the number of workstations by 100%, the request arrival rate, likewise, is assumed to increase by 100%. Letting $\lambda^{\text{new}} = 2 \times 8 = 16$, the model is re-solved to obtain the predicted measures.

$$U_{\text{proc}} = \lambda^{\text{new}} D_{\text{proc,aggr}} = 64\%$$

$$U_{\text{disk}} = \lambda^{\text{new}} D_{\text{disk,aggr}} = 96\%$$

$$R'_{\text{proc}} = D_{\text{proc,aggr}}/(1 - U_{\text{proc}}) = 0.111$$

$$R'_{\text{disk}} = D_{\text{disk,aggr}}/(1 - U_{\text{disk}}) = 1.5$$

$$R_{\text{request}} = R_{\text{proc}} + R_{\text{disk}} = 1.611$$

Therefore, if the number of workstations were doubled, the file server disk would saturate and the average request response time would increase from 0.174 sec to 1.611 sec, an 825% increase! The model clearly indicates that the server would be bogged down and users would suffer with long response times at the workstations.

Now consider some possible alternatives to support system expansion without impairing service levels. The current system performance will be used as a basis for the comparison of the various alternatives under consideration. Each alternative is evaluated by considering the relative change in system performance from the baseline model.

- *Server caching scheme.* A new version of the operating system that provides a cache for the server is available. According to the vendor, read and write cache hit ratios of 70% and 60%, respectively, can be achieved. To reduce the impact of unanticipated failures, every write operation to cache will also be applied to the disk. Thus, the server cache can then be modeled by reducing the visit ratio of read requests [i.e., $V_{\text{disk,read}}^{\text{new}} = (1 - \text{hit ratio})V_{\text{disk,read}}$]. To have a better understanding of the impact of the server cache on the performance of each class of the workload, a three-class model is solved using the predicted arrival rate and letting $D_{\text{disk,read}}^{\text{new}} = (1 - 0.7) \times 0.04 = 0.012$.
- *Client caching scheme.* In this case, when a read is issued at the workstation, the data read are stored in a local buffer pool, called *client cache* [8]. Subsequent remote reads may find the requested data in the local cache. This reduces significantly the number of requests that go to the server. It is assumed that due to reliability reasons, a write operation always goes to the disk in the server, after updating the client cache. The introduction of a client cache in the workstations of the environment can be modeled by reducing the arrival rate of read requests. Thus, $\lambda_{\text{read}}^{\text{new}} = (1 - \text{client hit ratio})\lambda_{\text{read}}$. Assuming a client hit ratio of 70%, the new value for the parameter that represents the change is given by $\lambda_{\text{read}}^{\text{new}} = (1 - 0.7) \times 10 = 3$.
- *Upgrade in disk subsystem.* The third alternative considered is to upgrade the storage subsystem and to install a second disk unit in the file server. This change is represented in the model by adding a third service center. The original disk service demand will be equally split between the two disks (i.e., $D_{\text{disk1},r}^{\text{new}} = D_{\text{disk2},r}^{\text{new}} = D_{\text{disk},r}/2$).

For each alternative, a three-class model is evaluated according to the formulas of Fig. 6.7. The model inputs consist of parameters from Table 6.8 and those that were calculated to represent each specific change in the baseline model. Table 6.9 summarizes the performance measures obtained for the three alternatives. To obtain a rank of the alternatives in terms of performance, aggregate response time is first calculated for each alternative, which is the

Table 6.9 Results of an Open Three-Class Model.

Alternative	Processor		Disk		Extra Disk	
	U (%)	R' (sec)	U (%)	R' (sec)	U (%)	R' (sec)
• Server cache						
Read	18	0.050	12	0.038	-	-
Write	36	0.250	40	0.313	-	-
Other	10	0.139	16	0.250	-	-
• Client cache						
Read	5.4	0.037	12	0.125	-	-
Write	36	0.185	40	0.313	-	-
Other	10	0.103	16	0.250	-	-
• Disk upgrade						
Read	18	0.050	20	0.038	20	0.038
Write	36	0.250	20	0.096	20	0.096
Other	10	0.139	8	0.077	8	0.077

average of the individual classes weighted by the class throughput. Table 6.10 displays the aggregate response times as well as the relative change in the response time from the baseline model. The *pure expansion* refers to the alternative that just increases the number of workstations. All alternatives assume that the number of workstations will be doubled.

From the file server perspective, the best alternative is the upgrade in the disk subsystem, because it considerably diminishes the demand on the original disk. The client cache, although seemingly worse than the server cache, may be the best alternative from the system viewpoint. The key issue in this alternative is the reduction in the number of times that a user process goes to the file server. This reduction implies less overhead of network access, which in most systems has a high cost. The network time spent by a request in a client server environment will be modeled with the techniques presented in Chap. 7.

Table 6.10 Performance of the Alternatives.

Alternative	Response Time (sec)	Variation (%)
Baseline	0.174	-
Pure expansion	1.611	825
Server cache	0.244	40
Client cache	0.354	103
Disk upgrade	0.227	30

6.6 MIXED MODELS

A mixed model with R classes of customers has C closed classes and O open classes, where $R = C + O$. In fact, a mixed model can be viewed as a combination of two separate submodels, a closed model and an open model, that happen to share the common resources of a computer system, as depicted in Fig. 6.8. The load intensity of a mixed queuing network model is defined by

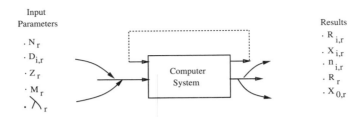

Input
Parameters

· N_r
· $D_{i,r}$
· Z_r
· M_r
· λ_r

Computer
System

Results

· $R_{i,r}$
· $X_{i,r}$
· $n_{i,r}$
· R_r
· $X_{0,r}$

Figure 6.8 Multiclass mixed models.

a pair of vectors $(\vec{C}, \vec{O})$, where $\vec{C} = (N_1, N_2, \ldots, N_C)$ specifies the customer populations of the closed submodel and $\vec{O} = (\lambda_1, \lambda_2, \ldots, \lambda_O)$ represents the arrival rates of the open submodel.

The basic approach to solve a mixed multiclass model is to solve their submodels independently, but with adjusted service demands to represent the impact on each other. Because the device utilizations do not depend on the closed submodel, the open submodel is solved first and the device utilizations due to the open classes are obtained. The effect of contention at a server due to customers of different submodels is represented by elongating the service demands for the closed submodel. To elongate the service demands appropriately, they are multiplied by a factor that is proportional to the inverse of the idle time remaining from the open submodel ([i.e., $1/(1 - U_{i,\text{open}})$] [13]). The closed submodel with the elongated service demands is then solved using the MVA algorithm. Response times of the open submodels are affected by the closed submodel. To account for this interference, the average queue lengths of closed customers is used in the calculation of response times of open customers (i.e., $n_{i,\text{closed}}$ is included in the number of customers seen by an arriving open customer). This approach is represented in the algorithm shown in Fig. 6.9.

Example

Reconsider the simple two-class model described in Sec. 6.2. Suppose now that the way of viewing the system has been changed by deciding to represent the query class as a transaction class, with arrival rate equal to 4.09 tps. Table 6.11 shows the input parameters of the mixed model. By following the algorithm of Fig. 6.9, the first step is to calculate the utilization due to the open class with $\lambda_1 = 4.09$.

Table 6.11 Measurement Data for the Transaction Processing System.

Class	Type	Service Demand			Multiprogramming Level	Arrival Rate
		Processor	Disk 1	Disk 2		
Query	Open	0.105	0.180	0	-	4.09
Update	Closed	0.375	0.480	0.240	1	-

Input Parameters

$D_{i,r}$, N_r, and λ_r

Steps

1. Solve the open submodel and obtain $U_{i,r}(\vec{O}) = \lambda_r D_{i,r}$
   $\forall\ r \in \{1, 2, \ldots, O\}$

2. Determine $U_{i,\text{open}} = \sum_{r=1}^{O} U_{i,r}$.

3. Elongate the service demands of the closed classes:

$$D_{i,r}^e = \frac{D_{i,r}}{1 - U_i}, \forall\ r \in \{1, 2, \ldots, C\}$$

4. Using the MVA algorithm, compute performance results for the closed model:

$$R_{i,r}'(\vec{C}),\ n_{i,r}(\vec{C}),\ X_{0,r}(\vec{C})\ \forall\ r \in \{1, 2, \ldots, C\}$$

5. Determine $n_{i,\text{closed}}(\vec{C}) = \sum_{r=1}^{C} n_{i,r}(\vec{C})$.

6. Compute the average residence time for the open submodel:

$$R_{i,r}'(\vec{O}) = \frac{D_{i,r}[1 + n_{i,\text{closed}}(\vec{C})]}{1 - U_{i,\text{open}}(\vec{O})}$$

$$n_{i,\text{open}}(\vec{O}) = \lambda_r R_{i,r}(\vec{O})$$

Figure 6.9 Algorithm for mixed multiclass models.

- Open submodel

$$\begin{aligned}
U_{\text{processor,query}} &= 0.105 \times 4.09 = 42.95\% \\
U_{\text{disk1,query}} &= 0.180 \times 4.09 = 73.62\% \\
U_{\text{disk2,query}} &= 0 \times 4.09 = 0.0\%
\end{aligned}$$

Using the utilizations due to the open class, the adjusted service demands are calculated for the closed submodel. By applying the MVA algorithm to solve the closed submodel with $N_1 = (1)$, the following are obtained:

- Closed submodel

$$\begin{aligned}
D_{\text{processor,update}} &= 0.375/(1 - 0.4295) = 0.657 \\
D_{\text{disk1,update}} &= 0.480/(1 - 0.7362) = 1.820 \\
D_{\text{disk2,update}} &= 0.240/(1 - 0.0) = 0.240 \\
R_{\text{update}} &= 2.717 \\
X_{\text{update}} &= 0.368 \\
n_{\text{processor,update}} &= 0.242 \\
n_{\text{disk1,update}} &= 0.67 \\
n_{\text{disk2,update}} &= 0.088
\end{aligned}$$

To compute the average response time of the open submodel, the queue lengths of the closed submodel are used to reflect the contention in the servers.

- Open submodel

$$R'_{processor,query} = \frac{0.105}{1 - 0.4295}(1 + 0.242) = 0.229$$

$$R'_{disk1,query} = \frac{0.180}{1 - 0.7362}(1 + 0.67) = 1.140$$

$$R_{query} = 1.369$$

As with the other types of models, mixed queuing networks can be used easily for predicting purposes. For example, what is the performance of the query transactions if the load of update jobs is doubled? In this case, it is only necessary to change the update multiprogramming level from 1 to 2 and re-solve the model. The new value for the response time of query transactions is 1.947, which corresponds to a 42% increase. □

6.7 CONCLUDING REMARKS

In this chapter queuing network models with multiple classes have been analyzed. These models are appropriate for describing workloads of actual systems. Usually, *"what if"* questions that appear in capacity planning are associated with individual classes of customers. Multiclass models provide performance results for individual class analysis. The discussion has concentrated on techniques for solving a special category of multiclass models, known as product-form, separable, or BCMP networks. The techniques are grouped into sections. One section refers to the exact and approximate solutions of closed models, where the load intensity is assumed to be constant. Another section shows how to solve open multiclass models, where external arrivals and departures of customers are allowed. Mixed models with both closed and open classes are solved by a combination of the two previous techniques.

Although product-form queuing networks have an efficient solution, they do not apply directly to modeling practical computer systems. For instance, in the examples examined in this chapter, memory constraints, which are always present in real systems, have been intentionally ignored. This has been done because separable models cannot directly represent the blocking effect caused by memory contention. The solution of models that incorporate features of practical systems such as memory constraints, priority scheduling, paging, and simultaneous resource possession are presented in Chap. 8.

6.8 EXERCISES

1. Consider the transaction system of Sec. 6.2. Calculate the performance measures of that model using the approximate MVA algorithm. Assume that the

stopping criterion is to have a maximum difference of 0.001 for successive values of $n_{i,r}$. Suppose now that the multiprogramming level of the update class is tripled. Recalculate the model's results using the exact and approximate techniques. Compare the computational effort required by the two algorithms.

2. In the example of the transaction system of Sec. 6.2 it is noted that query transactions only make use of disk 1, which increases its utilization and turns it into the bottleneck. Having observed this problem, the support analyst wants to know what would be the effect on performance if the I/O load due to query transactions were balanced among the two disks. Compare the results obtained with the current situation.

3. A computer system has a CPU and two disks, D1 and D2. The workload is divided into three classes: query (Q) transactions, update (U) transactions, and interactive (I) users. Table 6.12 gives the input parameters for these classes.

Table 6.12 Parameters for Exercise 3.

Class	D_{cpu}	D_{D1}	D_{D2}	N_r^{max}	λ_r	M_r	Z_r
Q	0.06	0.030	0.06	5	3.0	-	-
U	0.10	0.030	0.09	3	1.5	-	-
I	0.09	0.045	0.00	5	-	50	15

Use *QSolver/1* to answer the following *"what if"* questions:
(a) What is the average response time for each class?
(b) What is the impact on response time if the arrival rate of query transactions is increased by 95%?
(c) In the scenario with an increased arrival rate of query transactions, consider the following hardware upgrades and compare the performance improvements obtained with each one of them.
  • replace disk D1 by one twice as fast.
  • replace the CPU by one twice as fast.
(d) With the increased arrival rate for query transactions and with a twice-as-fast CPU, draw a graph of response time versus the number of terminals when the number of terminals varies from 50 to 250. What is the maximum number of terminals that can be supported to keep the response time for the interactive users below 1.5 sec?

BIBLIOGRAPHY

1. L. Dowdy, B. Carlson, A. Krantz, and S. Tripathi, Single-class bounds of multiclass queuing networks, *Journal of the ACM*, Vol. 39, No. 1, January 1992.

2. C. Woodside and S. Tripathi, Optimal allocation of file servers in a local network environment, *IEEE Transactions of Software Engineering*, Vol. SE-12, No. 8, August 1986.

3. F. Baskett, K. Chandy, R. Muntz, and F. Palacios, Open, closed, and mixed networks of queues with different classes of customers, *Journal of the ACM*, Vol. 22, No. 2, April 1975.

4. E. Lazowska, J. Zahorjan, S. Graham, and K. Sevcik, *Quantitative System Performance: Computer System Analysis Using Queueing Network Models*, Prentice Hall, Englewood Cliffs, N.J., 1984.

5. A. E. Conway and N. D. Georganas, *Queuing Networks - Exact Computational Algorithms: A Unified Theory Based on Decomposition and Aggregation*, MIT Press, Cambridge, Mass., 1989.

6. M. Reiser and S. Lavenberg, Mean-value analysis of closed multi-chain queuing networks, *Journal of the ACM*, Vol. 27, No. 2, 1980.

7. K. Sevcik and I. Mitrani, The distribution of queuing network states at input and output instants, *Journal of the ACM*, Vol. 28, No. 2, April 1981.

8. E. Drakopoulos and M. Merges, Performance analysis of client-server storage systems, *IEEE Transactions on Computers*, Vol. 41, No. 11, 1992.

9. E. Souza e Silva, S. Lavenberg, and R. Muntz, A perspective on iterative methods for the approximate analysis of closed queuing networks, in *Mathematical Computer Performance and Reliability*, North-Holland, Amsterdam, 1984.

10. Y. Bard, Some extensions to multiclass queuing network analysis, in *Performance of Computer Systems*, North Holland, Amsterdam, 1979.

11. P. Schweitzer, Approximate analysis of multiclass closed network of queues, in *International Conference on Stochastic Control and Optimization*, Amsterdam, 1979.

12. P. Heidelberger and S. Lavenberg, Computer performance methodology, *IEEE Transactions on Computers*, Vol. C-33, No. 12, December 1984.

13. S. Agrawal, *Metamodeling: A Study of Approximations in Queuing Models*, MIT Press, Cambridge, Mass., 1985.

Chapter **7**

Performance of Client-Server Architectures

7.1 INTRODUCTION

Desktop workstations are becoming more and more powerful each day in many respects: processing power, main memory, and local disk space. High-resolution color monitors allow for friendly user interfaces. Networking capabilities allow for several workstations to be interconnected and share resources such as files systems, databases, printers, wide area network gateways, and others through specialized servers. The flexibility and price-performance advantages of this new paradigm for structuring computation, often referred to as the *client-server* paradigm, have led many companies to move considerable portions of their operation from the traditional mainframe-centered model to the distributed client-server model. This is called *downsizing*. In this chapter we focus on performance models used to predict the performance of client-server architectures. As with the other chapters of this book, we start by studying a motivating example, in this case of a telemarketing company. To avoid confusion, we use the term *device* to designate queuing network servers; in this chapter the term *server* is reserved to the server in a client-server architecture.

7.2 THE TELEMARKETING COMPANY PROBLEM

A catalog marketing company sells brand-name and private-label merchandise by telemarketing. Customers call and place orders from a catalog. A telemarketing representative takes the order and gives the customer an order number, the total cost, and an estimate of how long it will take for the order to be mailed. A computer system based on a mainframe with one terminal per telemarketing representative is currently used to handle mail-order operations, customer service, and credit authorization. The company would like to migrate to a client-server architecture in which each telemarketing representative has a workstation (the client workstation in the client-server paradigm) with a nice graphical user interface to improve productivity and reduce the time needed to complete an interaction with the customer. All workstations would be interconnected through a local area network (LAN) to a database server that will store the customer file, orders file, and inventory file (see Fig. 7.1).

The company receives an average of 30,000 mail orders per day from its 5 million active customers. When a call comes in, it is placed on hold for the first available representative if all of them are busy. The company asked its capacity planning analyst, Alice, to answer the following question: *How many representatives are necessary to guarantee that each calling customer will not have to wait more than 5 sec, on the average, before being served given a proposed system configuration (LAN, server characteristics, and client workstation characteristics)?*

Before we solve this problem and introduce the modeling techniques necessary to handle it, let us first discuss the main considerations that affect

telemarketing representatives

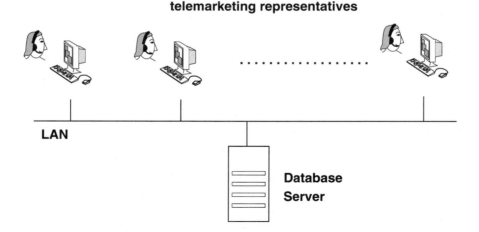

Figure 7.1 CS architecture for the telemarketing company.

performance in client-server (CS) architectures as well as workload characterization issues in these environments.

7.3 PERFORMANCE CONSIDERATIONS IN THE CS PARADIGM

In a client-server computing paradigm, one or more *clients* and one or more *servers*, along with the underlying operating system, interprocess communication system, and network protocols, form a composite system allowing distributed computation [1]. The client is a process that interacts with the user and is responsible for (1) implementing the user interface, (2) generating one or more requests to the server from the user queries or transactions, (3) transmitting the requests to the server via a suitable interprocess communication mechanism, and (4) receiving the results from the server and presenting them to the user. A server is a process, or set of processes, which collectively provide services to the clients in a manner that shields from the client the details of the architecture of the server hardware/software environment. A server does not initiate any dialogue with a client. It only responds to requests [1]. Servers control access to shared resources, such as file systems, databases, gateways to wide area networks (WANs), printers, and others.

Usually, clients and servers are located on different machines interconnected by a LAN. Figure 7.2 shows how a request generated at the client is serviced by the server. Typically, a request, say a file service request (e.g., "read block x from file foo") to a file server, is invoked at the client as a remote procedure call (RPC), a request that a procedure running at the server site (the remote machine) execute the request with the appropriate parameters (e.g., "x" and "foo") and return the result, via the network, to the calling client. Several network messages may be necessary to send the result from the server to the client. Figure 7.2 shows the general structure of an interaction between a client and a server in a CS architecture.

An example of a common client-server architecture for access to remote files is the Network File System (NFS) [2]. More details about client-server architectures and Remote Procedure Calls can be found in Refs. [1] and [3].

As we can see from Fig. 7.2, each user transaction in a CS paradigm has three components to its delay or response time:

$$\text{transaction response time} = \text{client delay} + \text{network delay} + \text{server delay} \quad (7.1)$$

The client delay includes CPU time at the client workstation plus any disk time at the client workstation. The client CPU time accounts for the time necessary to execute the user interface code, plus local preparation of the service request at the application level, plus the time necessary to process all protocol levels from the session layer (e.g., NetBIOS [4], SPX [5]) down to the transport/network layer (e.g., TCP/IP [6], UDP [7]). Some client workstations

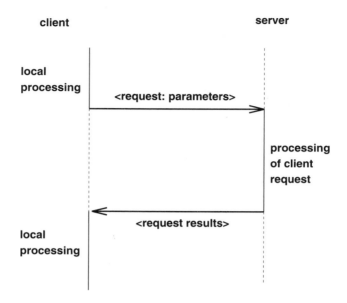

Figure 7.2 Client–server interaction.

may have local disks for paging purposes, to hold temporary files, or even to cache files or portions of files in order to reduce traffic with the server. The delay at the client is independent of the total system load and consists only of the service demands at the client CPU and disk (if any).

The network delay is composed of the time necessary to get access to the network through the appropriate medium access protocol (MAC), such as token-ring [8] or CSMA/CD (Ethernet) [9], plus the time necessary to transmit through the network the packets involved in the service request. The first component of the network delay (network access time) is clearly dependent on the network load. For instance, the number of collisions in a CSMA/CD network increases as more stations attempt to transmit at the same time. Similarly, the time for the token to return to a station, in a token-ring network, increases with the number of stations.

Finally, the server delay is decomposed into server CPU delay plus server disk delay. In both cases, queues may form at these devices since the server is a shared resource being used by all clients. The service demand at the server CPU accounts for the time necessary to process the incoming requests from the clients plus the time necessary to process all the protocol layers at the server side. The service demands at the server disks depend on the type of service provided by the server. For instance, a file server may provide services such as reading a block from a file or writing a block to a file, while a database server may provide a service such as executing an SQL query involving joining two or more database tables which could result in numerous physical I/Os.

The performance of CS systems is greatly influenced by the congestion levels at the shared resources (network, server CPU, and server disks). Caching can be used at various levels to decrease the demand on these resources as analyzed in Ref. [10] for a file server accessed by diskless workstations. File blocks can be cached at the client workstation to avoid sending a request to the server when that block is referenced again in the near future or file blocks may be cached at the server memory to avoid physical I/Os for recently read blocks. Client caching outperforms server caching since it reduces network and server contention, but it requires that a cache consistency protocol be used to guarantee that all caches remain mutually consistent. More on caching techniques for distributed file systems can be found in Ref. [11]. The performance of CS systems is also affected by the degree into which one is able to reduce overhead at various levels by amortizing it over larger units (e.g., disk blocks, network packets, etc.) [10].

7.4 WORKLOAD CHARACTERIZATION FOR CS ARCHITECTURES

One of the important steps in the performance analysis of any computer system is the characterization of the workload. In a CS architecture there are several candidates for the service request considered in the workload characterization step.

Lazowska et al. [10] defined a request as a transfer of 4 Kbytes of data, plus the average amount of "user mode" processing that occurs at the client workstation per 4 Kbytes transferred. They used this characterization to compare several design alternatives for remote access to a file server by diskless workstations.

Bodnarchuk et al. [12] built a workload model for a distributed system file server. A request in their study is characterized by NFS requests for file operations such as create, getattr, mkdir, rmdir, read, write, remove, and others. The factors they considered as relevant to characterize the workload were:

- *Request frequency distribution:* gives the percentage of each type of request with respect to the total number of requests during a measurement interval. Those requests that occur very infrequently can safely be omitted from the workload model with no significant effect on its accuracy. Bodnarchuk et al. [12] found that read requests outnumber write requests by a 3:1 margin.

- *Request interarrival time distribution:* workload component that describes the time interval elapsed between two consecutive requests to the file server. This factor depends on the speed of the clients and on the network speed and congestion. It may also depend on some factors related to the maximum size of a read/write request. For instance, in NFS, the maximum size of a write request is 8192 bytes. If a client application generates a logical write greater than 8 Kbytes, it will be decomposed at the client into several NFS calls which will arrive at the server in a burst. In the study carried out in Ref. [12] it was shown that the average size of a write request tends to be very large (> 8192 bytes).

- *File referencing behavior:* describes how file service requests are distributed among the several files of the entire file system. In Ref. [12] it was found that clients tend to request access to complete files rather than to partial files. It was also found that accesses tend to concentrate on a small subset of files rather than be scattered to all files. An important related consideration is the access mode. Ousterhout et al. [13] showed that 90% of the files tend to be accessed sequentially rather than randomly. In a lightly loaded system this tends to decrease the number of seeks per request at the disk server. As the load increases and congestion on the disk arm increases, the benefit of sequential access is lost.

- *Distribution of the sizes of read and write requests:* concerned with the amount of bytes requested by read and write requests. For instance, in Ref. [12] it was found that 64% of the read requests demanded a transfer of 8001 to 8192 bytes, and 26.62% were for very small requests (< 500 bytes). Writes requiring from 8001 to 8192 bytes comprised 74% of the requests.

Artificial NFS workload generators such as the *nhfsstone* (pronounced "nfs-stone") are now being used throughout industry [14]. This benchmark was shown to generate average server and network workload levels comparable to actual workloads [15]. The default mix—called the Legato mix—of NFS calls in this benchmark has the following distribution: getattr (13%), setattr (1%), lookup (34%), readlink (8%), read (22%), write (15%), create (2%), remove (1%), readdir (3%), and fsstat (1%).

Finally, another possible level of workload characterization is at the transaction level. A request could be an SQL request to an SQL server. The more complex the request, the fewer requests of lower complexity are sent to the server.

7.5 SOLVING THE TELEMARKETING COMPANY PROBLEM

Let us return to our telemarketing company problem and build a model that will allow us to answer the capacity planning question. Consider that the telemarketing application runs on a CS architecture with m client workstations and one SQL server. The server has one CPU and one disk. The client workstations are diskless. The network connecting the client workstations and the server is an Ethernet at 10 Mbps.

After building a prototype for the new application, service demands were measured for the various devices. The work unit for the workload characterization is an SQL request generated by a mail-order transaction.

Consider the following SQL-request-related parameters:

N_{sql} = average number of SQL requests per mail-order transaction
L_{sql} = average length (in bytes) of the result of an SQL request
D^{cl} = average time elapsed at the client workstation since a reply to a previous SQL command was received and a new one is issued; includes the time spent by the telemarketing representative to talk to the customer and enter a transaction, plus the processing time at the client workstation
D^{sv}_{cpu} = average CPU service demand per SQL request at the server
D_d = average disk service demand per SQL request at the server

Consider the following network-related parameters:

B = network bandwidth in bits per second (bps)
S = slot duration [i.e., the round-trip propagation time of the channel (time required for a collision to be detected by all stations)]
L_p = maximum packet length, in bits, including header and data field
$\overline{L_p}$ = average packet length, in bits
L_d = maximum length, in bits, of the data field of a packet

The average number of packets, NP_{sql}, generated per SQL request can be computed as follows. Assume that the request from the client to the server can always be sent in one packet. The number of packets necessary to send the result from the server to the client is given by $\lceil L_{sql}/L_d \rceil$. So

$$NP_{sql} = 1 + \left\lceil \frac{L_{sql}}{L_d} \right\rceil$$

Table 7.1 gives the values of all measured and computed parameters for our CS model.

The performance model for this problem, shown in Fig 7.3, is a hierarchical model consisting of two submodels: a higher-level model (a birth-death model) in which we represent the arrivals of calls, the queue for the next available representative, and one device for each of the m representatives. This model can be solved using the state-transition diagram techniques discussed in Chap. 4 if we are given the average arrival rate of calls (λ in our case) and the service rate, $X_{call}(k)$ [i.e., the rate at which calls are completed when there are k calls in the system (waiting or being served)]. The service rate $X_{call}(k)$ may be obtained by solving a lower-level model (the CS model) which captures the details of handling a call.

Next we show how to solve the birth-death and CS models.

Table 7.1 Parameters for the Telemarketing Problem.

SQL-request-related parameters	
N_{sql}	4 SQL commands/call
L_{sql}	1000 bytes
D^{cl}	45 sec
D^{sv}_{cpu}	0.12 sec
D_d	0.054 sec
Network Parameters	
B	10 Mbps
S	51.2 μsec
L_p	1518 bits
$\overline{L}_p$	1518 bits
L_d	1492 bits
Computed Parameter	
NP_{sql}	7 packets

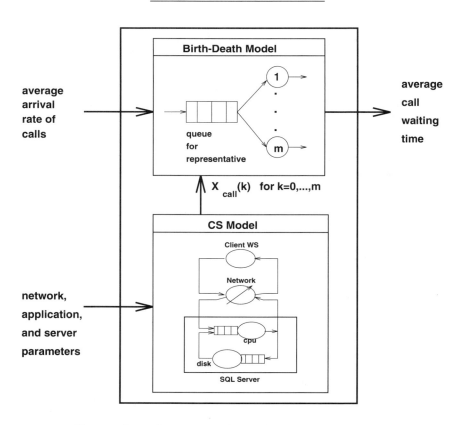

Figure 7.3 Performance model of the telemarketing problem.

7.5.1 Birth–Death Model

To answer the original capacity planning question "What is the number of telemarketing workstations necessary to guarantee that a calling customer will not have to wait more than 5 sec on the average?" we need to model the queue of waiting calls. For that purpose, we will use the method of state-transition diagrams explained in Chap. 4. A state here is the number k of customers (calls) in the system, including those being served by a telemarketing representative plus those which are waiting for the next available representative. So the possible states are $0, 1, \ldots, m, \ldots$. The average arrival rate of calls is computed below assuming that the system is available 12 hours a day and that traffic is balanced throughout the day.

$$\lambda = \frac{30,000 \text{ calls per day}}{12 \times 3600} = 0.69 \text{ calls/sec}$$

So the rate at which transitions occur from state k to state $k+1$ is constant and equal to λ. The rate at which transitions occur from state k to $k-1$ (number of calls served per second) depends on the number of customers in the system. The system throughput in calls per second, $X_{\text{call}}(k)$, is obtained from the CS model described in the next subsection.

Figure 7.4 shows the state-transition diagram for the birth-death model.

We use the general birth-death equation, derived in Chap. 4 and repeated below, to obtain the probability P_k that there are k calls in the system.

$$P_k = P_0 \prod_{i=0}^{k-1} \frac{\lambda_i}{\mu_{i+1}} \tag{7.2}$$

If we look at the diagram of Fig. 7.4, we see that $\lambda_i = \lambda$ for $i \geq 0$, $\mu_i = X_{\text{call}}(i)$ for $1 \leq i \leq m$, and $\mu_i = X_{\text{call}}(m) = \mu_m$ for $i \geq m$. Making these substitutions in Eq. (7.2), we get that

$$P_k = \begin{cases} P_0 \lambda^k / (\mu_1 \cdots \mu_k) & k \leq m \\ P_0 \lambda^k / [\mu_1 \cdots \mu_m (\mu_m)^{k-m}] & k > m \end{cases} \tag{7.3}$$

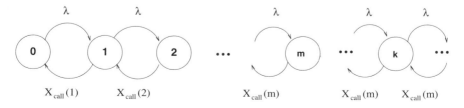

Figure 7.4 State-transition diagram.

where P_0 is obtained by requiring that all probabilities sum to 1. Hence,

$$
\begin{aligned}
P_0 &= \left[1 + \sum_{k=1}^{m} \lambda^k \frac{1}{\mu_1 \cdots \mu_k} + \sum_{k=m+1}^{\infty} \lambda^k \frac{1}{\mu_1 \cdots \mu_m (\mu_m)^{k-m}} \right]^{-1} \\
&= \left[1 + \sum_{k=1}^{m} \lambda^k \frac{1}{\mu_1 \cdots \mu_k} + \frac{\mu_m^m}{\mu_1 \cdots \mu_m} \sum_{k=m+1}^{\infty} \left(\frac{\lambda}{\mu_m} \right)^k \right]^{-1} \\
&= \left[1 + \left(\sum_{k=1}^{m} \lambda^k \frac{1}{\mu_1 \cdots \mu_k} \right) + \frac{\mu_m^m}{\mu_1 \cdots \mu_m} \frac{(\lambda/\mu_m)^{m+1}}{1 - (\lambda/\mu_m)} \right]^{-1}
\end{aligned}
\tag{7.4}
$$

The summation on the right-hand side of Eq. (7.4) converges only if $\lambda < \mu_m$, which is the equilibrium condition for the system.

To compute the average call waiting time, W, we use Little's result which when applied to the queue of waiting calls says that

$$
N_w = \lambda W \tag{7.5}
$$

where N_w is the average number of calls waiting to be served. Note that if we knew the probability P_k^w that k calls are waiting to be served, we could compute N_w as

$$
N_w = \sum_{k=1}^{\infty} k P_k^w \tag{7.6}
$$

But P_k^w can easily be obtained as a function of the probabilities P_k by observing that when the number of calls in the system is less than or equal to the number of representatives, the number of waiting calls is zero. After that point, the number of waiting calls is equal to the number of calls in the system minus the number of representatives. So

$$
P_k^w =
\begin{cases}
\sum_{j=0}^{m} P_j & \text{for } k = 0 \\
P_{k+m} & \text{for } k > 0
\end{cases}
\tag{7.7}
$$

Using Eq. (7.7) in Eq. (7.6), we get that

$$
\begin{aligned}
N_w &= \sum_{k=1}^{\infty} k P_{k+m} = \sum_{k=1}^{\infty} \frac{k P_0 \lambda^{k+m}}{\mu_1 \cdots \mu_m (\mu_m)^{k+m-m}} \\
&= \frac{P_0 \lambda^m}{\mu_1 \cdots \mu_m} \sum_{k=1}^{\infty} k \left(\frac{\lambda}{\mu_m} \right)^k \\
&= \frac{P_0 \lambda^m}{\mu_1 \cdots \mu_m} \frac{\lambda/\mu_m}{[1 - (\lambda/\mu_m)]^2}
\end{aligned}
\tag{7.8}
$$

The values of μ_i, equal to $X_{\text{call}}(i)$, are obtained by solving the CS model given in the next subsection.

7.5.2 CS Model

The CS model, depicted in Fig. 7.3, has a single class with a total of m customers in the population (the number of client workstations). This follows from the assumption that each client workstation cannot submit a new SQL request until it receives the answer to a previous one. The client workstations are represented by a single delay device whose service demand is D^{cl} since a request spends this amount of time at the client workstation before being submitted to the server.

Queuing devices represent the CPU and disk at the server. The service time per packet at the network is dependent on the number of workstations contending for it. As discussed in Chap. 3, the network has to be modeled as a load-dependent device. To solve the model we need to discuss how MVA can be extended to handle the existence of load-dependent devices.

Solving QNs with load-dependent devices.   Chapter 5 presented the three main relationships (repeated below) needed to solve a queuing network using MVA. They assume that service times are load-independent (LI).

$$R_i'(n) = \begin{cases} D_i & \text{if } i \text{ is a Delay device} \\ D_i[1 + \bar{n}_i\ (n-1)] & \text{otherwise} \end{cases} \tag{7.9}$$

$$X_0(n) = \frac{n}{\sum_{i=1}^{K} R_i'(n)} \tag{7.10}$$

$$\bar{n}_i(n) = X_0(n)\, R_i'(n) \tag{7.11}$$

For load-dependent (LD) devices, the service rate, and consequently, the response time will be a function of the distribution of customers at the device. Therefore, we need to adjust Eq. (7.9). Since Eq. (7.11) does not hold for load-dependent devices, we compute, in what follows, the queue length distribution at these devices to obtain the average queue length.

Let

$P_i(j \mid n)$ = probability that device i has j customers given that there are n customers in the queuing network

$\mu_i(j)$ = service rate of device i when there are j customers at the device

An arriving customer who finds $j-1$ customers at device i will have a response time equal to $j/\mu_i(j)$. The probability that an arrival finds $j-1$ at device i given that there are n customers in the queuing network is $P_i(j-1 \mid n-1)$, due to the arrival theorem. The average residence time can now be computed as the product of the average number of visits to the device by the average response time per visit. So

$$R_i'(n) = V_i \sum_{j=1}^{n} \text{response time given } j \text{ customers}$$

$$\times \text{ probability that arrival finds } (j-1) \text{ customers}$$

$$= V_i \sum_{j=1}^{n} \frac{j}{\mu_i(j)} P_i(j-1 \mid n-1) \tag{7.12}$$

The mean queue length at node i is given by

$$\bar{n}_i(n) = \sum_{j=1}^{n} j P_i(j \mid n) \tag{7.13}$$

We now need to compute the values of $P_i(j \mid n)$. By definition, $P_i(0 \mid 0) = 1$. If one applies the principle of flow equilibrium to the queuing network states [16], the probability of having j customers at device i for a queuing network with n customers can be expressed in terms of the probability of having $j-1$ customers at device i when there is one less customer in the queuing network. Hence,

$$P_i(j \mid n) = \begin{cases} [D_i X_0(n)/\alpha_i(j)] P_i(j-1 \mid n-1) & j = 1, \ldots, n \\ 1 - \sum_{k=1}^{n} P_i(k \mid n) & j = 0 \end{cases} \tag{7.14}$$

where $\alpha_i(j)$ is a *service-rate multiplier* defined in Ref. [17] as $\mu_i(j)/\mu_i(1)$. From Eq. (7.12) and the definition of the service-rate multipliers it follows that

$$R_i'(n) = \frac{V_i}{\mu_i(1)} \sum_{j=1}^{n} \frac{j}{\alpha_i(j)} P_i(j-1 \mid n-1) \tag{7.15}$$

The service time, S_i, when there is no congestion at device i is equal to $1/\mu_i(1)$. Since $D_i = V_i S_i$, it follows that

$$R_i'(n) = D_i \sum_{j=1}^{n} \frac{j}{\alpha_i(j)} P_i(j-1 \mid n-1) \tag{7.16}$$

The MVA algorithm for load-dependent devices is given in Fig. 7.5.

Example

A multiprocessor has two processors and one disk. Benchmarks indicate that a given two-processor machine is 1.8 times faster than the single-processor model for this type of machine. Then we have that

$$\alpha_{\text{cpu}}(j) = \begin{cases} 1 & j = 1 \\ 1.8 & j \geq 2 \end{cases}$$

Input Parameters: service demands (D_i's), N, K, and service-rate multipliers [$\alpha_i(j)$'s].

Initialization

For $i := 1$ to K do

$$\begin{cases} P_i(0 \mid 0) = 1 & \text{for LD devices} \\ \bar{n}_i(0) = 0 & \text{otherwise} \end{cases}$$

Iteration Loop

For $n := 1$ to N do

  Begin

    For $i := 1$ to K do

$$R_i'(n) = \begin{cases} D_i[1 + \bar{n}_i\,(n-1)] & \text{LI queuing device} \\[2mm] D_i & \text{delay device} \\[2mm] D_i \displaystyle\sum_{j=1}^{n} \frac{j \cdot P_i(j-1 \mid n-1)}{\alpha_i(j)} & \text{LD device} \end{cases}$$

$$R_0(n) = \sum_{i=1}^{K} R_i'(n)$$
$$X_0(n) = n/R_0(n)$$

    For $i := 1$ to K do

$$\begin{cases} \bar{n}_i(n) = X_0(n)R_i'(n) & \text{LI queuing} \\ & \text{or delay device} \\[2mm] \text{For } j := n \text{ down to 1 do} & \\ \quad P_i(j \mid n) = [D_i X_0(n)/\alpha_i(j)] & \\ \qquad\qquad \times P_i(j-1 \mid n-1) & \text{LD device} \\[2mm] P_i(0 \mid n) = 1 - \sum_{k=1}^{n} P_i(k \mid n) & \text{LD device} \end{cases}$$

  End

Figure 7.5 Single-class MVA algorithm with LD devices.

Let the service demand of a job at the disk be 0.06 sec and the service demand at the CPU be 0.1 sec. Let the degree of multiprogramming be 3 and let the average service time at the CPU be 0.1 sec. So, $\mu_{cpu}(1) = 1/0.1 = 10$ jobs/sec. The results obtained with the algorithm of Fig. 7.5 are shown in Table 7.2. They indicate that the average response time is 0.24 sec and the average throughput is 12.44 jobs/sec. □

Table 7.2 Example of Load-Dependent MVA.

n	R'_{cpu}	R'_{disk}	R_0	X_0	$\overline{n}_{cpu}$	$\overline{n}_{disk}$
0	-	-	-	0.00	0.00	0.00
	$p_{cpu}(0 \mid 0) = 1.0$					
1	0.10	0.06	0.16	6.25	0.63	0.37
	$p_{cpu}(0 \mid 1) = 0.375$; $p_{cpu}(1 \mid 1) = 0.625$					
	$U_{cpu} = 0.625$; $U_{disk} = 0.375$					
2	0.11	0.08	0.19	10.56	1.13	0.87
	$p_{cpu}(0 \mid 2) = 0.238$; $p_{cpu}(1 \mid 2) = 0.396$					
	$p_{cpu}(2 \mid 2) = 0.367$					
	$U_{cpu} = 0.763$; $U_{disk} = 0.633$					
3	0.13	0.11	0.24	12.44	1.60	1.40
	$p_{cpu}(0 \mid 3) = 0.177$; $p_{cpu}(1 \mid 3) = 0.296$					
	$p_{cpu}(2 \mid 3) = 0.274$; $p_{cpu}(3 \mid 3) = 0.253$					
	$U_{cpu} = 0.823$; $U_{disk} = 0.747$					

Using LD MVA in the telemarketing problem.   To apply the algorithm just described to the catalog marketing company problem, we need an expression for the service rate of the network as a function of the number of client workstations using it. This service rate, $\mu_{net}(m)$, measured in SQL requests per second, is given by

$$\mu_{net}(m) = \begin{cases} \mu_p(1)/NP_{sql} & m = 1 \\[2mm] \mu_p(m+1)/NP_{sql} & m \geq 2 \end{cases} \tag{7.17}$$

where $\mu_p(n)$ is the network throughput, in packets/sec, for a network with n stations. Note that when $m = 1$, even though there are two stations in the network (the server and the only client), the server transmits only when requested by the client and no collisions occur. For that reason, $\mu_p(1)$ is used in the expression for $\mu_{net}(1)$. An expression for $\mu_p(n)$ for an Ethernet network was derived in [17] and is given by

$$\mu_p(n) = \frac{\overline{L}_p/B}{\overline{L}_p/B + S \times C} \times \frac{B}{\overline{L}_p} = \frac{1}{\overline{L}_p/B + S \times C} \tag{7.18}$$

where C, the average number of collisions, is given by $(1 - A)/A$, where A, the probability of a successful transmission, is given by $(1 - 1/n)^{n-1}$.

If we use the algorithm of Fig. 7.5 with the parameters given in Table 7.1, we obtain the values of the throughput $X_{sql}(m)$ when there are m client workstations. Figure 7.6 shows the variation of X_{sql} as a function of the number of client workstations.

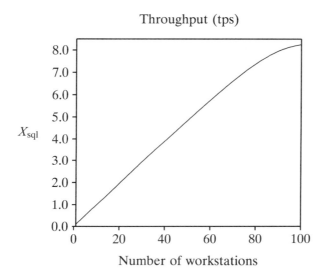

Throughput (tps)

Number of workstations

Figure 7.6 Throughput versus number of workstations.

The system throughput in calls per second, $X_{call}(k)$, when there are k calls in the system is given by

$$X_{call}(k) = \begin{cases} X_{sql}(k)/N_{sql} & k \leq m \\ X_{sql}(m)/N_{sql} & k > m \end{cases} \tag{7.19}$$

where the values of X_{sql} are obtained by solving the closed queuing network model just described.

If we now combine the results of the two submodels we obtain the average waiting time as a function of the number of representatives, as shown in Table 7.3.

As we can see, we need 175 representatives in order for the average waiting time per call not to exceed 5 sec.

7.6 CATEGORIES OF CS PERFORMANCE MODELS

In this section we analyze the different types of performance models that may be necessary to deal with situations involving CS architectures. We classify

Table 7.3 Average Waiting Time per Call.

Number of Representatives	Average Waiting Time (sec)
125	1398.0
130	36.8
135	19.4
140	13.4
145	10.5
150	8.7
155	7.5
160	6.6
165	6.0
170	5.5
175	**5.1**
180	4.7
185	4.5
190	4.2
195	4.0
200	3.9

the models according to the type of client workstations (single request versus multiple request) and to the type of client workstation-generated workload (homogeneous versus heterogeneous).

A client workstation is considered to be of the *single-request* type if it cannot issue a new service request to the server until a reply to a previous one has been received. This was the case in our telemarketing company example. *Multiple-request* workstations can issue several requests to the server before receiving a reply to requests previously pending. Consider for example, a workstation that allows the user to work on several windows simultaneously. File service requests can be generated to a file server from each of the windows open by the user.

We say that the load generated by the client workstations is *homogeneous* if all of them have a similar profile in terms of the load of requests generated to the server. Otherwise, we say that the load is *heterogeneous*. In the heterogeneous case, we may be able to group the client workstations into *clusters* of homogeneous workstations.

In the following four subsections we discuss the performance models needed to handle each possible combination of situations encountered when modeling CS architectures.

7.6.1 Single-Request Clients and Homogeneous Workloads

This is the case discussed in detail in the telemarketing company example. The set of client workstations is modeled by a delay device whose service demand represents the average time elapsed between the receipt of a reply from the server and the generation of a new request. Let this interval be called *client think time*. Since the workload is homogeneous, the analytic model has only one class of customers and the customer population is equal to the number of client workstations. The analytic model used to solve this performance model is the single-class MVA with load-dependent devices shown in Fig. 7.5. Load-dependent devices are needed because the local area network connecting client workstations and the server has a load-dependent service rate.

7.6.2 Single-Request Clients and Heterogeneous Workloads

Assume that there are R clusters of client workstations. Let N_r be the number of client workstations in cluster r. Let Z_r for $r = 1, \ldots, R$ be the average client think time for client workstations in cluster r. We model the set of all client workstations by a single delay device, denoted by cl, whose class r service demand $D_{\text{cl},r}$ is equal to Z_r. The analytic model used to solve this type of performance model is a multiclass closed queuing network model where the number of classes is equal to the number of clusters and the population of class r is equal to N_r for $r = 1, \ldots, R$. Given that the LAN is a load-dependent device, we need to be able to solve a multiclass MVA with load-dependent devices. This is discussed in Sec. 7.7.

7.6.3 Multiple-Request Clients and Homogeneous Workloads

Since client workstations may generate any number of requests to the server without receiving replies to outstanding requests, we consider that each client workstation generates requests at a rate equal to λ' requests/sec. Since there are m client workstations, the total arrival rate of requests to the server is equal to $\lambda = m\lambda'$. Once generated, each request has to go through the LAN and then be serviced by the server. We model this situation as a single-class open queuing network, as described in Chap. 6. There we only considered load-independent devices. To model the LAN we need to extend the solution of open queuing networks to allow for load-dependent devices. This will be done in Sec. 7.8 in the context of multiple classes, of which this discussion is a particular case.

7.6.4 Multiple-Request Clients and Heterogeneous Workloads

This discussion is an extension to multiple classes of the one in the preceding subsection. Each cluster r of workstations corresponds to a class in an open queuing network model. The total arrival rate of requests generated by cluster r is equal to $\lambda_r = N_r \times \lambda'_R$, where N_r is the number of workstations in cluster r and λ'_R is the average submission rate of requests per workstation in cluster r. Figure 7.7 displays a typical open network model for a multiple-request heterogeneous workload.

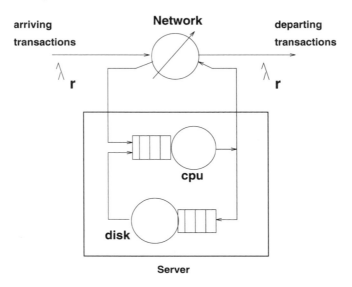

Figure 7.7 QN for multiple-request heterogeneous case.

7.7 MULTICLASS MVA WITH LOAD-DEPENDENT DEVICES

The algorithm for solving a multiple-class closed QN with load-dependent devices is given in this section. It is an extension of the approximate algorithm for multiple classes given in Chap. 6 with the ideas for incorporating load-dependent devices discussed previously in this chapter. We assume in this section that the service-rate multiplier of any load-dependent device is class independent [i.e., if i is load-dependent, then $\alpha_{i,r}(j) = \alpha_i(j)$ for all classes r].

The basis for the algorithm lies in obtaining an appropriate expression for the marginal probability, $P_i(j \mid \vec{N})$, of finding j customers at load-dependent device i given that the QN population vector is $\vec{N}$. This probability can be obtained from the local balance equations of the network states [16] as

$$P_i(j \mid \vec{N}) = \frac{1}{\alpha_i(j)} \sum_{r=1}^{R} U_{i,r}(\vec{N}) \, P_i(j-1 \mid \vec{N} - \vec{1}_r) \qquad j = 1, \ldots, |\vec{N}|$$

$$(7.20)$$

where $|\vec{N}| = \sum_{r=1}^{R} N_r$. As in the load-independent case, the dependency on values derived by removing one customer from each class makes an exact MVA solution for even moderate size QNs very expensive. To overcome this problem, we assume, as an approximation, that

$$P_i(j \mid \vec{N} - \vec{1}_r) \approx P_i(j \mid \vec{N}) \qquad j = 0, \dots, |\vec{N}| - 1 \qquad (7.21)$$

In other words, we are assuming that the removal from the QN of one customer of class r does not significantly affect the overall queue length distribution at device i [16]. Using Eq. (7.21) in Eq. (7.20) and the fact that $U_{i,r}(\vec{N}) = D_{i,r} X_{0,r}(\vec{N})$, we obtain

$$P_i(j \mid \vec{N}) \approx \frac{\sum_{r=1}^{R} U_{i,r}(\vec{N})}{\alpha_i(j)} P_i(j - 1 \mid \vec{N})$$

$$= \frac{\sum_{r=1}^{R} D_{i,r} X_{0,r}(\vec{N})}{\alpha_i(j)} P_i(j - 1 \mid \vec{N}) \qquad j = 1, \dots, |\vec{N}| \qquad (7.22)$$

Solving Eq. (7.22) recursively we obtain a closed-form expression for $P_i(j \mid \vec{N})$ as a function of $P_i(0 \mid \vec{N})$. $P_i(0 \mid \vec{N})$ can be obtained by requiring all probabilities to sum to 1 (see Exercise 3). Thus,

$$P_i(j \mid \vec{N}) = P_i(0 \mid \vec{N}) \prod_{k=1}^{j} \frac{\sum_{r=1}^{R} D_{i,r} X_{0,r}(\vec{N})}{\alpha_i(k)} \qquad j = 1, \dots, |\vec{N}| \qquad (7.23)$$

$$P_i(0 \mid \vec{N}) = \left[1 + \sum_{j=1}^{|\vec{N}|} \prod_{k=1}^{j} \frac{\sum_{r=1}^{R} D_{i,r} X_{0,r}(\vec{N})}{\alpha_i(k)} \right]^{-1} \qquad (7.24)$$

The generalization of Eq. (7.16) for the multiple-class case is

$$R'_{i,r}(\vec{N}) = D_{i,r} \sum_{j=1}^{|\vec{N}|} \frac{j}{\alpha_i(j)} P_i(j - 1 \mid \vec{N} - \vec{1}_r) \qquad (7.25)$$

Using the approximation given in Eq. (7.21) in Eq. (7.25), we obtain

$$R'_{i,r}(\vec{N}) = D_{i,r} \sum_{j=1}^{|\vec{N}|} \frac{j}{\alpha_i(j)} P_i(j - 1 \mid \vec{N}) \qquad (7.26)$$

We see that to compute the residence time $R'_{i,r}(\vec{N})$ we need the values of the probabilities $P_i(j - 1 \mid \vec{N})$. To compute these probabilities we need the values of the throughputs $X_{0,r}(\vec{N})$, which depend on the residence time values. We propose the following iterative approach:

1. Estimate initial values for the throughputs $X_{0,r}(\vec{N})$. These estimates can be obtained by approximating the throughput by its asymptotic upper bound, namely $X_{0,r} \leq \min\{N_r / \sum_{i=1}^{K} D_{i,r},\ 1/\max_i\{D_{i,r}\}\}$. Although this

is a rather loose upper bound, it is usually good enough as a starting point for the iteration discussed here.

2. Compute the probabilities $P_i(j - 1 \mid \vec{N})$ according to Eqs. (7.23) and (7.24).

3. Compute the residence times using Eq. (7.26).

4. Compute new values for the throughputs using Little's result as

$$X_{0,r}(\vec{N}) = N_r / \sum_{i=1}^{K} R'_{i,r}(\vec{N})$$

5. If the relative error between the throughputs obtained in the current iteration and the previous one is greater than a certain tolerance ϵ then go to step 2. Otherwise, compute the final metrics and stop.

This approach is specified in detail in the form of an algorithm in Fig. 7.8. Note that in the algorithm, the notation K_r is used to indicate the number of devices for which $D_{i,r} > 0$. A Pascal program that implements this algorithm is given on the disk that accompanies this book.

Example

A client-server architecture is used to process database transactions. There are a total of 35 client workstations and a database server. The database server has one CPU and one disk only. The transactions were categorized as being of three types: trivial, average, and complex, according to their use of database resources. Ten client workstations are responsible for submitting trivial transactions, 20 for submitting average transactions, and five for complex ones. Table 7.4 shows the results of measurement data. The average disk service time was measured to be 18 msec. The LAN is an Ethernet at 10 Mbps with a slot duration S of 51.2 μsec. The average network service demands per transaction class can be computed as average number packets $\times$ average packet length/network bandwidth. This gives the values 0.16, 0.41, and 1.27 msec for trivial, average, and complex transactions, respectively. The network is modeled as a load-dependent device with class independent service rate function $\mu(n)$. To use Eq. (7.18) for the Ethernet throughput, we need to compute the average packet length $\overline{L}_p$ over all classes as follows:

$$\overline{L}_p = 800 \times 0.164 + 1382 \times 0.639 + 1410 \times 0.193 = 1286 \text{ bits}$$

Table 7.4 Data for Example of Multiclass Load-Dependent MVA.

Trans. Type	Percent Trans.	Avg. Think Time (sec)	Avg. No. Packets/ Trans.	Avg. Packet Length per Trans. (bits)	No. Reads/ Trans.	No. Writes/ Trans.	Server CPU Demand (μsec)
Trivial	16.4	40	2	800	1	1	30
Average	63.9	20	3	1382	11	6	255
Complex	19.3	15	9	1410	30	11	615

Input Parameters: $D_{i,r}$'s, $\vec{N}$, K, R, ϵ, $\alpha_i(j)$'s
Initialization
For $r := 1$ to R do For $i := 1$ to K do if $D_{i,r} > 0$ then $\bar{n}_{i,r}(\vec{N}) = N_r/K_r$;
For $r := 1$ to R do $X_{0,r}^{prev} = \min\left\{N_r/\sum_{i=1}^{K} D_{i,r}, \ 1/\max_i\{D_{i,r}\}\right\}$;
Error $= \epsilon + 1$; { force entering loop for first time }
Iteration Loop
While Error $> \epsilon$ do
    Begin
        Compute Queue Lengths for Non-LD Devices
        For all non-LD device i do For $r := 1$ to R do

$$\bar{n}_i(\vec{N} - \vec{1}_r) = \frac{N_r - 1}{N_r}\bar{n}_{i,r}(\vec{N}) + \sum_{j=1 \ \& \ j \neq r}^{R}\bar{n}_{i,j}(\vec{N})$$

        Compute Probabilities for LD Devices
        For all LD device i do

$$
\begin{cases}
P_i(0 \mid \vec{N}) = \left[1 + \sum_{j=1}^{|\vec{N}|}\prod_{k=1}^{j}\dfrac{\sum_{r=1}^{R}D_{i,r}X_{0,r}^{prev}(\vec{N})}{\alpha_i(k)}\right]^{-1} \\[3ex]
P_i(j \mid \vec{N}) = P_i(0 \mid \vec{N})\prod_{k=1}^{j}\dfrac{\sum_{r=1}^{R}D_{i,r}X_{0,r}^{prev}(\vec{N})}{\alpha_i(k)} \\[2ex]
\qquad\qquad\qquad\qquad\qquad\qquad j = 1, \ldots, |\vec{N}|
\end{cases}
$$

        Compute Residence Times
        For $i := 1$ to K do
            For $r := 1$ to R do

$$
R'_{i,r}(\vec{N}) = \begin{cases}
D_{i,r}[1 + \bar{n}_i(\vec{N} - \vec{1}_r)] & \text{LI queuing device} \\
D_{i,r} & \text{delay device} \\
D_{i,r}\sum_{j=1}^{|\vec{N}|}[j/\alpha_i(j)]P_i(j-1 \mid \vec{N}) & \text{LD device}
\end{cases}
$$

        Compute Throughputs
        For $r := 1$ to R do $X_{0,r}^{curr}(\vec{N}) = N_r/\sum_{i=1}^{K}R'_{i,r}$
        Compute Queue Lengths per Class for Non-LD Devices
        For all non-LD device i do For $r := 1$ to R do
          $\bar{n}_{i,r}(\vec{N}) = X_{0,r}^{curr}(\vec{N}) \times R'_{i,r}(\vec{N})$

        Compute Relative Error Error $:= \max\limits_{r}\left|\dfrac{X_{0,r}^{curr}(\vec{N}) - X_{0,r}^{prev}(\vec{N})}{X_{0,r}^{curr}(\vec{N})}\right|$

        Prepare for Next Iteration
        For $r := 1$ to R do $X_{0,r}^{prev}(\vec{N}) := X_{0,r}^{curr}(\vec{N})$
    End ; { while }

Figure 7.8 Multiple-class MVA algorithm with LD devices.

The average number of packets per transaction, P_{tr}, is given by

$$P_{tr} = 2 \times 0.164 + 3 \times 0.639 + 9 \times 0.193 = 3.98 \text{ packets}$$

So, the service rate in tps for the network is equal to its service rate in packets/sec divided by the average number of packets per transaction. The average service demands at the disk are computed for each class by multiplying the number of reads and writes for the class by the average disk service time. The resulting values are 36, 306, and 738 μsec, for trivial, average, and complex transactions, respectively. Using the algorithm given in Fig 7.8, we obtain the performance metrics shown in Table 7.5. In this particular example, convergence was achieved after 11 iterations for a tolerance of 10^{-4}. □

Table 7.5 Metrics for Example of Multiclass Load-Dependent MVA.

Trans.	Residence Time (sec)			Response Time	Throughput
Type	Network	Server CPU	Server Disk	(sec)	(tps)
Trivial	0.00016	0.052	0.072	0.124	0.249
Average	0.00042	0.433	0.602	1.035	0.951
Complex	0.01271	1.020	1.414	2.447	0.287

7.8 MULTICLASS OPEN QUEUING NETWORKS WITH LOAD-DEPENDENT SERVERS

The algorithm discussed in this section is an extension of the algorithm presented in Chap. 6 for solving multiple-class open queuing networks. Load-dependent servers will be incorporated here. Similarly to the closed queuing network case, we assume in this section that the service-rate multiplier of any load-dependent device is class independent [i.e., if i is load-dependent, then $\alpha_{i,r}(j) = \alpha_i(j)$ for all classes r]. As discussed in Chap. 6, the solution to an open queuing network exists only if a stability condition is satisfied. In the case of load-dependent multiclass open networks with class-independent service multipliers, the stability condition is

$$\forall i \, \forall j \quad \left[\frac{U_i}{\alpha_i(j)} \right] < 1 \tag{7.27}$$

If i is a load-independent device, $\alpha_i(j) = 1$ for all j and the stability condition reduces to $\forall i \, U_i < 1$, as shown in Chap. 6.

Let $\vec{\lambda}$ be the vector $(\lambda_1, \ldots, \lambda_R)$ of arrival rates per class. Let $P_i(j \mid \vec{\lambda})$ be the probability that there are j customers irrespective of their classes at device i given that the arrival rate vector is $\vec{\lambda}$.

The residence time, $R'_{i,r}(\vec{\lambda})$, of a class r customer at device i is given by

$$R'_{i,r}(\vec{\lambda}) = V_{i,r} R_{i,r}(\vec{\lambda}) \tag{7.28}$$

where $R_{i,r}(\vec{\lambda})$ is the average response time per visit to device i of a class r customer, which can be computed from Little's result as

$$R_{i,r}(\vec{\lambda}) = \overline{N}_{i,r}(\vec{\lambda})/\lambda_{i,r} \tag{7.29}$$

where $\overline{N}_{i,r}(\vec{\lambda})$ is the average number of class r jobs at device i and $\lambda_{i,r}$ is the average arrival rate of class r jobs at device i. But it can be proved (see [16]) that

$$\overline{N}_{i,r}(\vec{\lambda}) = \frac{U_{i,r}}{U_i}\overline{N}_i(\vec{\lambda}) \tag{7.30}$$

where $\overline{N}_i(\vec{\lambda})$ is the average total number of customers at device i, which can be computed from the device probabilities as

$$\overline{N}_i(\vec{\lambda}) = \sum_{j=1}^{\infty} j P_i(j \mid \vec{\lambda}) \tag{7.31}$$

According to Ref. [16], the probability distribution of node i is given by

$$P_i(j \mid \vec{\lambda}) = P_i(0 \mid \vec{\lambda})\frac{U_i^j}{\beta(j)} \qquad j \geq 1 \tag{7.32}$$

where $\beta(j) = \alpha(1) \times \cdots \times \alpha(j)$. The probability $P_i(0 \mid \vec{\lambda})$ can easily be computed by requiring that all probabilities sum to 1. Thus,

$$P_i(0 \mid \vec{\lambda}) = \left[\sum_{j=0}^{\infty} \frac{U_i^j}{\beta(j)}\right]^{-1} \tag{7.33}$$

If we assume that the service-rate multipliers become constant after some value w_i, as it is true in most practical cases, we can obtain closed-form expressions for the probabilities $P_i(j \mid \vec{\lambda})$ and for $\overline{N}_i(\vec{\lambda})$. The stability condition in this case becomes $\forall i \; U_i/\alpha_i(w_i) < 1$. So, if we assume that $\alpha_i(j) = \alpha_i(w_i)$ for $j \geq w_i$ we get that (see Exercise 6)

$$P_i(j \mid \vec{\lambda}) = \begin{cases} P_i(0 \mid \vec{\lambda})[U_i^j/\beta_i(j)] & j = 1, \ldots, w_i \\[2mm] P_i(0 \mid \vec{\lambda})U_i^j/\{\beta_i(w_i)[\alpha_i(w_i)]^{j-w}\} & j > w_i \end{cases} \tag{7.34}$$

$$P_i(0 \mid \vec{\lambda}) = \left[\sum_{j=0}^{w_i} \frac{U_i^j}{\beta_i(j)} + \frac{[\alpha_i(w_i)]^{w_i}}{\beta_i(w_i)}\frac{[U_i/\alpha_i(w_i)]^{w_i+1}}{1 - U_i/\alpha_i(w_i)}\right]^{-1} \tag{7.35}$$

and

$$\overline{N}_i(\vec{\lambda}) = P_i(0 \mid \vec{\lambda})\left\{\sum_{j=1}^{w_i} j \frac{U_i^j}{\beta_i(j)} + \frac{U_i^{w_i+1}}{\beta_i(w_i)\alpha_i(w_i)}\right.$$
$$\left. \times \left[\frac{U_i/\alpha_i(w_i) + (w_i + 1)\left(1 - U_i/\alpha_i(w_i)\right)}{[1 - U_i/\alpha_i(w_i)]^2}\right]\right\} \tag{7.36}$$

If we use the utilization law and the forced flow law in the equations above, we can substitute $U_{i,r}$ by $\lambda_r D_{i,r}$ and U_i by $\sum_{r=1}^{R} \lambda_r D_{i,r}$ and obtain an algorithm to solve multiclass open queuing networks with load-dependent servers as a function of the class service demands and the class arrival rates. Figure 7.9 displays this algorithm, which is implemented in Pascal in the disk provided with this book. In the algorithm we use $R_{0,r}(\vec{\lambda})$ to denote the average response time of class r customers and $\overline{N}_r^s$ to denote the average number of class r customers in the system.

Example

A collection of workstations generate three types of requests to a file server: reads, writes, and other requests. Suppose that the LAN is an Ethernet at 10 Mbps with a slot duration S equal to 51.2 μsec. Table 7.6 shows data obtained from measurements.

Table 7.6 Data for Example of Multiclass Open QNs.

Request Type	Avg. Arrival Rate (req./sec)	Avg. No. Packets per Request	Avg. Packet Length (bits)	Server Service Demand (sec)	
				CPU	Disk
Read	0.30	80	1403	0.030	0.263
Write	0.10	25	1206	0.015	0.102
Other	0.05	6	1019	0.005	0.030

Let us show how the response time for read and write requests varies as a function of the increase in the average arrival rate of read requests.

The average packet length $\overline{L}_p$ over all types of requests can be computed as follows.

$$\overline{L}_p = 1403 \times \frac{0.3}{0.3 + 0.1 + 0.05} + 1206 \times \frac{0.10}{0.3 + 0.1 + 0.05}$$
$$+ 1019 \times \frac{0.05}{0.3 + 0.1 + 0.05}$$
$$= 1317 \text{ bits/packet}$$

The average number of packets per request, P_{req}, is given by

$$P_{req} = 80 \times \frac{0.3}{0.3 + 0.1 + 0.05} + 25 \times \frac{0.1}{0.3 + 0.1 + 0.05} + 6 \times \frac{0.05}{0.3 + 0.1 + 0.05}$$
$$= 60 \text{ packets/request}$$

So the network service rate, in requests/sec, is equal to its service rate in packets/sec divided by the average number of packets per request. The service demand per class at the network can be computed as average number packets $\times$ average packet length/network bandwidth. This gives the values 11.2, 3.02, and 0.611 msec, respectively, for read, write, and other requests. Using the algorithm shown in Fig. 7.9 for various values of the arrival rate of read requests, we obtain the graph shown in Fig. 7.10. $\square$

Input Parameters: $D_{i,r}$'s, $\vec{\lambda}$, K, R, $\alpha_i(j)$'s, w_i's

Compute Utilizations

For $i := 1$ to K do For $r := 1$ to R do $U_{i,r} := \lambda_r D_{i,r}$

For $i := 1$ to K do $U_i := \sum_{r=1}^{R} U_{i,r}$

Check Stability Condition

If $\exists\, i$ such that $[U_i/\alpha_i(w_i)] \geq 1$ then stop;

Compute Queue Lengths

For $i := 1$ to K do

  Begin

   If device i is LD

   Then Begin

$$P_i(0 \mid \vec{\lambda}) = \left[\sum_{j=0}^{w_i} \frac{U_i^j}{\beta_i(j)} + \frac{[\alpha_i(w_i)]^{w_i}}{\beta_i(w_i)} \frac{[U_i/\alpha_i(w_i)]^{w_i+1}}{1 - U_i/\alpha_i(w_i)} \right]^{-1}$$

$$\overline{N}_i(\vec{\lambda}) = P_i(0 \mid \vec{\lambda})$$

$$\left\{ \sum_{j=1}^{w_i} j \frac{U_i^j}{\beta_i(j)} + \frac{U_i^{w_i+1}}{\beta_i(w_i)\,\alpha_i(w_i)} \right.$$

$$\left. \times \left[\frac{U_i/\alpha_i(w_i) + (w_i+1)\,(1 - U_i/\alpha_i(w_i))}{(1 - U_i/\alpha_i(w_i))^2} \right] \right\}$$

   End ;

   For $r := 1$ to R do

$$N_{i,r}(\vec{\lambda}) = \begin{cases} U_{i,r} & \text{delay device} \\ U_{i,r}/(1 - U_i) & \text{queuing LI device} \\ (U_{i,r}/U_i)\,\overline{N}_i(\vec{\lambda}) & \text{LD device} \end{cases}$$

  End;

Compute Residence Times per Class

For $i := 1$ to K do For $r := 1$ to R do

$$R'_{i,r}(\vec{\lambda}) = \begin{cases} D_{i,r} & \text{delay device} \\ D_{i,r}/(1 - U_i) & \text{queuing LI device} \\ N_{i,r}/\lambda_r & \text{LD device} \end{cases}$$

Compute Response Times per Class

For $r := 1$ to R do For $i := 1$ to K do $R_{0,r}(\vec{\lambda}) := \sum_{i=1}^{K} R'_{i,r}$

Compute Number in System per Class

For $r := 1$ to R do For $i := 1$ to K do $\overline{N}_r^s(\vec{\lambda}) := \sum_{i=1}^{K} N_{i,r}(\vec{\lambda})$

Figure 7.9 Multiple-class open QN algorithm with LD devices.

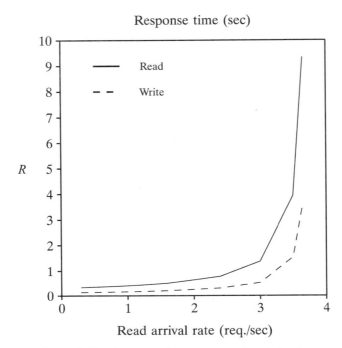

Response time (sec)

Read arrival rate (req./sec)

Figure 7.10   Response time versus read arrival rate.

7.9 CONCLUDING REMARKS

The techniques discussed in previous chapters were extended here to allow us to analyze the performance of client-server architectures. One of the important extensions is that of load-dependent servers as a means to model a local area network. Exact algorithms were presented for single class closed QNs with load-dependent servers and for single- and multiple-class open QNs with load-dependent servers. An approximate algorithm for multiple-class closed QNs was also given. Programs that implement these algorithms are provided with the disk that accompanies the book.

7.10 EXERCISES

1. Consider the CS model discussed in the telemarketing company problem and assume that the server will be upgraded by a two-processor server where each processor is identical to the original processor. If the same disk is used, solve the CS model assuming that the service rate, $\mu(j)$, for the server CPU is such that $\mu(2) = 1.8\mu(1)$.

2. An interactive computer system has M terminals used for a data-entry application. This application presents the user with a screen to be filled out before

submitting it to the mainframe for processing. The computing system has one CPU and two disks. The results of measurements taken during a 1 hour interval are shown in Table 7.7.

Table 7.7   Data for Exercise 2.

Number of requests completed	11,808
Number of terminals	100
U_{cpu}	0.26
U_{disk1}	0.41
U_{disk2}	0.33
Avg. response time (sec)	0.47

Main memory at the mainframe is such that at most 5 transactions may be executed simultaneously. The company intends to redesign the user interface to increase the productivity at each terminal so that the average think time may be reduced to 60% of its original value. Also, the company expects that the recovery of the economy will boost its business so that more terminals will be needed. Under this new scenario, determine the maximum number of terminals, M_{max}, the system will be able to handle before response time exceeds 3 sec. Plot a response time versus number of terminals curve. When the number of terminals is equal to M_{max}, how much of the transaction response time is spent in the computer system, and how much is spent queuing for memory? Compute the CPU and disk utilizations. What would be your recommendation for allowing the system to handle $1.2 \times M_{max}$ terminals while keeping the average response time at 3 sec? Justify your answer by using your model. In answering the questions above you should use MVA. To take memory queuing into account you should use MVA with load-dependent devices.

3. Show that Eqs. (7.23) and (7.24) are the solution to Eq. (7.22). [*Hint*: Using Eq. (7.22), write $P_i(1 \mid \vec{N})$ as a function of $P_i(0 \mid \vec{N})$. Then write $P_i(2 \mid \vec{N})$ in terms of $P_i(1 \mid \vec{N})$. Since $P_i(1 \mid \vec{N})$ is already known as a function of $P_i(0 \mid \vec{N})$, $P_i(2 \mid \vec{N})$ can be written as a function of $P_i(0 \mid \vec{N})$. If you continue this process one more step, you will be able to see what the general expression for $P_i(j \mid \vec{N})$ should be. $P_i(0 \mid \vec{N})$ can be computed by requiring that all probabilities sum to 1.]

4. The telemarketing company discussed in Sec. 7.2 posed the following problem to its capacity planner, Alice. Assume that the interaction time between the telemarketing representative and the customer could be cut down by 40% if the telemarketing representative had the capability of viewing digitized images of the products displayed in the catalog instead of having to browse the actual catalog to answer questions from the customer. This would require buying an additional disk to store the compressed digitized images. Consider that the additional service demand at this new disk is equal to 0.3 sec. Consider that each call requests two images, on the average, to be sent from the server to the client and that each compressed image is 100 Kbytes long. What is the minimum number of telemarketing representatives necessary to guarantee that each customer will not have to wait more than 5 sec on the average before being served?

5. Show that if device i is load-independent, Eqs. (7.32) and (7.33) reduce, as expected, to $P_i(j \mid \vec{\lambda}) = (1 - U_i) \, U_i^j$ for $j \geq 0$.
6. Use the fact that $\alpha_i(j) = \alpha_i(w_i)$ for $j \geq w_i$ in Eqs. (7.32), (7.33), and (7.31) to prove Eqs. (7.34), (7.35), and (7.36). (*Hint:* You will need to know that $\sum_{j=a}^{\infty} j\rho^j = \rho^a[\rho + a\,(1 - \rho)]/(1 - \rho)^2$ for $\rho < 1$.)
7. Consider the example given in Sec. 7.7. Assume that the number of workstations is to be doubled. The proportion of workstations that submit transactions of each type (trivial, average, and complex) will be kept constant, and so is the percentage of transactions of each type received by the server. Compute the new values of the response time and throughput. What would your recommendation be to guarantee that the response time for average transactions does not exceed 2 sec?

BIBLIOGRAPHY

1. A. Sinha, Client-server computing, *Communications of the ACM*, Vol. 35, No. 7, July 1992, pp. 77–98.
2. Sun Microsystems, *NFS: Network File System Protocol Specification; RFC 1094*, Network Working Group Request for Comments (RFC 1094), Network Information Center, SRI International, March 1989.
3. A. Silberschatz, J. Peterson, and P. Galvin, *Operating System Concepts*, 3rd ed., Addison-Wesley, Reading, Mass., 1991.
4. IBM Corporation, *IBM Local Area Network Technical Reference SC30-3383-2*, 1988.
5. Novell Inc., *Netware Loadable Module Library Reference*, Professional Development Series, C Network Compiler/386, Austin, Texas.
6. D. Comer, *Internetworking with TCP/IP: Principles, Protocols, and Architectures*, Prentice Hall, Englewood Cliffs, N.J., 1988.
7. J. B. Postel, User datagram protocol, *Internet Request for Comments RFC-768*, August, 1980.
8. IEEE, *Token Ring Access Method*, ANSI/IEEE Std. 802.5-1992; ISO/IEC IS 8802.5-1992., IEEE, Piscataway, N.J., 1992.
9. IEEE, *Carrier Sense Multiple Access with Collision Detection*, ANSI/IEEE Std. 802.3-1992; ISO/IEC IS 8802/3:1992, IEEE, Piscataway, N.J., 1992.
10. E. D. Lazowska, J. Zahorjan, D. Cheriton, and W. Zwaenepoel, File access performance of diskless workstations, *ACM Transactions on Computer Systems*, Vol. 4, No. 3, August 1986, pp. 238–268.
11. K. Smith, Caching techniques in distributed file systems: A survey, *CMG Transactions*, Winter 1990, pp. 93–98.
12. R. R. Bodnarchuk, R. B. Bunt, and K. Reid, The design and validation of a workload model for a distributed system file server, *Technical Report 91–2*, Laboratory for Performance Studies of Distributed Computing Systems, Department of Computational Science, University of Saskatchewan, Saskaton, Saskatchewan, June 1991.

13. J. K. Ousterhout, H. da Costa, D. Harrison, J. A. Kunze, M. Kupfer, and J. G. Thompson, A trace-driven analysis of the UNIX 4.2 BSD file system, *Proceedings of the 10th ACM Symposium on Operating Systems Principles*, Orcas Island, Wash., December 1–4, 1985, pp. 15–24.

14. Sun Microsystems, *Distributed File Service Networks—NFS Server Configuration, Performance Tuning, & Benchmarking Guide*, NFS Server Swat Team, February 1991.

15. B. Keith, Perspectives on NFS file server performance characterization, *USENIX Summer Conference Proceedings*, Anaheim, Calif., June 11–15, 1990, pp. 267–277.

16. K. Kant, *Introduction to Computer System Performance Evaluation*, McGraw-Hill, New York, 1992.

17. E. D. Lazowska, J. Zahorjan, G. S. Graham, and K. C. Sevcik, *Quantitative System Performance: Computer System Analysis Using Queuing Network Models*, Prentice Hall, Englewood Cliffs, N.J., 1984.

Chapter 8

Models of Practical Computer Systems

8.1 INTRODUCTION

Most practical computer systems exhibit features that violate the assumptions required by product-form networks. Some examples are memory queuing, CPU priority scheduling, and simultaneous resource possession (CPU and I/O concurrency). These features cannot be modeled directly by product-form networks. Thus, many algorithms have been developed to approximate the solution of models that incorporate non product-form features. These algorithms share the same basic idea. They accept a queuing network model that has some nonseparable features and transform it into an approximate network that obeys the BCMP conditions [1]. The approximate network has a product-form solution and gives approximate measures on the performance of the original model. The input parameters of the original model are either transformed by means of iterative process or by approximations that resemble the effects of the feature being modeled. Once the new parameters are obtained, an efficient algorithm calculates the performance measures of the approximate network. Some kind of transformation may be required to map the results of the approximate model back to the original one. The following sections present approximate techniques for modeling problems related to disk subsystems, memory queuing, processor scheduling, and multiprocessing.

8.2 MODELING MEMORY QUEUING

Multiprogramming is a central part of modern operating systems. It allows for several programs (jobs, transactions, processes, and requests) to be memory resident at the same time, sharing the system resources, such as processors and I/O devices. Most programs do not overlap their I/O and processing activities, so that while one program is making use of the processor, others are undergoing I/O processing. Therefore, multiprogramming leads to a better use of the system resources, by keeping I/O devices running concurrently with processors.

If the memory of a system were unlimited, its throughput would be a nondecreasing function of the multiprogramming level [2]. However, due to the finitude of real memory, the number of programs in execution may affect system performance. For example, in virtual memory systems, as the multiprogramming level increases, the paging and swapping activities also increase and may cause a reduction of throughput of productive work. Thus, there must be control of the maximum number of programs allowed to share memory at the same time. Usually, operating systems control the overall load by acting on the degree of multiprogramming. To illustrate the problem, consider the operation of a file server in a network environment. Usually, the file services are provided by a number of daemons (in UNIX terminology, daemons are processes not associated with any user but with systemwide functions) that run in the background waiting for service to appear. A number of daemons may be active simultaneously, executing several file service requests. This number depends on factors such as the available memory, the disk subsystem capacity, and the expected load on the server. When the number of requests being serviced reaches the maximum number of daemons, an arriving request must wait in the memory queue as illustrated in Fig. 8.1. When a request is completed, another request is selected from the memory queue to be executed in the system.

In a multiprogrammed system, jobs compete for resources. Before competing for processor and I/O devices, a job must acquire a memory partition or a scheduling token. Fig. 8.1 depicts a model of a system with memory constraint. The number of tokens available for the jobs is represented by the pool of tokens. If all partitions (or tokens) are occupied, an arriving job must wait. Once a job acquires a partition or token, it becomes ready to use processor and I/O components. In this case, the job holds two limited resources at the same time (i.e., processor-memory, I/O-memory), which represents a violation of the assumptions required by the product-form solution. After completing execution, the job releases the token, which is immediately assigned to a job in the memory queue. If the queue is empty, the token returns to the pool of available resources. Given that this model cannot be solved directly by the efficient algorithms (MVA and convolution) introduced in Chap. 5, an approximate solution is required. Techniques for solving non product-form models

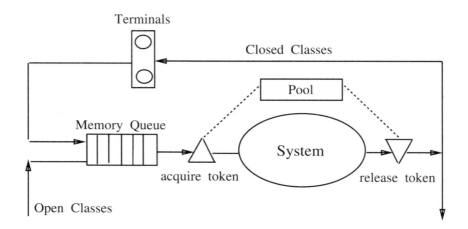

Figure 8.1 Models of system with memory constraints.

rely heavily on the use of the flow-equivalent concept, which was introduced in Chap. 5, as the decomposition/aggregation technique. We review and amplify that discussion in the next subsection.

8.2.1 Flow-Equivalent Method

Divide and conquer: This is a common approach to solving problems in computing. It also applies to solving non product-form networks. According to this principle, it is often efficient to solve a queuing network by partitioning it into several smaller subnetworks and then combining the solutions for the subnetworks into an approximate solution for the entire network. In the queuing network literature, this approach has been referred to as *decomposition and aggregation*. The basic idea here is to replace each subnetwork of queues by a single load-dependent queue, which is *flow-equivalent* to the subnetwork. To behave as the replaced subnetwork, the job flow through the single server must equal the job flow through the subnetwork. As a result, the mean service time of the single server given n jobs in the queue is $S(n) = 1/X(n)$, where $X(n)$ is the throughput of the subnetwork considered in isolation and under a constant load of n jobs. To specify the flow-equivalent server completely, we need to calculate the throughput of the subnetwork in isolation for each possible population size n.

When the flow-equivalent method is applied to closed single-class product-form models, it yields exact results [3]. In non product-form cases, some error is introduced. Courtois [4] has shown that little error is introduced with this approximation if the rate at which transitions occur within the subnetwork is much greater than the rate at which the subnetwork interacts with the rest of the network.

Example

Consider the queuing network model of Fig. 8.2, composed of one processor, three disks, and three jobs. The model parameters are: $S_0 = 0.1$ sec, $V_0 = 4$, $D_0 = 0.4$ sec, $S_1 = S_2 = S_3 = 1$ sec, $V_1 = V_2 = V_3 = 1$, $D_1 = D_2 = D_3 = 1$ sec, and $n = 3$. The goal of this example is to replace the I/O subsystem composed of three disks by a single load-dependent server using the flow-equivalent approach. The first step is the calculation of the throughput of the I/O subsystem in isolation, illustrated by Fig. 8.2b. For each job population ($n = 1, 2, 3$), we use the MVA algorithm to calculate the throughput of the disk subsystem; $X(1) = 0.333$ job/sec, $X(2) = 0.5$ job/sec, and $X(3) = 0.6$ job/sec. The mean service times of the flow-equivalent server are determined using the relation $S(n) = 1/X(n)$. Thus, $S(1) = 1/0.333 = 3$ sec, $S(2) = 1/0.5 = 2$ sec, and $S(3) = 1/0.6 = 1.667$ sec. The original system is then reduced to a network composed of the processor and the load-dependent server, as illustrated in Fig. 8.2c. As the original model has a product-form solution, the results calculated for the flow-equivalent model are exact. So if we use exact MVA (see Sec. 5.5) in the model of Fig. 8.2a and load-dependent MVA (see Sec. 7.7) in the model of Fig. 8.2c, we obtain the same results for the throughput and response time, namely 0.569 job/sec and 5.276 sec. □

8.2.2 Single Class

Consider a computer system with maximum multiprogramming level J, which indicates the maximum number of transactions that may be executed concurrently. When a transaction arrives and finds J transactions in execution, it has to wait outside the multiprogramming mix. When a transaction completes execution, another one, from the memory queue, is admitted in the

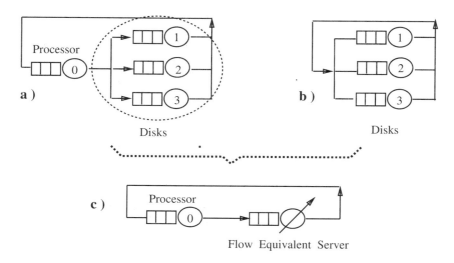

Figure 8.2 Flow-equivalent technique.

system. Let us use a single-class queuing model to represent the computer system with memory constraint. The workload consists of transactions processed by the system and can be modeled either by an open class (*transaction* type) or by a closed class (*interactive* type). In both cases, the memory constraint effects appear when the number of transactions to be executed exceeds the maximum multiprogramming level. This situation generates a memory queue, whose length varies with time. A *batch* class is treated as having a constant memory constraint, because the presence of a continuous backlog is assumed. However, its effects are not represented in the queuing model. When the multiprogramming level of a batch class (N_b) is not an integer, it means that the number of batch jobs in the system oscillates between two consecutive integers: the smallest integer greater than N_b and the greatest integer smaller than N_b. For instance, during the observation period of a computer system, the measured multiprogramming level of the batch class was 3.8. It indicates that the system had 4 batch jobs for most of the observation period and 3 jobs during the rest of the period. Performance measures of models with noninteger batch multiprogramming levels can be calculated directly by the approximate MVA algorithm. The solution of single-class models with memory queuing is typical of many other non product-form models. It proceeds in five steps.

1. Consider the computer system in isolation, ignoring the external arrivals of transactions.

2. For each feasible customer population (i.e., from 0 to J transactions), solve the model in isolation and obtain the throughput as a function of the population, $X(n)$, $n = 0, 1, 2, \ldots, J$. Use either the MVA or the convolution algorithm to solve the model.

3. Define a flow-equivalent server to replace the computer system. The service time of the flow-equivalent server depends on the load of the system and is given by:

$$S_{\text{FE}}(n) = \begin{cases} 1/X(n) & n \leq J \\ \\ 1/X(J) & n > J \end{cases}$$

4. Create a reduced model with the flow-equivalent server and the external workload. Fig. 8.3 shows the reduced models for the two representations of the workload. For an interactive workload, the reduced model is closed with population equal to M, the number of terminals or workstations associated with the class. In addition to the flow-equivalent server, the model has a delay server that represents the average think time (Z). The interactive model can be viewed as having M transactions, which alternate between execution in the flow-equivalent server and thinking in the delay server. The reduced model of the transaction class is an open model with a flow-equivalent server and arrival rate λ.

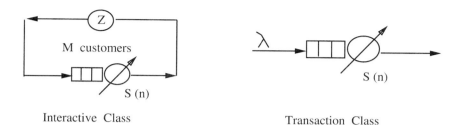

Interactive Class   Transaction Class

Figure 8.3 Reduced models of a system with memory queuing.

5. Solve the reduced model. The closed model can be solved using the single-class MVA algorithm with load-dependent devices, described in Chap. 7. The solution of the open model follows that of the birth-death model, also provided in Chap. 7.

Example

A database server consists of a processor and two large disks (D1 and D2). It is responsible for processing transactions that access the database. For workload characterization purposes, the transactions are grouped into a single class, which means that they are somehow similar. A typical transaction is characterized by the following service demands: $D_{cpu} = 0.1$ sec and $D_{D1} = D_{D2} = 0.45$ sec. The arrival rate is $\lambda = 1$ tps. Due to the installed capacity of the server, the maximum multiprogramming level was set to three (i.e., $J = 3$). The performance analyst wants to evaluate the effect of the memory constraint on the transaction response time. In other words, the model should be able to calculate the percentage of the response time that a transaction spends waiting for memory ($\%w$).

To answer the question, we need to calculate the average response time (R_s) and the average waiting time (R_w) for memory. From Little's result, we have

$$R_s = N_s/\lambda \qquad (8.1)$$

$$R_w = N_w/\lambda$$

$$\%w = (R_w \times 100)/R_s = (N_w \times 100)/N_s$$

where N_s is the average number of transactions in the system and N_w is the average number of transactions waiting for memory.

By following the steps to solve a non product-form model, we first calculate the server throughput in isolation, for all possible populations. In this case, because of the memory constraint, the server can have at most three transactions in execution ($n = 1, 2, 3$). Using the single-class MVA algorithm (Chap. 5), we obtain the following: $X(1) = 1$, $X(2) = 1.413$, and $X(3) = 1.623$. These results allow us to define a flow-equivalent server for the database system. Now we have to solve the reduced model, which is an open system with a load-dependent server and arrival rate λ. Using the results introduced in Sec. 7.5 for birth-death models, we are able to calculate P_k, the probability that there are k transactions in the system. Thus, letting $\lambda_i = \lambda$ and

$\mu_i = X(i)$, the probabilities $P_0 = 0.260$, $P_1 = 0.260$, $P_2 = 0.184$, and $P_3 = 0.113$ are obtained. An expression for the average number (N_w) of transactions waiting in the memory queue is also available in Sec. 7.5. Using the values calculated for P_k, we obtain $N_w = 0.474$. The average number of transactions in the system is given by

$$N_s = N_w + N_m \tag{8.2}$$

where N_m is the average number of transactions in memory (i.e., in multiprogrammed execution).

$$N_m = \sum_{k=1}^{J} k\,P_k + J \sum_{k>J} P_k = \sum_{k=1}^{J} k\,P_k + J \left(1 - \sum_{k=0}^{J} P_k \right) \tag{8.3}$$

Plugging the values of P_k and J into Eq. (8.3), we have $N_m = 1.516$. Thus, the average number of transactions in the system is 1.99 and the percentage of time that a typical transaction spends in the memory queue is $\%w = (0.474 \times 100)/1.99 = 23.8\%$. □

8.2.3 Multiple Classes

We have seen in Chap. 6 the importance of multiple-class models for capacity planning. Therefore, we need to generalize the solution of memory-constrained models to multiple classes. The queuing network models considered here contain K service centers and a number R of different classes of customers. Among the customer classes, C classes ($C \leq R$) have memory constraints, specified by the maximum multiprogramming level of each class, J_c, $c = 1, 2, \ldots, C$. For example, consider a simple two-class model with a processor and two disks. The workload consists of two classes of transactions: queries (q) and updates (u). The execution mix can have at most four queries and one update simultaneously (i.e., $J_q = 3$ and $J_u = 1$). The two classes are characterized by their arrival rates, $\lambda_q = 4.20$ tps and $\lambda_u = 0.20$ tps. Typical capacity planning questions are: What is the effect of the amount of available memory on the system performance? What will be the effect on the response time if the memory is doubled? To answer these questions, we need first to introduce approximate solution techniques for the memory queuing problem.

Brandwajn [5] and Menascé and Almeida [6] independently developed a noniterative solution technique for multiple-class models with memory constraints. Basically, the technique requires the calculation of throughputs for all possible combinations of customer populations. These throughputs feed a series of single-class models, whose results are then combined into the solution of the original problem. Although accurate, the technique has a high computational cost. An iterative approximation, developed by Brandwajn [5] and Lazowska and Zahorjan [7], circumvents the problem of computing throughputs for all populations. However, as pointed out in Ref. [8], the iterative algorithm tends to be less accurate than the first technique. The basic approach of the iterative technique developed in Ref. [7] is to reduce a multiclass model to a set of single-class models. To achieve this goal, two assumptions are introduced.

- *Independence.* It is assumed that the average class i population in the constrained model is independent of class j $(i \neq j)$ population.

- *Average Population.* It is assumed that the throughput of class i given n_i customers in the model depends only on the average population of the other classes.

The first assumption allows the creation of flow-equivalent servers for each constrained class c $(c = 1, 2, \ldots, C)$. The second assumption avoids the calculation of throughputs for all possible population configurations. The throughput of a given class i with population n_i, $X_i(n_i)$, is obtained from the evaluation of the multiclass model with n_i class i customers and with other class populations fixed at their average values, $n_j = \bar{n}_j$, $j \neq i$. The average customer population can be obtained by an iterative process that evaluates the single-class model of each constrained class. The full description of the algorithm proposed by Lazowska and Zahorjan [7] for multiple-class population constrained models is as follows.

1. Initialize the average population of each memory-constrained class. To obtain an initial estimate for the average population of each constrained class, solve the original multiclass models without memory constraints. If class c is of type *transaction* it should be modeled as an open class. If class c is of type *interactive* it should be modeled as a closed class. The techniques for solving the unconstrained model are given in Chap. 6 for closed, open, and mixed multiclass queuing networks. For each memory constrained class, set the estimate $\bar{n}_c$ to the minimum between J_c and the average class c population obtained by solving the unconstrained model. Thus, the outcome of this step is a set of estimates for $\bar{n}_c$.

2. Create a transformed multiclass model. The type of a memory-constrained class is either *transaction* or *interactive*. Change the original type to *batch*, with population equal to $\bar{n}_c$. The unconstrained classes remain unchanged.

3. For each memory-constrained class $c = 1, \ldots, C$ do:

   (a) Calculate the throughputs $X_c(n_c)$ for $n_c = 1, \ldots, J_c$. These throughputs are obtained through the solution of the transformed multiclass model when $\bar{n}_c$ is substituted for $1, 2, \ldots, J_c$. The population for class s $(s \neq c)$ remains fixed at $\bar{n}_s$. The model has to be solved J_c times.

   (b) Define a single-class model with memory queuing and throughputs $X_c(n_c)$.

   (c) Using the FESC-based algorithm of Sec. 8.2.2, solve the single-class model.

   (d) Using Eq. (8.3), calculate $N_{m,c}$, the average number of class c customers in memory. Let $\bar{n}_c = N_{m,c}$.

4. Repeat step 3 until successive values of $\bar{n}_c$ are sufficiently close (i.e., the percentage difference between successive iterations is smaller than a set tolerance).

5. Obtain performance results for the C constrained classes from the solution of the C single-class models of step 3.

6. Obtain performance results for the $(C - R)$ unconstrained classes from the solution of the transformed multiclass model (step 2), which take as input parameter for the memory-constrained classes the final values for $\bar{n}_c$, obtained in step 3.

Example

Consider again the simple two-class model described in the beginning of this section. Table 8.1 displays the parameters that characterize the model.

Table 8.1 Input Parameters for the Two-Class Model.

| Class | Service Demand (sec) | | | Arrival Rate, λ | Maximum MPL, J |
	Processor	Disk 1	Disk 2		
Query	0.105	0.180	0	4.20	4
Update	0.375	0.480	0.240	0.20	1

Step 1 of the algorithm requires us to solve an open multiclass unconstrained model as given in Chap. 6. The resulting values of the average population are 6.0192 and 0.8540 transactions for classes query and update, respectively. So $\bar{n}_Q$ and $\bar{n}_U$ are initialized as $\bar{n}_Q = \min\{4, 6.0192\} = 4$ and $\bar{n}_U = \min\{1, 0.8540\} = 0.8540$. Table 8.2 shows the first four iterations of step 3 of the algorithm.

Table 8.2 First Four Iterations for Multiclass Example.

| Iteration | Query | | | | | Update | |
	$X_Q(1)$	$X_Q(2)$	$X_Q(3)$	$X_Q(4)$	$\bar{n}_Q$	$X_U(1)$	$\bar{n}_U$
1	2.542	3.577	4.115	4.434	3.648	0.342	0.585
2	2.789	3.835	4.350	4.645	3.355	0.381	0.525
3	2.850	3.897	4.407	4.695	3.289	0.386	0.518
4	2.857	3.904	4.412	4.700	3.282	0.386	0.518

The columns labeled $X_Q(1)$ through $X_Q(4)$ display the throughputs obtained in step 3a for class *query*, and the column labeled $X_U(1)$ shows the throughput obtained in the same step for class *update*. The columns labeled $\bar{n}_Q$ and $\bar{n}_U$ display the values obtained in step 3d derived from the solution of a FESC model for classes *query* and *update*, respectively. For instance, if we wanted to stop at iteration 4, the response time for *update* transactions would be obtained by dividing the average number of transactions in the system (N_s) obtained by solving the FESC model (1.077 in this case) by the average arrival rate (0.2 tps). The resulting response time would then be 5.83 sec. Table 8.3 shows the solution of this example for a tolerance of 10^{-2}.

Table 8.3 Response Time Profile per Service Center.

Class	Response Time (sec)				
	Average	Memory	Processor	Disk 1	Disk 2
Query	2.17	1.39	0.19	0.59	-
Update	5.36	2.77	0.68	1.67	0.24

We note from this table that an update transaction spends, on the average, 51.74% of the response time waiting for memory. It is clear that the system is short of memory. Using the same model, one would be able to investigate what would be the effect of a memory expansion on the performance of update transactions. Assume that the maximum multiprogramming level of update transactions is doubled. Thus, letting $J_u = 2$ and solving the model again, we obtain 3.09 and 2.33 sec for the average response times of updates and queries, respectively. In this case, an update transaction would spend only 0.29 sec waiting for memory. With the removal of the memory bottleneck, disk 1 will become the new bottleneck. □

8.3 MODELING DISK SUBSYSTEMS

Contemporary disk subsystems involve several components between a disk unit and main memory. String controllers, control units, and channels are some of these components whose function is to improve the performance and reliability of I/O subsystems. Thus far, the performance models considered have been composed of service centers representing only processors and disks. Based on this observation, the reader may be wondering if queuing models ignore important components of real systems. Fortunately, they do not. Components of an I/O subsystem are represented implicitly in the values of the disk service demands.

Although queuing models do account for the time spent on the components of an I/O architecture, there is still a problem with this way of representing an I/O subsystem. As an example, consider a computer system with one processor, one disk controller, and eight disks, connected to a single I/O channel. Due to the poor response time, the analyst decided to investigate the performance of the I/O subsystem. Having identified the channel as the bottleneck, the analyst wishes to use a model to assess the cost/benefit of installing one additional channel and disk controller to split the disk drives evenly into two independent strings. Therefore, the question is: How could the proposed modification be represented in the performance model? A possible answer is to change the disk service demands accordingly. But in what amount? Clearly, we need techniques to quantify the contributions of each I/O component to the formation of disk service demands. The purpose of this section is to show how to estimate the delays associated with the main components of an I/O subsystem. Once the delays are calculated, one would be able to express a modification to the I/O architecture in terms of changes of service demands.

8.3.1 I/O Subsystem Architecture

An I/O subsystem is a set of components responsible for controlling and executing I/O operations. Disk drives are connected to main memory via a series of devices that form the I/O interface. The complexity of an I/O interface varies as a function of its performance, reliability, and cost. For instance, a low-end workstation could have an SCSI interface (*small computer system interface*) to connect a disk unit directly to the CPU. A file server could have a separate SCSI disk controller to support a number of disk drives [9], as illustrated in Fig. 8.4.

Mainframes typically have complex I/O interfaces, composed of several control devices. Figure 8.5 exhibits the structure and main components of a typical I/O architecture for mainframes. Moving outward the memory, the first component is a *channel*, which provides a communication path between memory and I/O devices. A channel is busy when it is transferring data. The next component is the *control unit* or *disk controller*, also called the *storage director* in the IBM terminology. A control unit decodes the device specific I/O commands (e.g., seek and transfer) into control signals for the associated disks. It also makes the connection between many channels and many disks. A string of disks is attached to a device called *head of string (HOS)* or *string controller*, which is responsible for controlling communications between control units and disks. The outermost component of the I/O subsystem is the disk unit, which can be viewed as a single server that services one request at a time. An *I/O path* is a physical connection between memory and an I/O device. In the case of Fig. 8.5, it includes a channel, a control unit, and a head of string. A path is considered busy if any part of it is busy. To improve availability and performance, I/O subsystems have redundant paths from memory to I/O devices. Switching devices placed at the level of the head of string (called the string switch) and at the control unit level (called the channel switch)

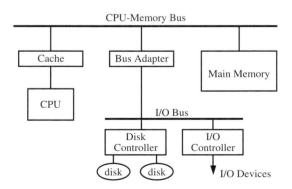

Figure 8.4 Typical I/O architecture.

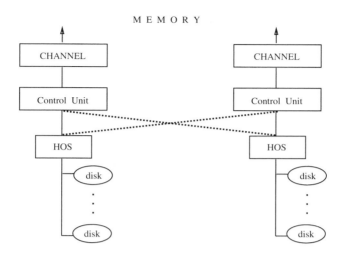

Figure 8.5 Typical I/O subsystem architecture for mainframes.

provide multiple and redundant paths to disk units. In Fig. 8.5, the dashed lines indicate the existence of a string switch that allows a disk to be accessed by the two channels. The control devices shared by a number of disk drives provide multiple pathways between memory and disks.

The basic disk service time consists of three parts: seek time, latency time, and data transfer time. The seek time corresponds to the time required to move the read/write heads over the desired position. A disk unit is capable of doing this operation independently, which means that during the seek, the control unit, string controller, and channel are free to take on other activities. Once the read/write heads have moved into place, the device has to wait until a particular sector of the disk comes under the heads. This time is referred to as *latency*. Old disk models required a full path dedicated to this operation.

Disks with a feature called *rotational position sensing* (RPS) allow the channel, control unit, and head of string to be free during the latency time. When an RPS-disk is just about to have the data under the heads, it contacts the control devices to establish an I/O path to transfer the data. If any of the devices of the I/O path is busy at that instant (transferring data on behalf of other disk units), the disk must wait a complete revolution until the data are in position again. This situation is known as an *RPS miss*. The RPS reconnect delay arises from the lack of buffers in the disk and from the timing constraints of the operation. Depending on the number of misses, the RPS reconnect time may become too long, degrading disk performance. It is clear that the reconnect time is a function of the load on the I/O subsystem. The busier the paths, the higher the number of RPS misses. The third component of the service time corresponds to the time to transfer the data between the device and main memory. The magnitude of the three components of disk service time varies according to the device's cost and performance. But in general, seek time is much longer than transfer time. Depending on the I/O load, RPS reconnect time can be longer than seek time.

One important capability found in modern disks is that of connecting and disconnecting from the I/O path. Most disks support independent seek and latency operations, which leads to an overlap of multiple I/O operations, increasing the overall I/O throughput. There is a trend toward intelligent devices [10, 11], which absorb part of the functions performed by I/O controllers. For example, there are SCSI-compatible drives that incorporate low-level tasks from the control unit and relax time constraints by queuing the desired data into track buffers. This type of drive does not suffer from the RPS problem. Thus, on a SCSI string, various disks can be active simultaneously. For example, a number of disks can be seeking and others filling their track buffer while only one is transferring data between its buffer and main memory, over the SCSI bus.

8.3.2 I/O Service Time

In general, the service demand of disk i is calculated using the following equation:

$$D_i = V_i S_i = \frac{U_i \times T}{C_0} \tag{8.4}$$

where U_i indicates the utilization of disk i, T the monitoring period, and C_0 the number of I/O operations carried out during T. The product $U_i \times T$ represents the time that disk i was busy. U_i and C_0 are obtained from measurement data collected from the system being modeled. A disk is considered busy while the I/O operation lasts. Thus, all delays that occur during the execution of an I/O operation are accounted for in the busy time of the disk. Timing analysis of the execution of a typical I/O operation leads to the identification of four main elements:

1. *Queuing time*, which is the waiting time due to the fact that the device is already busy servicing other I/O requests.

2. *Basic service time*, which corresponds to the time required to perform the device operations (i.e., seek, latency, and transfer).

3. *Delays*, which are caused by blocking and queuing within the I/O subsystem. For example, if the channel is busy, the reconnect after a seek operation is delayed. RPS delays are also examples of this type of delay.

4. *Controller time*, which is the overhead required by control devices to perform a disk I/O operation.

The disk service time comprises items 2 through 4. Part of the service time is due to basic work being performed by the disk unit (i.e., seek, latency, and transfer operations). This part does not depend on the load of the system. In a noncontention system, the I/O service time is reduced to this component. The rest of the disk service time consists of delays due to contention in the I/O subsystem. Item 3 represents the queuing time for common I/O paths that are shared by multiple-disk units. This component is variable and depends on the contention for the resources of the I/O path. The higher the load on the I/O subsystem, the longer the queuing delays. The queuing time described in item 1 is not part of the disk service time. As a matter of fact, queuing time plus disk service time form the disk response time, which can be calculated by performance models.

When one monitors the operation of a computer system and measures the disk busy time, we get the disk service time, which includes the basic service time plus the contention time. In actuality, what is obtained from measurement data is called effective service time and can be viewed as a combination of two parts:

effective service time   =   basic service time   +   contention time

where "contention time" refers to the delays described in items 3 and 4 above. Assuming that input parameters for a queuing network model are based on effective service times, it is clear that the components of an I/O subsystem are all represented implicitly in the model. In light of the definition of effective service time, Eq. (8.4) can be rewritten as follows:

$$D_i = V_i S_i = V_i(\text{seek}_i + \text{latency}_i + \text{transfer}_i + \text{contention}_i) \qquad (8.5)$$

8.3.3 Estimating Delays within the I/O Subsystem

We notice from Eq. (8.5) that contention is one of the components of effective service demands. To assess the effect of each I/O element on the disk service demand, we need to learn how to estimate the delays associated with each I/O element. This is the purpose of this section.

RPS reconnect delay.   In the case of the RPS feature, the disk attempts to reconnect to the I/O path. If the channel/path is busy, the disk unit waits one full revolution until the data are under the heads and then again attempts to reconnect. This step is repeated until an attempt succeeds. Thus, the waiting time in this step is an integral multiple of a full disk revolution time. The first step to calculate the RPS reconnect delay is determining NRPS_i, the average number of missed reconnects before a successful connect by disk i.

Let $P_i(\text{path busy})$ denote the probability that the I/O path for disk i is busy. $P_i(\text{path busy})$ is also the probability that a reconnect fails and

$1 - P_i$(path busy) the probability of a successful reconnect. Considering that reconnect attempts are independent, we can write that the probability of having k RPS misses is $[1 - P_i(\text{path busy})] \times [P_i(\text{path busy})]^k$. The average number of misses is then given by:

$$\text{NRPS}_i = \sum_{k=1}^{\infty} k[1 - P_i(\text{path busy})] \times [P_i(\text{path busy})]^k$$

$$= \frac{P_i(\text{path busy})}{1 - P_i(\text{path busy})} \tag{8.6}$$

Multiplying the average number of missed reconnects by the rotation time of disk i, we obtain the average RPS delay, DRPS_i.

$$\text{DRPS}_i = \text{NRPS}_i \times \text{rotation}_i \tag{8.7}$$

To complete the analysis of the RPS delay, we need to determine P_i(path busy), the probability of having the I/O path of disk i busy. Initially, let us assume that the channel is the major delay component of an I/O path, so that the delays caused by the other elements of the pathway are negligible. As a result, the I/O path can be viewed as being the channel. In this case, we have

$$P_i(\text{path busy}) = P_i'(\text{channel busy}) \tag{8.8}$$

where P_i'(channel busy) is the probability that disk i *sees* the channel busy. This is slightly different from the probability of the channel being busy, which is equal to the channel utilization, U_{ch}. The probability P_i'(channel busy) refers to situations when the disk is not using the I/O path and is potentially capable of attempting to connect the path (i.e., when *disk i is not transferring data*) [12]. Thus,

$$P_i'(\text{channel busy}) = P_i(\text{channel busy} \mid \text{disk } i \text{ not transferring data}) \tag{8.9}$$

From the definition of conditional probability, $P(A|B) = P(A \cap B)/P(B)$. From Eq. (8.9), we have that

$$P_i'(\text{channel busy}) = \frac{P_i(\text{channel busy} \cap \text{disk } i \text{ not transferring data})}{P_i(\text{disk } i \text{ not transferring data})} \tag{8.10}$$

We have seen that a system is considered busy when one or more customers are in the system, which is indicated by the utilization of the server. Thus, we have

$$P_i'(\text{channel busy}) = \frac{[\sum_{k=1}^{K} U_{\text{ch}}(k)] - U_i(\text{transferring})}{1 - U_i(\text{transferring})} \tag{8.11}$$

where $\sum_{k=1}^{K} U_{\text{ch}}(k)$ represents the utilization of the channel by all the K devices attached to it. When disk i is transferring data, it is using the channel, which means that the time disk i is dedicated to transferring data is equal to the time the channel is busy transferring data on behalf of disk i. Thus, we can say that utilization of disk i, due to transfers, $U_i(\text{transferring})$, is equal to utilization of the channel due to the transfers of disk i, $U_{\text{ch}}(i)$. Letting $U_{\text{ch}} = \sum_{k=1}^{K} U_{\text{ch}}(k)$ and substituting Eq. (8.11) in Eq. (8.6), we have

$$\text{NRPS}_i = \frac{U_{\text{ch}} - U_{\text{ch}}(i)}{1 - U_{\text{ch}}} \tag{8.12}$$

So far in this analysis, we have viewed an I/O path as composed of only one element: a channel. Now, let us extend the results to include a disk controller in the I/O path. Through switching devices, a channel may be shared by several controllers. The approach adopted here to calculate reconnect delays taking into consideration the effect of disk controllers is based on Lazowska et al. [12]. To determine the average number of misses [Eq. (8.6)], we need first to estimate the probability that the I/O path is busy, which is given by

$$P_i(\text{path busy}) = P_i'(\text{controller busy})$$
$$+ P_i'(\text{controller free and channel busy}) \tag{8.13}$$

where $P_i'(E)$ represents the probability of event E as seen by device i. Following the procedure used in this section to calculate $P_i'(\text{channel busy})$, we have

$$P_i'(\text{controller busy}) = \frac{\left[\sum_{k=1}^{K} U_{\text{ctr}}(k)\right] - U_{\text{ctr}}(i)}{1 - U_i(\text{transferring})} \tag{8.14}$$

where $\sum_{k=1}^{K} U_{\text{ctr}}(k)$ is the utilization of the controller by all disks connected to it and $U_{\text{ctr}}(i)$ is the utilization due to disk i. The $P_i'(\text{controller free and channel busy})$ term in Eq. (8.13) can be rewritten as

$P_i(\text{controller free and channel busy} \mid \text{disk } i \text{ not transferring})$

$$= \frac{P_i(\text{controller free and channel busy and disk } i \text{ not transferring})}{P_i(\text{disk } i \text{ not transferring})} \tag{8.15}$$

When the controller is free, disk i is not transferring, because the controller is part of its I/O path. Thus,

$$P_i'(\text{controller free and channel busy}) = \frac{U_{\text{ch}} - U_{\text{ch}}(\text{ctr})}{1 - U_i(\text{transferring})} \tag{8.16}$$

where $U_{\text{ch}}(\text{ctr})$ is the channel utilization due to the controller in question. Combining Eqs. (8.14) and (8.16) and substituting $U_i(\text{transferring})$ for $U_{\text{ch}}(i)$, we obtain the probability that the I/O path for disk i is busy.

$$P_i(\text{path busy}) = \frac{U_{\text{ch}} - U_{\text{ch}}(\text{ctr}) + U_{\text{ctr}} - U_{\text{ctr}}(i)}{1 - U_{\text{ch}}(i)} \tag{8.17}$$

Substituting for $P_i(\text{path busy})$ in Eq. (8.6), we obtain the average number of missed reconnects for the case of an I/O path represented by the channel and disk controller. In a similar way, extensions can be made to incorporate other elements in the calculation of P_i(path busy).

Channel contention. Consider the case of intelligent disks that are capable of performing seek and latency independently and have track buffers for queuing results. These disks do not suffer from RPS problems. However, a disk may still have to wait while the channel (or I/O bus) is busy transferring data of other disks. This kind of delay arises due to channel contention. The problem here is to estimate this delay. An approximate method for calculating the delay is to view the channel as an open single server, receiving requests from disks that want to transfer data. When disk i attempts to seize the channel to transfer data, it may find a number of requests from other disks waiting for the channel. In an open system with a single server (see Chap. 4), the average queue length seen by an arriving customer is $U/(1 - U)$, where U is the system utilization. As the channel is being viewed as an open system, the average number of requests (NCH$_i$) seen by disk i is given by

$$\text{NCH}_i = \frac{P_i'(\text{channel busy})}{1 - P_i'(\text{channel busy})} \quad (8.18)$$

Considering that each disk can only have one I/O request at a time, P_i'(channel busy) represents the probability that the channel is busy given that disk i is not transferring data. Therefore, by following the procedure used previously, we have

$$\text{NCH}_i = \frac{U_{\text{ch}} - U_{\text{ch}}(i)}{1 - U_{\text{ch}}} \quad (8.19)$$

Assuming that *transfer* is the average time for transferring data over the channel, we can express the average waiting time (TCH$_i$) of disk i due to contention as:

$$\text{TCH}_i = \text{NCH}_i \times \text{transfer} \quad (8.20)$$

This analysis can be extended in a straightforward manner to other elements of an I/O path. A detailed treatment of RPS, multipathing, and other features of IBM I/O technology can be found in Refs. [13] and [12].

Example

Consider a database server with a processor and an I/O subsystem consisting of an I/O bus (i.e., the channel), a disk controller, and two disk drives (A and B). The server executes on the average 2 transactions per second. A typical transaction requires 0.2 sec of CPU and performs 8 I/O operations on disk A and 14 on disk B. The size of the block transferred in each operation is 0.5 Kbytes. The disks rotate at 3600 rpm (rotations per minute), the advertised average seek time is 15 msec, the transfer rate is 2 Mbytes/sec, and the controller overhead is 1 msec. We want to calculate the average transaction response time for three models corresponding to situations that:

1. Ignore contention within the I/O subsystem

2. Consider contention and assume that the disks have the RPS feature
3. Consider contention and assume that the disks have a track buffer

Before constructing an analytical open model to represent server performance, the first step is to determine the disk demands for each situation under analysis. The basic service time of a disk is

$$S_b = \text{seek} + \text{latency} + \text{transfer} \tag{8.21}$$

The latency is typically considered to be one half of the disk rotation period (i.e., $1/2 \times 1/3600 = 8.3$ msec). The average transfer time for 512 bytes equals $0.5/2 = 0.25$ msec. Plugging these values into Eq. (8.21), we have

$$S_b = 15 + 8.3 + 0.25 = 23.55 \text{ msec}$$

The effective service time can then be expressed as

$$S_{\text{ef}} = S_b + \text{controller time} + \text{contention} = 24.55 + \text{contention} \tag{8.22}$$

The problem now is to estimate contention for the three situations of the example. In the first case, we ignore contention and $S_{\text{ef}} = 24.55$. The service demands for disks A and B are $24.55 \times 8 = 196$ msec and $24.55 \times 14 = 343.7$ msec, respectively.

For the RPS disks, let us proceed to calculate DRPS_i, the average RPS delay for disk i. To do that, we first need to estimate the average number of misses, NRPS_i. The channel utilization due to disk i is $U_{\text{ch}}(i) = X_0 \times V_i \times$ transfer time. Thus, $U_{\text{ch}}(A) = 2 \times 8 \times 0.25 = 4\%$, $U_{\text{ch}}(B) = 2 \times 14 \times 0.25 = 7\%$, and the total channel utilization is $U_{\text{ch}} = 11\%$. Using Eq. (8.6), we obtain

$$\text{NRPS}_A = \frac{0.11 - 0.04}{1 - 0.11} = 0.079$$

$$\text{NRPS}_B = \frac{0.11 - 0.07}{1 - 0.11} = 0.045$$

The average delays for the two disks are $\text{DRPS}_A = 0.079 \times 16.6 = 1.311$ msec and $\text{DRPS}_B = 0.045 \times 16.6 = 0.747$ msec. With the RPS reconnect delays estimated, we are able to calculate the effective service time and consequently, the disk demands. Thus, $D_A = (24.55 + 1.311) \times 8 = 206.89$ msec and $D_B = (24.55 + 0.747) \times 14 = 354.16$ msec.

Disks with track buffer do not suffer from the RPS problem, because they store the desired data into local buffers. However, contention for the I/O bus remains. Using Eq. (8.20), we determine the average waiting time of a disk due to bus contention. $\text{TCH}_A = 0.079 \times 0.25 = 0.0198$ msec and $\text{TCH}_B = 0.045 \times 0.25 = 0.0113$ msec. The disk service demands for this case are as follows: $D_A = (24.55 + 0.0198) \times 8 = 196.56$ msec and $D_B = (24.55 + 0.0113) \times 14 = 343.86$ msec. Recall from Chap. 6 the equation $R_i = D_i/(1 - U_i)$, which gives the response time of server i in an open model. Using this equation, we obtain the performance results shown in Table 8.4. We notice from Table 8.4 that ignoring the RPS reconnect delay leads to optimistic results. The response time of the result that represents the RPS effect is about 8.3% higher than the model that ignores the I/O feature. In this example, because transfer time is much smaller than rotation time, the delay caused by bus contention is insignificant when compared to the RPS delay. Two comments are worth noting.

Table 8.4 Performance Results of Three Models of an I/O Subsystem.

Case	Response Time (sec)			
	R_{cpu}	R_A	R_B	R_{total}
No contention	0.333	0.322	1.099	1.754
RPS disks	0.333	0.353	1.214	1.900
Disks with buffer	0.333	0.324	1.102	1.759

1. In this example, we have used information that is typically provided by disk manufacturers, such as average seek time, transfer rate, and rotational speed. Using information from product specification is like a double-edge sword. On one hand, it facilitates the process of obtaining input parameters for models. On the other hand, manufacturer information may not reflect the behavior of a disk when processing real workloads. For example, when one takes the advertised average seek time, we may be overestimating the basic service demand. The reason stems from the spatial and temporal locality found in the pattern of disk accesses of a real workload. It has been observed [10] in real workloads that the great majority of seeks concentrate on short distances. The simplest way to estimate the average transfer time is to divide the average number of bytes transferred by the transfer rate. In actuality, this simple procedure introduces some error, because it ignores the several bytes of control information that are transferred with each block of data. There are alternative ways to obtain the basic service time of a disk. For example, transfer time can be estimated from measurement data using the following relation: average transfer $= U_{\text{ch}}/(V\, X_0)$. Channel utilization, number of I/O operations (V) executed by a channel, and system throughput are usually provided by software monitors and accounting systems, as discussed in Chap. 9. Once you have obtained the average transfer time and latency, the average seek time can be estimated using the following equation:

$$\text{seek}_i = \frac{D_i}{V_i} - \text{latency}_i - \text{transfer}_i - \text{contention}_i \qquad (8.23)$$

where D_i and V_i are measurement data and contention can be calculated by the techniques described in this section.

2. The example concerns an open system whose load is characterized by an arrival rate. Considering the system in operational equilibrium, we know that the arrival rate equals the throughput. Knowing the throughput in advance makes easy calculation of the contention within the I/O subsystem, as indicated by the equations of Sec. 8.3.3. However, there are systems that are better represented by closed models, where the throughput is not known until the model is solved. In the next section we detail an iterative technique to estimate I/O delays in closed models. □

8.3.4 Modeling I/O Contention in Closed Systems

In Sec. 8.3.3 we showed how one can determine the delays associated with channel contention and RPS reconnect delay. These delays were computed as a function of the utilization of the channel, which can be obtained from the throughput by using the forced flow law and the utilization law. For instance, using the utilization law, the channel utilization, U_{ch}, may be written as

$$U_{ch} = X_{ch} \times \text{average transfer time}$$

where X_{ch} is the channel throughput. Using the forced flow law, we get that

$$U_{ch} = X_0 \times \text{average number of transfers} \times \text{average transfer time}$$

If the system is being modeled as a closed queuing network, the throughput X_0 is not known ahead of time. In fact, this is one of the performance metrics computed by the algorithm. But to solve the model, we need the throughput to be able to compute the delays associated with various I/O system components. This seems like an impasse. These situations arise very often in performance modeling situations. To break the impasse, we use an iterative procedure in which an initial value for the throughput is assumed (zero for instance) and the delays associated with the I/O components are computed. The closed queuing network is then solved and a new value of the throughput is obtained. This new value is used to recompute the I/O delay figures, and the process iterates until successive values for the throughput are sufficiently close. More precisely, the iterative procedure is:

1. (Initialization) $i \leftarrow 0$; $X_0^i = 0$.

2. Compute disk demands by using the expressions that take into account the appropriate contention factors (e.g., channel contention, RPS reconnection delay). These measures are a function of X_0^i.

3. $i \leftarrow i + 1$.

4. Solve the closed queuing network and obtain the throughput X_0^i.

5. (*Convergence Test*) If $| (X_0^i - X_0^{i-1}) / X_0^i | >$ tolerance, then go to step 2; else stop.

Example

Let us apply the procedure outlined above for the database server considered in Sec. 8.3.3. In this case, assume that the degree of multiprogramming is 5, the disks have the RPS feature, and the block size is 4 Kbytes. Table 8.5 shows the results of several iterations. The last column shows the response time obtained when the closed queuing network is solved using the service demands for disks A and B, given by columns labeled D_A and D_B, respectively. The entry under the throughput column in the following line shows the corresponding throughput. In this example, the algorithm converges in four iterations. □

Table 8.5 Results for a Closed Model of an I/O Subsystem.

X_0	$U_{ch}(A)$	$U_{ch}(B)$	$NRPS_A$	$NRPS_B$	$DRPS_A$	$DRPS_B$	D_A	D_B	R (sec)
0.0000	0.0000	0.0000	0.0000	0.0000	0.0000	0.000	0.2104	0.3682	2.0301
2.4629	0.0394	0.0690	0.0773	0.0442	0.00128	0.00073	0.2207	0.3785	2.0863
2.3966	0.0383	0.0671	0.0750	0.0429	0.00125	0.00071	0.2204	0.3782	2.0846
2.3985	0.0384	0.0672	0.0751	0.0429	0.00125	0.00071	0.2204	0.3782	2.0846

8.4 MODELING CPU SCHEDULING PRIORITIES

Most operating systems use job priorities as a way to implement a CPU scheduling policy. Newly arriving high-priority jobs are given the CPU, even though jobs of lower priority may have been waiting longer for the CPU. Priority scheduling may be preemptive or nonpreemptive. In the preemptive case, jobs lose control of the CPU when jobs of higher priority arrive. The suspended jobs resume their execution when there are no jobs of higher priority waiting for the CPU. This is called *preemptive resume priority scheduling*. This is the type of priority scheduling that is considered in this section. In the nonpreemptive case, low-priority jobs are never interrupted by jobs of higher priority while being served. Unfortunately, the use of priority as a scheduling discipline violates the conditions given in Chap. 6 for the existence of a product-form solution for QNs. This means that we need to use an approximate solution. We introduce the idea that motivates the approximation through an example. Then, we generalize the algorithm.

8.4.1 Two-Priority Example

Consider a computer system composed of a CPU and two disks (D1 and D2) used to support an interactive system with 35 terminals. The total workload may be further decomposed into two workloads: production and development. Table 8.6 presents the service demands and workload intensity parameters for the two workloads.

Table 8.6 Input Parameters for Priority Example.

Parameter	Class	
	Production	Development
Service Demand (sec)		
CPU	0.30	1.00
D1	0.08	0.05
D2	0.10	0.06
Number of terminals	20	15
Think time (sec)	20	15
Max. degree of multiprogramming	20	15

Since production commands have a more strict response time requirement, we would like to answer the following questions. How would the response time of the production and development workloads classes change if we assigned a higher CPU scheduling priority to the production class? Would the response time for the development class be increased significantly?

Before we answer these questions, let us use the models we know to obtain the average response time of both classes when both of them have the same priority. The model is composed of four devices: a delay device to represent the think time at the terminals, three queuing load-independent devices to represent the CPU, and the two disks. This model can be solved by the multiclass MVA algorithm given in Chap. 6. If we use program ClosedQN provided in the disk that accompanies this book we obtain that the response time for the production class is 2.69 sec and 8.19 sec for the development class.

Let us now examine how we can model the use of priorities. For that matter, we follow the approach called *stepwise inclusion of classes* (SWIC) presented in Ref. [14]. We start by noting that commands from the development class do not interfere at all with production commands at the CPU since the latter have preemptive priority at the CPU over the former. So, in this respect, production commands see the CPU as if it were dedicated to them. On the other hand, development commands see the portion of the CPU that is left after production commands have used it. On the remaining part of the computer system (i.e., the I/O subsystem), both classes have the same priority.

We start by obtaining an estimate of the CPU utilization due to the production class only. This can be done by building a model with the production class as the only class. We then build a model with both the production and development classes and an additional CPU, called *shadow CPU* (see Fig. 8.6).

The use of the original and shadow CPUs by production and development classes is governed by the following rules:

- Production commands use only the original CPU.
- Development commands use only the shadow CPU.

The problem now is how to compute the service demands of the original and shadow CPUs, $D_{\text{cpu},r}^{\text{org}}$ and $D_{\text{cpu},r}^{\text{shw}}$ respectively, for class r, where r may be p (for production) or d (for development). Since each class uses only its own dedicated CPU, we have that

$$D_{\text{cpu},d}^{\text{org}} = 0 \qquad \text{and} \qquad D_{\text{cpu},p}^{\text{shw}} = 0$$

Since the production class has higher priority over the development class, its service demand at the original CPU is equal to its CPU service demand $D_{\text{cpu},p}$. So

$$D_{\text{cpu},p}^{\text{org}} = D_{\text{cpu},p}$$

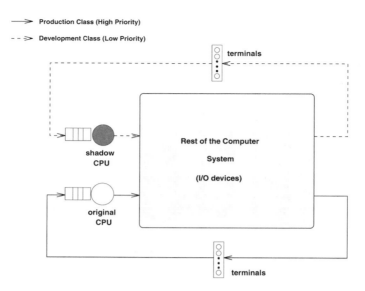

Figure 8.6 Shadow CPU for Priority Modeling.

The CPU service demand of development commands at the shadow CPU has to be inflated to reflect the fact that it will take these commands longer to go through the CPU due to the presence of higher-priority commands. The higher the CPU utilization due to production commands, the more the service demand of development commands has to be inflated. The inflation factor $1/(1 - U_{\text{cpu},p})$ has the desired properties. Thus,

$$D_{\text{cpu},d}^{\text{shw}} = \frac{D_{\text{cpu},d}}{1 - U_{\text{cpu},p}}$$

Let us now follow all the steps necessary to solve our priority model.

1. *Build a single-class model.* This model includes the production class only, the original CPU, the terminals, and the disks. Using the parameters of Table 8.6 in the MVA algorithm, we get that the throughput of the production class is 0.97 command/sec. Therefore, the CPU utilization can be computed as $U_{\text{cpu},p} = D_{\text{cpu},p} \times X_{0,p} = 0.3 \times 0.97 = 0.291$.

2. *Add the shadow CPU and the development class.* We compute the service demands at the shadow and original CPUs as follows:

$$D_{\text{cpu},d}^{\text{org}} = 0 \qquad \text{and} \qquad D_{\text{cpu},p}^{\text{shw}} = 0$$

$$D_{\text{cpu},p}^{\text{org}} = D_{\text{cpu},p} = 0.3 \text{ sec}$$

$$D_{\text{cpu},d}^{\text{shw}} = \frac{D_{\text{cpu},d}}{1 - U_{\text{cpu},p}} = \frac{1.00}{1 - 0.291} = 1.41 \text{ sec}$$

Using the MVA algorithm, we get that the response time for the production class is 0.62 sec and for the development class is 8.66 sec. So there was a significant improvement in the response time of the production class (from 2.69 sec to 0.62 sec) with very little increase in the response time of the development class (5.7% increase). The reason is that the production class has a much smaller service demand at the CPU than that of the development class. So, giving priority to this class at the CPU does not hurt the lower-priority class too much.

In the next section we generalize the algorithm presented in this example to the case of more than two priorities.

8.4.2 SWIC Priority Algorithm

Using the notation introduced in Chap. 3, consider that we have P priority groups numbered from 1 to P. Let Prior(r) denote the priority of class r customers. Classes in priority group 1 have the highest priority, while those in group P have the lowest one. The SWIC algorithm builds P different models. The first model contains all classes of the highest priority (priority 1) only. The second model contains all classes of priority 1 and 2 and a shadow CPU to be used exclusively by customers of priority 2. As in the previous example, the service demand at this shadow CPU has to be inflated by dividing the original service demand by (1 − CPU utilization of higher-priority customers). In general, at each step, we introduce an additional priority, an additional shadow CPU, and we inflate the service demand of the classes just included in the model. The P different QN models considered by the SWIC algorithm are denoted $\mathcal{Q}_1, \ldots, \mathcal{Q}_P$. Figure 8.7 shows the SWIC algorithm. We use the notation $D^p_{\text{cpu},r}$ to indicate the service demand of a class r job of priority p at shadow CPU p. The notation $D_{\text{cpu},r}$ stands, as usual, for the service demand of class r jobs at the CPU. We denote by $\Omega(p)$ the set of classes of priority p. Thus, $\Omega(p) = \{r \mid \text{Prior}(r) = p\}$.

The SWIC algorithm was shown to be very accurate. In Ref. [14], the authors compare the results obtained with SWIC with exact results obtained by solving global balance equations and with results from other approximations. The global balance equation method (explained in Chap. 4) can only be used in very small examples since the number of states grows very fast with the degree of multiprogramming. Other approximations have been proposed. Agrawal presents a nice treatment of various approximation methods for modeling priorities (see Ref. [15]). Lazowska et al. propose another method, which is also based on the notion of shadow CPUs and service demand inflation, but is iterative in nature [12]. A discussion of this method is left as an exercise.

Input Parameters: service demands ($D_{i,r}$'s) and Prior(r)'s
Iteration Loop
For $p := 1$ to P do
　　Begin
　　　　Build a QN model $\mathcal{Q}_p$ containing classes r such that Prior(r) $\leq p$.
　　　　Model $\mathcal{Q}_p$ should contain p shadow CPUs.
　　Compute Inflated Service Demands for Shadow CPUs
　　　　For r such that Prior(r) $\leq p$ do

$$
D_{cpu,r}^{p} = \begin{cases} 0 & r \notin \Omega(p) \\ D_{cpu,r}/(1 - \sum_{q=1}^{p-1} \sum_{s \in \Omega(q)} U_{cpu,s}) & \text{otherwise} \end{cases}
$$

　　　　Solve model $\mathcal{Q}_p$ and obtain the throughputs $X_{0,r}$ for all classes r
　　　　such that Prior(r) $\leq p$.
　　Compute Utilizations
　　　　For all r such that Prior(r) $\leq p$ do $U_{cpu,r} = D_{cpu,r} X_{0,r}$
　　End ;
Compute Final Metrics
The residence times for the I/O devices are obtained from model $\mathcal{Q}_P$.
The residence times at the CPU per class are obtained from the corresponding shadow CPU in model $\mathcal{Q}_P$.

Figure 8.7　SWIC algorithm for priority modeling.

Example

Table 8.7 contains parameters for an example of the execution of the SWIC algorithm. The example has four classes and three priorities. The assignment of priorities to classes is reflected in the following Ω function: $\Omega(1) = \{1, 2\}$, $\Omega(2) = \{3\}$, and $\Omega(3) = \{4\}$. The system in question has one CPU and only one disk.

Table 8.7　Input Parameters for SWIC Algorithm Example.

Class	Priority	$D_{cpu,r}$ (sec)	$D_{disk,r}$ (sec)	Degree of Multiprogramming
1	1	0.10	0.50	3
2	1	0.15	0.35	4
3	2	0.80	0.20	2
4	3	0.90	0.06	1

Table 8.8 shows the results of the execution of the algorithm. The response times per class are 4.03, 2.93, 3.34, and 4.08 sec, for classes 1 through 4, respectively. □

Table 8.8 Results for SWIC Algorithm Example.

	Model		
	$\mathcal{Q}_1$	$\mathcal{Q}_2$	$\mathcal{Q}_3$
$D^1_{\text{cpu},1}$	0.10	0.10	0.10
$D^1_{\text{cpu},2}$	0.15	0.15	0.15
$D^2_{\text{cpu},3}$	-	$0.8/(1-0.327)=1.19$	$0.8/(1-0.287)=1.12$
$D^3_{\text{cpu},4}$	-	-	$0.9/(1-0.747)=3.56$
$U_{\text{cpu},1}$	$0.87\times0.1=0.087$	$0.77\times0.1=0.077$	$0.75\times0.1=0.075$
$U_{\text{cpu},2}$	$1.58\times0.15=0.237$	$1.40\times0.15=0.210$	$1.36\times0.15=0.204$
$U_{\text{cpu},3}$	-	$0.58\times0.8=0.464$	$0.60\times0.8=0.480$
$U_{\text{cpu},4}$	-	-	$0.25\times0.9=0.225$
$\sum_r U_{\text{cpu},r}$	0.324	0.751	0.984

8.5 MODELING PAGING ACTIVITY

Most modern computer systems have paging disks that hold the pages of the virtual addresses of the several processes. As a process page fault rate (number of page faults divided by the number of memory references) increases, a greater portion of the process execution time is spent on the paging device. The load on the paging device affects all processes in execution. In this section we show how paging activity can be taken into account when modeling computer systems.

Let pag be the index of the paging device. Since this device may also be used to store files other than process address spaces, a process service demand at the paging device may be decomposed into two components: one due to paging (D^P_{pag}) and another not due to paging (D^{NP}_{pag}) which is a given parameter. So

$$D_{\text{pag}} = D^{NP}_{\text{pag}} + D^P_{\text{pag}} \tag{8.24}$$

Our problem is how to estimate D^P_{pag}. We can say that the average service demand at the paging device due to paging is equal to the average number of page faults multiplied by the average disk time to service a page fault S_{pag}. So

$$D^P_{\text{pag}} = \text{average number of page faults} \times S_{\text{pag}} \tag{8.25}$$

Since the average service time per page fault can easily be computed as a function of the disk physical characteristics and the size of a virtual page, our problem reduces to estimating the average number of page faults per process.

Let f be the number of pages frames allocated to a process in main memory. Let IFT(f) be a function that gives the *interfault time* of a process when f page frames are allocated to the process. The interfault time is defined as the average time between consecutive page faults. So, if we divide the total CPU time of a process (D_{cpu}) by the value of the IFT function, we obtain the average number of page faults. The graph of the IFT function is monotonically increasing, as shown in Fig. 8.8, except for page replacement policies such as FIFO that exhibit Belady's anomaly [16]. Initially, the interfault time grows very fast as the process acquires more page frames. However, as the number of page frames approaches the size of the process working set, the rate of increase of the interfault time decreases sharply and tends to zero as the number of page frames allocated to the process approaches its total number of pages. At this point there are no page faults and the interfault time becomes equal to the total CPU time for the process. A possible expression for such as function is

$$\text{IFT}(f) = \frac{D_{\text{cpu}}}{1 + (a/f)^2 - (a/F)^2} \tag{8.26}$$

where F is the number of virtual pages that compose a process address space and the constant a may be obtained from measurement data. Other examples of interfault time functions are given in Ref. [17]. Let NP be the total number of page frames to be divided by all processes and let n be the multiprogramming level. Assuming that the page frames are equally divided among all processes, each will be allocated a number of frames f given by NP/n. Hence, the service demand due to paging can be written as

$$D_{\text{pag}}^{P} = \frac{D_{\text{cpu}}}{\text{IFT}(\text{NP}/n)} \times S_{\text{pag}} \tag{8.27}$$

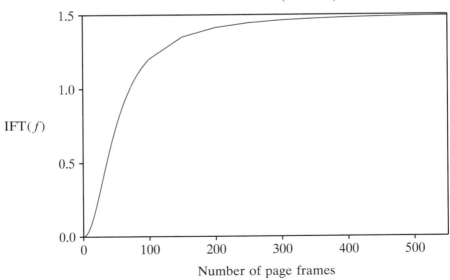

Figure 8.8   Interfault time versus number of page frames.

Using Eq. (8.26) in Eq. (8.27), we get that

$$D_{pag}^P = \left[1 + \left(\frac{a}{NP/n}\right)^2 - \left(\frac{a}{F}\right)^2\right] \times S_{pag} \qquad (8.28)$$

Therefore, using Eq. (8.28) in Eq. (8.24) we get that

$$D_{pag} = D_{pag}^{NP} + \left[1 + \left(\frac{a}{NP/n}\right)^2 - \left(\frac{a}{F}\right)^2\right] \times S_{pag} \qquad (8.29)$$

Note that Eq. (8.29) is valid only when the degree of multiprogramming is such that there are not enough page frames to store the complete address space of all processes (i.e., when $n \times F > NP$). Otherwise, there are no page faults and the paging device service demand due to paging activity is zero.

We can now use Eq. (8.29) to adjust the residence time recurrence expression for the paging device in the MVA algorithm as given in Eq. (8.30). So,

$$R'_{pag}(n) = \begin{cases} \left\{D_{pag}^{NP} + \left[1 + \left(\frac{a}{NP/n}\right)^2 - \left(\frac{a}{F}\right)^2\right] \times S_{pag}\right\} \\ \qquad \times [1 + \bar{n}_{pag}(n-1)] & n > NP/F \qquad (8.30) \\ \\ D_{pag}^{NP} & n \leq NP/F \end{cases}$$

The residence time for the nonpaging devices follow the well-known expressions for MVA given in Chap. 5.

Example

A computer system has one CPU and two disks (disks D1 and D2). Disk D2 is used for paging purposes only. The service demands at the CPU and at disk D1 are 0.2 and 0.06 sec, respectively. The paging disk has an average service time equal to 30 msec. The system has 10 Mbytes of memory available for paging. The size of the page frame is equal to 1024 bytes. The address space of each process is equal to 2 Mbytes. The constant a for the interfault time function is assumed to be equal to 4000. Plot a graph of the throughput versus the multiprogramming level.

We need to compute the model parameters from the problem data. The number of virtual pages per address space, F, is equal to $2 \times 1024 \times 1024/1024 = 2048$ pages. The total number of page frames is equal to $NP = 10 \times 1024 \times 1024/1024 = 10,240$ pages. Also, $D_2^{NP} = 0$ since the paging disk is used for paging only, and $S_{pag} = 0.03$ sec. We can now use the MVA algorithm and compute the throughput for various values of the degree of multiprogramming n. We need to use Eq. (8.30) for the residence time of the paging disk. For the other devices we use the normal residence time equation. In this example, the residence time equation becomes

$$R'_{D2}(n) = \left[1 + \left(\frac{4000}{10,240}n\right)^2 - \left(\frac{4000}{2048}\right)^2\right] \times 0.030 \times [1 + \bar{n}_{pag}(n-1)]$$

$$= (1 + 0.153n^2 - 3.81) \times 0.030 \times [1 + \bar{n}_{pag}(n-1)] \qquad n = 1, \ldots, N$$

for $n > 5 = 10,240/2048$. For $n \leq 5$, $R'_{D2}(n) = 0$. The resulting throughput graph is given in Fig. 8.9. It predicts the expected result, namely that at the beginning, the throughput increases with the degree of multiprogramming. After the paging activity starts to increase, the load on the paging device increases and it eventually becomes the bottleneck. The throughput decreases and eventually goes to zero. This phenomenon is called *thrashing* (see Exercise 4). □

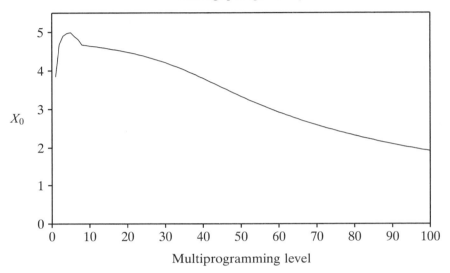

Figure 8.9 Throughput versus multiprogramming level.

8.6 MODELING MULTIPROCESSING

Multiprocessing is a very important issue in both commercial and scientific computing. Systems with multiple independent processors aim basically at two goals: performance and availability. With regard to performance, multiprocessing has been employed primarily to increase system throughput. For example, OLPT applications demand rapid and interactive processing for a large volume of simple transactions that access large databases. No single transaction takes less CPU time than in a uniprocessor, but more independent transactions can be completed per time unit in a multiprocessor system. Thus, the waiting time component of the response time is shortened. However, the other component, the execution time, remains unaltered. There are cases, however, where multiprocessing has been used to cut down on execution time. In parallel processing, many processors work simultaneously on the execution of the same problem, reducing its execution time. In addition to delivering high-performance computing, multiprocessing has been used in the construction of fault-tolerant systems, which offer high availability and reliability. Transaction processing (e.g., ATM), electronic funds transfers, and communications are some of the growing number of applications that make use of fault-tolerant computing. Multiprocessors have been classified as tightly coupled and loosely coupled systems. In this section we focus on approximate techniques for modeling performance of both classes of multiprocessors.

8.6.1 Tightly Coupled Multiprocessors

In *tightly coupled systems*, a set of processors are connected to a common main memory via an interconnection network (e.g., cross-bar, high-speed buses, etc.). Under the coordination of a single operating system, processors communicate through the shared main memory and operate toward a common goal, such as to increase throughput or reduce response time. Because tightly coupled systems can tolerate a high degree of interactions between processors, without a significant degradation of performance, we can view the set of processors as a single entity. This view forms the basis of the approximate technique for modeling performance of this class of system.

The idea here is to model the tightly coupled multiprocessor as a single server with a single queue for job scheduling. Whenever a processor becomes free, the next job from the common queue is taken up for execution. But there is a problem. What is the speed of the service center that represents the multiple processors? As an example, consider a system with eight processors. The service rate of the single server must vary according to the number of jobs in the queue. Ideally, when there are four jobs in the queue, the service rate would be four times as high as the rate of the system with only one job. However, due to software contention (e.g., protecting critical regions with semaphores) and operating system overhead, there is a performance degradation that reduces the effective processor speed. For instance, experiments reported in Ref. [18] show that the effective CPU powers for 2 and 4 processors are 1.78 and 3.03, respectively. These numbers refer to a compilation workload. It should be noted that software contention in a multiprocessor is highly dependent on the nature of the workload. Therefore, the performance of a tightly coupled multiprocessor can be modeled approximately by a queuing network model, with a load-dependent server representing the processors. The solution of queuing networks with load-dependent devices (see Chap. 7) requires the definition of a service rate multiplier (α) that indicates the speed of the server. In this case, the speed indicator is given by

$$\alpha_{\text{mult}}(j) = \begin{cases} j\phi & j \le P \\ P\phi & j > P \end{cases} \tag{8.31}$$

where P is the number of processors, j indicates the number of jobs in the queue for processors, and ϕ is the contention factor that reduces the effective power of the system ($\phi \leq 1$).

8.6.2 Loosely Coupled Multiprocessors

A *loosely coupled system*, also called a multicomputer, consists of a set of autonomous processors, where each processor has a large local memory and may have I/O devices. Unlike tightly coupled systems, processors do not have a common shared memory; they communicate by exchanging messages through an interconnecting network (IN), as illustrated in Fig. 8.10. The approach used to model a loosely coupled system is to view each processor as an independent service center and the multiprocessor as a network of interconnected servers, as shown in Fig. 8.10. We assume that the system is divided into compute and I/O processors.

A transaction is submitted to the system and directed to a compute processor. When a processor needs an I/O operation to be performed on behalf of the transaction, it sends a message to another server—an I/O processor—requesting that it perform the I/O. The transaction execution may be viewed as a sequence of visits by the transaction to the processors of the system [19].

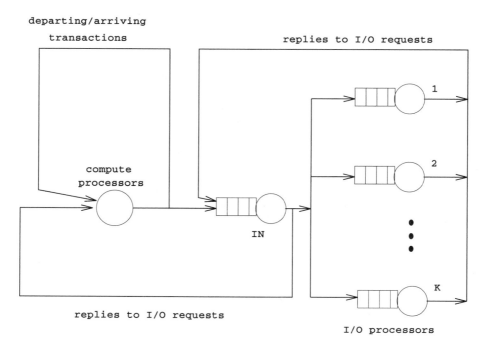

Figure 8.10 Queuing network model of a loosely coupled system.

We assume that once a transaction is started at a compute processor it completes at that processor. This is a fair assumption since process migration has a considerable overhead associated with it. The transaction residence time in the multiprocessor can be regarded as composed of three components: the time spent in a compute processor, the time in different I/O processors, and the time in the interconnection network.

To carry out a detailed analyis of a loosely coupled system, we represent it by a closed queuing network with $K + 2$ servers. One server represents the P processors, one for each of the K I/O processors, and one to represent the interconnection network. The service demand at an I/O processor comprises the total time spent at that processor by a transaction. This includes not only I/O time but also the I/O request processing time. As usual, this service demand does not include any queuing time. This is computed by the model.

The service demand, D_{in}^p, at the interconnection network by transactions executed at processor p may be estimated as follows

$$D_{in}^p = \sum_{i=1}^{K} V_{i,p} \times (\text{request message delay}_{i,p} + \text{reply message delay}_{i,p}) \quad (8.32)$$

where $V_{i,p}$ is the average number of I/O requests sent by a transaction running at compute processor p to I/O processor i, request message delay$_{i,p}$ is the average time neeeded to transmit an I/O request generated by compute processor p to I/O processor i, and reply message delay$_{i,p}$ is the corresponding time spent by reply messages sent by I/O processor i to compute processor p. Note that the service demands at the interconnection network do not include queuing at the interconnection network.

Assume that the compute processors are not multiprogrammed, that is, once they start a transaction, they do not take up any other activity to execute until they complete the transaction. So, once transactions return from the I/O processors they find no queue at their compute processors. Thus, the compute processors can be modeled as a single delay server. Assuming that all transactions submitted at the same compute processor have the same resource demands and that the system is under heavy load, that is, there is always one transaction in execution at each processor, we may model the system as a closed queuing network with P classes of customers, one per compute processor.

Example

Consider a loosely coupled multiprocessor with 10 compute processors and 3 identical I/O processors. The total processor time per transaction is 0.6 sec. So the service demand at the delay server that represents the compute processors is equal to 0.6 sec for all classes $p = 1, \ldots, 10$. Each transaction requires $V_{io} = 6$ I/O operations from each I/O processor. The average service time per disk operation is 20 msec. There is an additional processing time at the I/O processor per I/O request equal to 13 msec.

So the total I/O service demand at any device, D_{io}, per transaction is given by

$$D_{io} = V_{io} \times (\text{disk service time} + \text{I/O processing time})$$

$$= 6 \times (0.020 + 0.013) = 0.198 \text{ sec}$$

Each I/O request message takes 20 μsec and each reply takes 146 μsec. Since there are 3 I/O processors, the service demand, D_{in}, at the interconnection network is equal to

$$D_{in} = 3 \times V_{io} \times (20 + 146)\mu\text{sec} = 18 \times 166 \ \mu\text{sec} = 0.003 \text{ sec}$$

The resulting QN model has 5 servers (one delay server for all compute processors, one server for the interconnection network, and one server per I/O processor) and 10 classes (one class per compute processor). The population of each class is 1. If we solve the corresponding closed queuing network (using program ClosedQN provided with the book), we obtain an average response time of 2.58 sec per transaction and a total throughput of 3.87 tps. The throughput per class (i.e., per processor) is equal to $3.87/10 = 0.387$ tps. Therefore, the utilization of each compute processor is equal to $0.387 \times 0.6 = 23.2\%$. If we increase the number of compute processors to 20, the response time increases to 4.49 sec and the throughput decreases to 2.22 tps. The response time increases because I/O is the bottleneck with 10 compute processors. The situation gets worse when we increase the number of compute processors since congestion on the I/O processors will increase even more. The utilization of each compute processor in this case is $2.22/20 \times 0.6 = 6.7\%$. $\square$

8.7 CONCLUDING REMARKS

Several important aspects of actual computer systems such as priority scheduling at the CPU, paging, memory queuing, complex I/O subsystems, and multiprocessing are not amenable to modeling with exact queuing network models. Approximations to deal with these situations were presented in this chapter.

8.8 EXERCISES

1. Consider the example of Sec. 8.2.3.
   (a) Use the open multiclass model of Chap. 6 to solve the unconstrained model.
   (b) Compute the values of line 1 of Table 8.2.
   (c) Use *QSolver/1* to solve the model and confirm the values of Table 8.3.
2. Consider the example of Sec. 8.4.1. Assume that the development commands have priority at the CPU over production commands. Compute the resulting response time.
3. An iterative approach for modeling priorities was presented by Lazowska et al. [12]. In their approach they suggest that one model with P shadow CPUs be built. The service demands have to be inflated properly in the same way as discussed in the algorithm given in Fig. 8.7. However, this requires knowing

the values of the utilizations for the various classes. Since the utilization $U_{cpu,r}$ is equal to $X_{0,r} \times D_{cpu,r}$, the algorithm starts by assuming an initial value of zero for all throughputs. MVA can now be used to solve the QN and obtain new values of the throughputs, which are used to compute the utilizations and therefore new values of the service demands for the shadow CPUs. This process continues until the throughput values converge within a given tolerance. Modify program ClosedQN to implement this algorithm. Use the modified program to solve the example given in Sec. 8.4.2.

4. Show that when the degree of multiprogramming goes to infinity, the throughput goes to zero in a paging system. [*Hint:* Take the limit of Eq. (8.30) as $n \to \infty$].

5. Imagine that the system described in the paging example of Sec. 8.5 is used to support an interactive system with 40 terminals and think time equal to 15 sec. The maximum multiprogramming level is 20. Compute the average response time by replacing the entire computer system by a load-dependent device. Proceed as follows. The rate, $\mu(n)$ of the device that replaces the computer system should be computed as

$$\mu(n) = \begin{cases} X_0(n) & n \le 20 \\ X_0(20) & n > 20 \end{cases}$$

where $X_0(n)$ is the system throughput when there are n commands in execution. This throughput can be obtained by using the MVA approach for paging systems explained in Sec. 8.5. Now model the terminals as a delay server and the computer system as a load-dependent device. Use MVA with load-dependent devices to solve this two-device queuing network. Where is a command spending most of its time? At the queue for memory or being processed? What is the effect of adding more memory so that the maximum degree of multiprogramming can be increased to 30?

6. Consider the example discussed in Sec. 8.3.4. Compute the average response time assuming that the disks have a track buffer.

7. Consider the example of Sec. 8.6.2. Keep the number of compute processors fixed at 10 and investigate the performance improvement that you would obtain by increasing the number of I/O processors. Assume that the initial I/O load is distributed uniformly over all I/O processors.

8. Consider the decomposition example of Sec. 8.2.1. Use program ClosedQN provided with the book to solve the complete QN of Fig. 8.2a and the network of Fig. 8.2c. Compare the results.

9. Consider the example of Sec. 8.2.3. What is the effect of upgrading disk 1 to a disk twice as fast for a maximum multiprogramming degree of 2 for update transactions?

BIBLIOGRAPHY

1. F. Baskett, K. Chandy, R. Muntz, and F. Palacios, Open, closed, and mixed networks of queues with different classes of customers, *Journal of the ACM*, Vol. 22, No. 2, April 1975.

2. L. W. Dowdy, D. Eager, K. Gordon, and L. Saxton, Throughput concavity and response time convexity, *Information Processing Letters*, No. 19, 1984.

3. K. Chandy and E. Sauer, Approximate methods for analyzing queuing network models of computing systems, *ACM Computing Surveys*, Vol. 10, No. 3, September 1978.

4. P. Courtois, Decomposability, instabilities and saturation in multiprogramming systems, *Communications of the ACM*, Vol. 18, No. 7, 1975.

5. A. Brandwajn, Fast approximate solution of multiprogrammed models, *Proceedings of 1982 SIGMETRICS Conference on Measurement and Modeling of Computer Systems*, Seattle, Wash., 1982.

6. D. A. Menascé, and V. A. Almeida, Operational analysis of multiclass systems with variable multiprogramming level and memory queuing, *Computer Performance*, Vol. 3, No. 3, September 1982.

7. E. Lazowska and J. Zahorjan, Multiple class memory constrained queuing network, *Proceedings 1982 ACM SIGMETRICS Conference on Measurement and Modeling of Computer Systems*, Seattle, Wash., 1982.

8. A. Thomasian and P. Bay, Analysis of queuing network models with population size constraints and delayed blocked customers, *Proceedings 1984 ACM SIGMETRICS Conference on Measurement and Modeling of Computer Systems*, Boston, 1984.

9. R. Katz, G. Gibson, and D. Patterson, Disk system architecture for high performance computing, *Proceedings of the IEEE*, Vol. 77, No. 12, December 1989.

10. J. Hennessy and D. Patterson, *Computer Architecture: A Quantitative Approach*, Morgan Kaufmann, San Mateo, Calif., 1990.

11. G. Houtekamer, The local disk controller, *Proceedings of the 1985 ACM SIGMETRICS Conference on Measurement and Modeling of Computer Systems*, Austin, Texas, 1985.

12. E. Lazowska, J. Zahorjan, S. Graham, and K. Sevcik, *Quantitative System Performance: Computer System Analysis Using Queuing Network Models*, Prentice Hall, Englewood Cliffs, N.J., 1984.

13. J. P. Buzen and A. Shum, A unified operational treatment of RPS reconnect delays, *Proceedings of the 1985 ACM SIGMETRICS Conference on Measurement and Modeling of Computer Systems*, Canada, 1987.

14. V. A. Almeida and D.A. Menascé, Approximate modeling of CPU preemptive resume priority scheduling using operational analysis, *Proceedings of the 10th European Computer Measurement Association (ECOMA) Conference on Computer Measurement*, Munich, October 12–15, 1982.

15. S. Agrawal, *Metamodeling: A Study of Approximations in Queuing Models*, MIT Press, Cambridge, Mass., 1985.

16. Tanembaum, A., *Modern Operating Systems*, Prentice Hall, Englewood Cliffs, N.J., 1992.

17. P. Harrison and N. Patel, *Performance Modelling of Communication Networks and Computer Architectures*, Addison-Wesley, Reading, Mass., 1993.

18. G. Bier and M. Vernon, Measurement and prediction of contention in multiprocessor operating systems with scientific application workload, *Proceedings of the International Conference on Supercomputing*, ACM Press, New York, 1990.

19. P. J. Denning, Queuing in network of computers, *American Scientist*, Vol. 79, May–June 1991.

Chapter 9

Obtaining Input Parameters

9.1 INTRODUCTION

Performance models aim at representing the behavior of real systems in terms of their performance. The input parameters for performance models describe the hardware configuration, the software environment, and the workload of the system under study. The representativeness of a model depends directly on the quality of its input parameters. Therefore, a key issue in conducting practical capacity planning projects is the determination of input parameters for performance models. Two practical questions naturally arise when one thinks of modeling a real computer system:

- What are the information sources for determining input parameters?
- What techniques are used to calculate input parameters?

The main source of information is the set of performance measurements collected from the observation of the real system under study. Further information can also be obtained from product specifications provided by manufacturers. However, typical measurement data do not coincide with the kind of information required as input by performance models. For modeling purposes, typical measurement data need to be reworked to become useful. We begin this chapter with a motivating example that introduces the basic problem of obtaining input parameters. Next, we discuss the main issues in the process of measuring performance of real computer systems. Because the particulars vary from system to system, we do not focus on any specific product or manufacturer. Instead, we present general procedures for transforming typical measurement data into input parameters. The procedures can be thought of as a set of major guidelines for obtaining input parameters for performance models. A case study illustrates the application of the general procedures to measurement data from actual systems.

Consider the example of a company that has a computer system dedicated to support phone orders. The system configuration consists of a single CPU, three disks (A, B, and C), and 30 terminals, as indicated by the upper part of Fig. 9.1. The two most used functions are:

- *Order Entry*, which performs on-line validation, updates customer and inventory information, and creates an order detail record
- *Order Inquiry*, which provides information about the status of pending orders

The order processing application runs on a software environment composed of an operating system (e.g., DEC/VMS, IBM/VSE, UNIX), a

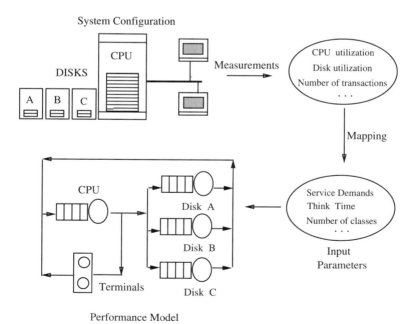

Figure 9.1 Input parameters for performance models.

transaction processing monitor (e.g., DEC/ACMS, IBM/CICS, Tandem/ Pathway, UNIX/Tuxedo, Unisys TIP, Transarc/Encina, NCR/TopEnd), and a data-base management system (e.g., Oracle, Sybase, DB2). The application uses three major databases: *Customers, Inventory,* and *Orders,* which are located on disks A and B, respectively. Disk C is used entirely for paging. Management is concerned about the service level, which has been considered poor by the terminal operators. During peak hours, the average response time observed for the order entry function is 3.1 sec. Therefore, management decided to contract a capacity planning study.

After analyzing the behavior of the system, the capacity planner developed a closed model to represent its performance, as illustrated in the lower part of Fig. 9.1. The analyst also identified three classes of transactions for the model: order entry, order inquiry, and one that represents all other processing activities. The analyst monitored the system during the peak period using the available software tools and obtained a set of measurements, such as CPU and disk utilizations, number of transactions processed, average page fault rate, and average response time. However, the kind of performance data collected do not match the input parameter requirements. Typical input parameters required by performance models are service demands, think time, level of multiprogramming, and number of terminals. Therefore, the basic question answered in this chapter is: How could one map typical measurement data into input parameters for performance models?

9.2 MEASUREMENT TECHNIQUES

What are the most used resources of a given computer system? How much CPU time does the electronic mail system consume daily? These are examples of typical questions that managers of computer system installations face frequently. To answer quantitative questions about the behavior of a computer system, one has to measure it. But what does this really mean? System measurement can be viewed as a process that observes the operation of a computer system over a period of time and records the values of the variables that are relevant for a quantitative understanding of the system [1]. As illustrated in Fig. 9.2, a measurement process involves three major steps.

1. *Specify measurements.* In this step one should decide on the performance variables to be measured. For example, suppose that we are interested in analyzing the behavior of a virtual memory policy of an operating system. Performance variables such as page fault rate and throughput of paging disks will certainly be among those required by the model.

2. *Instrument and gather data.* After selecting variables to be observed, one should install measurement tools to instrument the system. This involves configuring the tools so that the specified variables are measured

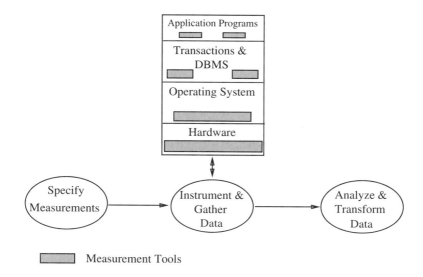

Figure 9.2 A representation of the measurement process.

during the observation period and the required information is recorded. A computer system can be viewed as a series of layers that create an environment for the execution of application programs, as shown in Fig. 9.2. According to the variables selected, one may have to install several measurement tools across the layers. For instance, if one is interested in obtaining service demands for transactions, measurement tools are required at both the operating system level and the transaction monitor level.

3. *Analyze and transform data.* Measurement tools gather huge amounts of raw data, which correspond to a detailed observation of the system operation. Usually, raw data specify time intervals, event counts, percentages, and so on, that have to be related to the logical functions of a system. To be useful, these bulky data must be analyzed and transformed into significant information. For instance, information recorded by software measurement tools typically include a record for each process that starts or completes during the observation period. These records must then be summarized to yield useful results, such as average execution time, number of processes executed, and so on.

In any performance measurement process, the key point is to understand what is being measured and how accurate and reliable the resulting numbers are. Thus, it is essential to know the measurement tools, and their capabilities and limitations.

9.2.1 Monitor Tools

Monitors are tools used for measuring the level of activity of a computer system [2]. The main function of a measurement monitor is to collect data regarding a system's operation. Ideally, a monitor must be an observer of the computer system under study and not in any way a participant. The monitoring must be done in such a way as not to affect the operation of the system being measured. This means that the monitoring process should minimally degrade the performance of the system.

At this point it is important to call attention to two issues that characterize a monitor: mode and type. Monitors perform data collection in two different modes: event trace and sampling. There are three types of implementations for measurement monitors: hardware, software, and hybrid. We discuss each of these attributes in some detail.

Hardware monitors

A *hardware monitor* is a measurement tool that detects events within a computer system by sensing predefined signals. A hardware monitor examines the state of the computer system under study via electronic probes that are attached to its circuitry and records the measurements. The electronic probes can sense the state of hardware components of the systems, such as registers, memory locations, and I/O channels. For example, a hardware monitor may detect a memory-read operation by sensing that the read probe to the memory module changes from the inactive to the active state [3, 4, 5].

There are several advantages to hardware monitors. As they are external to the measured system, they do not consume resources from the system. This means that hardware monitors typically do not place any overhead on the monitored system. Another important feature is portability. Usually, it is possible to move a hardware monitor to different types of computer systems; they do not depend on the operating systems.

One of the major problems of hardware monitors is the expertise required to handle them; they lack ease of use. Typically, they demand a great deal of effort to set up a measurement experiment. Software features are also difficult to detect using these monitors. They do not have access to software-related information such as the identification of the process that triggered a given event. For instance, data about classes of workload, and number of transactions executed are difficult to obtain via hardware monitors.

Software monitors

A *software monitor* consists of routines inserted into the software of a computer system with the aim of recording status and events of the system [1, 4]. They gather performance data about the execution of one or more programs and about the components of the hardware configuration. The routines can be activated either by the occurrence of specific events or by timer interrupts, depending on the mode of the monitor, which is discussed in the following sections.

Software monitors can basically record any information that is available to programs and operating systems. This feature, along with great flexibility to select and reduce performance data, makes software monitors a powerful tool for analyzing computer systems. The IBM Resource Management Facility (RMF) and the Unisys Software Instrumentation (SIP) are examples of software monitors that provide performance information such as throughput, device utilizations, I/O activity, and so on. However, as software monitors use resources they are to measure to run their routines, they interfere with the system significantly. Depending on the level of overhead introduced, the monitoring may yield meaningless results. Software monitors are easy to install and easy to use. These are some of their advantages. The main shortcomings are the overhead and the dependency on the operating system.

There are some classes of tools that may be regarded as software monitors, in the sense that they monitor, via a set of appropriate routines, the behavior of hardware and software systems. Due to their specific uses, they receive special names: accounting systems and program analyzers.

Accounting systems. These are tools primarily intended as means of apportioning charges to users of a system [6, 7]. They are usually an integral part of most multiuser operating systems. The IBM/SMF (System Management Facility) is a standard feature of the operating system MVS that collects and records data related to job executions. Other examples of accounting systems include the VMS ACCOUNTING, and the UNIX/sar (System Activity Reporter) [8].

Although their main purpose is billing, accounting tools can be used as a data source for capacity planning studies. Accounting systems are the easiest way to gather some very important performance information. They should be viewed as the first recourse when one begins a measurement effort. In general, accounting data include three groups of information.

- *Identification*, which specifies user, program, project, accounting number, and class
- *Resource usage*, which indicates the resource consumed by the program, such as CPU time, I/O operations, network operations, and memory required
- *Execution time*, which shows the start and completion times of program execution

Although accounting monitors provide a lot of useful data, there are some problems with the use of their data for performance modeling.

Accounting monitors do not capture the use of resources by operating systems (i.e., they do not include any unaccountable system overhead). Another problem refers to the way that accounting systems view some special programs, such as database management systems (DBMS) and transaction monitors. These programs have transactions and processes that execute within them. As accounting systems treat those special programs as single entities, they do not collect any information about what is being executed inside the programs. However, if one wants to model transaction response time, one needs to feed the model with information about individual transactions. Thus, special monitors are required to examine performance of some programs.

Program analyzers.   Instead of monitoring the entire system, *program analyzers* are software tools intended to collect information about the execution of individual programs. They can also be used to identify those parts of a program that consume significant computing resources [7]. For example, most of the workload of large corporations is due to transaction processing (TP), which is usually controlled by single programs such as CICS, ACMS, and Tuxedo. Consider a capacity planning project of a transaction processing system, controlled by a program such as CICS. For performance modeling purposes, the information provided by the accounting logs and software monitors does not suffice. Both tools do not look inside the program. As those tools view a TP system as a single entity, they capture only global resource usage data. Thus, what is needed is a tool capable of observing and recording events internal to the execution of specific programs. In the case of transaction monitors, program analyzers provide information such as transaction count, average transaction response time, mean CPU time per transaction, mean number of I/O operations per transaction, and transaction mix. Examples of program analyzers include monitors for special programs such as IBM's database products, DB2 and IMS, and transaction processing product, CICS.

Hybrid monitors

The combination of hardware and software monitors results in a hybrid monitor, which shares the best features of both types. Basically, software routines are responsible for sensing events and moving information to special monitoring registers. The hardware component performs the data recording function, avoiding interference in the I/O activities of the system monitored. A problem associated with hybrid monitors is the requirement of special hardware (e.g., monitor registers and performance test points) in the system being measured. Unless hybrid monitors are designed as an integral part of the system architecture, their practical use is limited.

9.2.2 Monitoring Modes

The technique used for data collection defines the monitoring mode [2]. Event trace and sampling are the two most important performance measurement techniques. In the paragraphs that follow we explain how the techniques work, as well as their pros and cons.

Event trace mode.   An I/O interrupt that indicates the completion of a disk read/write operation can be viewed as an *event* that changes the state of a computer system. The state of a system is specified by a set of variables. At the operating system level, the state of the system is usually defined as the number of processes that are in the ready queue, blocked queue, and running. Examples of events at this level are a call to operating system modules and an I/O request. At a higher level, where the number of transactions in memory represents the state of the system, the completion of a transaction can also be considered an event. An *event trace monitor* collects information at the occurrence of specific events.

Usually, an event trace software monitor consists of special codes inserted at specific points of the operating system. Upon detection of an event, the special code calls an appropriate routine that generates a record containing information such as date, time, and type of the event. In addition to that, the record contains some kind of event-related data. For instance, a record corresponding to the completion of a process would contain the CPU time used by the process, the number of page faults initiated, the number of I/O operations executed, the amount of memory required, and so on. In general, monitors record the information corresponding to the occurrence of events in buffers, which are later transferred to disk or tape.

When the event rate becomes very high, the monitor routines are executed very often, which may introduce a large overhead in the measurement process. The overhead corresponds to the load placed by the monitor on the system resources. Depending on both the events selected and the event rate, the overhead may reach unbearable levels, such as 30%. Overheads up to 5% are regarded as acceptable for measurement activities [7]. As the event rate cannot be controlled by the monitor, the measurement overhead becomes unpredictable, which constitutes one of the major shortcomings of this class of monitors.

Sampling mode.   A *sampling monitor* collects information about the system at specified time instants. Instead of being triggered by the occurrence of an event, the data collection routines of a sampling software monitor are activated at predetermined times, which are specified at the start of the monitoring session. The sampling is driven by timer interrupts, based on a hardware clock.

The overhead introduced by a sampling monitor depends on two factors: the number of variables measured at each sampling and the size of the sampling interval. With the ability of specifying both factors, a sampling monitor is also able to control its overhead. On one hand, long intervals result in low overhead. On the other hand, if the intervals are too long, the number of samples decreases and reduces the confidence interval of the variables of interest. Thus, there exists a clear trade-off between overhead and accuracy of measurement results. The higher the accuracy, the higher the overhead. When compared to event trace mode, sampling provides a less detailed observation of a computer system. Errors may also be introduced because of masked interrupts. For example, if some routines of the operating system cannot be interruptible by the timer, their contribution to the CPU utilization will be not accounted for by a sampling monitor [3].

Sampling monitors typically provide information that can be classified as system level statistics: for example, the number of processes in execution and resource use, such as CPU and disk utilization. Process-level statistics are usually generated by event trace monitors, for it is easy to associate events to the start and completion of processes. Hereafter, let us call *system monitors* those monitoring tools (hardware or software) that collect global performance statistics (i.e., do not attempt to distinguish among workload classes).

9.3 INPUT PARAMETER DESCRIPTION

The input parameters for performance models describe the hardware configuration, the software, and the workload of the system under study. These parameters include four groups of information:

- Servers or devices
- Workload classes
- Workload intensity
- Service demands

Servers, devices, or service centers are components of performance models intended to represent the resources of a computer system. A server may be either queuing or delay, depending on the nature of the component it represents. Terminals, for instance, are usually represented by delay servers, whereas processors are typically queuing servers. The first step in obtaining input parameters is the definition of the servers that make up the model.

The scope of the capacity planning project helps to select which servers are relevant to the performance model. Consider the case of a distributed system composed of file servers and workstations connected via a LAN. The capacity planner wants to examine the impact caused on the system by the replacement of the uniprocessor file server by a four-processor server. The specific focus of the project may be used to define the components of a performance model. For example, the system under study could be well represented by an open queuing network model consisting of three devices, which correspond to the file server configuration: processor and two disks. The workstations are represented implicitly by the request arrival rate, which corresponds to the read and write requests generated by the workstations. A different performance model, with other servers, would be required if the planner were interested in studying the effect of the LAN on the performance of the distributed system.

In order to increase the model's representativeness, workloads are partitioned into classes of somehow similar components. Programs that are alike concerning the resource usage may be grouped into workload classes. Depending on the way a given class is processed by a computer system, it may be classified as one of three types: *transaction*, *terminal* or *interactive*, and *batch*. The second step in determining the input parameters for a performance model concerns the definition of class types.

The nature of the real workload is the main factor that influences the choice of the class type. A class that represents the set of read and write requests that arrive at a file server may naturally be classified as transaction type. Another example is that of a workload generated by data-entry operators, which may adequately be typed as terminal. Although the nature of the real workload has a strong influence on the class-type determination, it is not the only factor to be considered. Performance modeling considerations are equally important. Consider again the order-processing example, where we have a computer system with 30 terminal operators supporting phone-order activities. At first sight, one would classify the workload as terminal, because of the nature of the work carried out by the operators. However, for capacity planning purposes, it would be preferable to view the workload as a transaction class. The transaction type is specially suited for estimating workload growth, because the forecast can be performed in terms of business units. In our example it would be possible to associate the transaction arrival rate with the number of customers. Consequently, the arrival rate growth may be estimated taking as a basis the forecasted number of customers.

9.3.1 Workload Intensity

Workload intensity parameters give an indication of the number of transactions, processes, programs, or jobs that contend for the resources of a computer system. Each type of class is characterized by a different set of parameters.

- *Batch class.* The batch class refers to jobs with large resource requirements that come at prescheduled times. Because they demand large amount of resources, there are few batch jobs running simultaneously on any given system. Usually, each batch job has exclusive control of its files and other resources it uses [9]. For modeling purposes, it is assumed that there is always a batch job waiting to be loaded into memory, which implies the presence of continuous backlog. In this case, the multiprogramming level (i.e., the average number of active jobs in the system) specifies the intensity of a batch class.

- *Interactive class.* This type of workload describes the typical interactive processing mode. The users at terminals generate requests that arrive at the computer system to be processed. After completing the processing of a request, the system sends the response back to the user at the terminal. After a certain period of time, the think time, the user generates a new request and the cycle is repeated. It is evident that the greater the number of terminals, the greater the volume of requests generated. It is also evident that the shorter the think time, the larger the number of requests submitted to the system per unit time. Therefore, both the number of active terminals (M) and the average think time (Z) specify the intensity of a terminal-type class.

- *Transaction class.* The transaction class describes user requests that arrive at random at a computer system. Instead of running arbitrary programs, users of transaction processing systems execute certain functions out of a predefined set of functions [9]. A user request corresponds to a well-defined unit of work, the transaction. Usually, there are a number of transaction types, characterized by different resource usage patterns. Similar transactions may be grouped into classes. The arrival rate (λ) indicates the intensity of a transaction class.

9.3.2 Service Demands

Queuing network models represent resources of a computer system. Although they may be used to model software resources (e.g., database locks), queuing networks have most frequently been applied to represent hardware resources. However, in modern computer systems, application programs do not see the hardware resources directly. Instead, they view the computer system as a set of services, provided by various layers of software. Clearly, there exists a gap between the application program view and the representation provided by a queuing network model. For example, a file server attached to a LAN provides a common service to all the other systems on the LAN. The primary service of the file server is to provide all the file management capabilities found on a time-sharing system. Thus, when a user program running on a networked workstation executes a command to read a file, it does not need to know where the file is loaded. Several pieces of software implement a network file system that provides the service requested by the read command.

Then, the following question arises: How are the services provided by software systems represented in a queuing network model? The answer lies in full understanding of the concept of service demand.

By definition, the service demand of a program at a server specifies the total amount of service time required by the program during its execution at the server. It is worth repeating that service demand refers only to the time a program spends actually receiving service. It does not include waiting times. Recall that V_i denotes the average number of visits that a program makes to server i and S_i represents the mean service time per visit to server i. The service demand of a program at server i is given by $D_i = V_i S_i$.

Another view of service demand is that derived from measurement data. Consider that a computer system is monitored for a period of time $\mathcal{T}$. During that period, the utilization of server i was U_i, which means that the server was busy $U_i \mathcal{T}$ units of time. If the count of completed programs during the period indicated is C_0, we can write that $D_i = U_i \mathcal{T}/C_0$.

Now let us examine how the services provided by software layers of a computer system may be represented by the service demand parameters. Figure 9.3 exhibits various execution environments for application programs, ranging from the least complex environment, the bare machine, to sophisticated environments with multiple operating systems. Looking at the definition of service demand, $D_i = U_i \mathcal{T}/C_0$, we note that U_i is the only factor amenable to different interpretations, according to the specific environment. The meaning of U_i is the key point to understand the concept of service demand in different execution environments. Let U_i' denote the total utilization of device i measured by a system monitor and $U_{i,r}$ represent the utilization of device i by class r.

Bare machine.   From the system viewpoint, the simplest environment in which to execute an application program is none. An application program runs directly on top of hardware resources. In this case, the program has

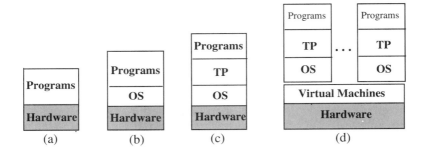

Figure 9.3 Execution environments for application programs.

complete control over the machine and no service is available, as shown in Fig. 9.3a. Looking at the CPU, for instance, we know that U_{cpu}^t represents the fraction of time the CPU was busy doing only one type of activity: executing program's instructions. Thus, we can write that

$$U_{cpu}^t = U_{cpu,prog} \tag{9.1}$$

where $U_{cpu,prog}$ refers to the fraction of actual CPU time consumed by application programs. In a bare machine, it is reasonable to assume that only one program is executing at a time. In other words, a single program of class r monopolizes the CPU, which means that

$$U_{cpu,r} = U_{cpu}^t \tag{9.2}$$

From the definition of service demand and from Eqs. (9.1) and (9.2) we can write that the CPU demand of the single class r is given by

$$D_{cpu,r} = U_{cpu,prog} \times \frac{T}{C_{0,r}} \tag{9.3}$$

In the case of a bare machine, we note from Eq. (9.3) that the CPU demand includes only the actual time a program spends executing at the CPU.

Example

Consider an early computer system with no operating system. The computer executes a job at a time. During an observation period of 1800 sec, a hardware monitor measured a utilization of 40% for the CPU and counted 100 batch job completions. Using Eq. (9.3), we compute the average CPU demand for these jobs, which is is equal to $0.4 \times 1800/100 = 7.2$ sec. □

Operating system. The next environment consists of an operating system on top of hardware resources. An application program, by its turn, runs on top of the operating system as illustrated in Fig. 9.3b. An operating system (OS) provides an execution environment for application programs. The role of an operating system is twofold; it is responsible for managing computer resources, such as allocation of main memory, CPU scheduling, and so on. It also acts as an interface, interacting directly with the hardware and providing common services to application programs. Among the services provided by an OS are program execution, access to I/O devices, memory management (e.g., swapping and paging), controlled access to files, error detection, and accounting [10]. The range of services provided and the efficiency with which they are performed vary from one operating system to another.

To analyze the impact of the operating system on service demands, let us focus on the meaning of the CPU utilization. It indicates the fraction of time the CPU was busy doing two types of activities: processing program's instructions and executing routines of the operating system. The hardware resource use by the operating system is known as *overhead*. We may then write the CPU utilization as composed of two parts:

$$U_{\text{cpu}}^t = U_{\text{cpu,os}} + U_{\text{cpu,prog}} \tag{9.4}$$

where $U_{\text{cpu,os}}$ corresponds to system overhead, typified by activities such as handling I/O operations, paging, and swapping.

Consider the case of a system with R classes. The device utilization due to each class of the workload is a fraction of the total device utilization. We can then write that:

$$U_{\text{cpu},r} = U_{\text{cpu}}^t \times f_{\text{cpu},r} \tag{9.5}$$

where $f_{\text{cpu},r}$ is the relative fraction of the total utilization by class r. In the case of a single-class model ($R = 1$), we have $f_{\text{cpu},1} = 1$. Various ways of calculating $f_{\text{cpu},r}$ are discussed later in this chapter. From Eqs. (9.4) and (9.5) it follows that the CPU demand is given by

$$D_{\text{cpu},r} = (U_{\text{cpu,os}} + U_{\text{cpu,prog}}) \times f_{\text{cpu},r} \times \frac{T}{C_{0,r}} \tag{9.6}$$

It can be noted from Eq. (9.6) that the effects of the OS on the performance is incorporated into the model implicitly through the way service demand is calculated. For instance, the larger the overhead represented by $U_{\text{cpu,os}}$, the larger the CPU demand.

Example

Consider a computer system running batch programs and interactive commands. The system was monitored for 1800 sec and a software monitor indicated a total CPU utilization of 60%. For the same period of time, the accounting log of the operating system recorded the CPU time for batch jobs and interactive commands separately. From the accounting data, the analyst got the CPU utilization by class: *batch* = 40% and *interactive* = 12%, and the number of interactive commands, 1200. Note that since the accounting data do not capture the OS usage of the CPU, these two utilizations do not add up to the total CPU utilization. Using these measurement data, the CPU demand for the class *interactive* is given by

$$D_{\text{cpu,interactive}} = 0.6 \times \frac{0.12}{0.12 + 0.40} \times \frac{1800}{1200} = 0.208 \text{ sec} \qquad \square$$

Transaction processing monitor. A transaction processing system (TP), such as the IBM/CICS, DEC/ACMS, or Unisys/TIP, is an on-line real-time multiuser system that receives requests, processes them, and returns response to these requests [11]. The processing of a request usually involves accessing databases. A key component of a transaction system is a *TP monitor*, which has the responsibility of managing and coordinating the flow of transactions through the system. The TP monitor provides a collection of services, such as communications control, terminal management, presentation

services, program management, and authorization. Thus, a TP monitor provides a transaction execution environment on top of a conventional operating
system, as illustrated in Fig. 9.3c. The total CPU utilization may then be
viewed as a combination of three different components:

$$U_{cpu}^t = U_{cpu,os} + U_{cpu,tp} + U_{cpu,prog} \qquad (9.7)$$

where $U_{cpu,tp}$ indicates CPU utilization by the TP monitor.

Consider now a system where multiple classes of workload run on top
of the OS. Each class may be a transaction monitor (TP), on top of which
transactions execute. We are interested in analyzing the demands of a given
class of transactions. For class r we have

$$U_{cpu,r} = U_{cpu}^t \times \frac{U_{cpu,tp}^{os}}{\sum_{\forall \text{ class } s} U_{cpu,s}^{os}} \times f_{cpu,r} \qquad (9.8)$$

where $U_{cpu,s}^{os}$ denotes the class s CPU utilization, measured by the accounting
system of the OS. In Eq. (9.8) we note that the total CPU utilization (U_{cpu}^t)
is first apportioned to the class represented by the TP monitor. Using $f_{cpu,r}$,
this value is then apportioned to class r within the TP monitor. The fraction
of CPU allocated to transactions of class r may be defined as

$$f_{cpu,r} = \frac{T_{cpu,r}^{tp}}{\sum_{\forall \text{ class } s} T_{cpu,s}^{tp}} \qquad (9.9)$$

where $T_{cpu,r}^{tp}$ is the within-TP CPU time of class r transactions, measured by
a performance tool of the TP monitor. From Eqs. (9.7) and (9.8), the CPU
demand of class r transactions can be expressed as

$$D_{cpu,r} = (U_{cpu,os} + U_{cpu,tp} + U_{cpu,prog}) \times \frac{U_{cpu,tp}^{os}}{\sum_{\forall \text{ class } s} U_{cpu,s}^{os}} \times f_{cpu,r} \times \frac{T}{C_{0,r}} \qquad (9.10)$$

The terms $U_{cpu,os}$ and $U_{cpu,tp}$ of Eq. (9.10) indicate that OS and TP overheads
are included as a part of the CPU demand of class r.

Example

Consider a mainframe that processes three classes of workload: *batch* (B), *interactive*
(I), and *transactions* (T). Classes B and I run directly on top of the operating system,
whereas user transactions execute within the TP monitor. There are two distinct
classes of transactions: *query* and *update*. The performance analyst wants to calculate
the CPU demand of transactions of class *update*. Measurements collected by a system
monitor for 1800 sec indicate a total CPU utilization of 72%. The accounting facility
recorded CPU utilization on a per-class basis, giving the following: $U_{cpu,B}^{os} = 32\%$,
$U_{cpu,I}^{os} = 10\%$, and $U_{cpu,T}^{os} = 28\%$. The program analyzer of the TP monitor provided
the following statistics for the period: 1200 *query* transactions and 400 *update* ones

were completed and consumed 120 and 140 sec of CPU time, respectively. Using Eqs. (9.9) and (9.10), the CPU demand of class *update* is equal to

$$D_{\text{cpu,update}} = 0.72 \times \frac{0.28}{0.32 + 0.28 + 0.10} \times \frac{140}{120 + 140} \times \frac{1800}{400} = 0.698 \text{ sec}$$

Note that if we just divided the total 140 sec of CPU time spent by all update transactions by the number of such transactions executed (400), we would obtain an average of 0.35 sec per transaction, which is about half of the true service demand value computed above. This is due to the fact that the simplistic computation just mentioned did not take into account the operating system overhead. □

Virtual machine: multiple operating systems. The ability to run multiple operating systems on a single processor has been provided by software-based partitioning mechanisms. By using processor scheduling and virtual memory mechanisms, an operating system is able to create the illusion of virtual machines, each executing on its own processor and own memory. Several virtual machines share an underlying common hardware complex.

The usual mode of sharing is multiplexing, which involves allocating time slices of the physical processor to several virtual machines that contend for processor cycles. Virtual machines enable the creation of various different execution environments over a single processor. However, there is a price to pay for this flexibility. Sharing by multiplexing leads to degraded performance on the virtual machines. The larger the number of virtual machines, the higher the performance degradation.

VM is IBM's implementation of virtual machines on its mainframes. VM provides both interactive processing facilities and the capability to run *guest operating systems*. For instance, on a single mainframe it is possible to have a situation where several versions of different guest operating systems (e.g., MVS and VSE) run simultaneously with interactive users (e.g., CMS) on top of a VM system. Fig. 9.3d illustrates the existence of various execution environments on top of virtual machines that share a common hardware complex. The point here is to answer the following question: How does the service demand reflect the existence of various virtual machines on top of a single real processor?

In the execution environment provided by virtual machines, we view the CPU shared by different layers of software, which can be expressed by the following [12]:

$$U_{\text{cpu}}^t = U_{\text{cpu,vm}} + U_{\text{cpu,os}} + U_{\text{cpu,tp}} + U_{\text{cpu,prog}} \qquad (9.11)$$

where $U_{\text{cpu,vm}}$ represents the CPU utilization by the host operating system responsible for implementing virtual machines to different guest operating systems. Thus, we may have j different guest operating systems and, on top of each of them, we may have k different classes of workload, including TPs. Additionally, it is possible to have r different classes of transactions within the

TP monitor. The CPU utilization by class r transactions running on top of guest operating system os can be written in a general form as follows:

$$U_{\text{cpu},r} = U_{\text{cpu}}^{t} \times \frac{U_{\text{cpu,os}}^{\text{vm}}}{\sum\limits_{\forall \text{ OS } j} U_{\text{cpu},j}^{\text{vm}}} \times \frac{U_{\text{cpu,tp}}^{\text{os}}}{\sum\limits_{\forall \text{ class } k} U_{\text{cpu},k}^{\text{os}}} \times f_{\text{cpu},r} \qquad (9.12)$$

Equation (9.12) can be viewed as a product of the total CPU utilization by three factors, each representing the *fraction* of CPU time received by each layer (i.e., VM, OS, and TP) that make up the execution environment. The total CPU utilization is allocated to an individual guest operating system OS by the following fraction:

$$\frac{U_{\text{cpu,os}}^{\text{vm}}}{\sum\limits_{\forall \text{ OS } j} U_{\text{cpu},j}^{\text{vm}}} \qquad (9.13)$$

The other fractions were explained in Eqs. (9.8) and (9.10), developed for the transaction processing environment. From Eqs. (9.11) and (9.12), we can write the following expression for the CPU demand of class r:

$$D_{\text{cpu},r} = (U_{\text{cpu,vm}} + U_{\text{cpu,os}} + U_{\text{cpu,tp}} + U_{\text{cpu,prog}})$$

$$\times \frac{U_{\text{cpu,os}}^{\text{vm}}}{\sum\limits_{\forall \text{ OS } j} U_{\text{cpu},j}^{\text{vm}}} \times \frac{U_{\text{cpu,tp}}^{\text{os}}}{\sum\limits_{\forall \text{ class } k} U_{\text{cpu},k}^{\text{os}}} \times f_{\text{cpu},r} \times \frac{T}{C_{0,r}} \qquad (9.14)$$

Example

Consider a virtual machine (VM) scheme that supports an execution environment with several guest operating systems: one for production (e.g., MVS1), one for development activities (e.g., MVS2), and a number of interactive users (e.g., CMS). The multiple operating system environment runs on top of a mainframe with a single processor. The production OS processes two workload classes: batch (B) and transaction (TP). The TP monitor supports the execution of two classes of transactions: *query* and *update*. Our goal in this example is calculating the average CPU demand for the class of update transactions.

A system monitor observed the behavior of the mainframe for 1800 sec and recorded a CPU utilization equal to 97%. For the same period, the software monitor of the VM system measured the following utilizations for the guest operating system: $U_{\text{cpu,mvs1}}^{\text{vm}} = 50\%$, $U_{\text{cpu,mvs2}}^{\text{vm}} = 14\%$, and $U_{\text{cpu,cms}}^{\text{vm}} = 20\%$. This last measurement indicates the total CPU utilization by all CMS users. The accounting system of the MVS1 collected statistics per workload, which are $U_{\text{cpu,B}}^{\text{os}} = 30\%$ and $U_{\text{cpu,TP}}^{\text{os}} = 60\%$. Performance figures from the TP monitor show that 1200 *query* transactions and 400 *update* ones were completed and consumed 120 and 140 sec of CPU time, respectively. Using Eq. (9.14), the CPU demand of class *update* is equal to

$$D_{\text{cpu,update}} = 0.97 \times \frac{50}{14 + 50 + 20} \times \frac{60}{60 + 30} \times \frac{140}{120 + 140} \times \frac{1800}{400} = 0.933 \text{ sec}$$

Now suppose that we want to estimate the CPU demand for the batch jobs that run on the production system. The count of production batch jobs for the observation period is 80. Adapting Eq. (9.14) to this situation (i.e., considering only the CPU allocation to the production OS and the corresponding suballocation to the batch class) we have

$$D_{\text{cpu,batch}} = 0.97 \times \frac{50}{14 + 50 + 20} \times \frac{30}{60 + 30} \times \frac{1800}{80} = 4.33 \text{ sec} \quad \square$$

9.3.3 Overhead Representation

Overhead denotes resource use by the operating system. It can be viewed as composed of two parts: a constant one and a variable one. The former corresponds to those activities performed by an OS that do not depend on the level of system load, such as the CPU time to handle an I/O interrupt. The variable component of overhead stems from activities that are closely associated with the system load. For instance, as the number of jobs in memory increases, the work done by memory management modules also increases.

Basically, there are two approaches for representing overhead in performance models. One approach uses a special class of the model for representing the overhead of the OS activities performed on behalf of application programs. There are problems associated with this approach. Because of its variable component, the service demands of the special class have to be made load-dependent. Thus, whenever the intensity parameters (e.g., multiprogramming level and arrival rate) of the application classes change, the service demands of the overhead class also have to be modified. The interdependency between overhead parameters and multiprogramming mix may make this approach impractical.

Unless the operating system load is itself a subject of the performance analysis, it is not a good modeling assumption to represent overhead as an independent class of the model. The usual modeling approach attempts to distribute overhead among the classes of application programs. As we will see in the next section, the problem with this approach is the calculation of breakdown ratios for distributing overhead among the classes in correct proportions.

9.4 PARAMETER ESTIMATION

Parameter estimation deals with the determination of input parameters from measurement data. Many times, monitors do not provide enough information for calculating the input parameters required by a performance model. Therefore, inferences have to be made to derive the desired parameters. In this section we discuss general procedures for estimating input parameters.

Measurement data that are commonly provided by current monitors can be grouped into two clusters, according to the information scope [13].

- *System-level statistics*, which show system-wide resource usage statistics, such as global CPU and disk utilization, total number of physical I/O operations, and page fault rate. This kind of information is usually provided by software monitors that run at the operating system level. As a rule, system monitors do not collect statistics by class of application programs.
- *Program-level statistics*, which show program-related information such as program identification, elapsed time, CPU time, number of I/O operations per execution, and physical memory use. Accounting systems constitute the most common source of program execution information.

9.4.1 Steps in Obtaining Input Parameters

Once the performance model has been specified and the solution techniques selected, the analyst faces the problem of estimating input parameters for the model. In this section we outline the basic steps for obtaining the most common input parameters for performance models. The techniques presented here attempt to use to the maximum extent possible the data that are commonly provided by current commercial monitors.

1. Identify the type of execution environment. In other words, the analyst has to find out what software layers are underneath application programs and on top of the hardware. The type of environment determines the way of estimating the workload service demands.
2. Specify the measurement process. Once the environment has been typified, the next step involves basic definitions concerning the monitoring tools to be used, the data to be obtained, and the measurement interval (i.e., starting time and duration).
3. Monitor the system and collect performance data. The measurement data will be used to estimate the input parameters.
4. Estimate input parameters. According to the type of environment and measurement data obtained, calculate input parameters using the appropriate techniques and formulas described in the next sections.

9.4.2 Arrival Rate

For a relatively long measurement interval, the arrival rate can be approximated by the throughput of the system. In other words, we assume that the system experiences an operational equilibrium; the difference between arrivals and completions is small compared to the number of completions. Thus, the arrival rate of class r can be estimated by

$$\lambda_r = \frac{C_{0,r}}{T} \tag{9.15}$$

where T is the length of the measurement interval and $C_{0,r}$ denotes the count of class r transactions or programs completed during T. Counts of completed transactions are usually provided by software monitors and program analyzers.

Example

A total of 5140 order-entry transactions were processed by a system during the monitoring period of 1 hour. According to Eq. (9.15), the estimated arrival rate is $5140/3600 = 1.428$ tps □.

The measurement interval should be long enough to minimize *end effects*, which are represented by those transactions that are executed partially within and partially outside the measurement interval. In most cases it is impractical to avoid end conditions. Therefore, it is important to attempt to reduce their bad effects on the accuracy of measurement results. The larger the number of transactions observed, the lower the impact of end conditions. Because the number of transactions processed is proportional to the length of the interval, end effects for long intervals are less significant than those for short intervals.

9.4.3 Multiprogramming Level

There are several different methods for obtaining the multiprogramming level of a batch class. For instance, software monitors are able to measure and report the time-averaged number of jobs actually in execution in memory during the measurement interval [1]. If the elapsed times of the n jobs executed during the measurement interval are available from the accounting logs, the average degree of multiprogramming of class r $(\overline{N}_r)$ can be estimated as follows:

$$\overline{N}_r = \frac{\sum_{i=1}^{n} e_{i,r}}{T} \tag{9.16}$$

where $e_{i,r}$ is the elapsed time of job i of class r.

Example

Consider the example of Fig. 9.4, which shows a time diagram of the execution of four jobs (A, B, C, and D) and their respective elapsed times. Using Eq. (9.16), the average degree of multiprogramming is $(20 + 14 + 32 + 38)/50 = 2.08$. □

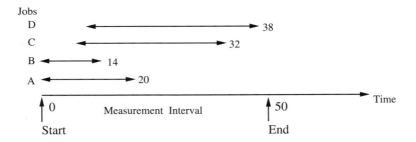

Figure 9.4 Average multiprogramming level.

Alternatively, if the average response time for class r jobs and the arrival rate of class r are available, Little's result can be used to calculate the average degree of multiprogramming as follows:

$$\overline{N}_r = \lambda_r R_r \tag{9.17}$$

9.4.4 Number of Active Terminals and Think Time

Possible approaches to estimate the number of active terminals of class r (M_r) include:

- Use information provided by software monitors concerning the average number of logged on users, who performed some activity during the monitoring interval.
- Use measurement data provided by accounting logs to calculate the number of active terminals, as follows:

$$\overline{M}_r = \frac{\sum_{i=1}^{n} s_{i,r}}{T} \tag{9.18}$$

where $s_{i,r}$ is the measured length of terminal session i of class r users. To use Eq. (9.18), one should have available records of all sessions performed during the monitoring period.

The average think time (Z_r) for users of class r can be obtained either from software monitors or from measurement data and from the interactive response time law, as indicated by the following expression:

$$Z_r = \frac{M_r \times T}{C_{0,r}} - R_r \tag{9.19}$$

where R_r denotes the measured average response time of class r.

Example

Suppose that a time-sharing system supports the program development activities of 40 programmers. The workload consists of commands entered by the programmers. During a monitoring period of 1 hour when the 40 programmers were logged on, the system executed 4900 commands and the measured average response time was 2.5 sec. According to Eq. (9.19), the average think time for this interactive workload is $40 \times 3600/4900 - 2.5 = 26.9$ sec. □

In the case of using data from software monitors, one should assure that what is being reported is think time. There are different views for this parameter. In our view, think time corresponds to the time interval that elapses from the beginning of a response from the system and the end of inputting the next command by the user.

9.4.5 CPU Service Demand

The basic formula for deriving the average CPU demand of class r is

$$D_{\text{cpu},r} = \frac{U_{\text{cpu},r} \times T}{C_{0,r}} \tag{9.20}$$

From Eq. (9.20) we note that we need to obtain CPU utilization on a per-class basis (i.e, $U_{\text{cpu},r}$). In general, system monitors obtain total device utilizations but do not collect these statistics by class. Partial device utilizations by workload class are typically derived from accounting data. As most accounting systems are intended primarily for billing purposes, they do not include any unaccountable system overhead. Consequently, it is usual to have the following relation:

$$\sum_{\forall \text{ class } r} U_{\text{cpu},r}^{\text{os}} < U_{\text{cpu}}^{t} \tag{9.21}$$

where $U_{\text{cpu},r}^{\text{os}}$ is the CPU utilization of class r measured by an accounting software of the OS. In other words, the resource usage of all programs does not add up to the global utilization observed by a software monitor. There are reasons for this inconsistency. First, some resource use by the operating system on behalf of application programs is not charged to them. Accounting softwares do not collect CPU time expended by the system in activities such as job initiation/termination, job scheduler, multiprogramming, and virtual storage support. Second, when a monitor operates on a sampling basis, the resource usage between the last sample and the instant a program ends is lost. The CPU time not collected by measurement tools is known as *uncaptured time*. The problem is how to distribute all unaccounted resource use among the classes of a workload. Since most of the unattributed CPU time is likely to be overhead, let us examine alternatives for spreading it over the workload classes.

The partial CPU utilization by each class can be written as

$$U_{cpu,r} = U_{cpu}^t \times f_{cpu,r} \qquad (9.22)$$

where $f_{cpu,r}$ is the relative fraction of the total CPU time used by class r. The relative fraction $f_{cpu,r}$ may be estimated in different ways, which depend on the assumptions about the workload and the execution environment (hardware and operating system) [4].

- Assuming that the unaccounted CPU time is proportional to the number of programs executed in each class during the monitoring period, we define the following:

$$f_{cpu,r} = \frac{C_{0,r}}{\displaystyle\sum_{\forall \text{ class } s} C_{0,s}} \qquad (9.23)$$

In this case, we are associating the overhead with the tasks performed by the operating system to control program execution. The shortcoming is that the nature of programs executed is not considered.

- Based on the assumption that the amount of unaccounted time is proportional to the accounted CPU time, we have the following relation:

$$f_{cpu,r} = \frac{U_{cpu,r}^{os}}{\displaystyle\sum_{\forall \text{ class } s} U_{cpu,s}^{os}} \qquad (9.24)$$

The problem with this approximation is that the unattributed CPU time may not be related to the accounted time. For instance, the amount of CPU time accumulated for interactive applications built on top of time-sharing systems (e.g., IBM's TSO) is considerably less than the same work done in batch mode [14].

- Assuming that most overhead is connected with the execution of I/O requests, the relative fraction for CPU time is given by

$$f_{cpu,r} = \frac{\text{number of I/O operations by class } r}{\text{total number of I/O operations by all classes}} \qquad (9.25)$$

Because of the uncertainties to determine $f_{cpu,r}$, one should select the approximations that seems to fit best one's particular problem. After solving the model, the results obtained are to be used to validate the approximation selected.

Capture ratio. The portion of time captured by accounting systems varies with both the nature of the workload and the type of operating system. The proportion of total CPU time that is captured by measurement tools is known as the *capture ratio*, which can be written as

$$c_r = \frac{\text{measured CPU time for class } r}{\text{real CPU time for class } r} \tag{9.26}$$

where c_r denotes the capture ratio of class r. For example, for IBM's MVS environment, the capture ratio varies from 0.27 for an interactive workload up to 0.82 for a scientific computation [14]. In general, the literature [15] reports a range from 0.40 to 0.85 for the variation of capture ratio, for different types of workload and computer system. Although the concept of capture ratio has been defined for CPU time, it also applies to other resource categories. In a more general way, we can define the resource usage capture ratio as the ratio of the resource use accounted to programs, to the resource usage measured by system monitors.

Example

Consider a computer system that processes two types of workloads: program development and scientific programs (e.g., simulation and numerical computation). The former is processed interactively, whereas the latter is executed via batch. During a period of 2 hours, the system was monitored and the accounting system recorded the same amount of CPU time for both workload classes (i.e., 1500 sec). For the same period, a system monitor indicated a CPU utilization of 64%. Based on the accounting data, we calculate the CPU utilization for each class: $1500/7200 = 20.8\%$ for both classes. The discrepancy between the value measured by the system monitor (64%) and the value calculated from the accounting data ($2 \times 20.8 = 41.6\%$) stems from the unaccounted system overhead.

   Assume that batch scientific processing has a capture ratio of 0.80 and that interactive program development has a capture ratio of 0.60. Thus, the true CPU time for scientific processing is $1500/0.80 = 1875$ sec and the true interactive time is $1500/0.60 = 2500$ sec. Using the adjusted values of CPU time, we obtain the following CPU utilization: $(1875 + 2500)/7200 = 61\%$, which approximates the value obtained by the software monitor.   □

   Once we have obtained the capture ratio, it is easy to estimate the true utilization per class:

$$U_{\text{cpu},r} = \frac{U_{\text{cpu},r}^{\text{os}}}{c_r} \tag{9.27}$$

Now that we have understood how to use the capture ratio to allocate unaccounted resource usage, the natural question that arises is: How could one determine the capture ratio for a particular workload and computer system?

   If only one class of application is running in a system, the capture ratio is defined to be the total CPU time obtained from accounting data divided by the total CPU time measured by a system monitor. A table with capture ratios for single workloads on a particular system can then be constructed. For a system with multiple classes, one can use c_r from tables or from data provided by manufacturers. Calibration of the values of c_r may be required to validate the results of a multiclass model.

9.4.6 I/O Service Demands

There exists a variety of I/O devices with different features, such as function (e.g., input, output, or storage) and data transfer rate. Some of the I/O devices connected to computer systems include keyboard, mouse, laser printers, networks, magnetic tapes, and disks. Most of them are immaterial with respect to computer system performance. Because of their critical role to performance, we concentrate on the study of disks and their service demand parameters.

The service time for a disk is equal to the seek time plus the rotational latency time plus the data transfer time plus the controller time. Between a disk and the main memory there are a hierarchy of I/O components (e.g., channel, control units, switches, etc.) that are shared by several disk units. The controller time refers to the overhead the control units impose to perform an I/O operation plus the contention for the common resources.

The two most commonly used approximations for deriving disk service demands for performance models with multiple classes are given as follows.

$$D_{i,r} = \frac{U_i^t \times T}{C_{0,r}} \times f_{i,r} \qquad (9.28)$$

$$D_{i,r} = \frac{\text{IOC}_i \times \text{MST}_i}{C_{0,r}} \times f_{i,r} \qquad (9.29)$$

where IOC_i denotes the number of physical I/O operations to disk i, MST_i is the mean service time of disk i, and $f_{i,r}$ represents the fraction of total activity (i.e., utilization or I/O count) of a disk i due to workload class r. The choice between the two approximations depends mainly on the type of measurement data provided by the available monitoring tools. For instance, the IBM Resource Measurement Facility (RMF) software monitor reports device utilizations as well as average service times and I/O count per device.

Considering that either utilization or I/O counts can easily be obtained from performance tools, the crucial step to calculate disk demands is estimating $f_{i,r}$. Thus, the basic problem is how to determine the fraction of I/O to each device, which is attributable to each workload class, as illustrated in Fig. 9.5. As software monitors do not usually provide statistics by class, inferences have to be made from measurement data to derive $f_{i,r}$. Several practical cases of estimating $f_{i,r}$ are presented next.

Single-class disk. When disk i is dedicated to a single class r, there is no need to breakdown its total utilization (or I/O count) (i.e., $f_{i,r} = 1$).

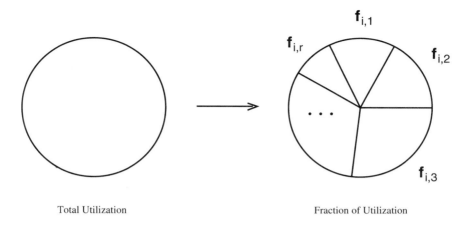

Total Utilization   Fraction of Utilization

Figure 9.5 Allocating the utilization of device i among r classes.

User disk.   When a disk contains only user data and is shared by several workload classes, the fraction will be approximately proportional to the number of I/O operations performed by each class. Thus,

$$f_{i,r} = \frac{\text{number of I/O operations to disk } i \text{ by class } r}{\text{total number of I/O operations to disk } i \text{ by all classes}} \qquad (9.30)$$

At this point, we should comment on the assumptions behind this estimate. To understand the I/O characteristics of an application, let us make a distinction between two types of operations. *Logical I/O operations* refer to the requests made by application programs to access file records. *Physical I/O operations* correspond to actions performed by the I/O subsystem to exchange blocks of data with peripherals. There is not always a one-to-one correspondence between logical and physical operations. At one extreme, when the data required by a logical operation are already in memory (e.g., I/O buffers), no physical operation needs to be carried out. At the other extreme, operations such as file open and keyed access may require several physical operations to complete. In general, accounting systems record logical operations, whereas system monitors count physical operations. Because system monitors do not collect statistics by class of application programs, in Eq. (9.30) we use the number of logical I/O operations. Consequently, we are assuming that the proportion of physical I/O operations toward disk i equals the proportion of logical operations.

Swap disk.   Swapping is a memory management mechanism that moves entire processes from main memory to disk and back. In most operating systems, the majority of swapping is due to interactive users. To represent swapping in performance models, one should specify, for each class, the service demand at each disk used for swapping purposes. Swapping activity is measured by the number of swap I/O operations, which include swap-ins and swap-outs. The former refers to processes moved from disk to memory, whereas the latter corresponds to processes moved from memory to disk. The swapping requests can be apportioned among the classes proportionally to the number of swap operations attributed to each class. Thus, we can write that

$$f_{i,r} = \frac{\text{number of swap I/Os to disk } i \text{ by class } r}{\text{total number of swap I/Os to disk } i} \tag{9.31}$$

where the number of swap I/O operations can be obtained from accounting data.

Paging disk.   Paging moves individual pages of processes from main memory to disk and back. Paging activity generates I/O traffic and should be included in performance models of systems that have virtual memory. This activity can be represented by the service demand of each class at the disks used for paging. The intensity of paging activities is measured by page-ins, or pages moved from disk to memory, and page-outs, or pages moved from memory to disk. Page-ins cause delay to a program's progress, since it has to wait until the page transfer completes. Thus, I/O operations due to page-ins should be considered part of a program's demand for I/O service. Page-outs, on the other hand, cause no direct delay on a program's execution and are, usually, modeled as part of the system overhead [16, 17]. When disk i is used for paging, the fraction $f_{i,r}$ will be approximately proportional to the number of page-ins generated by workload class r, as follows:

$$f_{i,r} = \frac{\text{number of page-in operations to disk } i \text{ by class } r}{\text{total number of page-in operations to disk } i} \tag{9.32}$$

The basic rule to map real I/O devices into components of a model is the assumption that each server in the model is capable of independent operation. For example, consider a group of tape drives connected to a single I/O channel. If only one tape drive can actively be transferring data at a time, the entire group would be represented by a single server. The most used approach to model I/O subsystems is to have a single service center representing each disk. However, there are situations where several disks can be represented by a single server, with no damage to the result's accuracy. The disk aggregation technique [15, 17] replaces all low utilization drives (less than 5%) by a single delay server. Programs visiting low utilization disks experience no queuing delay. Thus, the use of a single server with fixed delay seems to be a good approximation that simplifies the solution of a model. The service demand of class r at the delay server is given by

$$D_{i,r} = \frac{T}{C_{0,r}} \times \sum_{\forall \text{ disk } i} f_{i,r} U_i^t \tag{9.33}$$

where the sum in Eq. (9.33) corresponds to the fraction of utilization attributed to class r on all low-utilization disks.

9.5 ORDER PROCESSING SYSTEM EXAMPLE

To obtain a better understanding of the problem, let us plug typical numbers into the order processing example described at the beginning of this chapter. Figure 9.1 depicts the performance model, which consists of a network of four queuing servers, one for the CPU and one for each disk. The system under study has available two monitoring tools: the system monitor and the accounting log. The former provides system-level statistics, whereas the latter describes performance information concerning the various transactions executed.

As stated earlier, the workload can be viewed as composed of three classes of transactions: *order entry* (OE), *order inquiry* (OI), and *others* (Ot), which represent all other processing activities. The next step in determining the input parameters is to define the type of each workload class. In this example, the workload classes are generated by operators at terminals. However, the operators work in response to requests from customers (e.g., order entry and inquiries). For planning purposes, the workload intensity is better described in terms of request arrival rates. Thus, the three classes are modeled as being of transaction type.

Using the available measurement tools, the performance analyst monitored the system for 1 hour during the peak period and collected the data listed in Table 9.1. The model proposed for the system consists of three transaction processing classes to represent the workload described. Table 9.2 displays the input parameters required by the model. Only the line corresponding to the multiprogramming level could be filled out directly from Table 9.1. The question that arises here is: How can we map the information shown in Table 9.1 into the information required by Table 9.2?

When examining the data in Table 9.1, we identify problems that will appear in the attempt to map one table into another.

Table 9.1 Summary of Measurement Data.

System-Level Statistics		Transaction-Level Statistics			
Device	Utilization (%)	Measurement	OE	OI	Ot
CPU	79	Transaction count	5140	2980	1100
Disk A	48	CPU time (sec)	1650	294	210
Disk B	41	I/O operations	52,428	12,814	10,010
Disk C	18	Maximum multiprogr.	10	5	5
-	-	Page fault/trans.	4.9	1.1	2.3
Monitoring period	3600 sec	Response time (sec)	3.25	1.09	2.44

Table 9.2 Input Parameters for a Performance Model.

	Class		
Parameters	OE	OI	Ot
CPU demand	?	?	?
Disk A demand	?	?	?
Disk B demand	?	?	?
Disk C demand	?	?	?
Average arrival rate	?	?	?
Maximum multipr. level	10	5	5

Performance models require disk demands specified per device for each class of workload. However, the data provided by the measurement tools lack the number of I/O operations to the disk by transaction class. They only include the total number of I/O operations per class. If we had the disk I/O count statistics per transaction per disk, it would be easy to allocate the disk utilization to each class. Because of the lack of these statistics per class, the problem here is to determine the relative fraction of the disk utilization for each class.

The measurement data indicate a 79% CPU utilization for a monitoring period of 3600 sec. Therefore, the workload demanded $3600 \times 0.79 = 2844$ sec of CPU time. If we add up the CPU time allocated to the transactions (Tab. 9.1) in the same period, we obtain 2154 sec. The discrepancy in the two values stems primarily from the fact that a portion of the CPU time used by system processes is not captured by the accounting system.

Having as a starting point the measurement data of Table 9.1, we carry out the input parameter calculation on a step-by-step basis.

9.5.1 Average Arrival Rate

The average arrival rate for each class is assumed to be equivalent to the measured throughput rate per workload class (X_i). The arrival rates, expressed in tps, for classes OE, OI, and Ot are $5140/3600 = 1.428$, $2980/3600 = 0.828$, and $1100/3600 = 0.306$, respectively.

9.5.2 CPU Demand

Consider the CPU utilization measured by the system monitor, which accounts for application time and overhead. Our modeling strategy considers overhead as an integral part of the workload. Our goal is therefore to distribute the total CPU utilization among the classes in the correct proportions. The expression used is

$$\text{CPU utilization by class } (r) \; = \; \text{total CPU utilization} \times f_r \qquad (9.34)$$

$$f_r \; = \; \frac{\text{class } r \text{ CPU seconds}}{\text{total CPU seconds}} \qquad (9.35)$$

where f_r is the relative fraction of CPU time for class r. The fraction f_r is approximated by the ratio of the accounted CPU time of class i to the total CPU time. The CPU demands are given by

$$\text{CPU demand per class} = \frac{\text{CPU utilization per class}}{\text{class throughput}} \tag{9.36}$$

Considering the total CPU utilization of 79%, we calculate the relative CPU utilizations and demands, as shown in Table 9.3.

Table 9.3   CPU Demands.

r	f_r	Relative CPU (%)	X_r (tps)	Demand (sec)
OE	1650/2154	60.52	1.428	0.424
OI	294/2154	10.78	0.828	0.130
Ot	210/2154	7.70	0.306	0.251

9.5.3 Disk Demands

The main problem in this step is to allocate properly the total disk utilization measured by the monitor among the workload classes. The basic question is: What criteria should be used for apportioning global disk utilization to the workload classes?

We learned from the system staff that the files are loaded onto disks as follows:

- *Disk A: CUSTOMER*, SYSTEM, and miscellaneous
- *Disk B: INVENTORY* and *ORDERS*
- *Disk C:* paging

The measurement data displayed in Table 9.1 do not provide the number of I/O operations to disk by class. Thus, we need to find a way to infer these numbers. Interviews with the analysts reveal details of the application logic, which will allow us to build Table 9.4.

For instance, a typical order-entry transaction performs, on the average, 3 logical I/O operations to file CUSTOMER, 4 operations to the INVENTORY, and 2 operations to create a detail record on the file ORDERS. The number of logical operations per transaction becomes the breakdown ratio for distributing the physical I/O operations among the files. From Table 9.1 we know that the class of order-entry transactions performed a total of 52,428 I/O operations. To estimate the number of physical I/O operations to file CUSTOMER by each class, we use the relative fraction of the number of logical operations. In fact, we are making the assumption that the fraction of physical I/O operations toward the disks is equal to the fraction of logical operations, listed in Table 9.4 Therefore, the number of I/O operations for class OE to file

CUSTOMER is $52,428 \times 3/(3+4+2) = 17,476$. We calculate the number of operations to the other files, similarly, as shown in Table 9.4. To allocate the operations performed by transactions of class Ot to file SYSTEM and miscellaneous, we use a proportion factor given by the system staff.

Table 9.4   Distribution of Physical and Logical Operations per File.

Files	Logical Operation			Physical I/O Operation		
	OE	OI	Ot	OE	OI	Ot
Customer	3	2	-	17,476	6,407	-
Inventory	4	-	-	23,301	-	-
Orders	2	2	-	11,651	6,407	-
Miscellaneous	-	-	7	-	-	7,007
System	-	-	3	-	-	3,003
Total				52,428	12,814	10,010

Once we know where the files are loaded and the number of operations to each file, we are then able to find the number of physical operations per disk by each class. For example, disk B contains only two files: *Inventory* and *Orders*. The number of I/O operations to the two files are 23,301 and 11,651 I/O operations, respectively, which results in 34,952 I/O operations to disk B by class OE transactions. As disk C is dedicated to paging, its total utilization can be allocated to the three classes using the total number of page faults per class as the basis for apportionment. For instance, Tab. 9.1 indicates 2980 class OI transactions and 1.1 page faults per transaction, which gives $2980 \times 1.1 = 3278$ page faults for this class. In the same way, we obtain 25,186 and 2530 page faults for classes OE and Ot, respectively. Table 9.5 summarizes the distribution of operations per disk unit.

Table 9.5   Distribution of Physical I/O Operations per Class and Disk.

Disk	Class			Total
	OE	OI	Ot	
A	17,476	6,407	10,010	33,893
B	34,952	6,407	-	41,359
C	25,186	3,278	2,530	30,994

To allocate the overall disk utilization to each class, we estimate a relative disk utilization for each class, proportional to the number of physical I/O operations to the disk. Thus, we have

$$U_{\text{disk},r} = U_{\text{disk}}^{t} \times f_{\text{disk},r} \qquad (9.37)$$

where U_{disk}^{t} is the overall disk utilization, $U_{\text{disk},r}$ denotes the estimated utilization of device disk by class r, and $f_{\text{disk},r}$ is the relative fraction, defined as follows:

$$f_{\text{disk},r} = \frac{\text{number of I/O operations to disk by class } r}{\text{total number of I/O operations to disk by all classes}} \quad (9.38)$$

The estimated utilization for disk B by class OE is computed as follows: $U_{\text{disk B,OE}} = 0.41 \times (34,952/41,359) = 0.3465$. The results for all classes and disks are listed in the leftmost part of Table 9.6.

Table 9.6   Estimated Disk Demands.

Disk	Total Utilization (%)	Relative Utilization (%)			Disk Demand (sec)		
		OE	OI	Ot	OE	OI	Ot
A	48	24.75	9.07	14.18	0.173	0.110	0.463
B	41	34.65	6.35	0.00	0.243	0.077	0.000
C	18	14.63	1.90	1.47	0.102	0.023	0.048

To convert the estimated disk utilization into the required service demands, we use the following relationship:

$$D_{\text{disk},r} = \frac{U_{\text{disk},r}}{X_{0,r}} \quad (9.39)$$

where $U_{\text{disk},r}$ denotes the relative utilization by class r and $X_{0,r}$ represents the throughput of class r. Using the values of $U_{\text{disk},r}$ and $X_{0,r}$ shown in Tab. 9.6 and Tab. 9.3, we calculate the disk demands for all classes and disks, as displayed in Tab. 9.6. At this point, we have a complete parametric description of the transaction processing system under study.

9.6 CONCLUDING REMARKS

There are two key issues in the process of obtaining input parameters for performance models: performance measurement and parameter estimation. With regard to measurement, it is essential to understand what is being measured, how accurate the measurements are, and how reliable the resulting numbers are. In this chapter we discussed several aspects of the measurement process and showed tools used for monitoring the level of activity of a computer system.

Parameter estimation deals with the determination of input parameters from measurement data. Many times, monitors do not provide enough information for calculating the input parameters required by a performance model. In most cases of real systems, assumptions have to be taken about the behavior of the system and inferences need to be made to derive the desired parameters.

Although this chapter does not focus on any particular product or manufacturer, it provides a set of general guidelines for transforming typical measurement data into typical input parameters. The guidelines can be applied to

real problems in a straightforward manner. Because of the uncertainties associated with the process of estimating parameters, it is indispensable to validate
the model. The validation process may require a parameter calibration, which
may involve reviewing assumptions and inferences made during the parameter
estimating step. In Chap. 10 we provide an in-depth discussion of validation
and calibration techniques.

9.7 EXERCISES

1. Select from published literature or from product specification manuals two performance monitors. Briefly describe the two products and show the measurements provided by each monitor. Considering that your purpose is to obtain
   input parameters for a performance model, discuss the good and bad points of
   each of the two tools selected.

2. A performance analyst monitored a computer system with one CPU and three
   disks (D1, D2, and D3) for 1 hour. The system processes three different types
   of transactions: A, B, and C. Using data collected by the software monitor
   and the accounting facility, the analyst obtained the following measurements:
   $U_{cpu}^t = 82\%$, $U_{D1}^t = 28\%$, $U_{D2}^t = 20\%$, $U_{D3}^t = 35\%$, $C_{0,A} = 2200$, $C_{0,B} = 4000$,
   $C_{0,C} = 1000$. Determine the service demands for this workload and comment
   on the pros and cons of the used approximations.

3. Consider a server dedicated to handling transactions generated by phone orders
   from customers. The server consists of a single processor and two disks (A and
   B). Disk A has customer data and disk B is used for paging. The analyst
   responsible for studying the system performance decided to build an analytic
   model with 3 service centers and 2 classes, one for order-entry transactions
   and one for representing the system overhead. Here are the measurement data
   obtained from the system monitor: $T = 900$ sec, $C_{0,trans} = 1800$, $U_{cpu} = 65\%$,
   $U_{disk\ A} = 20\%$, $U_{disk\ B} = 35\%$, page-ins = 22,500, and page-outs = 10,000.
   $C_{0,trans}$ is the number of user transactions completed during the monitoring
   period. The total CPU time for user transactions recorded by the accounting
   system is 567 sec. You may assume that:

   - The system vendor informed that the CPU times to handle a page-in and a
     page-out operation are 0.0015 and 0.0042 sec, respectively.
   - Page-ins should be viewed as a part of the workload demand for I/O services.
     On the other hand, page-out should be included in the system overhead.

   Find the input parameters for the model.

BIBLIOGRAPHY

1. C. Rose, A measurement procedure for queuing network models of computer
   systems, *ACM Computing Surveys*, Vol. 10, No. 3, September 1978.
2. D. Ferrari, G. Serazzi, and A. Zeigner, *Measurement and Tuning of Computer
   Systems*, Prentice Hall, Englewood Cliffs, N.J., 1983.

3. P. Heidelberger and S. Lavenberg, Computer performance methodology, *IEEE Transactions on Computers*, Vol. C-33, No. 12, December 1984.

4. M. Kienzle, Measurements of computers systems for queuing network models, *Technical Report CSRG-86*, Department of Computer Science, University of Toronto, Canada, October 1977.

5. D. Lavery, The design of a hardware monitor for the Cedar supercomputer, *CSRD Report No. 866*, University of Illinois at Urbana-Champaign, May 1989.

6. I. Borovits and S. Neuman, *Computer System Performance Evaluation*, Lexington Books, Lexington, Mass., 1979.

7. J. Cady and B. Howarth, *Computer System Performance Management and Capacity Planning*, Prentice Hall, Brookvale, New South Wales, Australia, 1990.

8. M. Loukides, *System Performance Tuning*, A Nutshell Handbook, O'Reilly & Associates, Sebastopol, Calif., 1991.

9. J. Gray and A. Reuter, *Transaction Processing: Concepts and Techniques*, Morgan Kaufmann, San Mateo, Calif., 1992.

10. J. Peterson and A. Silberschatz, *Operating Systems Concepts*, Addison-Wesley, Reading, Mass., 1991.

11. W. Highleyman, *Performance Analysis of Transaction Processing Systems*, Prentice Hall, Englewood Cliffs, N.J., 1989.

12. BGS Systems, Building a baseline model of a mixed VM/370 system, *Technical Note 17*, BGS Systems, Waltham, Mass., February 1982.

13. S. Agrawal, Determining VAX/VMS workloads, their resource usage and service levels, *Proceedings of the CMG'90, International Conference on Management and Performance Evaluation of Computer Systems*, Computer Measurement Group, December 1990.

14. J. Cooper, Capacity planning methodology, *IBM Systems Journal*, Vol. 19, No. 1, 1980.

15. E. Lazowska, J. Zahorjan, G. S. Graham, and K. C. Sevcik, *Quantitative System Performance: Computer System Analysis Using Queuing Network Models*, Prentice Hall, Englewood Cliffs, N.J., 1984.

16. J. P. Buzen, A queuing network model of MVS, *ACM Computing Surveys*, Vol. 10, No. 3, September 1978.

17. J. Silvester and A. Thomasian, Performance modeling of a large scale multiprogrammed computer using BEST/1, *Proceedings of the International Conference on Computer Capacity Mangement*, Chicago, 1981.

Chapter 10

Model Calibration and Validation

10.1 INTRODUCTION

Regrettably, the following scenario happens all too often. After the system analyst carefully selects an appropriate model of the system, after accurate measurements have been taken, after the necessary parameters have been obtained for the model, and after the model has been solved using an appropriate solution technique, the performance metrics from the model do not match (i.e., are not even *close* to) the measured performance metrics of the system. Even after careful examination and reexamination of each aspect of the modeling process, significant differences between the model and the actual system can result. Aside from sheer frustration, the system analyst must admit to either not being able to know some aspect(s) of the system or not being able to model certain known aspects accurately. That is, two fundamental sources of errors in the modeling process are:[1]

- An unknown system attribute which, by definition, cannot be modeled
- A known system attribute which by its nature cannot be, or is chosen not to be, modeled accurately, usually for reasons of model complexity

[1]Significant portions of this chapter have been contributed by Craig Lowery and Amy Apon.

(Of course, a good system analyst *always* opts for the second of these two justifications even when the first justification is the more truthful!)

In the final analysis, when discrepancies exist between the model and observed behavior, the analyst may have no other option than to *calibrate* the model. Calibration is the changing of the model to force it to match the actual system. In many scientific disciplines, calibration is both expected and respected as a necessary aspect of the modeling process. Unfortunately, in the computer system modeling discipline, calibration is often viewed with disrespect since it is associated with the admission of a perceived lack of knowledge and failure on the part of the analyst. In this chapter (after having ample experience being the recipients of the latter view), we aspire to the former view, that calibration is an expected, respected, and necessary aspect of the modeling process. In succeeding sections we discuss different techniques of calibration and how effective each of these might be for different prediction tasks.

10.1.1 Review of the Basic Modeling Paradigm

In Chap. 4 a modeling paradigm was presented. A slightly altered version is presented in Fig. 10.1. Errors can be introduced at any step of the modeling process. Therefore, the baseline model is likely to be imperfect and not match the actual system. The first step is to select and construct an appropriate model. The second step is to obtain measurements from the computer system. The third step is to characterize the workload by abstracting the required model parameters from the measurement data. The fourth step is to solve the model. The fifth step is to compare the performance metrics of the model (e.g., processor utilizations, user response times, system throughput) against the measurements from the actual system. If the comparison is acceptable, the model can be used to predict the performance of the system. If the comparison is not acceptable, the model must be calibrated. These five steps are repeated until the calibrated baseline model is acceptable.

10.2 CALIBRATION EXAMPLE

Consider the queuing network model of an example system shown in Fig. 10.2. The example system has one CPU, one disk, and a set of two active terminals. This system represents a typical workstation with one active user at the main console and another customer using the system via remote login. (*Note:* An alternative view of this model is a single workstation with a single user who is actively using two windows. However, to avoid confusion, the "two-terminal" view is adopted.) The routing probabilities, 0.99 and 0.01, represent the relative probabilities of a request which, upon finishing at the CPU, next requires service from the disk or next requires service from the requesting terminal, respectively. The two interactive customers use the system. Using a

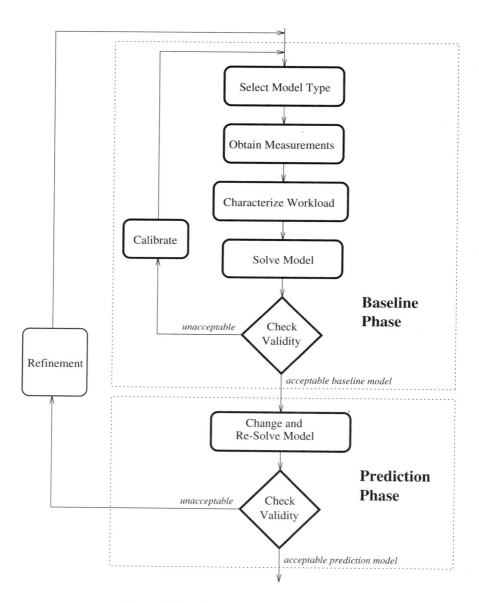

Figure 10.1 The predictive modeling task.

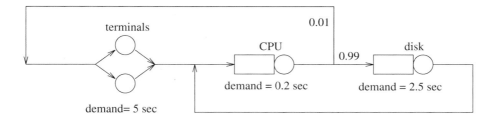

Figure 10.2 Queuing network model of an example system.

performance monitor, suppose that the analyst measures the average service times of transactions to be 25 msec at the disk, 2 msec at the CPU, and 5 sec at the terminal (i.e., user think time). Taking the inverse of these measurements gives service rates in units of transactions per msec, as shown in Table 10.1. The system monitor measures that upon leaving the CPU there is a 99% chance a transaction will go to the disk and a 1% chance it will return to its terminal. That is, an average user transaction requires 99 disk requests and 100 CPU visits per terminal request. Hence, the CPU and disk service demands are obtained as follows: $D_{\text{cpu}} = V_{\text{cpu}} S_{\text{cpu}} = 100 \times 0.002 = 0.2$ sec and $D_{\text{disk}} = V_{\text{disk}} S_{\text{disk}} = 99 \times 0.025 = 2.5$ sec. These probabilities are shown in Fig. 10.2.

Table 10.1 Service Rates (Transactions per Millisecond) for the Example System.

Device	Rate
CPU	0.5000
Disk	0.0400
Terminal	0.0002

The analyst makes several assumptions in order to allow the simplest model to be constructed that is consistent with the measurement data. These assumptions include the following.

- Measurements made by the monitor are assumed to be correct.
- Since there are two terminals, the analyst assumes that there is one transaction in the system for each terminal at all times. This transaction may be competing actively for system resources (e.g., the CPU or the disk) or may be at the terminal waiting for the next user request (e.g., a user's think time). Thus, *type-ahead*, where a user submits two requests at the same time, is not allowed.
- The multiprogramming level (MPL) is assumed to be two and is assumed to be constant.

- Since the monitor reports only averages, the analyst assumes that all transactions are statistically identical (i.e., a single-class system).
- Other assumptions about the system are made so that the model can be solved using product-form techniques (e.g., all service times are assumed to be exponentially distributed).

It may be, however, that the monitor reports user process statistics but not system process statistics. Thus, the multiprogramming level may actually be higher than 2, and these two types of processes may have quite different resource requirements. Inaccurate measurements affect the service rates and routing probabilities. It may be that each terminal has more than one transaction associated with it and that each transaction's service demand at a device is different. It may be that some service times are drawn from a more general distribution, or that the multiprogramming level is not constant (due to the user processes forking and joining), or that scheduling is based on a priority queue for some devices, such as the CPU. Thus, the assumptions for the model may be inaccurate, but it may be impossible or not convenient (or just not worth it) to arrive at better ones.

Suppose that the analyst has observed directly that the average response time of the actual system (i.e., the time elapsed from when a request is made at the terminal until its response) is 2.7 sec. However, analytically solving the example model of Fig. 10.2 gives a response time of 3.5 sec.

If the criterion for an acceptable model is that system response time closely match measured response time, the model of Fig. 10.2 may not be acceptable. The analyst reevaluates the model, making some change that will reduce the response time of the model so that it matches the actual system response time of 2.7 sec. Perhaps the simplest way that the analyst may change the model is to scale (i.e., apply a "fudge" factor to) the output response time by 0.77 (i.e., whatever response time the model outputs, reduce it by 23%). This changing of the model to force it to match the actual system is referred to as the *calibration procedure*.

A calibration is a change to some *target parameter* of the analytic model. The *target parameter* may be any input or output parameter of the analytic model. For example, in the analytic model of Fig. 10.2, the target parameter of the calibration is the response time of the model, since it is the parameter that is directly changed. The goal in performing a calibration is to force the analytic model to match the actual system for some objective performance metric. The *objective performance metric* is the output metric of the actual system, which will match in the baseline analytic model after a successful calibration procedure. The objective performance metric in the analytic model of Fig. 10.2 is response time. As another example, suppose that system X has an actual throughput of 20 jobs per time unit. Suppose, also, that an analytic model is created of system X, and the throughput of the analytic model is 18 jobs per time unit. If the model is calibrated, say, by changing the MPL of the model so that the throughput of the model is exactly 20 jobs per time unit, the objective performance metric of the calibration is throughput and the target parameter is the MPL. The objective performance metric may be chosen to be any output metric of the analytic model. Usual output metrics, which are objective performance metrics for calibration, are system throughput, system response time, the utilization of a device, or the queue length of a device.

10.3 TYPES OF CALIBRATIONS

There are many different types of calibrations. Altering the disk or CPU speeds, or varying the routing probabilities, can cause the response time of the model to change to where it matches the observed measurement value. Other possibilities exist, such as making a multiclass model, or modeling a non-constant multiprogramming level distribution. Generally, any input or output parameter of the analytic model may be a target parameter for calibration, and the target parameter may be altered in different ways. The target parameter may be altered in:

- The direction of change
- The scale of change

The target parameter may be:

- An input parameter to the queuing network model
- An output parameter of the queuing network model

The direction of change to the target parameter may be up or down. For example, if the MPL in the model is 6, and the MPL is to be changed, it may be changed up, so that MPL = 7, or it may be changed down, so that MPL = 5.

The scale of change of the target parameter may be by either an absolute or a percentage amount. For example, if the service demand at a device is 10, and it is to be increased, it may be changed by an absolute amount, such as 2. In this case, the calibrated model would have a service demand of 12 at this device, and the calibration is termed *absolute difference*. Or, the service demand at the device may be changed by a percentage amount, such as 20%. If the service demand starts at 10 and is increased by 20%, the calibrated model would have the service demand equal to 12. In this case the calibration is termed *percentage difference*. A change may be made using an absolute scale to a target parameter which is either an input or output parameter of the analytic model. A change made using a percentage scale is usually made to a target parameter which is an output parameter of the analytic model.

The target parameter for calibration may be any input parameter to the analytic model. For example, the input parameters to a product-form queuing network model are [1]:

- *Multiprogramming level.* This is the number of jobs or transactions in the system. The multiprogramming level is specified only for closed systems (or closed classes of customers). For closed queuing network models this is normally a constant integer.
- *Customer arrival rate.* This is the rate at which external customers arrive to the system. It is applicable to open or mixed systems.
- *Number of devices.* This is the number of service stations in the system and is a constant integer.
- *Number of classes of customers.* This is the number of distinct customer classes. Each class may contain any number of separate (but statistically identical) customers. In a single-class queuing network model the number of customer classes is 1.
- *Service demand for each class of customers at each device.* This value may be specified as a fixed number, independent of the number of customers at the device (i.e., load-independent); or this number may vary, depending on the number of customers currently at the device (i.e., load-dependent).
- *Scheduling discipline at each device.* For a product-form queuing network model this must be processor sharing (PS), infinite server (IS), last come first served preemptive resume (LCFS-PR), or first come first served (FCFS).

In non product-form queuing network models, additional input parameters are possible. For example, it may be possible to (1) change the scheduling discipline at a service center, (2) change the number of buffers available at a service center, (3) change priorities of customer's classes, or (4) adjust the routing probabilities for customers in the network. Any input parameter may be changed up or down, and by an absolute or a percentage amount. When a model is calibrated by altering an input parameter, the baseline calibrated model may be used directly for performance prediction. In this case the model is again altered for the purposes of predicting performance (i.e., the prediction phase in Fig. 10.1). The metrics of the altered (calibrated) baseline model give the predicted performance of the system.

The target parameter for calibration may be any output parameter of the analytic model. A special situation exists when an output parameter is the target of the calibration (i.e., it is the parameter of the model that is to be changed). In this case, this same output parameter is also the objective performance metric of the calibration. The usual performance metrics of interest are:

- Throughput of the system
- Response time of the system
- Utilizations of the various devices
- Queue lengths at the various devices

The output parameter may be changed up or down, and by an absolute or percentage amount. The model is made to match the actual system simply by scaling the objective performance metric by an absolute or a percentage amount. No other changes in the model are made.

When the model is calibrated by altering an output parameter, the baseline calibrated model may be used for performance prediction, but an additional step is required to obtain the prediction metrics. The output metrics of the prediction model must be altered in the same manner as was done in calibrating the baseline model in order to obtain the predicted performance metrics. For example, consider the system of Fig. 10.2. The model is calibrated using a percentage difference of the output metric, response time. The response time of the baseline model is scaled by a factor of 0.77. After the baseline model is calibrated, suppose that it is modified for the purposes of performance prediction (the prediction phase in Fig. 10.1). To obtain the predicted response time after modification, the calculated response time is multiplied by a factor of 0.77. The same percentage difference is applied to the prediction model as was applied to the baseline model in order to obtain the predicted performance of the system.

10.4 EFFECT OF CALIBRATIONS

The effect of some calibrations is known for some target parameters and for some types of models. Some calibrations can only increase the output performance metrics of the baseline model. Some calibrations can only decrease the output performance metrics of the baseline model. Some calibrations may do either. If this information is known before the calibrated model is solved, it can be helpful in selecting an appropriate calibration. However, this information is not always known before the calibrated model is solved. It is possible to attempt a calibration procedure, only to find that the solution to the calibrated model is *further* from the actual system than the uncalibrated model. In that case, the calibration chosen is not effective, and the calibration (or at least the target parameter's direction of change) must be altered.

If the calibration is a change to an output parameter of the model, only the objective performance metric will be affected by the calibration. However, if the calibration is a change to an input parameter of the model, all performance metrics in the baseline model will be affected in some way. In general, if the calibration causes a decrease (increase) in throughput, there is a corresponding increase (decrease) in response time, and vice versa. Also, in general, the utilizations and queue lengths at a device will either both increase or both decrease. It is possible that a calibration to an input parameter of the model will cause an increase in the utilization of a device but cause either an increase or a decrease in the throughput, depending on the specific system being modeled.

The effect of the major techniques used for calibration are described in this section. The primary calibration techniques considered here are:

- *Percent difference.* Alter the value of the objective performance metric in the baseline model by a percent difference to make it match the actual system.

- *Absolute difference.* Alter the value of the objective performance metric in the baseline model by an absolute difference to make it match the actual system.

- *Mean multiprogramming level.* Adjust the number of users in the baseline model (i.e., the multiprogramming level) until the objective performance metric is matched.

- *Multiprogramming level distribution.* Solve the model for several multiprogramming level values and use the distribution of the multiprogramming level to calculate the performance metrics of the calibrated model.

- *Multiclass calibration.* Add a new class of customers and shift demand from one class to another in the model.

- *Absolute demands.* Change the service demand at every server by the same absolute amount until the objective performance metric is matched.

- *Demand at the bottleneck device.* Adjust the demand at the most heavily utilized server until the objective performance metric is matched.

- *Ghost server.* Add a delay server (i.e., ghost server) to the model and set the demand at this new server so that the objective performance metric is matched.

10.4.1 Percent and Absolute Difference

The easiest calibrations to perform are those that alter the value of the objective performance metric by some amount. This is a calibration on the output parameter of the model and is applicable to any type of model. The change may be either an absolute amount or a percentage difference. Since the effect to the baseline model is only to the specific output metric being altered, it is easy to understand exactly what change to make to the baseline model. No further understanding of the model is required to force the baseline model to match the actual system.

Since these are calibrations on an output metric of the model, the prediction performance metrics are not obtained directly. Instead, the metric obtained from the prediction model must be altered in exactly the same way as is done in the baseline model to obtain the predicted performance of the system. Although these calibrations are easy to do, the disadvantage of this method of calibration is that the effect on the prediction model may lead to a poor performance prediction. The accuracy of the prediction depends on the specific system being modeled and may vary greatly from system to system.

10.4.2 Calibration on the Mean Multiprogramming Level

A common calibration is to adjust the mean multiprogramming level of the model. The mean multiprogramming level can be adjusted up or down, and is usually adjusted by an absolute amount. An adjustment on the multiprogramming level is easy to perform and may be applied to any model. This is a calibration on an input parameter, so the prediction performance metrics can be obtained directly simply by altering the calibrated baseline model.

For single-class product-form models, two facts about the behavior of the performance metrics throughput, utilization, and queue lengths help in determining the amount and direction of the change that will be required to the multiprogramming level for the model to match the actual system. The first fact is that for single-class product-form models, when the multiprogramming level is increased these performance metrics will also increase, and when the multiprogramming level is decreased these performance metrics will decrease. In other words, the throughput, utilization, and queue lengths are monotonically increasing as a function of the multiprogramming level. The second fact is that for single-class product-form models, a $p\%$ increase in the multiprogramming level will lead to a less than $p\%$ increase in the throughput of the model. This is true because the throughput of the model is an increasing, concave-down function of the multiprogramming level. Figure 10.3 is a graph of the throughput of a single-class product-form model with respect to the multiprogramming level. For example, suppose that the throughput of the model is 4.0 and the throughput of the actual system is 5.0. Suppose also that the model is a single-class product-form model and that the MPL is 20 in both the model and the actual system. Since the throughput in the model is less than the throughput of the system, the first fact indicates that an increase in the multiprogramming level of the model will cause an increase in the throughput of the model. Since the throughput of the model is 20% less than the throughput of the actual system, the second fact indicates that the multiprogramming level must be increased by at least 20% in order to have the model throughput come close to the actual system throughput. Therefore, an appropriate calibration is to solve the model with a multiprogramming level of 24, a 20% increase, to see if the performance metrics match.

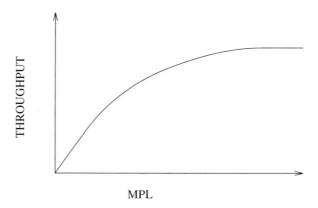

Figure 10.3 Graph of throughput versus multiprogramming level.

For non product-form models, and for multiclass or load-dependent product-form models, an increase in the multiprogramming level may or may not lead to an increase in the output performance metrics. Also, with multiclass models, it is possible to increase the multiprogramming level in one class but not in another. The effect on the output performance metrics of the baseline model will depend on the specific system being modeled.

10.4.3 Multiprogramming Level Distribution

Another calibration technique is to solve the model using a distribution of the multiprogramming level. The multiprogramming level in a queuing network model is normally constant, but when modeling systems have a large variance in the multiprogramming level, a more effective model can be constructed by solving the model for two (or even several) values of the multiprogramming level and taking the average performance of the two models. For instance, if the average multiprogramming level is 5, instead of solving the baseline model with a constant MPL = 5, a calibrated model is constructed by solving two models, one with MPL = 3 and one with MPL = 7 and taking the average performance of the two models. This can be viewed as a calibration on an output metric of the model, since a calculation (the average) is being performed on the output performance metrics of the model(s). Since it is a calibration on an output metric, the performance metrics of the prediction model are not obtained directly, but must be obtained by performing the same calculation on the prediction model as is performed on the baseline (calibrated) model.

As is the case with a calibration on the mean multiprogramming level, the effect to the baseline model is known with single-class product-form queuing networks, but the effect is not known in general. With single-class product-form queuing networks, an increase in the variance of the multiprogramming level will cause the throughput of the baseline calibrated model to decrease. That is, the throughput in a model with a constant MPL of 5 is higher than the average throughput of two models, one with MPL = 3 and one with MPL = 7. The average MPL is the same in both cases (i.e., 5), but the latter has a higher MPL variance and exhibits poorer performance.

10.4.4 Multiclass Calibration

It is possible to add classes of customers and shift service demand from one class to another in the baseline model. This is a calibration on an input parameter of the queuing network. If the uncalibrated model is a single-class product-form queuing network, and the calibration is to create two or more classes while maintaining the same mean service demand at a device, the effect on the performance metrics in the baseline model is known. The throughput of the calibrated baseline model will be no less than the throughput in the un-calibrated model. The response time of the calibrated baseline model will be no more than the response time in the uncalibrated model. The relative uti-lizations at each of the devices in the calibrated model will be the same as the relative utilizations in the uncalibrated model, but the actual utilizations in the calibrated model will be higher than those in the uncalibrated model. Thus, changing a model from a single-class model to a multiclass model generally improves performance. The intuitive reasoning is that in multiclass models, the customers in different classes tend to stay out of each other's way. Thus, there is generally less queuing in a multiclass model and this leads to improved performance.

If the uncalibrated model is multiclass, and the calibration is to add more classes, or to shift demands from one class to another, it is possible for the performance metrics in the calibrated model to increase or decrease. Thus, there are many possible multiclass calibration variations.

10.4.5 Absolute Demand Calibration

A common calibration is to adjust the service demand at every device to make the model match the actual system. If this change is done by a percentage amount at every device, the calibration is exactly the same as the percentage change calibration to the output performance metrics. However, the effect is different if this change is done by an absolute amount at every device. In a single-class model, this adjustment affects all customers equally. In this case, a decrease (increase) in the service demand at all devices will cause an increase (decrease) in the throughput of the model. It is possible, however, for utilizations and queue lengths to either increase or decrease.

In a multiclass model, a change in the service demand at a device does not affect all customers equally, but depends on the relative class throughputs for each of the classes. A decrease in the service demand for a class at the device which is the most heavily utilized for that class will cause an increase in the throughput for that class. However, the throughput for other classes may increase or decrease as a result, so that the total throughput of the model may increase or decrease. If the model is multiclass and the service demands are changed at the devices for all classes, the effect on the output performance metrics of the model will depend on the specific system being modeled.

10.4.6 Calibration on the Bottleneck Device

It is possible to adjust the service demand at only the bottleneck device of the system, the device with the highest utilization. This calibration may be done by either an absolute amount or by a percentage amount. If the system is single-class, a decrease (increase) in the demand at the bottleneck device will cause an increase (decrease) to the throughput. If the system is multiclass, the effect on the baseline model will depend on the specific system being modeled.

10.4.7 Ghost Server Calibration

In cases where the throughput of the baseline model is too high, it is possible to reduce the throughput in the calibrated model by adding a delay server. This is a calibration to an input parameter of the model (the number of service centers). This calibration is especially useful in systems where there exist possible software delays. Adding a ghost server mimics these delays. Delays of this type include the paging activity that cannot be measured, but is known to exist as the multiprogramming level increases. In some cases the delay is not able to be measured, yet the analyst can be certain that the delay is there.

10.5 CASE STUDY OF A THEORETICAL SYSTEM

This case study is an application of calibration to a theoretical system. Consider the theoretical system described by the queuing network diagram of Fig. 10.4. This is a closed system of N jobs circulating between a "host" and a "database server" consisting of three parallel processors. Such a system could be used for keyword queries in large database applications, where users enter keywords at three terminals (not shown) connected to the host. The result of each query is a list of entries that contain the keyword. Each request (i.e., job) is submitted to the database server, shown in the dashed box, for processing. The database server comprises three parallel processors, each responsible for searching a partition of the database. Each job forks into three subjobs, each of which is assigned to a unique processor. The solution of a general fork-join system is intractable. Therefore, a small number of servers (e.g., three) and a small number of users (e.g., three) are chosen to keep the analysis tractable

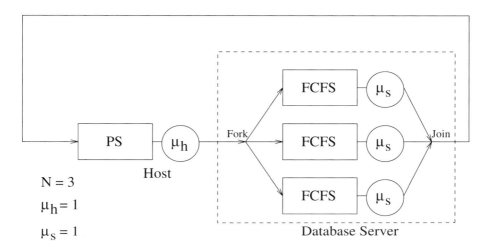

Figure 10.4 Exact queuing network model of fork-join system.

while retaining the characteristics of fork-join. The result of a query is formed when all three subjobs complete. The results of each processor's search are merged (i.e., joined) and these results are then reported to the user.

The queuing discipline is processor sharing at the host and FCFS at each of the parallel processors. The number of users (or, terminals) is represented by the multiprogramming level (N) and indicates the maximum number of outstanding queries at any time. Forking and joining are instantaneous events. The only blocking that occurs is at the join point. The subjobs wait at the join point until all subjobs belonging to the same job complete. The parallel processors continue service as long as subjobs are present in their respective queues. Service time distributions at the host and at each parallel server are assumed to be negative exponentials with means equal to 1.

This model is considered to exactly represent an actual computer system. Because of the forking and joining of jobs, there does not exist a product-form solution of this system. But since the system is small, it is possible to analyze the underlying Markov chain directly to determine the performance of the system. The throughput for the actual system is $X_A = 0.6340$. Utilization of the host is $U_h = 0.6340$, and utilization of the database server is $U_d = 0.8942$. The mean number of customers in the system is $N = 3$.

A typical analyst will not know about all of the complexities of this system. Only the external measurements (the throughput, utilizations, and multiprogramming level) are known. Figure 10.5 shows the view that a typical analyst would have of the system. The analyst must make assumptions about the hidden details of the servers, construct a model, and evaluate its accuracy by comparing the model's output to the known measurements of the actual system. A natural assumption is that each server consists of a single queue and

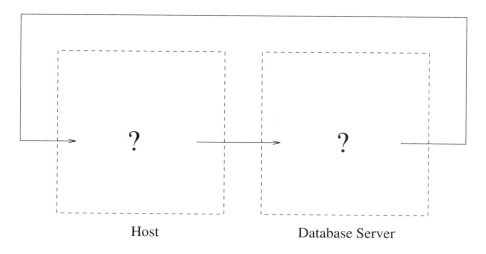

Figure 10.5 Analyst's view of the fork-join system.

a single server. To parameterize this model, the service rate of each server is needed. Knowing that throughput of any server is the product of its utilization and mean rate, the mean service rate of the database server, μ_d, is found as

$$\mu_d = \frac{X_A}{U_d} = \frac{0.6340}{0.8942} = 0.7090$$

The mean service rate of the host server, μ_h, is

$$\mu_h = \frac{X_A}{U_h} = \frac{0.6340}{0.6340} = 1.0000$$

Without other information, the analyst might assume a PS scheduling discipline at both servers. Thus, the uncalibrated baseline model shown in Fig. 10.6 is constructed. By comparing the actual system to its baseline model, it is easy to see that the modeling of the database server is in error. The uncalibrated baseline model of Fig. 10.6 has an efficient product-form solution. The throughput of the uncalibrated baseline model is found to be $X_U = 0.6105$, a 4% difference from the known throughput $X_A = 0.6340$. The analyst may consider a 4% error acceptable and use the uncalibrated baseline model for prediction studies. If a better match is desired, a more detailed baseline model must be constructed, or the original baseline model must be calibrated. Since no extra information is available, the analyst must calibrate to reduce the error.

10.5.1 Calibrated Models

Each of the calibrations described in Sec. 10.4 is now considered with respect to the uncalibrated model. The sign of the error value determines a set

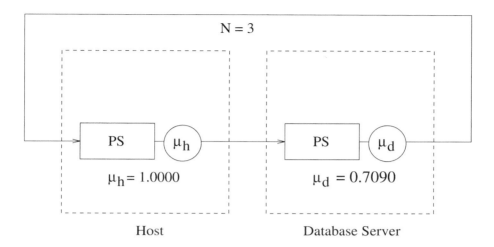

Figure 10.6 Uncalibrated baseline model of fork-join system.

of calibrations which can be applied, according to the direction of the error. In this case, since the error is negative (i.e., the uncalibrated model underpredicts throughput) only calibrations that increase the value of throughput are appropriate. [Note that not all calibrations that increase the throughput value will necessarily work. Service rates are bounded on the left by zero, meaning that if a device is made infinitely fast (i.e., if it is removed from the model), throughput may still not increase sufficiently.] If a calibration is suitable (i.e., will cause throughput to increase from 0.6105 to 0.6340) and has a natural and obvious implementation given the modeling circumstances, it is applied to the uncalibrated model. The result is a calibrated model that matches the actual system's throughput at the baseline. A description of each calibration follows. If a calibration is suitable, its application is described. If a calibration is not suitable, the reason is given.

- *Percent difference.* The percent difference calibration is bidirectional and is a candidate calibration. To implement the calibration, one determines a constant k by which the uncalibrated model's throughput is multiplied, yielding the calibrated throughput. The factor k is based on the actual throughput and the uncalibrated throughput at the baseline.

$$k = \frac{X_{A_b}}{X_{U_b}}$$

Therefore, the value of k for the fork-join example is found to be

$$k = \frac{0.6340}{0.6105} = 1.038$$

- *Absolute difference.* The absolute difference calibration is bidirectional and is a candidate calibration. To implement this calibration, one determines a constant c to which the uncalibrated model's throughput is added, yielding the calibrated throughput. The constant c is based on the actual throughput and the uncalibrated throughput at the baseline.

$$c = X_{A_b} - X_{U_b}$$

Therefore, the value of c for the fork-join example is found to be

$$c = 0.6340 - 0.6105 = 0.0235$$

- *MPL mean.* Since the MPL mean calibration is bidirectional, it is a candidate calibration. The appropriate calibration is found by determining the value of N at which the desired throughput is achieved. At $N = 3$, the throughput of the uncalibrated model is 0.6105. At $N = 4$, the throughput of the uncalibrated model is 0.6454. Using linear interpolation, the value for N at which throughput is modeled at 0.6340 is $N = 3.673$. Therefore, increasing the multiprogramming level from 3 to 3.673 yields a calibrated baseline model (i.e., one that matches the observed actual throughput).

- *MPL variance.* The MPL variance calibration is a unidirectional decreasing calibration. It is not suitable in this case since the objective is to increase throughput.

- *Multiclass.* Since the multiclass calibration is unidirectional increasing, it is a candidate calibration. There are three cases to consider: multiclass at the host, multiclass at the database server, and global multiclass. Starting with the single-class baseline system (in which all customers place the same demands on the devices), a group of customers are designated "fast" customers (i.e., these will place less demand on the devices), "slow" customers (i.e., these will place more demand on the devices), and "medium" customers (i.e., these customer demands do not change). Customer demands in the fast class are increasingly shifted to the customers of the slow class until the desired throughput is attained (if it can be attained). The distribution of customers among classes can be done in many ways. Since there are three customers in the system, one natural way is to put one in the slow class, one in the fast class, and leave one as it is (i.e., in the medium class). Using this technique, it is necessary to move 53.13% of the fast customer's host demand to the slow customer. Alternatively, when 33.17% of the fast customer's database server demand is shifted to the slow customer, the throughputs of the model and the actual system match.

    There are several ways in which a global multiclass calibration can be implemented. Unfortunately, the large number of parameters (i.e., number of classes, distribution of customers across classes, demands in each class) makes consistent application difficult. One natural interpretation is to have a systemwide slow class and a systemwide fast class in which a percentage of demand at each device is shifted. This calibration is equivalent to the percent difference calibration. Other implementations of this calibration are possible but are not considered here.

- *Speed mean.* The speed mean calibration is bidirectional and therefore a candidate calibration. To apply the calibration, one increases or decreases the speed of a device by decreasing or increasing all demands at that device by a common percentage amount. This can be done locally (i.e., at each station) or globally (i.e., at all stations). When the calibration is applied locally at the host, reducing the demand of jobs to 87.22% of the observed demand yields a model with the desired throughput. Similarly, reducing the demand at the database server to 94.58% of the observed demand produces a match. Reducing the demands at both servers to 96.30% of the observed demands also yields a matching model. This global speed mean calibration, however, is equivalent to the percent difference calibration, which is easier to implement (it is an output transformation). Therefore, only local speed mean calibrations are considered.

- *Delay/ghost server.* This calibration is unidirectional decreasing and is therefore not suitable in this case.

Thus, the following seven calibrated models have been identified as being suitable calibrations: percent difference, absolute difference, mean MPL, multiclass at the host, multiclass at the database server, host speed, and database server speed.

10.5.2 Prediction Tasks

By construction, each calibrated model matches the observed performance at the baseline case. However, each calibrated model exhibits different predictive capabilities. That is, even though calibration A and calibration B match at the baseline case, using A to predict what will happen if the system is altered in some fashion can yield quite different predictions from those found using B. Calibrations have different predictive capabilities. Such behavior, when applied to the theoretical system case study, is investigated in this subsection.

In determining a set of prediction tasks to be investigated, each assumption and parameter that contributes to the model is considered to be variable. Not all prediction tasks identified in this manner are natural or feasible to implement. For example, the assumption of negative exponential service distributions cannot be replaced with a general distribution since product-form solution techniques (e.g., convolution, mean value analysis) cannot accommodate general distributions. Moreover, depending on the prediction task, not all calibrations are applicable. For example, the MPL variance calibration is not easily applied to a prediction study in which the MPL is varied. The following eight prediction tasks are considered suitable for study. Those instances in which certain calibrations cannot be used in the prediction task are noted and explained.

- *Mean host demand.* In the baseline system, the average demand placed on the host device by each job is observed to be $1/\mu_h$. For x in the [0.1, 3.0] interval, let the demand that each job places on the host be x/μ_h. The calibrated models are solved and the actual system modified. This predicts the effects of hardware changes to the host. The graph of Fig. 10.7 compares the throughput curves of each calibrated model with the actual throughput curve as the value of x changes.

- *Mean database server demand.* In the baseline system, the average demand placed on the database server by each job is observed to be $1/\mu_d$. For x in the [0.1, 3.0] interval, let the demand each job places on the database server be x/μ_d. For the calibrated models, this is the demand placed on the single database server. For the actual system, this is the demand placed on each of the parallel database servers. This predicts the effects of hardware changes to the database server. The graph of Fig. 10.8 compares the throughput curves of each calibrated model with the actual throughput curve as the value of x changes.

- *Mean global demand.* For x in the [0.1, 3.0] interval, let the demand that each job places on each device be scaled by x, in the manner described above. This predicts the effects of hardware changes to both the host and the database server. The graph of Fig. 10.9 compares the throughput curves of each calibrated model with the actual throughput curve as the value of x changes.

- *Mean MPL.* In this prediction task, the number of jobs in the system N (i.e., the multiprogramming level) is varied from 1 to 20. Each calibrated model is solved and the actual system is modified at each point. This predicts the effect of changing the mean number of system users (i.e., jobs). Application of the mean MPL calibration to this prediction task is not appropriate and is, therefore, omitted. The graph of Fig. 10.10 compares the throughput curves of each calibrated model with the actual throughput curve as the value of N changes.

- *Multiclass at host.* The jobs in the original baseline model are assumed to be statistically identical (i.e., single-class). In this prediction it is assumed that the three customers place different demands on the host. Three classes of one customer each are created: slow, medium, and fast. For x in the [0.0, 0.9] interval, the host demand of the slow class is increased by a factor of x while the host demand of the fast class is reduced by x (i.e., $100x\%$ of the host demand is shifted from the fast class to the slow

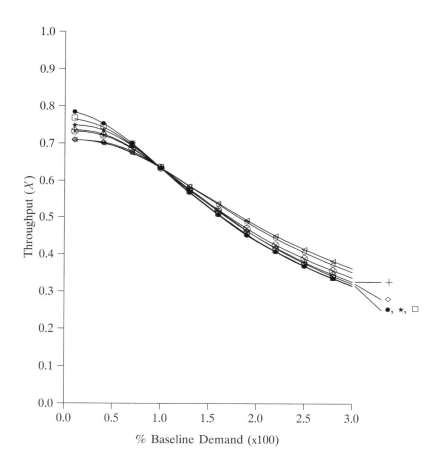

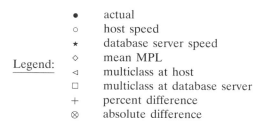

Legend:
- • actual
- ○ host speed
- ★ database server speed
- ◇ mean MPL
- ◁ multiclass at host
- □ multiclass at database server
- + percent difference
- ⊗ absolute difference

Figure 10.7   Fork-join: prediction = mean host demand.

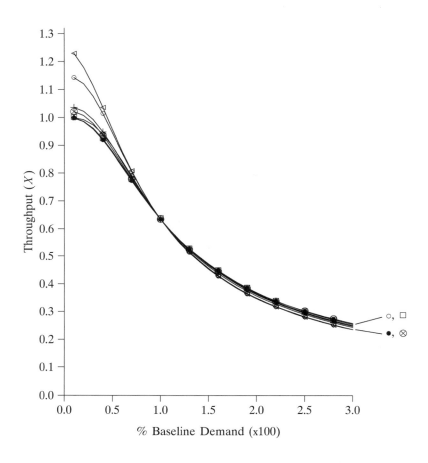

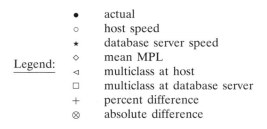

Legend:
- $\bullet$ actual
- $\circ$ host speed
- $\star$ database server speed
- $\diamond$ mean MPL
- $\triangleleft$ multiclass at host
- $\square$ multiclass at database server
- $+$ percent difference
- $\otimes$ absolute difference

Figure 10.8   Fork-join: prediction = mean database server demand.

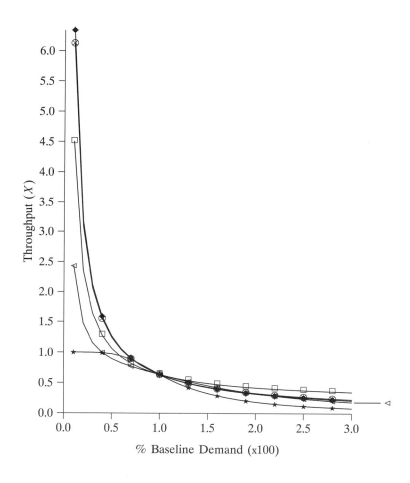

% Baseline Demand (x100)

Legend:

●	actual
○	host speed
★	database server speed
◇	mean MPL
◁	multiclass at host
□	multiclass at database server
+	percent difference
⊗	absolute difference

Figure 10.9 Fork-join: prediction = mean global demand.

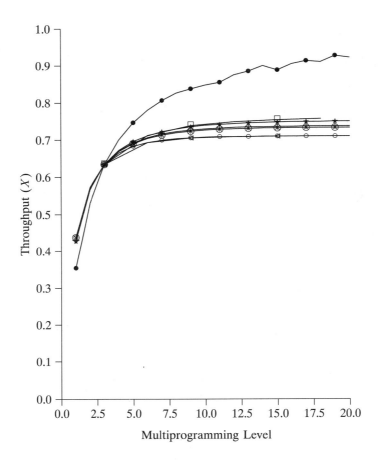

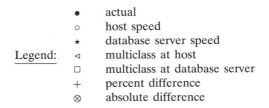

Figure 10.10 Fork-join: prediction = mean MPL.

class). This predicts the effects of the variance between the workload jobs. Application of the mean MPL calibration to this prediction task is not appropriate since there is no natural way to distribute a nonintegral value of N (i.e., $N = 3.672$) among the three classes. The graph of Fig. 10.11 compares the throughput curves.

- *Multiclass at database server.* In this prediction it is assumed that the three customers place different demands on the database server. Again, three classes of one customer each are created: slow, medium, and fast. For x in the [0.0, 0.9] interval, the database server demand of the slow class is increased by a factor of x while the database server demand of the fast class is reduced by x (i.e., $100x\%$ of the database server demand is shifted from the fast class to the slow class). As in the previous prediction, application of the mean MPL calibration to this prediction task is not appropriate. The graph of Fig. 10.12 compares the throughput curves of the calibrated models and the actual systems.

- *Multiple processors at host.* For $j = 1$ to 10, let there be j servers at the host. This predicts what happens when a uniprocessor becomes a multiprocessor having j processing elements. The graph of Fig. 10.13 compares the throughput curves of the calibrated models and the actual system.

- *MPL variance.* The multiprogramming level of the original model is assumed to be constant at 3. In this prediction task, the multiprogramming level of the actual system is drawn from a distribution other than a constant distribution. The mean multiprogramming level remains 3. One way to implement this calibration is to solve the system at two values of N such that the average of the two N's is 3. The average of the two throughputs is taken as the predicted throughput. For $j = 0$ to 3, throughputs $X(3 - j)$ and $X(3 + j)$ are solved for in the calibrated models and the actual system. (j is referred to as the MPL offset.) The predicted throughput for each model and the actual system is

$$\frac{X(3 - j) + X(3 + j)}{2}$$

When $j = 0$, the variance of the multiprogramming level is 0 (i.e., the baseline case). As j increases, the variance of the multiprogramming level increases. This predicts the effect of a variable workload where sometimes there are fewer customers and at other times there are more customers. The multiclass calibrations are not applicable in this prediction task since a value of N divisible by 3 is required. The mean MPL calibration is also not applicable. The graph of Fig. 10.14 compares the throughput curves of the calibrated models and the actual system.

In viewing each graph, one can determine which calibrations are performing well (i.e., producing throughput curves which closely match that of

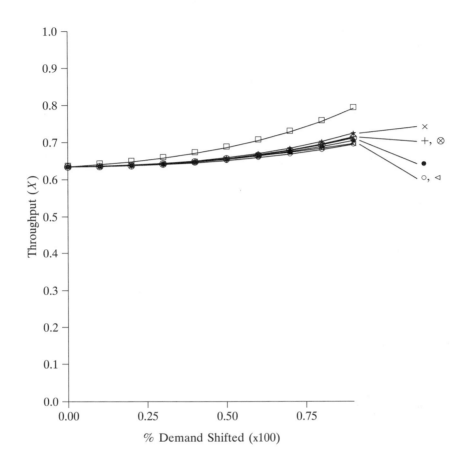

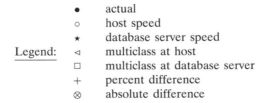

Figure 10.11   Fork-join: prediction = multiclass at host.

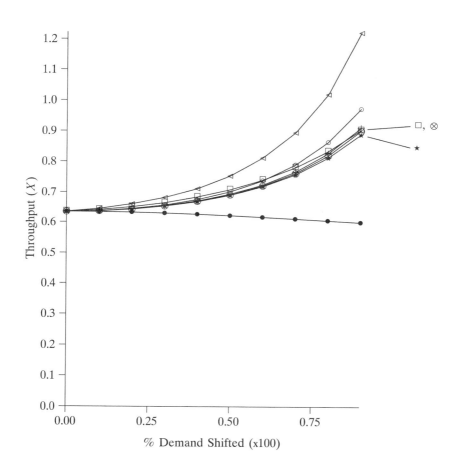

Figure 10.12 Fork-join: prediction = multiclass at database server.

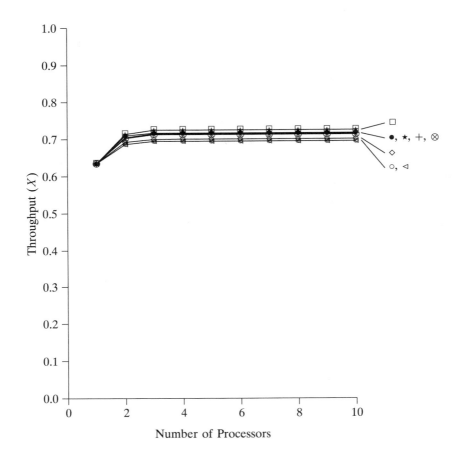

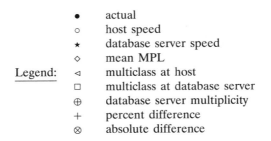

Figure 10.13 Fork-join: prediction = multiple processors at host.

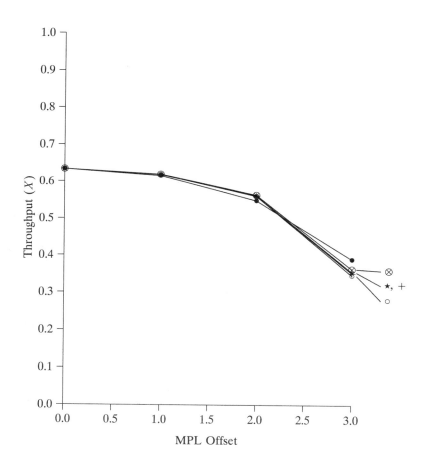

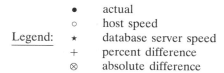

Figure 10.14 Fork-join: prediction = MPL variance.

the actual throughput curve) and which calibrations are performing poorly. To aid in determining a ranking of calibrations by accuracy for each prediction task, a scoring function g is adopted.

$$g = \frac{\sum_{i=1}^{K}(X_{A_i} - X_{P_i})^2}{K}$$

where X_{A_i} is the actual throughput at prediction point i and X_{P_i} is the predicted throughput at prediction point i. Therefore, g is the variance of the distance between the actual and predicted throughput curves at K points. This variance is referred to as the g-score of the calibration with respect to that prediction. The smaller the value of g, the more accurate the calibrated model's prediction. The value of g for each prediction for each calibration is shown in Table 10.2. Since the models are calibrated at the baseline point b, $X_{A_b} = X_{P_b}$ regardless of the prediction task and calibration. This point, the baseline calibration point, can be identified in each graph as the point through which all throughput curves pass. For example, Fig. 10.10 shows throughput curves of the actual system and the calibrated models, with each curve plotting throughput at each multiprogramming level value, and with each curve matching at $N = 3$, the baseline point. To obtain a g-score for a particular calibration, the sum of the squares of the distances between the actual throughput and the predicted throughput at each value of N is averaged.

Calibrations can be ranked within each prediction task by ordering them by ascending g-scores. These rankings are shown in Table 10.3.

Table 10.2 g-Scores for Fork-Join Models.

	Prediction Task							
Calibration	Mean host demand	Mean database server demand	Mean global demand	Mean MPL	Multiclass at host	Multiclass at database server	Multiclass at Multiple processors at host	MPL variance
Multiclass at database server	0.00034	0.000009	0.154724	0.011944	0.001860	0.020277	0.000053	n/a
Database server speed	0.000110	0.000027	1.173100	0.014191	0.000074	0.016708	0.000053	0.000335
Percent difference	0.000309	0.000266	0.000000	0.016481	0.000017	0.019095	0.000006	0.000382
Absolute difference	0.000491	0.000070	0.002038	0.017314	0.000008	0.017899	0.000018	0.000229
Mean MPL	0.000715	0.000285	0.000000	n/a	n/a	n/a	0.000237	n/a
Host speed	0.001385	0.002608	0.000000	0.022213	0.000026	0.026408	0.000440	0.000501
Multiclass at host	0.001698	0.004929	0.655089	0.020706	0.000011	0.070877	0.000440	n/a

Note: An entry of n/a indicates that the calibration is not applicable for the prediction task.

Table 10.3 Relative Rankings of Calibrations for Fork-Join.

Calibration	Mean host demand	Mean database server demand	Mean global demand	Mean MPL	Multiclass at host	Multiclass at database server	Multiple processors at host	MPL variance
	Prediction Task							
Multiclass at database server	1	1	5	1	6	4	4	n/a
Database server speed	2	2	7	2	5	1	3	2
Percent difference	3	4	3	3	3	3	1	3
Absolute difference	4	3	4	4	1	2	2	1
Mean MPL	5	5	2	n/a	n/a	n/a	5	n/a
Host speed	6	6	1	6	4	5	6	4
Multiclass at host	7	7	6	5	2	6	7	n/a

Note: An entry of n/a indicates that the calibration is not applicable for the prediction task.

By looking across a row in the table and observing the various rankings a calibration achieves in the various prediction tasks, one can obtain an estimate of that calibration's overall accuracy in this particular fork-join case. For example, percent difference and absolute difference calibrations tend to have good rankings (i.e., closer to 1), while the host speed and multiclass at host calibrations tend to have poor rankings (i.e., closer to 7). That is, for this example, calibrations on the output parameter (i.e., percent and absolute difference) do well and calibrations affecting the host (i.e., host speed and multiclass at host) do poorly. It should be kept in mind, however, that rankings across prediction tasks are relative to each prediction task. Although they are useful, they can be used informally only for determining which calibrations are the best overall.

10.6 RULES OF THUMB

In general, the only correct model of the system is the system itself, and any abstract model will be an approximation of the system. The way to make better models of the system is to understand the system better. Calibration is an attempt to bring the model closer to the system by adjusting different input or output parameters of the model.

Any calibration technique can be the best in a particular situation, but all calibration techniques fail at times. Predicting which calibration technique will work best in a given situation is hard. Some general rules of thumb have been developed which can guide the choice of a calibration technique:

1. Alterations to demands on the bottleneck device are more accurate than alterations to nonbottleneck devices. For example, if a device is underutilized (i.e., if the device is not the bottleneck), changing its service demand will have little effect on the performance of the system, and the resulting calibration will be ineffective.

2. Calibration via adjusting the multiprogramming level should not be done if the resulting calibrated model is saturated, especially if the prediction causes the system to become unsaturated. For example, when the system is saturated, changes in the multiprogramming level will have little effect on overall performance. The resulting multiprogramming level calibration will not be effective.

3. Calibrations that alter the performance outputs of the model appear to be more effective than those which alter the input parameters of the model. For example, adjusting the throughput either by a percent difference or an absolute difference appears to be more effective than adjusting the loadings at the individual devices.

4. The model should not be calibrated in the same way that it is to be altered for performance prediction. For example, if the performance prediction is to increase the multiprogramming level, the model should not be calibrated by adjusting the multiprogramming level.

10.7 A MORE FORMAL VIEW

Calibration can be viewed more formally as an approximation technique. The goal of approximation is to reduce the solution complexity of the model so that it can be solved. The disadvantage of approximation solutions is less accuracy. However, approximations that consistently yield results within an acceptable range of error are valuable.

A general procedure for approximations is described in Fig. 10.15. First, an exact model of a computer system is constructed. But the exact model cannot be solved analytically using standard solution tools or techniques. It is intractable. The exact model is transformed into an approximate model using a forward mapping $\mathcal{F}$. The approximate model can be solved exactly. It is tractable. The results of the exact solution of the approximate model are transformed using a reverse mapping $\mathcal{F}^{-1}$ which adjusts (i.e., calibrates) the answer to account for information lost during forward mapping.

This view of approximation is particularly useful when the analytic model is to be used for prediction. Suppose that two terminals are to be added to the example system of Fig. 10.2. The analytic model of Fig. 10.2 is to be used for predicting the performance of the system as the multiprogramming level increases from 2 to 4. Suppose that the calibration procedure chosen is

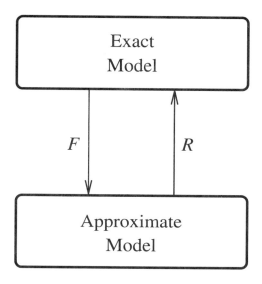

Figure 10.15 General approximation procedure.

to scale the response time of the model by a factor of 0.77. The calibration procedure is included in the process of predicting the performance of the system as follows:

1. The analytic model of Fig. 10.2 is constructed. The response time of the model differs from the response time of the system. The response time of the model, R_{model}, is calculated from the actual response time of the system, R_{actual}, as

$$R_{model} = \frac{R_{actual}}{0.77}$$

   In this case, the forward mapping function, $\mathcal{F}$, is

$$R_{model} = \mathcal{F}(R_{actual}) = \frac{R_{actual}}{0.77}$$

   The inverse mapping function $\mathcal{F}^{-1}$ is

$$R_{actual} = \mathcal{F}^{-1}(R_{model}) = (0.77)R_{model}$$

2. The multiprogramming level of the model is changed to 4.
3. The model is solved.
4. The actual predicted response time is calculated using the reverse mapping function $\mathcal{F}^{-1}$ as

$$R_{actual\ (pred)} = \mathcal{F}^{-1}(R_{model\ (pred)}) = (0.77)R_{model\ (pred)}$$

Calibration is an approximation process. The calibration procedure of scaling the output of the model by a percentage will not in general give the exact value for the actual predicted response time. In many cases the results are close enough.

10.8 CONCLUDING REMARKS

In this chapter, issues of calibration have been addressed. The goal is to develop a proper view of calibration. In an ideal situation, the modeler is so wise as to not require calibration. However, none (well, only a few) of us have risen to that level of sainthood. Calibration is a necessary step in the modeling process. There are many different calibration techniques and several of them have been compared in this chapter. The unfortunate fact is that there is no single best calibration technique. Each calibration technique works well in certain situations, and each calibration technique fails in certain situations. Thus, calibration is an art. The approach to calibration taken in this chapter has been to apply the scientific method to its evaluation, that is, identify the various alternatives, perform a well-designed set of experiments, and evaluate the effectiveness of each calibration technique in each situation. Perhaps the most important side benefit of a rigorous calibration study is that it forces the modeler to spend time analyzing and experimenting with the system being modeled. In this way, the modeler understands the system better, creates better models as a result, and makes the calibration issue moot. Additional material relevant to model calibration can be found in Refs. [2, 3, 4].

10.9 EXERCISES

1. It is not hard to find a system in which an absolute demand calibration to every device in the system causes the utilization of one device to increase, and the utilization of another device to decrease. Give an example.
2. Suppose that the model you are using is a single-class product-form queuing network model. Show, using asymptotic bounds analysis, the effect on system throughput by a calibration (up or down) on the bottleneck device.
3. Suppose that the model you are using is a single-class product-form queuing network model. Show, using asymptotic bounds analysis, the effect on system response time by a calibration (up or down) on the bottleneck device.
4. Reconsider the case study given in Sec. 10.5. Suppose that there are only two servers in the database server instead of three. Solve the exact system and construct the seven calibrated models as illustrated in Sec. 10.5.1.
5. Continue the analysis of the previous problem, by mimicking the eight prediction tasks given in Sec. 10.5.2. Compare the various calibrations, using the g-scoring function and by giving the relative rankings. Compare the results to those given in the text.

6. Consider a workstation to which you have access. To carry on this project, the workstation needs to have at least two local disks and must run a UNIX-like operating system. The following steps will guide you through a complete calibration project.

(a) Write a workload generator program in C according to the following algorithm. The workload generator consists of a parent process (P) and multiple instances of children processes (C) which are forked by the parent. The parent process is responsible for obtaining the parameters that will determine the service demands on the CPU and disks of the children processes, controlling the experiment, and computing final statistics. The children processes are the core of the workload generator and they will use the CPU and the two disks as shown below. The parent process P will make sure that there is always a fixed number N (the degree of multiprogramming) of children processes running. The entire experiment must be run for a time interval (*total time*) equal to at least 100 times the execution time of a C process (*max time*) to minimize end effects when measuring the throughput. Measure the throughput as the number of completed C processes divided by the total time of the experiment. Figure 10.16 shows the algorithm for processes P and C. At the baseline, an average[2] of 20,000 iterations of a computationally intensive (i.e., memory, register, and arithmetic operations) code are performed per CPU phase (i.e., "visit" to the CPU). For the prediction studies, the CPU demand parameter will vary by changing the number of iterations of this loop. For example, to double the CPU demand, the workload generating program was configured to iterate the loop 40,000 times instead of 20,000 times. Visits to both disks must be weighted equally for the baseline model, with the average number of bytes written during each visit being 1250 Kbytes at each device. If your workstation is connected to a file server, make sure that the files you will be using in the experiment are local to your workstation. Also, make sure that there is nobody else logged into your workstation during the time you are running your experiment.

(b) Build a performance model with one CPU and two disks. The performance model should consider only the type C processes. Obtain the service demands for the three devices.

(c) Solve the model and obtain the baseline model throughput.

(d) Determine which calibration techniques are applicable to move the throughput in the right direction (up or down).

(e) Calibrate the model according to all techniques specified in the previous item.

(f) Carry out the following prediction studies using all calibrated models:

- *Mean MPL.* The multiprogramming level N (i.e., the number of processes running simultaneously) is varied from 1 to 6.

---

[2]The workload generating program draws each value (both CPU phase iterations and size of disk and tape transfers) from a negative exponential distribution having the desired mean obtained from a random number generator.

Process P:
> Get parameters (mean number of loops during CPU burn,
>> ratio of disk 1 to disk 2 visits, mean transfer
>> size for disks 1 and 2)
>
> Open one file on disk 1 and another on disk 2
> Fork *N* processes of type C
> Wait on the completion of any process of type C
> Upon completion of a type C process do:
>> update experiment time (*total time*)
>> if *total time* < *max time*
>> then fork another child C
>> else compute and print throughput and stop

Process C:
> Loop
>> Burn CPU time
>> Decide to visit disk 1 or disk 2
>> Determine size of transfer
>> Write from memory to chosen device
>
> Endloop

Figure 10.16 Workload generator algorithm.

- *Mean CPU demand.* Two experiments besides the baseline are conducted: (1) at 50% of the observed CPU demand, and (2) at 150% of the observed CPU demand. The demands are changed in the actual system by scaling the number of times the CPU phase computation loop of the workload generator is executed.

- *Mean disk 1 demand.* Two experiments besides the baseline are conducted: (1) at 50% and (2) at 150% of the observed demand. The demands are changed in the actual system by scaling the number of bytes written to disk 1. In each calibrated model, the time required to perform the operation is scaled. The assumption is that by halving the number of bytes written to the disk, the time taken to perform the write will also be halved. This assumption may be in error since channel path contention, queuing for service by the controller, and seek and rotational latency are factors that do not necessarily scale linearly with the size of the transfer. However, this is a natural assumption to make without further information.

- *Mean disk 2 demand.* Two experiments besides the baseline are conducted: (1) at 50% and (2) at 150% of the observed demand. The demands are changed in the actual system by scaling the number of bytes written to disk 2. In each calibrated model, the time required to perform the operation is scaled.

- *Split disk 1/disk 2.* The ratio of the number of visits made to disk 1 and disk 2 is scaled by making 30% of disk 1 visits become disk 2 visits, and vice versa.

(g) Compute *g*-scores and build a table for all calibration techniques and all prediction studies.

BIBLIOGRAPHY

1. F. Baskett, K. Chandy, R. Muntz, and F. Palacios, Open, closed, and mixed networks of queues with different classes of customers, *Journal of the ACM*, Vol. 22, No. 2, April 1975, pp. 248–260.
2. J. C. Lowery, Calibration and predictive modeling of computer systems, Ph.D. dissertation, Vanderbilt University, Nashville, Tenn., 1992.
3. J. P. Buzen and A. Shum, Model calibration, *Proceedings of the 1989 CMG Conference*, Reno, Nevada, December 1989, pp. 808–811.
4. J. Flowers and L. W. Dowdy, A comparison of calibration techniques for queuing network models, *Proceedings of the 1989 CMG Conference,* Reno, Nevada, December, 1989, pp. 644–655.

Chapter 11

Performance of New Applications

11.1 INTRODUCTION

Several techniques and examples have been presented that predict performance when a change to an existing system occurs, either with respect to the system workload or with respect to the system hardware. Capacity planning involves building performance models for existing workloads and predicting the effects of possible upgrades. Measurements taken on existing workloads are used to parameterize the service demands required by the performance model, as indicated in Fig. 11.1.

However, in many capacity planning situations one is confronted with the problem of predicting the performance of *new* applications. Two types of new applications should be considered:

- *Internally developed products.* In this case, new applications are developed by a team of in-house programmers. This implies that the software structure and the target architecture are well known.
- *Externally developed products.* In this case, software products are developed by a third party, and the software structure and the assumed target architecture are unknown.

Typically, the role of performance is of secondary importance in the development of new applications [1]. Most applications are designed,

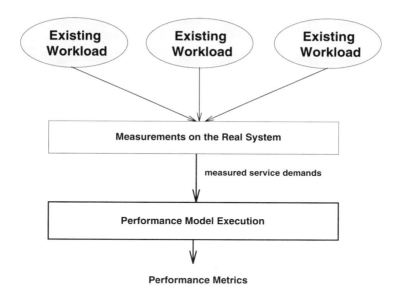

Figure 11.1   Capacity planning for existing workloads.

implemented, and installed without prior (much less proper) performance considerations. As seen throughout this text, performance depends critically upon the particular combination of logical requirements, physical design, and the operating environment. The consequence of this neglect is that many applications are abandoned soon after (and sometimes before!) implementation. Often, such applications require expensive software rewrites and an increase in the current system's capacity.

Correct functionality of an application should not be its only requirement. New applications should also be required to meet certain specified performance service levels. Analysts and designers should be concerned with the performance requirements of new systems from the beginning stages of the early design. This requires being able to translate from a relatively high-level logical description of the application and a relatively high-level description of the target architecture with its supporting software platform into appropriate service demands of the application. This is called *application sizing (AS)*.

Figure 11.2 depicts the role of application sizing in a capacity planning study. If a new application will be running with existing applications, a performance model is needed that provides a performance assessment of the new application as well as an estimate on the impact, called the *environmental impact*, on already existing applications. Therefore, the inputs to the performance model are the estimated service demands for the new application and the measured service demands for the existing applications.

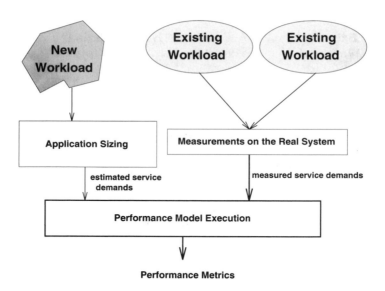

Figure 11.2 Application sizing.

The process of constructing software systems that meet performance objectives has been called *software performance engineering* (SPE). SPE is used to identify those designs which are likely to yield satisfactory performance. At the same time, SPE is used to discard those designs that are likely to exhibit unacceptable performance. Such identifications are required before significant time is spent on the application's development. In this chapter we illustrate how performance models can be used in the SPE process. The presentation is motivated by a typical credit card problem.

11.2 THE CREDIT CARD PROBLEM

Consider a chain of department stores which are distributed over several cities. In the board meeting it was decided that the company should start offering its own credit card as a means of increasing sales. The systems software department was requested to develop the necessary software to support the new credit card. The capacity planning staff immediately started to worry about the potential impact that the new credit card software would have on the service levels of existing applications. They were also anxious to assess whether or not acceptable service levels for the new credit card application could be supported by the existing system.

It would be unfortunate if the credit card application were fully implemented before it was discovered that it performs poorly and that it consumes a significant amount of resources. Restructuring the software to remedy the problems may be too costly and too time consuming. Rather, it would have been preferable if the entire software development process were integrated with performance prediction studies. Such studies provide software designers with early performance information to guide their design and to compare alternatives at each stage in the design process.

The capacity planning staff met with the application programmers and system analysts and were given the following description of the credit card application. Each cashier is to have a point-of-sale (POS) terminal connected to the DP facility as shown in Fig. 11.3. Each use of a credit card is to generate an on-line transaction, called a *sale*. A sale first checks the customer's current balance and credit limit to determine whether the customer has enough credit for the purchase. If the customer has sufficient credit, the sale is recorded and an authorization code is returned to the requesting terminal. If the customer has insufficient credit, a credit rejection message is returned to the terminal.

Summary reports are to be generated every day by a batch application called *statement*. The due dates for customer balances are assigned in such a way as to distribute the processing load uniformly throughout the month. The statement application scans all customer records. If a bill is to be issued on that day for a customer, the application scans all transactions, purchase or refund, for the customer during the billing period in order to generate the bill.

The following information about the operation of the new system has been provided by the marketing and sales personnel:

- A total of 180,000 credit cards are expected to be issued.

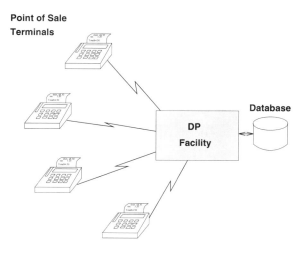

Figure 11.3   Credit card application environment.

- On the average, each customer will use the credit card on four different shopping days per month.
- Each customer will perform an average of three credit card transactions on each day they shop.
- An average of 30% of the sales are expected to occur between noon and 1:00 p.m.
- Approximately 10% of the credit card transactions are expected to be rejected due to insufficient credit.

The following service levels for the credit card application have been established by management:

- The average response time for a *sale* transaction should not exceed 2 sec, taking into account that this type of transaction will share the DP facility resources with other on-line applications.
- The *statement* application should be able to issue all daily statements in 2 hours during the night batch window.

To address the capacity planning issues, estimates are needed for the service demand and workload intensity parameters for the credit card system. These estimates will be used to parameterize performance prediction models similar to those constructed in previous chapters.

11.3 SIZING THE CREDIT CARD APPLICATION

Before performance prediction techniques used to size applications are formalized, reconsider the credit card example. Consider the workload intensity parameter for the *sale* transaction. The total number of transactions generated per month can be computed as:

$$180,000 \text{ customers} \times \frac{4 \text{ shopping days}}{\text{month} \times \text{customer}} \times \frac{3 \text{ transactions}}{\text{shopping day}}$$

$$= 2,160,000 \text{ tr./month}$$

Assuming that the store remains open seven days a week, and that 30% of the daily transactions occur during the peak time from noon to 1:00 p.m., the average arrival rate, in tps, during the peak period is:

$$0.3 \times \frac{2,160,000 \text{ tr./month}}{30 \text{ days/month}} = 21,600 \text{ tr./hr} = \frac{21,600 \text{ tr./hr}}{3600 \text{ sec/hr}} = 6 \text{ tps}$$

Now consider the service demands for the *sales* transaction at the CPU and I/O devices. For this, a more precise description of the transaction is needed. The following details have been obtained from the application developers. As shown in Fig. 11.4, each customer record is retrieved from a CUSTOMER file, which is keyed by credit card number. If the available credit limit is insufficient for the requested purchase, a reject message is returned to the terminal. This occurs 10% of the time. Otherwise, the transaction is posted in a SALES file. One such file is generated each day and contains all transactions performed on that day. If the purchase is approved, a message with the authorization code is returned to the POS terminal.

Consider the four boxes labeled (a) through (d) in Fig. 11.4. The service demand, D_i^{sales}, at any device i for the *sales* transaction can be written as a function of the service demands at the same device at each of the boxes. The contribution of each box to the total service demand depends on the logic of the application and on the relative frequency at which each box is executed. For instance,

$$D_i^{sales} = D_i^a + 0.1 \times D_i^b + 0.9(D_i^c + D_i^d) \tag{11.1}$$

The remaining problem now is how to compute the individual components D_i^a through D_i^d. This computation depends, among other things, on the type of the device. For instance, assume that two disks, D1 and D2, are to be used for the credit card database. Suppose that the CUSTOMER file will reside

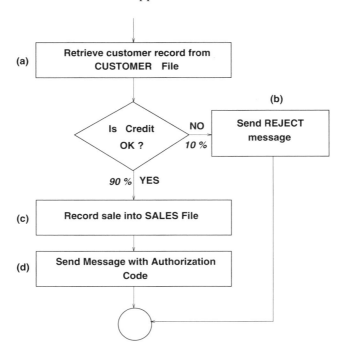

Figure 11.4 Sale transaction.

on D1 and the SALES file will reside on D2. Since boxes (b) and (d) do not access any file, $D_{D1}^b = D_{D1}^d = D_{D2}^b = D_{D2}^d = 0$. Also, since box (a) does not access the SALES file and box (c) does not access the CUSTOMER file, $D_{D2}^a = D_{D1}^c = 0$.

The next issue is how to estimate the nonzero service demands on the two disks. This requires an estimate of the number of I/O operations on each file per box, as well as the average service time per I/O operation. The application developers were asked what kind of access method would be used for the CUSTOMER and SALES files. The CUSTOMER file is to be supported by a B-tree based access method [2] (such as IBM's VSAM [3]), and entries to the SALES file are to be appended sequentially. Given the following assumptions, the height of the B-tree can be estimated as 3 (see Fig. 11.5).

- Disk blocks at the leaf nodes of the tree contain 10 complete customer records each. Thus, since there are a total of 180,000 credit cards, there are a total of 18,000 (180,000/10) disk blocks at this level.
- Blocks at nonleaf nodes contain only keys and pointers used to reach the appropriate leaf block containing a customer record with a given key. Each such block holds 200 (key + pointer) cells. Thus, there are 90 (18,000/200) blocks at the level just above the leaf nodes. Above this level, only one block (the root of the tree) is needed to point to the 90 blocks at the next lower level.

Assume that the physical characteristics of disks D1 and D2 are those given in Table 11.1. Assuming that the root block will be in the memory buffer at all times, two physical I/Os are required (one per lower level) for each access to a record in the CUSTOMER file. Assume further that each physical I/O reads a 4 Kbyte disk block. Thus, the average service time, S_{D1}, per read on disk D1 can be computed as the sum of the average seek, average latency, and transfer time: $S_{D1} = 28 + 8.33 + 4/2.2 = 38$ msec. Hence, the average service demand on disk D1 due to box (a) is $2S_{D1}$ since each access

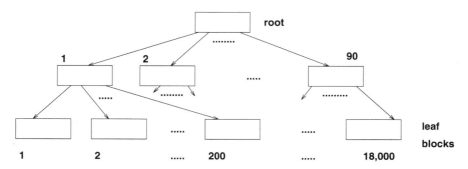

Figure 11.5 B-tree organization of CUSTOMER file.

Table 11.1 Physical Disk Characteristics.

Device	Average Seek (msec)	Latency (msec)	Transfer Rate (MB/sec)
D1	28.0	8.33	2.2
D2	18.5	8.33	2.8

to the CUSTOMER file requires two physical I/Os. Thus, $D^a_{D1} = 2 \times S_{D1} = 76$ msec.

Each access to the SALES file in box (c) requires only one physical I/O. Assuming the disk characteristics of Table 11.1 and assuming that each sales record is 0.1 Kbytes long, the service demand on disk D2 due to box (c) is estimated to be $D^c_{D2} = 18.5 + 8.33 + 0.1/2.8 = 27$ msec. Table 11.2 summarizes the service demand values for the two disks at each box for the *sales* transaction using Eq. (11.1).

The next step is to estimate the service demands at the CPU for each of the boxes of the *sales* transaction. The three main sources for CPU use are user code, operating system code (including file management system and network protocol processing), and software support code (e.g., DBMS, transaction monitors, graphical packages, etc.). The CPU demand by the user code is difficult to estimate during the early stages of the design because little is known about the application. For this reason, application CPU usage is often ignored because I/O activity dominates system performance and the I/O demands are easier to estimate [4]. In fact, it has been argued that user code contributes to less than 5% of the total response time in most applications [1]. Thus, the CPU usage in boxes (a) and (c) is first estimated by considering only the CPU usage attributed to the operating system to perform the I/O operations required in these boxes. Then, the CPU usage of boxes (b) and (d) is estimated as the CPU time needed to format and build messages.

One technique used to obtain the above estimates is to construct small benchmarks for certain components of the proposed system [5]. These benchmark programs may be subject to performance testing and measurement. For instance, suppose that one wanted to estimate the CPU usage of an access to a record in the CUSTOMER file using the B-tree based access method. Two programs, A and B, could be constructed as shown in Fig. 11.6. These two

Table 11.2 Disk Service Demands for Sales Transaction.

Box	Disk D1 (msec)	Disk D2 (msec)
(a)	76.0	0.0
(b)	0.0	0.0
(c)	0.0	27.0
(d)	0.0	0.0
sales	76.0	24.3

```
Program A: [ Includes I/O access]

For  n := 1 to 100 do
    begin
        Generate a key K randomly ;
        Retrieve   record with key = K from file
               CUSTOMER;
    end;
```

```
Program B: [Does not include I/O's]

For n:= 1 to 100 do
    Generate a key K randomly  ;
```

Figure 11.6 Programs A and B to estimate CPU service demand.

programs could then be executed and the total CPU time, t_A and t_B, could be monitored for each run. By subtracting t_B from t_A, the total CPU time required to execute one hundred retrieve operations from file CUSTOMER can be obtained. Hence, the average CPU service demand due to box (a) can be estimated as

$$D_{cpu}^a = \frac{t_A - t_B}{100}.$$

Note that D_{CPU}^a includes all the CPU time spent by the access method and the operating system to retrieve a record from the CUSTOMER file. The same approach is used to obtain the CPU demand estimate for box (c).

Similarly, one could construct programs C and D, shown in Fig. 11.7, to estimate the CPU time spent by the network protocols and operating system to send one message. Again, the CPU times, t_C and t_D, of both programs would be measured. By subtracting t_D from t_C one obtains the time needed to create and send 100 messages. Thus,

$$D_{cpu}^b = D_{cpu}^d = \frac{t_C - t_D}{100}.$$

Table 11.3 shows the results of following the procedures above to obtain D_{cpu}^a through D_{cpu}^d. The resulting CPU service demand for the *sales* transaction is computed using Eq. (11.1) and included in Table 11.3.

Attention is now focused on the *statement* application. It is assumed that at the end of every day, before the *statement* application executes, an index is created for the SALES file generated on that day. An example of such an index file is shown in Fig. 11.8. The generation of this index file is assumed to take approximately two hours given that an average of 72,000 sales are expected per day.

```
Program C: [sending dummy message]

For n := 1 to 100 do
   begin
      create a dummy message ;
      send dummy message ;
   end;
```

```
Program D:[plain loop]

For n := 1 to 100 do
   begin
   end;
```

Figure 11.7   Programs C and D to estimate CPU service demand.

Table 11.3 CPU Demands for Sales Transaction.

Box	D_{cpu} (msec)
(a)	40.0
(b)	20.0
(c)	15.0
(d)	20.0
sales	71.7

The flow diagram of the *statement* application is shown in Fig. 11.9. As seen, the application executes a loop 180,000 times, one per customer. For each customer, the customer record is retrieved from the CUSTOMER file and the statement closing date is checked. If no statement is to be printed on this date for this customer, the next customer record is examined. Otherwise, the SALES files, one for each of the 30 days in the billing period, are scanned. For each file, the first SALES record for the customer in question is obtained. If no such record is found, the next SALES file is processed. Otherwise, the application keeps retrieving all additional SALES records from the file. After all SALES files have been scanned, the customer's statement is generated and printed.

It is worth examining the branching probabilities at each branching point (i.e., the diamond shaped boxes) in the diagram of Fig. 11.9. The first branching point follows the YES path with probability 1/30 since it is assumed that 1/30 of the statements are printed daily. The second branching point follows the YES path if there is any SALES record for that day for a particular

Index to SALES file

Card#	
09123	01012
21345	00001,00003,01010
54678	00002,00005,01011
	......
88976	00004,60691
	......

SALES file for 1 day

	CARD #	Transaction
00001	21345	
00002	54678	
00003	21345	
00004	88976	
00005	54678	
	......	......
01010	21345	
01011	54678	
01012	09123	
	......	......
60691	88976	

Figure 11.8 Index on SALES file.

customer. Since it is assumed that each customer will go shopping 4 times a month on the average, the probability of shopping on any given day is 4/30. This assumes that visits to the store are uniformly distributed over the month. This assumption is a bit simplistic since weekend shopping is considerably heavier than weekday activity. Including a daily shopping activity distribution is possible, but not included here. The graphical notation used to indicate that a certain portion of the code is executed a certain number of times on the average has been proposed by Smith [6] and is shown in Fig. 11.10.

It is now possible to formulate an equation for the average service demand, D_i^{stat}. This is the demand of the *statement* application placed on device i as a function of the service demands at boxes (a) through (d) at device i.

$$D_i^{\text{stat}} = 180{,}000 \times \left\{ D_i^a + \frac{1}{30} \left[30 \times \left(D_i^b + \frac{4}{30} \times 2 \times D_i^c \right) + D_i^d \right] \right\}$$

$$= 180{,}000 \times \left(D_i^a + D_i^b + \frac{4}{15} \times D_i^c + \frac{1}{30} D_i^d \right) \tag{11.2}$$

The same type of analysis can be used to obtain D_i^a through D_i^d, for $i =$ CPU, D1, and D2. It is assumed that only one I/O operation to disk D1 is necessary in box (a) of the *statement* application since the customer records are scanned sequentially and not by the key as was done in the *sale* transaction

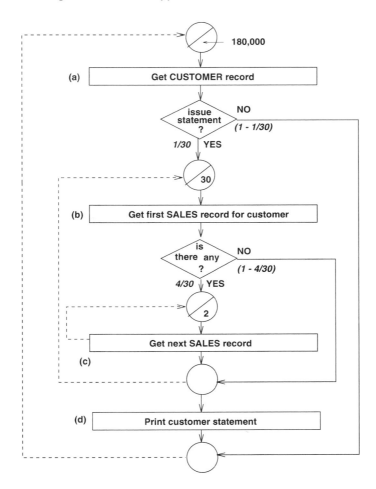

Figure 11.9 Statement job.

to the CUSTOMER file. Table 11.4 shows these service demands as well as the service demands for the entire application computed using Eq. (11.2). The last line of Table 11.4 shows the service demands for the *statement* application in hours. It can be seen that a lower bound on the application's turnaround time is equal to 8.5 hours (i.e., the sum of all service demands). Even without taking into account any queuing delays, it is obvious that the turnaround time for this application will significantly exceed the desired service level of 2 hours. This observation emphasizes that the mere exercise of computing the service demands for a new application can reveal important insights into its future performance. In Sec. 11.6, software restructuring alternatives to mitigate the problem of this application are discussed.

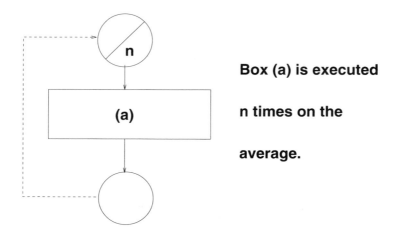

Box (a) is executed

n times on the

average.

Figure 11.10   Convention for representing loops.

Table 11.4   Service Demands for the Statement Application (in Seconds).

Box	D_{CPU}	D_{D1}	D_{D2}
(a)	0.035	0.038	0.000
(b)	0.030	0.000	0.054
(c)	0.028	0.000	0.027
(d)	0.050	0.000	0.000
statement	13.3×10^3	6.8×10^3	11×10^3
Service Demand (hours)			
statement	3.7	1.8	3.0

11.4 TECHNIQUES FOR SPE

In this section, software performance engineering techniques are discussed. These techniques can be integrated into the software development life cycle. Also discussed are techniques related to data collection for SPE.

11.4.1 Software Development Life Cycle and SPE

Several methodologies for software development have been proposed and used successfully in the software industry. A widely used methodology, the waterfall model, is described here and how each step in this methodology can provide input data for a SPE study.

The waterfall model introduced by Boehm [7] decomposes the software development life cycle into five main phases: requirement analysis and specification, system design, program design, program coding, and system testing.

Figure 11.11 illustrates these various phases. The relationships between each phase and SPE activities and/or data for SPE studies are shown. These relationships are indicated above each of the boxes that represent the various phases of the software development life cycle.

The requirement analysis and specification phase describes the problem to be solved by the new software. As a result of this phase, two types of requirements are generated: functional and nonfunctional requirements. The functional requirements describe the functions that the new system is supposed to perform. The nonfunctional requirements may include service levels (e.g., response times, throughputs, etc.) as well as a specification of the target hardware/software platform. This includes the specification of the CPU, I/O devices, operating system, database management system, transaction processing monitors, and compilers of the target hardware/software platform.

The system design phase describes the solution to the problem specified in the previous requirements phase. The system is decomposed into modules and pseudocode for each module to be generated. The relationship between modules is established and the type of data used by each module is specified. The number of invocations per module can be derived from the system design. This allows a first approximation of the service demands to be obtained. Performance predictions obtained with SPE data collected during this phase should be within 30% of the performance of the actual application [1].

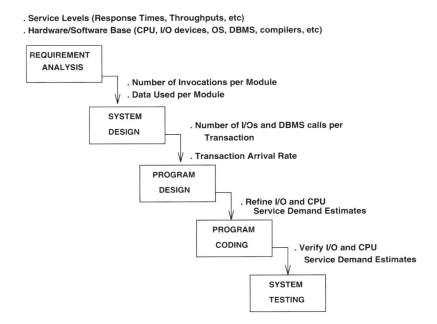

Figure 11.11   Waterfall model of software development.

The third phase, program design, describes the mechanisms that best implement the solution. Algorithms and data structures are specified in this phase. Each of the modules resulting from the System Design Phase is mapped into one or more programs. A complete specification of each transaction is given in this phase. This specification is generally given in some form of pseudocode and is independent of the target programming language. More precise estimates of the transaction service demands may be obtained in this phase since the number of I/O operations and/or DBMS calls can be derived from the transaction description. The accuracy of the predictions obtained in this phase is expected to be in the range 15 to 20% [1].

The actual implementation occurs during the program coding phase. This phase is used to refine the I/O and CPU service demands for the various transactions as they are implemented.

The final phase is system testing. In this phase, an overall verification of I/O and service demand estimates is performed.

Each phase of the software development life cycle increases the level of accuracy of the service demand estimates. The initial models developed during the early stages of the design can only be expected to provide gross order-of-magnitude performance predictions. Ref. [5] indicates the type of data than can be captured in each phase of the software development life cycle using the spiral methodology for software development.

11.4.2 Obtaining Data for SPE

Application sizing involves cooperating with people from other departments, mainly the developers. This may pose problems of a managerial nature. Developers must be educated on the importance of SPE so that they assign it enough importance and give priority to it [1]. Ref. [8] describes numerous approaches that can be used to obtain cooperation from people that should provide data for SPE.

The main difficulties in obtaining the right data may arise from [1]:

- Inadequate communication between designers and capacity planners.
- Low priority given by designers to obtain SPE data.
- Inadequate understanding by designers of the relevant SPE data. Some inputs are more important than others, and designers are not always aware of which parameters will affect performance most. For instance, the volume of physical I/O is an important factor in determining service demands at the peripherals and at the CPU.

It should also be realized that not all transactions will have a strong impact on performance. In fact, as observed by many authors [9, 10], more than 80% of the user's interactions typically invoke less than 20% of the transactions. This 80-20 rule of thumb calls for giving priority to obtaining SPE data for the 20% most frequent transactions.

Whenever there is a high uncertainty over the value of a given service demand or workload intensity parameter, one should use best-case and worst-case analysis [9]. In the process of refining the estimates, one should identify the resources that will have a greatest impact on performance and concentrate most of the effort in trying to obtain better estimates for them [9].

There are several elements to be determined to compute the values of service demands for SPE models. The number of logical I/Os or DBMS calls, the access method or DBMS call execution logic, and the placement of files into disks are key elements in determining the number of physical I/Os per transaction, V_i^f, to the portion of a given file f resident at device i. The average record size, block size, and device physical characteristics (e.g., seek time, latency, data transfer rate) can be used to determine the average service time, S_i^f, at device i due to accesses to file f. S_i^f is given by

$$S_i^f = \left\lceil \frac{\text{RecordSize}_f}{\text{BlockSize}_f} \right\rceil \times \left(\text{Seek}_i + \text{Latency}_i + \frac{\text{BlockSize}_f}{\text{TransferRate}_i} \right) \qquad (11.3)$$

where RecordSize_f, BlockSize_f, Seek_i, Latency_i, and TransferRate_i are the file record size, the file block size, the average seek time at device i, the average latency at device i, and the transfer rate of device i. The average service demand D_i is then computed by summing the contributions to the service demand from all files resident at the device. Hence,

$$D_i = \sum_{\forall \text{ file } f} V_i^f S_i^f \qquad (11.4)$$

The CPU service demand is obtained by adding the CPU time spent executing the access method or DBMS code for each logical I/O request or DBMS call, plus the time spent in network protocol processing, plus the time spent in user code. Table 11.5 summarizes the main elements to be determined for an SPE study as well as the relevant model parameters.

Table 11.5 Main Elements to Be Determined in an SPE Study.

Elements	Parameter Influenced
Number of logical I/Os, access method, and file placement	Number of physical I/Os to file f at device i (V_i^f)
Avg. record size, block size, and device physical characteristics	Average service time to file f at device i (S_i^f)
Access method and DBMS processing, number of logical I/Os or DBMS calls, protocol processing, and user code	CPU service demand (D_{cpu})

The flow of control of each transaction or application must be used to determine the number of times that a certain portion of the code will be executed on the average. At any design stage, a transaction may be specified as a sequence of computational and I/O functions. These functions are depicted as building blocks or boxes, as shown in Fig. 11.4 and 11.9. The complexity of the function performed by each box varies with the level of detail of the design. At early stages, there are fewer complex boxes, while at later stages of the design, more complex boxes exist. The flow of control through the various boxes will be determined by the way the various boxes are sequenced. As shown in Fig. 11.12, several constructs may be used to arrange elementary boxes: a sequence of boxes (Fig. 11.12a), a loop construct (Fig. 11.12b), an if-then-else construct (Fig. 11.12c), and a case construct (Fig. 11.12d). The figure also shows for each of the four basic constructs the contribution, Δ_i, of each construct to the service demand of device i. By applying the rules in Fig. 11.12 successively, one can determine an expression for the service demand of the entire transaction at any given device i, as a function of the component boxes.

11.5 ENVIRONMENT FOR SPE

As seen in Sec. 11.2, one must be able to determine the service demands of a given procedure from its description and from the service demand contributions of each of its primitive building blocks. If done manually, this process may be quite time consuming and error prone. It is desirable to automate the procedure so that one may generate the data needed to drive performance prediction models.

For SPE to be automated, one needs to be able to specify the transactions in a machine-readable format. One approach is to use a language that could be used to specify transactions for SPE purposes. Such a language should allow for the specification of the following elements:

- *Hardware description:* specification of the relevant hardware environment used by the new application, such as processors, disks, and networks

- *Basic software description:* specification of compilers, database management systems, and any other external modules (e.g., graphical packages) used by the application

- *File description:* specification of the files used by the application as well as their attributes, such as file size, record size, block size, and access modes

- *Workload description:* specification of the different workloads of the application as well as their types and intensity parameters

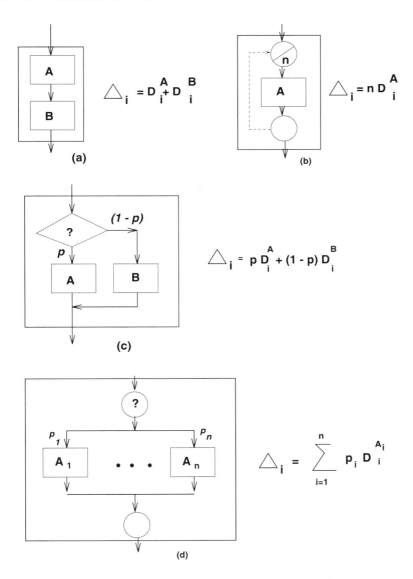

Figure 11.12 Service demand computation rules.

- *Procedure description:* specification of the procedures that compose the application

There are some commercial automated tools for SPE. Examples include BGS's Crystal [11], ICL's VCSR, and Metron's SCERT. We use, for illustration purposes, the language described in Ref. [12]. The language is called

ADL (Application Description Language) and the compiler built for it generates input parameters for analytic models (see Fig. 11.13). The compiler takes a description of an application in the ADL language and computes the service demands using the rules shown in Fig. 11.12 along with a quantitative characterization of elements such as CPUs, I/O devices, access methods, DBMS calls, network protocols, and compilers, obtained by the compiler from the Environment DB, which is part of the ADL system. Examples of the type of values found in this DB are CPU MIPS ratings, physical characteristics of I/O devices (e.g., seek time, latency, and transfer rate), number of I/Os per access methods or DBMS call, and average number of machine instructions generated by a compiler per high-level language statement.

Figure 11.14 shows an example of how the procedural part of the *statement* job, shown in Fig. 11.9, would be specified using ADL. The words in boldface indicate ADL statements or reserved words. The text that follows a ! sign is regarded as a comment. The REPEAT statement specifies the average number of times that a certain block of statements is going to be executed. The IF-THEN-ELSE statement specifies a probability of executing the THEN branch. The LINES statement seen in this picture is used to give a rough estimate on the number of high-level statements of a given language that are necessary to perform a given task. This guess has to be supplied by experienced analysts or programmers. The information contained in the Environment DB is used by the ADL compiler to translate this number into

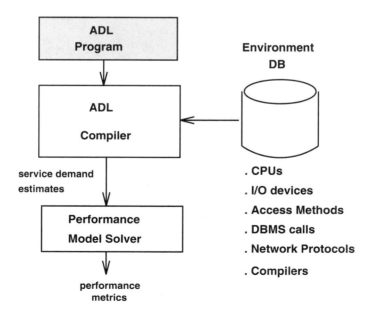

Figure 11.13 An environment for SPE.

```
PROCEDURE     Statement    ;
   REPEAT    180000   ! scan all customers
        READ    CUSTOMERS  (indexed);
       IF    1/30      ! Statement must be issued
      THEN REPEAT      30
                   READ  SALES (indexed) ;
                  IF   4/30   ! found at least one SALES record
                  REPEAT     2  ! retrieve additional  SALES records
                     READ SALES (sequential) ;
                  END-REPEAT     ;
                  END-IF ;
              END-REPEAT;
            LINES    (COBOL, 1000) ;  ! print statement
        END-IF;
   END-REPEAT;
```

Figure 11.14 Description of the job statement in ADL.

the service demand contribution of a LINES statement. In general, the service demand contribution, $\Delta_{\text{LINES}}^{\text{comp},n}$, of a LINES (comp,n) statement can be estimated as

$$\Delta_{\text{LINE}}^{\text{comp},n} = \frac{n \times \text{machine instructions per comp statement}}{\text{CPU speed}} \qquad (11.5)$$

The ENVIRONMENT section of an ADL program is used to describe the elements of the environment to be used in the application. An example of the ENVIRONMENT section for the credit card application is shown in Fig. 11.15.

```
ENVIRONMENT
   CPU  IBM_9121/320 (1)  ;
   DEVICE  D1   TYPE  3380 ;
           D2   TYPE  3380 ;
   COMPILER   COBOL  ;
   NETWORK   X.25  ;
END-ENVIRONMENT ;
```

Figure 11.15 Environment section of ADL program.

The mapping between files and disks, as well as the file attribute, are given in the FILE section of an ADL program. Figure 11.16 shows an example of such a section for the credit card application.

```
FILE
    CUSTOMERS IN D1 ;
                FILE-SIZE = 180000 ;
                RECORD-SIZE = 400

                ACCESS-MODE = (indexed, sequential);
                BLOCK-SIZE = 4096 ;


        SALES IN D2 ;
                FILE-SIZE = 72000 ;
                RECORD-SIZE = 100 ;
                ACCESS-MODE = sequential ;
                BLOCK-SIZE = 1024;

    END-FILE ;
```

Figure 11.16 File section of ADL program.

11.6 CREDIT CARD PROBLEM REVISITED

The future performance of the new credit card application as well as its environmental impact can now be predicted. Reconsider the *sales* transaction shown in Fig. 11.4. It is assumed that this new workload will run concurrently with two other workloads: *development* and *production*. The *development* workload is associated with the programmers and analysts in charge of developing new applications and maintaining existing ones and is modeled as an interactive workload. The *production* workload aggregates all transactions that belong to the current systems already in production and is modeled as a transaction-processing workload. Table 11.6 shows the intensity parameters and average service demands for the three workloads. It also shows the response times obtained by solving the corresponding performance model with *QSolver/1* (the queuing network solver package that accompanies this book). The response times thus obtained reflect only the time spent by the transaction in the computer system. In the case of the *sales* workload one should add the communication time to send the transaction to the computer system plus the time for the reply to be sent from the computer system to the terminal. This total communication time, assumed to be 0.6 sec, has to be added to the response time shown in Table 11.6 bringing the total response time for *sales* transactions to 1 sec, well below the desired service level of 2 sec.

Table 11.6 Performance Prediction for Sale Transaction.

		Workload	
	Sales	Development	Production
N^{max}	5	5	1
λ (tps)	6	-	1
Prior	1	3	2
No. terminals	-	20	-
Z (sec)	-	5	-
Service Demand (msec)			
CPU	71.7	35.0	20.0
Disk 1	76.0	40.0	30.0
Disk 2	24.3	50.0	35.0
Response Time (sec)			
	0.40	0.33	0.23

Since the marketing department was not so certain about their estimates on the number of customers that will apply for the new credit card, they requested a sensitivity analysis on the arrival rate of *sales* transactions. The results are displayed in Fig. 11.17, which shows that when the arrival rate of *sales* transactions approaches 8.4 tps, the response time tends to infinity (solid curve). The reason can be seen by analyzing the output graphs and

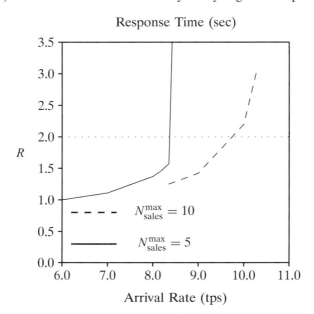

Figure 11.17 Sensitivity analysis for λ_{sales}.

reports of *QSolver/1*. *Sales* transactions spend 51% of their time in the memory queue when the arrival rate is equal to 8.35 tps. If the maximum degree of multiprogramming is increased from 5 to 10 (dashed curve), the arrival rate can be increased up to 10.4 tps before the response time goes to infinity. However, the service level requirement of 2 sec will be violated for an arrival rate of approximately 9.7 tps.

Now consider the *statement* application. As seen in Sec. 11.2, this application would require at least 8.5 hours every night, which is unacceptable. One member of the development staff suggested the following modification of the system:

- Add a new field, consisting of a bit vector of length 30, to each customer record. Each bit is associated to one day of the month. Whenever a sale ocurrs on a certain day, the corresponding bit is set, and the customer record is updated.

- Modify the *statement* application to retrieve sales from SALES files that correspond to days that have the bits set on the customer record. After the statement for a given customer is generated, its record in the CUSTOMER file has to be updated with all bits reset to zero.

Figure 11.18 shows the new proposed flow of control for the statement job. The new equation for the service demand at device i is given by

$$D_i = 180,000 \times \left[D_i^a + \frac{1}{30} \left(30 \times \frac{4}{30} \times 3D_i^b + D_i^c + D_i^d \right) \right]$$

$$= 180,000 \times \left[D_i^a + 0.4D_i^b + \frac{1}{30}(D_i^c + D_i^d) \right]$$

Adapting the values of service demands obtained during the previous analysis of the *statement* job, new service demand values are obtained and shown in Table 11.7. A comparison of Tables 11.4 and 11.7 shows that the new version of the *statement* job has a minimum execution time (sum of all service demands) equal to 5.2 hours, an improvement of 3.3 hours over the previous version! It is necessary to assess the impact on the *sales* transaction due to the additional I/O for updating the customer record (to modify the bit vector). The new logic for the modified *sales* transaction is shown in Fig. 11.19. It can be seen that for 90% of the transactions, an additional I/O to disk D1 will be required. This will increase the service demand on this disk by 34.2 msec (0.9×38). If *QSolver/1* is re-executed, it is seen that the maximum achievable arrival rate for *sales* transactions is equal to 5.3 tps for a maximum degree of multiprogramming equal to 10. The average response time in this

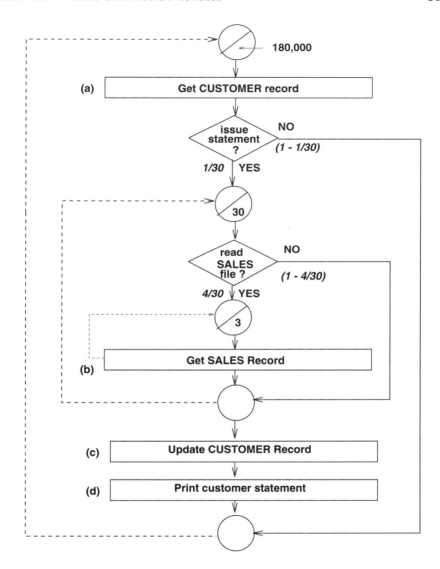

Figure 11.18 Modified statement job.

case is equal to 1.25 sec. Disk D1 becomes the bottleneck, with transactions spending 71% of their time queuing or being served at it. Even though the modification just discussed improves the execution time for the *statement* job, it is not able to bring it below the required limit of 2 hours. Moreover, the modification to the *sales* transaction made it impossible to achieve the 6 tps throughput required.

Table 11.7 Service Demands for New Statement Job (in Seconds).

Box	D_{CPU}	D_{D1}	D_{D2}
(a)	0.035	0.038	0.000
(b)	0.029	0.000	0.036
(c)	0.035	0.038	0.000
(d)	0.050	0.000	0.000
statement	8.9×10^3	7.0×10^3	2.6×10^3
Service Demand (hours)			
statement	2.5	2.0	0.7

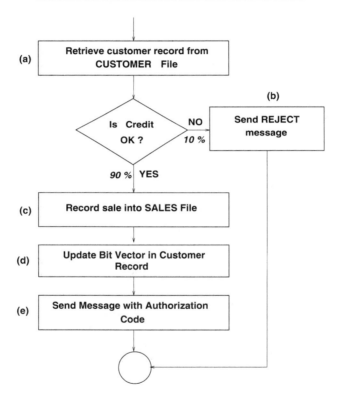

Figure 11.19   Modified sale transaction.

When these results were presented to the developers, one of the analysts suggested that two digits of the credit card number be used to indicate the day of the month when a statement should be generated. The CUSTOMER file would be decomposed into 30 files, one per statement closing date. Each such file would have 1/30 of the total number of customers, for a total of 6000 (180,000/30) customer records per file. The access method to each such file would still be based on a B-tree. Using the same assumptions as before, the height of this tree can be computed as follows:

- There are a total of 600 (6000/10) leaf blocks.
- There are 3 (600/200) nonleaf blocks at the level above the leaves. Above this level, only one block (the root of the tree) is needed to point to the 3 blocks at the level below.

So the tree still has height of 3. If it were assumed that the root for each of the 30 files is kept in the buffer, two physical I/Os would still be needed to access each customer record. Reconsider the original design for the *sales* transaction (see Fig. 11.4). The only difference is that box (a) would determine the appropriate CUSTOMER file to access from the credit card number. It can be safely assumed that this does not significantly change the CPU service demand at this box. So the results obtained for the original version of the *sales* transaction are still valid. The main difference has to do with the *statement* job. Instead of scanning all customer records each day, one has to scan only one of the 30 files. The flow of control for this version of the *statement* job is the same as the one shown in Fig. 11.9, except that the main loop is executed 6000 times instead of 180,000. This reduces all service demands by a factor of 30. Thus, the minimum execution time (i.e., the sum of all service demands) decreases from 8.5 hours to 17 minutes!

The examples above show how SPE techniques can be used successfully to compare different design alternatives before any major development takes place.

11.7 CONCLUDING REMARKS

It has been observed that minor modifications to the design of a transaction or to the physical database design can lead to factors of 5 to 10 in response time improvement [5, 10]. Modifications in the design are much less costly during the system design phase than in the system testing phase. Performance problems found in the late phases of the software development life cycle may require major software rewrites to fix them.

As shown in this chapter, software performance engineering techniques, should be employed in any software development project to allow for alternative designs to be compared before any major development effort takes place. The main difficulty in applying SPE techniques lies in estimating service demands for nonexisting applications. Service demand estimates will become increasingly accurate as the software development progresses. At the very early stages of development, even gross order-of-magnitude predictions are preferable to no estimates at all. One should concentrate the effort of application sizing on the subset of transactions that will be most frequently invoked.

11.8 EXERCISES

1. Consider the flow of control diagram given in Fig. 11.20. Give an expression
   for the average service demand, D_i, at any device i as a function of the service
   demands D_i^a through D_i^f.

2. A bank is considering the development of a new application to support a phone
   banking system. Customers would be allowed to dial to the bank and choose,
   from a touch-tone phone, one of two transactions: access balances and transfer
   funds. If they choose to access balances they can select from checking or savings
   accounts. If they select to transfer funds, they will be asked to specify the type
   of account (checking or savings) to transfer from and the type of account to
   transfer to. They will then be requested to enter the amount to be transferred.
   A transfer confirmation number is given to the customer. Estimate the service
   demands for this new application and plot the response time as a function of the
   arrival rate. For which value of the arrival rate will the response time exceed
   1 sec? Consider the following assumptions:

   - The computer system consists of a CPU and two disks (D1 and D2). The
     physical characteristics of the disks are the same as given in Table 11.1.
   - Every customer has an identification number (ID) and a password that must
     be entered before any transaction can take place.
   - The following files will be managed by the application: CUSTOMERS
     (contains one record per customer—keyed by the customer ID),
     CHK_ACCOUNTS (for checking accounts—keyed by the customer ID),

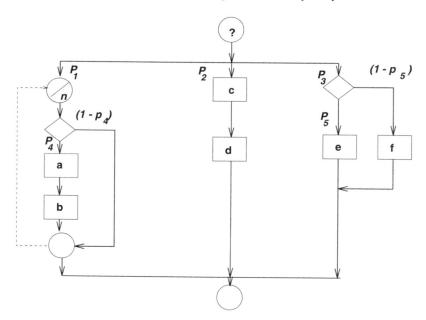

Figure 11.20   Figure for exercise 1.

SAV_ACCOUNTS (for saving accounts—keyed by customer ID), HISTORY (contains a log of all transactions executed).

- Each account (savings or checking) record is 200 bytes long, each customer record is 250 bytes long, and each history record is 100 bytes long.
- Two physical I/O operations are needed on the average to retrieve an account record or a customer given a customer ID from either the CUSTOMER, CHK_ACCOUNTS, or SAV_ACCOUNTS files.
- A total of 60% of the calls are expected to request balance information on one account only, 30% will first request balance information on one account and will then request a funds transfer involving this account and another account, and 10% will request funds transfer without requesting balance information first.
- The CPU time per I/O and per message sent are the same as given in Sec. 11.3 for the *sales* transaction.

Make your own assumptions about the file distributions on the two disks.

3. A health insurance company wants to cut down on the personnel and time involved in processing claim forms submitted by participating doctors. They plan to develop an application by which claims can be filed electronically from the doctor's office. Each doctor would be given a copy of a program to run on their personal computers. The program would collect all the information on the claim and would generate a small file to be transmitted to the health insurance company by dialing to their mainframe. When dialing to the health insurance company, users would be given two alternatives: upload a claim file or query the status of a previous claim. The claim file contains information about the doctor, the patient, the services rendered, and the associated charges. The main files managed by the health insurance company system are: MEMBER, which contains information on each member of the health insurance plan, CLAIMS, which contains pending claims, and DOCTORS, which contains information on participating doctors. Develop an application sizing study for this application. You should make your own assumptions about hardware platform and file distribution.

4. A university wants to develop a new application that would allow students to register by phone before each semester. Students would dial a special number and would be requested to enter their student identification number and the codes for the courses and sections they want to register in. Conduct an application sizing to compare the following two alternatives:

- *Minimal consistency check.* In this alternative, the only consistency checks that are performed on-line involve verifying if the selected courses and sections are indeed being offered. The student's registration request is recorded into a file in the order of arrival to be processed later in batch mode. No registration confirmation is issued by the on-line transaction.
- *Complete Registration Processing.* In this case, besides checking the validity of the courses and sections requested, the transaction should check whether the student has completed all prerequisites and whether the classes selected are still open. If any class is not open the student should be placed on a waiting list. A registration confirmation number is given back to the student by the system.

Use the same assumptions about the hardware platform of Exercise 11.2. Make any other assumptions necessary to determine for each case the service demands of the on-line transaction. Assuming that the university has 25,000 students, that the system will be on-line for phone registration 24 hours a day for two weeks, and that each student requests enrollment in three courses on the average, determine the average response time for each case.

BIBLIOGRAPHY

1. C. Wilson, Performance engineering—better bred than dead, *Proceedings of the Computer Measurement Group Conference*, Nashville, Tennessee, December 9–13, 1991, pp. 464–470.

2. D. Comer, The Ubiquitous B-Tree, *ACM Computer Surveys*, Vol. 11, No. 2, 1979, pp. 121–137.

3. *OS/VS Virtual Storage Access Method (VSAM) Logic*, Order SY26-3841, IBM, Armonk, N.Y.

4. C. U. Smith, How to obtain data for software performance engineering, *Proceedings of the Computer Measurement Group Conference*, Dallas, Texas, December 12–16, 1988, pp. 321–329.

5. J. Gunther, Capacity planning for new applications throughout a typical development life cycle, *Proceedings of the Computer Measurement Group Conference*, Nashville, Tennessee, December 9–13, 1991.

6. C. U. Smith, *Performance Engineering of Software Systems*, Addison-Wesley, Reading, Mass., 1990.

7. B. Boehm, Software engineering, *IEEE Transactions on Computers*, Vol. C-25, No. 12, December 1976, pp. 1226–1241.

8. L. Lipner, Sizing applications by cooperating: Mastering the unmeasurable, *Proceedings of the Computer Measurement Group Conference*, Nashville, Tennessee, December 9–13, 1991, pp. 977–985.

9. C. U. Smith, Software performance engineering tutorial, *Proceedings of the Computer Measurement Group Conference*, Orlando, Fla., December 10–14, 1990, pp. 1311–1318.

10. A. Grummitt, A performance engineer's view of systems development and trials, *Proceedings of the Computer Measurement Group Conference*, Nashville, Tennessee, December 9–13, 1991, pp. 455–463.

11. *CRYSTAL Performance Evaluator User's Manual*, Document 90010-00, BGS Systems, Waltham, Mass.

12. R. E. M. Maia, A tool for performance prediction of new software systems, M.Sc. Dissertation, Departamento de Informática, PUC-RIO, Rio de Janeiro, Brazil, July 1991.

Chapter 12

Concluding Remarks

The field of performance prediction (i.e., answering *"what if"* questions) of computer systems is the basis for capacity planning. This field has witnessed a tremendous evolution in the past 20 years. Some of the milestones are the convolution algorithm, introduced by Buzen; the BCMP theorem, by Baskett, Chandy, Muntz, and Palacios-Gomes; the field of decomposition/aggregation, beginning with the application of Norton's theorem introduced by Chandy, Herzog, and Woo and fully developed by Courtois; the theory of operational analysis, introduced by Buzen and later expanded to queuing networks by Denning and Buzen; and the mean value analysis algorithm, based on the arrival theorem and Little's result, developed independently by Reiser and Lavenberg and Mitrani and Sevcik. Nelson [1] contains a good survey of the mathematics behind product-form queuing networks. Several other important techniques have been developed for the exact and approximate analysis of large multiclass queuing networks, priority CPU scheduling, memory queuing, I/O modeling, and the modeling of parallelism. Such techniques have allowed the theory of capacity planning to be put into practice. Many commercial packages have incorporated these theoretical techniques and have made it possible for efficient performance prediction models to become a standard component of the capacity planning practice.

One of the best known commercial packages is Best/1 from BGS Systems. Initially, Best/1 was developed as a general purpose capacity planning

package to be used for modeling different architectures and operating systems. Due to its generality, some specific features of some environments were
hard to model. As a consequence, BGS Systems developed different versions
of BEST/1 tailored to specific processing environments such as BEST/1 for
MVS, VM, UNIX, and DEC OpenVMS. Best/1 for UNIX systems allows the
capacity planner to build performance models of client-server environments.
BGS Systems has also developed a complete suite of monitoring tools to automate the process of workload characterization for different environments.
These tools use data measured by the operating system and transaction processing monitors to automatically build a performance model. Best/1 continues
to be widely used.

TeamQuest Corporation has developed a family of CMF packages for Unisys systems. The Capacity Management Facility database
(CMF.database) product collects data from the Software Instrumentation
Package (SIP/Unisys), the system log, and the MAPPER log. This data is
used to construct a workload characterization model. Using the workload
characterization model as input data, an Automated Model Builder automatically builds a baseline model of the underlying Unisys system. This model can
then be solved by the package CMF.model. CMF.model is a general purpose
performance modeling package that can be used to model other environments
as well. Automatic model builders for a variety of environments are being
developed.

Another example of a capacity planning and performance evaluation
package is MODEL 300 by Boole & Babbage. It includes features for
workload characterization in MVS environments and performs validation of
baseline models. Metron Systems Inc (MSI) distributes Athene, a modeling
package with versions for IBM MVS and UNIX environments. Examples of
software performance engineering products include CRYSTAL from BGS
Systems, SPE·ED from L&S Computer Technology, SES/workbench and
SES Client/Server Model from SES. Several other packages have been
developed including QNAP, PAWS, SPNP, and GreatSPN.

The architecture of most performance prediction tools are composed
of three functions: data collection, solution of a performance model, and
visualization of the input data and the output performance results. While
the data collection can take place only at the system being modeled (e.g.,
mainframe, multiprocessor, parallel system, file server), the solution of a
performance model may be done on a variety of systems, typically on a
PC workstation. For instance, the basic software package included with this
book is an example of a performance prediction tool that runs on a PC
and may be used to solve performance models of many different hardware
and software environments. The visualization function of a performance
tool is best carried out at a PC or workstation with a flexible graphical
user interface. This is the approach taken by most existing commercial
packages.

When the prediction models are complex and the number of alternatives to consider is large, it may become impossible or too time-consuming to analyze all the possible alternatives. Pruning options and judiciously exploring the search space is necessary. A recent development is the use of expert systems to analyze performance prediction results to suggest the configuration alternatives that achieve the desired goals in the most cost-effective fashion. A series of papers on the use of expert systems in capacity planning can be found in [2]. An example of such a commercial expert system package is CP-Expert by CMS Computer Management Sciences. It is designed to analyze automatically performance problems in IBM MVS/XA or MVA/ESA environments. It uses information from the system and from performance databases to generate reports that explain possible performance problems and suggest improvements.

Performance models require input parameters that are obtained from the performance monitors of the systems being modeled. There is often a lack of coordination between the designers of performance monitors (e.g., of operating systems, transaction systems, database management systems, and network operating systems) and the designers of performance prediction tools. Most often, the data provided by these performance monitors require a significant amount of massaging before they can be used as input to performance models. Also, too often, certain parameters required by the model are not measured by the system monitor and/or certain assumptions made by the model cannot be validated by the system monitor data. Many designers of performance prediction tools have been forced to develop their own data collection facilities to derive the input parameters for the performance prediction models. It is true that the situation has improved, but many further improvements are still required.

The primary purpose of this book is to address the various steps needed to carry out a complete capacity planning study. The driving motivation for capacity planning is performance prediction. Important issues such as workload characterization, model validation and calibration, data collection, and software performance engineering are also discussed. Several novel aspects are introduced, not only in the subjects addressed, but also in the approach taken. For instance, workload characterization material is scattered throughout the capacity planning literature. A coherent and unified view is given in Chapter 2. Chapters 4 and 5 introduce the seemingly complex material of theoretical modeling in an intuitive and appealing manner. Chapters 7 and 10 deal with issues not typically found, namely client-server architecture performance models and model validation and calibration. The theory is presented in an intuitive fashion, and the formalism is minimized. The presentation is example-based throughout. We believe that the insight provided is essential for those who are (or who intend to be) seriously involved in capacity planning and performance prediction.

To remain informed of the developments in the area, we recommend the following specialized publications: *ACM Sigmetrics Performance Evaluation Review*, Computer Measurement Group (CMG) *Transactions* and *Proceedings*, *EDP Performance Review*, and *Performance Evaluation*. For those who have access to the Internet, there exists a Sigmetrics bulletin board newsgroup.

We hope you have enjoyed the book!

BIBLIOGRAPHY

1. R. D. Nelson, The mathematics of product-form queuing networks, *ACM Computing Surveys*, Vol. 25, No. 3, Sept. 1993.
2. *CMG Transactions*, Special issue on expert systems and automated operations, Fall 1992.

Glossary of Terms

Accounting Systems Tools intended primarily as means of apportioning charges to users of a system.

Active Resource Resource that delivers a certain service to a job or transaction at a finite rate or speed.

Application Sizing Process of translating the logical description of an application running on a particular hardware and basic software platform into service demands.

Arrival Theorem The number of customers seen by an arriving customer to a system is equal to the mean number of customers found in steady-state if the arriving customer were removed from the system.

Artificial Models Models that do not make use of any basic component of the real workload. Instead, these models are constructed out of special-purpose programs and descriptive parameters.

Asymptotic Bound Analysis (ABA) Quick bounding technique that is exact for light-load and heavy-load situations. It provides upper bound estimates for system throughput.

Availability   Metric used to represent the percentage of time a system is available during an observation period.

Average Degree of Multiprogramming   Average number of transactions or jobs that are concurrently in execution.

Balance Job Bound Analysis (BJB)   Quick bounding technique that provides both upper and lower bound estimates for system throughput.

Bandwidth   Specifies the amount of data that can be transmitted over the channel per unit of time, usually measured in bits per second.

Baseline Model   Performance model of a computer system in its current situation (i.e., before any modifications on the parameters are investigated). The baseline model must be calibrated and validated using measurements of performance metrics from the actual system.

Basic Component   Generic unit of work that arrives at a system from an external source.

Batch   Class of components executed in batch mode, which can be described by the number of active jobs in the system.

Batch Window   Period of time (usually at night) where only batch jobs are being executed.

Benchmarking   Running a set of standard programs on a machine to compare its performance with that of others.

Bottleneck   Device that saturates first as the workload intensity increases. It is the device with the highest service demand.

Buzen's Technique   Elegant iterative technique for efficiently finding the normalization constant G(MPL) in closed queuing networks. It iterates across the number of system devices.

Calibration   Technique used to alter the parameters (either the input or the output parameters) of a base model of an actual system, so that the output parameters of the resulting calibrated model match the performance of the actual system being modeled.

Capacity Planning   Process of predicting if and when system saturation is going to occur, taking into consideration the evolution of the workload due to existing and new applications, and the desired service levels.

Capture Ratio   Proportion of total CPU time that is captured by measurement tools, such as accounting systems.

Central Server Model   Queueing model with a particular server (i.e., the central server) through which all customers must visit. The central server model is useful for modeling multiprogrammed computer systems. Basically, the processor acts as the central service center (or server) and the disks are the peripheral servers. When entering the system, each customer goes directly to the processor. After receiving service at the processor, a customer may either proceed to a peripheral device or finish, leaving the system. After completing service at a peripheral device, a customer returns to the processor.

Class (of Transaction)   Concept used in a performance model to abstract the parameters of a workload which are relevant to performance.

Class Population   Maximum number of customers of a class.

Client   Process that interacts with the user and is responsible for (1) implementing the user interface, (2) generating one or more requests to the server from the user queries or transactions, (3) transmitting the requests to the server via a suitable interprocess communication mechanism, and (4) receiving the results from the server and presenting them to the user.

Client-Server (CS) computing paradigm   Model for distributed computation involving one or more *clients* and one or more *servers*, along with the underlying operating system, interprocess communication system, and network protocols.

Client Think Time   Average time elapsed between the receipt of a reply from the server and the generation of a new request.

Closed System Model   Queuing model of a system with a fixed number of customers. Customers circulate among the system resources. The number of customers in the system at all times is fixed and the number of possible system states is finite.

Clustering Analysis   Process in which a large number of components are grouped into clusters of similar components.

Cluster (of Client Workstations)   Collection of client workstations that generate a homogeneous workload.

Command   Unit of user-submitted work in an interactive system.

Conservation of Total Probability Equation   Equation that specifies that the sum of the steady-state probabilities is 1. That is, the system must always be in one of the known system states.

Convolution   Another term for Buzen's technique.

Customer   Entities that flow through a system receiving service from its various servers.

Decomposition/Aggregation   Solution technique that partitions the system into subsystems, solves each separately, and combines the separate solutions into the global solution of the complete aggregate system.

Delay Server   Server where no queueing is allowed.

Device Saturation   State that occurs when utilization of the device reaches 1.

Disk Controller   Device that decodes the device-specific I/O commands (e.g., seek and transfer) into control signals for the associated disks.

Effective Capacity   Greatest system throughput at which response time remains within the service levels.

Elapsed Time   Total time spent by a job from its submission until its completion. This corresponds to the response time concept, except that it is generally used for batch workloads.

Environmental Impact   Impact of a new application on the performance of existing applications.

Event Trace Monitor   Monitor that collects information at the occurrence of specific events.

Flow Balance Equations   Linear equations that equate the customer's rate of flow into a system state to the customer's rate of flow out of the system state.

Flow-Equivalent Service Centers (FESC)   Devices used in the decomposition/aggregation method to represent the individual subsystems. Basically, they replace several servers by a single FESC.

Functional Characterization   Description of the programs or applications that make up the workload.

Global Balance Equations   Equations that are formed by equating the total flow into a system state to the total flow out of a system state. There is one global balance equation per system state.

Global Workload   Set of transactions or jobs submitted to a computer system.

Heterogeneous Client Workload   Load generated to the server when the client workstations have different profiles in terms of the load of requests generated to the server.

Homogeneous Client Workload   Load generated to the server when all client workstations have a similar profile in terms of the load of requests generated to the server.

Interactive or Terminal   On-line processing class with components generated by a given number of terminals or workstations with a given think time.

Interfault Time: Average time between consecutive page faults.

I/O Path   Physical connection between memory and an I/O device.

Last Come First Served Preemptive Resume (LCFS-PR)   Server scheduling discipline under which whenever a new customer arrives, the server ceases (i.e., preempts) servicing the customer (if any) and proceeds to serve the new arrival. When a customer completes, the server resumes its previous activity.

Little's Result   Fundamental and general result which states that the number of customers in a system is equal to the product of the arrival rate of customers to the system and the mean time that each customer stays in the system (i.e., the customer's mean response time).

Load-Dependent Server   Server whose rate of service delivery is not constant but rather is a function of the number of customers in the server.

Local Balance Equations   Equations that are formed by equating the flow into a system state due to an arrival at a queue to the flow out of the system state due to a departure from the queue. There are generally several local balance equations per system state.

Logical I/O Operations   Requests made by application programs to access file records.

Maximum Degree of Multiprogramming   Maximum number of transactions or jobs of a class that can be in execution at a given time.

Mean Value Analysis (MVA)   Elegant iterative technique for solving closed queuing networks. It iterates across the number of customers.

Mission-Critical Applications   Those applications that are fundamental to running the business.

Model Validation   Ability of a model to capture accurately key aspects of a system. As a rule of thumb, if a model can accurately predict various changes to the system, the model is termed "validated."

Model Calibration   Indicates that a model is able to match, or has been modified to match, the performance of the system at a number of observation points.

Modification Analysis   Analysis of the variation of the performance behavior of a system as a function of the variation of its workload, hardware, and software parameters.

Monitors   Tools used for measuring the level of activity of a computer system.

Multiclass Systems   Those systems where customers may be partitioned into different classes. Each class has unique device service demands and routing behavior.

Multiple-Request Workstation   Workstation that can issue several requests to the server before receiving a reply to pending requests.

Open System Model   Queuing model of a system with an infinite customer population where customers arrive from the outside world, receive service, and exit. The number of customers in the system at any one time is variable. Usually, infinite buffer sizes are assumed and the number of possible system states is infinite.

Operational Analysis   Assumes that the input parameters of the system model are all based on measured quantities.

Overhead   Hardware resource usage by the operating system.

Pairing-of-the-Arcs Equations   Equations that are formed by equating the flows between two system states. There are generally several of these equations per system state.

Passive Resource   Resource that is needed for the execution of a transaction or job but which is not characterized by a speed of service delivery. Once holding the appropriate number of instances of a passive resource, execution of the transaction progresses at a rate that is independent of any characteristic of the passive resource.

Path Length   Number of instructions executed by an instance of a given transaction or job type.

Physical I/O Operations   Operations that correspond to actions performed by an I/O subsystem to exchange blocks of data with peripherals.

Prediction Model   Model that, once calibrated, is used to answer "what if" performance prediction questions.

Preemptive Resume Scheduling Policy   Scheduling policy where higher-priority customers preempt customers of lower priority from a device. Preempted customers resume their service when no customers of higher priority are present at the device.

Priority Scheduling   Device scheduling discipline that allocates the device to customers according to externally assigned customer priorities. Customers of the same priority are served in FIFO order.

Processor Sharing (PS)   Server scheduling discipline under which customers receive service at a rate of $1/n$ units of work per unit of time when the queue length is equal to n.

Product-Form   Class of systems whose solution can be represented as a (normalized) product of the device relative utilizations.

Program Analyzers   Software tools intended to collect information about the execution of individual programs.

Queue   Set composed of a server and its associated waiting queue.

Queue Length   Average number of customers in the system, including both customers in service as well as enqueued customers.

Queueing Network   Set of interconnected queues.

Real Workloads   All the original programs, transactions, and commands processed during a given period of time.

Reliability   Measures of the occurrence of failures during the processing of services.

Residence Time   Time spent by a job or transaction once it is loaded into memory.

Resource-Oriented Characterization   Description of the consumption of the system resources by the workload.

Response Time   Time from when a customer arrives to the system until the customer completes service and exits the system.

Rotational Position Sensing (RPS)   Disk feature that allows the channel, control unit, and head of string to be free during the latency time.

Rules of Thumb   Rules that are used to determine overall system capacity as a function of the utilization of key individual components.

Sampling Monitor   Monitor that collects information about the system at specified instants of time.

Scheduling Policies   Policies that are responsible for assigning customers to be executed by a server over time in order to reach system objectives, such as minimizing average response time or maximizing throughput.

Separable   Another term for product-form. It indicates that each server can be analyzed independently (i.e., separately).

Server (in the CS paradigm)   Process, or set of processes, which collectively provide services to clients in a manner that shields from the client the details of the architecture of the server hardware/software environment. A server does not initiate any dialogue with a client; it only responds to requests. Servers control access to shared resources.

Service Demand   Sum of the service times at a resource (e.g., CPU, disks) over all visits to that resource during execution of the transaction or job.

Service Level Value of a performance metric, such as response time or throughput, which sets a limit for performance. Service levels are defined for each workload.

Service-Rate Multiplier Ratio of the service rate of a load-dependent device under a certain load n to the service rate of this device with just one customer.

Service Time Time spent at a resource (e.g., CPU, disks) receiving service from it each time a transaction or job visits that resource.

Shared Domain Environment where more than one class shares a maximum multiprogramming degree.

Simultaneous Resource Possession Situation where two or more resources must be used simultaneously by a customer.

Single-Class Systems Those systems where all customers are indistinguishable with respect to their device service demands and routing behavior.

Single-Request Workstation Workstation that does not issue a new service request to the server until a reply to an earlier request has been received.

Software Performance Engineering Process of constructing software systems that meet performance objectives.

Steady State Long-term average behavior after any initial transient effects have dissipated.

Stepwise Inclusion of Classes (SWIC) Approximate algorithm to model CPU preemptive resume priority.

Stochastic Analysis Assumes that the input parameters of the system model (e.g., the customer inter-arrival time, the customer's service requirements) are random variables with known distributions.

Stretch Factor Ratio of the residence time to the service demand of jobs at a device.

String Controller Device responsible for controlling communications between control units and disks.

Synthetic Models Models that are constructed using basic components of the real workload as building blocks.

System Monitors Those monitoring tools (hardware or software) that collect global performance statistics (i.e., do not attempt to distinguish among workload classes).

Target Parameter May be any input or output parameter of the analytical model which is altered directly by the analyst in an effort to force the model to match the performance of the actual system.

Terminal Response Time   Time interval elapsed between the instant a transaction or command is submitted until the answer to it begins to appear at the user's terminal.

Theoretical Capacity   Maximum rate at which a computing system can perform work.

Think Time   Interval of time that elapses since the user receives the prompt until he/she receives a new transaction.

Throughput   Rate at which customers depart the system measured in number of departures per unit time.

Time Windows   Intervals of time during which the system, the workload, and the performance indexes are observed.

Transaction   On-line processing class that groups components that arrive at a computer system with a given arrival rate.

Utilization of a Device   Fraction of time that the device is busy, or equivalently, the percentage of time that at least one customer is in the system receiving service.

Validation   Desirable characteristic of a model, seldom achieved in practice. A validated model of a system accurately mimics the actual behavior of the system in all aspects and can be used to predict the performance of the system under system or workload changes. The only truly validated model of a system is the system itself.

Workload Characterization   Process of partitioning the global workload of a computer system into smaller sets or workload components which are composed of transactions or jobs which have similar characteristics, and assigning numbers that represent their typical resource demand and intensity.

Workload Model   Representation that mimics the real workload under study.

Workload Saturation   State that is said to have been reached for a given workload when the service level for that workload is violated.

Glossary of Notation

- $\alpha_i(j)$: service-rate multiplier for load-dependent device i when the queue length at the device is j. It is defined as $\mu_i(j)/\mu_i(1)$.
- $\beta(j)$: product of service-rate multipliers. Defined as $\prod_{k=1}^{j} \alpha(k)$.
- Φ: power, defined as the ratio of the throughput to the response time of a system.
- λ: state-independent arrival rate of customers to the system.
- λ_k: state-dependent arrival rate of customers to the system when k customers are in the system.
- λ_r: average arrival rate of class r customers.
- $\vec{\lambda}$: vector $(\lambda_1, \ldots, \lambda_R)$ of average arrival rates per class.
- μ: state independent service rate of the server.
- $\mu_i(j)$: service rate of device i when the queue length at the device is j.
- μ_k: state-dependent service rate of the server when k customers are in the system.
- $\Omega(p)$: set of classes that have priority p.
- A_i: total number of service requests (i.e., arrivals) to device i in the observation period $\mathcal{T}$.

- $A_{i,j}$: number of service requests from device i that next request service at device j in the observation period T.
- A_0: total number of arrivals to the system in the observation period T. It is equal to $\sum_{i=1}^{K} A_{0,i}$.
- $A_{0,i}$: number of service requests (i.e., arrivals) to device i that arrived directly from the outside world and not from another device in the observation period T.
- B_i: total busy time of device i in the observation period T.
- c_r: capture ratio.
- C_0: total number of jobs completed by the system in the observation period T.
- C_i: total number of service completions from device i in the observation period T.
- $C_{i,j}$: number of times a job completing service at device i requests service next at device j in the observation period T.
- $C_{i,0}$: number of service completions (i.e., job completions) at device i that "exit" the system to the outside world and do not visit further devices during T.
- $C_{0,r}$: count of class r transactions or programs completed during T.
- $CT_i(\mathrm{MPL})$: the cycle time (i.e., the return time) of a customer to device i when the system multiprogramming level is MPL.
- $D_{\mathrm{cpu},r}^p$: service demand of class r jobs at shadow CPU p.
- D_i: service demand at device i (single-class model).
- $D_{i,r}$: service demand of transactions of class r at device i.
- $\mathrm{Dom}(r)$: domain of class r.
- DRPS_i: average RPS delay of disk i.
- $e_{i,r}$: elapsed time of job i of class r.
- $f_{i,r}$: fraction of total activity of a device i due to workload class r.
- F: number of pages in the virtual space of a process.
- $FESC_i$: the flow-equivalent service center for the ith subsystem.
- $G(\mathrm{MPL})$: the normalization constant of a system with a multiprogramming level of MPL.
- $\mathrm{IFT}(f)$: average interfault time when the process has f page frames allocated to it.
- IOC_i: number of physical I/O operations to disk i.
- K: total number of devices.
- M: number of terminals in an interactive system.
- MST_i: mean service time of disk i.
- M_r: number of active terminals of class r.

- $\overline{N}$: average degree of multiprogramming.
- NCH_i: average number of I/O requests seen by disk i at the channel.
- NP: total number of page frames in main memory.
- $\overline{N}_r$: average degree of multiprogramming of class r.
- $\overline{N}_i$ $(\vec{\lambda})$: average total number of customers at device i given that the arrival rate vector is $\vec{\lambda}$.
- $\overline{N}_{i,r}$ $(\vec{\lambda})$: average number of class r jobs at device i given that the arrival rate vector is $\vec{\lambda}$.
- $N^{\max}$: maximum degree of multiprogramming.
- N_r: class r population.
- $\overline{N}_r^s$: average number of class r customers in the system given that the arrival rate vector is $\vec{\lambda}$.
- $NRPS_i$: average number of missed reconnects before a successful connect by disk i.
- $\mathcal{P}$: the stochastic routing probability matrix, which gives the routing probabilities between servers. The row sums of $\mathcal{P}$ are all 1.
- $P_i(j \mid n)$: probability that device i has j customers given that there are n customers in a single-class queuing network.
- $P_i(j \mid \vec{N})$: marginal probability of finding j customers at device i given that the multiclass QN population vector is $\vec{N}$.
- $P_i(j \mid \vec{\lambda})$: probability that there are j customers irrespective of their classes at device i given that the arrival rate vector is $\vec{\lambda}$.
- P_k: steady-state probability that there are k customers in the system, either in service or enqueued.
- Prior(r): priority of class r.
- R: number of transaction or job classes.
- $R_{i,r}(\vec{\lambda})$: average response time per visit to device i of a class r customer given that the arrival rate vector is $\vec{\lambda}$.
- $R'_{i,r}(\vec{\lambda})$: average residence time of a class r customer at device i given that the arrival rate vector is $\vec{\lambda}$.
- R_r: measured average response time of class r.
- $R_{0,r}(\vec{\lambda})$: average response time of class r customers given that the arrival rate vector is $\vec{\lambda}$.
- $s_{i,r}$: measured length of session i of class r.
- S_i: mean service time between completions at device i. It is equal to $S_i = B_i/C_i$.
- S_i^f: average service time per operation to the portion of file f stored at I/O device i.
- $S_{i,r}$: average service time of class r customers at device i.

- $\mathcal{T}$: monitoring interval.
- T: average response time.
- $T_{\min}$: minimum average response time.
- TCH_i: average delay due to channel contention seen by disk i.
- $\mathcal{U}_i$: relative utilization of server i.
- $U_{\text{ch}}(\text{ctr})$: channel utilization due to controller ctr.
- $U_{\text{ch}}(i)$: utilization of an I/O channel due to I/O device i.
- U_i: utilization of device i.
- $U_i{}^t$: total utilization of device i.
- $U_{i,r}$: utilization of device i by class r.
- V_i: average number of visits (i.e., the visit count) per job to device i.
- $\mathcal{V}_i$: relative average number of visits to server i per transaction.
- V_i^f: average number of visits to I/O device i caused by operations on file f.
- $V_{i,r}$: average visit ratio of class r customers at device i.
- $\mathcal{X}_i$: relative throughput of server i.
- X_i: throughput of device i.
- $X_{i,r}$: class r throughput at device i.
- X_0: systems throughput.
- $X_{0,r}$: class r system throughput.
- Z: average think time.
- Z_r: average think time for users of class r.

Formulas

z Score:

$$z \text{ score} = \frac{\text{measured value} - \text{mean value}}{\text{standard deviation}}$$

Moving average:

$$f_{t+1} = \frac{y_t + y_{t-1} + \cdots + y_{t-n+1}}{n}$$

Mean squared error (MSE):

$$\text{MSE} = \frac{\sum_{t=1}^{n}(y_t - f_t)^2}{n}$$

Exponential smoothing:

$$f_{t+1} = f_t + \alpha(y_t - f_t)$$

Simple linear regression:

$$y = a + bx$$

$$b = \frac{\sum_{i=1}^{n} x_i y_i - n\bar{x}\bar{y}}{\sum_{i=1}^{n} x_i^2 - n(\bar{x}^2)}$$

$$a = \bar{y} - b\bar{x}$$

$$\bar{y} = \frac{1}{n} \sum_{i=1}^{n} y_i$$

$$\bar{x} = \frac{1}{n} \sum_{i=1}^{n} x_i$$

Service demand:

$$D_i = \frac{U_{i,r} \times T}{C_{0,r}} = \frac{U_{i,r}}{X_{0,r}}$$

Single-server system:

$$P_k = \left(\frac{\lambda}{\mu}\right)^k \left(1 - \frac{\lambda}{\mu}\right)$$

$$\text{utilization} = \frac{\lambda}{\mu}$$

$$\text{queue length} = \frac{\lambda}{\mu - \lambda}$$

$$\text{response time} = \frac{1}{\mu - \lambda}$$

Little's result:

$$\begin{array}{ccc} \text{average number of} \\ \text{customers in a system} \end{array} = \begin{array}{c} \text{arrival rate} \\ \text{at the system} \end{array} \times \begin{array}{c} \text{average time spent} \\ \text{in the system} \end{array}$$

Generalized birth-death model:

$$\text{flow in} = \text{flow out}$$

$$\mu_1 P_1 = \lambda_0 P_0$$

$$\lambda_0 P_0 + \mu_2 P_2 = \lambda_1 P_1 + \mu_1 P_1$$

$$\vdots$$

$$\lambda_{k-1} P_{k-1} + \mu_{k+1} P_{k+1} = \lambda_k P_k + \mu_k P_k$$

$$\vdots$$

$$P_k = \left[\sum_{j=0}^{\infty} \prod_{i=0}^{j-1} \frac{\lambda_i}{\mu_{i+1}} \right]^{-1} \prod_{i=0}^{k-1} \frac{\lambda_i}{\mu_{i+1}} \qquad \text{for } k = 0, 1, 2, \dots$$

$$\text{utilization} = P_1 + P_2 + \cdots = 1 - P_0$$

$$\text{throughput} = \mu_1 P_1 + \mu_2 P_2 + \cdots = \sum_{k=1}^{\infty} \mu_k P_k$$

$$\text{queue length} = 0P_0 + 1P_1 + 2P_2 + \cdots = \sum_{k=1}^{\infty} k P_k$$

$$\text{response time} = \frac{\text{queue length}}{\text{throughput}} = \frac{\sum_{k=1}^{\infty} k P_k}{\sum_{k=1}^{\infty} \mu_k P_k}$$

Operational relationships:

Arrival rate: $\lambda_r = \dfrac{C_{0,r}}{T}$

Multiprogramming level: $\overline{N}_r = \dfrac{\sum_{i=1}^{n} e_{i,r}}{T}$

Utilization law: $U_{i,r} = S_{i,r} X_{i,r}$

Interactive response time law:

$$R_r = \frac{M_r}{X_{0,r}} - Z_r$$

Forced flow law: $X_{i,r} = V_{i,r} X_{0,r}$

Convolution technique:

$$G(MPL) \equiv g(\text{MPL}, K) = g(\text{MPL}, K-1) + \mathcal{U}_K g(\text{MPL}-1, K)$$

$$G(0) = g(0, k) = 1 \qquad k = 1, \ldots, K$$

$$g(m, 1) = \mathcal{U}_1^m \qquad m = 0, \ldots, \text{MPL}$$

$$X_i(\text{MPL}) = \mu_i \mathcal{U}_i \frac{G(\text{MPL}-1)}{G(\text{MPL})}$$

$$U_i(\text{MPL}) = \mathcal{U}_i \frac{G(\text{MPL}-1)}{G(\text{MPL})}$$

$$\bar{n}_i(\text{MPL}) = \sum_{m=1}^{\text{MPL}} \mathcal{U}_i^m \frac{G(\text{MPL}-m)}{G(\text{MPL})}$$

$$R_i(\text{MPL}) = \frac{\sum_{m=1}^{\text{MPL}} \mathcal{U}_i^{m-1} G(\text{MPL}-m)}{\mu_i G(\text{MPL}-1)}$$

Single-class MVA:

$$R_i'(n) = V_i R_i(n) = D_i [1 + \bar{n}_i(n-1)]$$

$$X_0(n) = \frac{n}{\sum_{k=1}^{K} R_k'(n)}$$

$$\bar{n}_i(n) = X_0(n) R_i'(n)$$

Stretch factor:

$$SF_i(n) = \frac{R_i(n)}{S_i} = \frac{R'_i(n)}{D_i}$$

ABA bounds:

$$X_{\text{system}}(\text{MPL}) \leq \min\left[\frac{\text{MPL}}{\sum_{k=1}^{K} V_k S_k}, \frac{1}{\max_{i=1}^{K}\{V_i S_i\}}\right]$$

BJB bounds:

$$\frac{\text{MPL}}{(\max_{i=1}^{K}\{V_i S_i\})(K + \text{MPL} - 1)} \leq X_{\text{system}}(\text{MPL})$$

$$\leq \frac{\text{MPL}}{[(\sum_{i=1}^{K} V_i S_i)/K](K + \text{MPL} - 1)}$$

Multiple-class load-independent exact MVA:

$$R'_{i,r}(\vec{N}) = V_{i,r} R_{i,r}$$

$$= \begin{cases} D_{i,r} & \text{delay} \\ D_{i,r}(1 + \bar{n}_i(\vec{N} - \vec{1}_r)) & \text{queuing} \end{cases}$$

$$X_{0,r}(\vec{N}) = \frac{N_r}{Z_r + \sum_{i=1}^{K} R'_{i,r}(\vec{N})}$$

$$\bar{n}_i(\vec{N}) = \sum_{r=1}^{R} X_{0,r}(\vec{N}) R'_{i,r}(\vec{N})$$

Multiple-class load-independent approximate MVA:

$$\bar{n}_{i,r}(\vec{N} - \vec{1}_t) = \begin{cases} \bar{n}_{i,r}(\vec{N}) & t \neq r \\ \dfrac{N_r - 1}{N_r}\, \bar{n}_{i,r}(\vec{N}) & t = r \end{cases}$$

$$R'_{i,r}(\vec{N}) = \begin{cases} D_{i,r} & \text{delay} \\ D_{i,r}\left[1 + \sum_{t=1}^{R} n_{i,t}(\vec{N} - \vec{1}_r)\right] & \text{queuing} \end{cases}$$

$$X_{0,r}(\vec{N}) = \frac{N_r}{\sum_{i=1}^{K} R'_{i,r}(\vec{N})}$$

$$\bar{n}_{i,r}(\vec{N}) = X_{0,r}(\vec{N}) R'_{i,r}(\vec{N})$$

Multiple-class load-independent open QN model:

$$U_{i,r}(\vec{\lambda}) = \lambda_r V_{i,r} S_{i,r} = \lambda_r D_{i,r}$$

$$U_i(\vec{\lambda}) = \sum_{r=1}^{R} U_{i,r}(\vec{\lambda})$$

$$\bar{n}_{i,r}(\vec{\lambda}) = \frac{U_{i,r}(\vec{\lambda})}{1 - U_i(\vec{\lambda})}$$

$$R_{i,r}(\vec{\lambda}) = \begin{cases} D_{i,r} & \text{delay} \\ \dfrac{D_{i,r}}{1 - U_i(\vec{\lambda})} & \text{queuing} \end{cases}$$

$$R_r(\vec{\lambda}) = \sum_{i=1}^{K} R_{i,r}(\vec{\lambda})$$

$$n_i(\vec{\lambda}) = \sum_{r=1}^{R} n_{i,r}(\vec{\lambda})$$

Single-class load-dependent MVA:

$$R_i'(n) = \begin{cases} D_i[1 + \bar{n}_i(n-1)] & \text{LI queuing device} \\ D_i & \text{delay device} \\ D_i \sum_{j=1}^{n} [j/\alpha_i(j)] P_i(j-1 \mid n-1) & \text{LD device} \end{cases}$$

$$X_0(n) = n / \sum_{i=1}^{K} R_i'(n)$$

$$\bar{n}_i(n) = \sum_{j=1}^{n} j P_i(j \mid n)$$

$$P_i(j \mid n) = \begin{cases} \dfrac{D_i X_0(n)}{\alpha_i(j)} P_i(j-1 \mid n-1) & j = 1, \ldots, n \\[2ex] 1 - \sum_{k=1}^{n} P_i(k \mid n) & j = 0 \end{cases}$$

Multiple-class load-dependent approximate MVA:

$$P_i(j \mid \vec{N}) = P_i(0 \mid \vec{N}) \prod_{k=1}^{j} \frac{\sum_{r=1}^{R} D_{i,r} X_{0,r}(\vec{N})}{\alpha_i(k)} \qquad j = 1, \ldots, |\vec{N}|$$

$$P_i(0 \mid \vec{N}) = \left[1 + \sum_{j=1}^{|\vec{N}|} \prod_{k=1}^{j} \frac{\sum_{r=1}^{R} D_{i,r} X_{0,r}(\vec{N})}{\alpha_i(k)} \right]^{-1}$$

$$R'_{i,r}(\vec{N}) = \begin{cases} D_{i,r}[1 + \bar{n}_i(\vec{N} - \vec{1}_r)] & \text{LI queuing device} \\ D_{i,r} & \text{delay device} \\ D_{i,r} \sum_{j=1}^{|\vec{N}|} [j/\alpha_i(j)] P_i(j-1 \mid \vec{N}) & \text{LD device} \end{cases}$$

$$X_{0,r}(\vec{N}) = N_r / \sum_{i=1}^{K} R'_{i,r}$$

$$\bar{n}_{i,r}(\vec{N}) = X_{0,r}(\vec{N}) \times R'_{i,r}(\vec{N})$$

$$\bar{n}_{i,r}(\vec{N} - \vec{1}_t) = \begin{cases} \bar{n}_{i,r}(\vec{N}) & t \neq r \\ \frac{N_r - 1}{N_r} \bar{n}_{i,r}(\vec{N}) & t = r \end{cases}$$

Multiple-class load-dependent open QN models:

$$U_{i,r} = \lambda_r D_{i,r}$$

$$P_i(0 \mid \vec{\lambda}) = P_i(0 \mid \lambda) = \left[\sum_{j=0}^{w_i} \frac{U_i^j}{\beta_i(j)} + \frac{[\alpha_i(w_i)]^{w_i}}{\beta_i(w_i)} \frac{[U_i/\alpha_i(w_i)]^{w_i+1}}{1 - U_i/\alpha_i(w_i)} \right]^{-1}$$

$$\overline{N}_i(\vec{\lambda}) = P_i(0 \mid \vec{\lambda}) \left[\sum_{j=1}^{w_i} j \frac{U_i^j}{\beta_i(j)} + \frac{U_i^{w_i+1}}{\beta_i(w_i)\alpha_i(w_i)} \right.$$

$$\left. \times \left[\frac{[U_i/\alpha_i(w_i)] + (w_i + 1)(1 - U_i/\alpha_i(w_i))}{(1 - \frac{U_i}{\alpha_i(w_i)})^2} \right] \right]$$

$$N_{i,r}(\vec{\lambda}) = \begin{cases} U_{i,r} & \text{delay device} \\ U_{i,r}/(1 - U_i) & \text{queuing LI device} \\ \frac{U_{i,r}}{U_i} \overline{N}_i(\vec{\lambda}) & \text{LD device} \end{cases}$$

$$R'_{i,r}(\vec{\lambda}) = \begin{cases} D_{i,r} & \text{delay device} \\ D_{i,r}/(1 - U_i) & \text{queuing LI device} \\ N_{i,r}/\lambda_r & \text{LD device} \end{cases}$$

I/O channel utilization:

$$U_{ch}(i) = X_0 \times \text{average number of transfers from disk } i \times \text{transfer time}$$

$$U_{ch} = \sum_{i=1}^{K} U_{ch}(i)$$

RPS reconnect delay:

$$\text{NRPS}_i = \frac{P_i(\text{path busy})}{1 - P_i(\text{path busy})}$$

$$\text{DRPS}_i = \text{NRPS}_i \times \text{rotation}_i$$

$$P_i(\text{path busy}) = \frac{U_{ch} - U_{ch}(\text{ctr}) + U_{ctr} - U_{ctr}(i)}{1 - U_{ch}(i)}$$

Channel contention delay:

$$\text{NCH}_i = \frac{U_{ch} - U_{ch}(i)}{1 - U_{ch}}$$

$$\text{TCH}_i = \text{NCH}_i \times \text{transfer}$$

Inter page-fault time function:

$$\text{IFT}(f) = \frac{D_{cpu}}{1 + (a/f)^2 - (a/F)^2}$$

Residence time at the paging device:

$$R'_{pag}(n) = \begin{cases} \dfrac{\left[D_{pag}^{NP} + \left[1 + \left(\dfrac{a}{NP/n} \right)^2 - \left(\dfrac{a}{F} \right)^2 \right] \times S_{pag} \right]}{\left[1 + \bar{n}_{pag}(n-1) \right]} & n > NP/F \\ \\ D_{pag}^{NP} & n \leq NP/F \end{cases}$$

Quick Manual for *QSolver/1*[1]

D1. Introduction. *QSolver/1* is a capacity planning tool that runs on PC computers with MS-DOS environments. Based on the input parameters that describe the computing environment, this tool calculates performance measures corresponding to the computing environment. Capacity planning projects often involve *"what if"* questions. As an example, consider the case of an IS manager who wants to know what will be the response time if the number of terminals connected to the transaction processing system is increased by 30%? Using a tool like *QSolver/1*, *"what if"* questions are easily answered by changing the input parameters accordingly. Fig. D.1 shows an overall view of *QSolver/1*.

Basically, it works with three entities: devices, workloads, and domains. *Devices* are used to specify the components of the computer system configuration that are able to carry out independent work. For instance, processors, disks, control units, tape units, and networks can be designated as devices. Components such as memory and terminals have a different specification, as we will see later. The *workload* represents all the processing requests (jobs, transactions, commands, etc) submitted to the system by the users during a

---

[1]©1989–1993 by Daniel A. Menascé and Virgilio A. F. Almeida. All Rights Reserved.

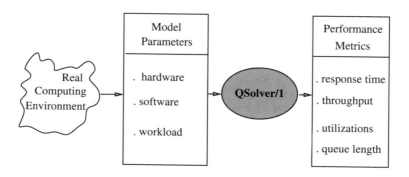

Figure D.1 Overview of *QSolver/1*.

given period of time. To represent the various collections of heterogeneous components, *QSolver/1* allows the capacity planner to specify different classes of workloads. Each class is specified by its type, which defines its mode of processing: batch, transaction, and terminal.

- *Interactive* or *Terminal* [TS]: it is an online processing class with components generated by a given number of terminals or workstations with a given think time. The number of terminals, the average think time, and the maximum degree of multiprogramming are the parameters that define this class.

- *Transaction* [TP]: it is an online processing class that groups components that arrive at a computer system with a given arrival rate. Thus, this class is defined by the arrival rate and the maximum degree of multiprogramming.

- *Batch* [BP]: it refers to components executed in batch mode that can be described by the number of active jobs in the system, i.e., the average degree of multiprogramming.

It is clear from above definitions that the available memory and the number of terminals are specified in the definition of the type of the class. *QSolver/1* allows the user to specify shared domains and priority for workload classes (see Chap. 3). In a multiclass performance model, one may have P priority groups. Many classes may have the same relative priority. The priority of a class is a number in the range $[1, \ldots, P]$. It is assumed that the highest priority is numbered 1, and that the priority number increases as the priority decreases.

D.2 Installation.   *QSolver/1* does not require a hard disk to run. An arithmetic coprocessor is not necessary but it is advisable to run larger models The contents of the disk that accompanies this book is shown in Table D.1.

Table D.1   Contents of the Disk.

QSOLVER1.EXE	Capacity planning software
PC1.CNF	Configuration file for the printers
EXAMPLE.PC1	Example of a *QSolver/1* model
MANUAL.TXT	This manual
CLOSEDQN.EXE	Program to solve closed multiple-class
	queuing models with LD servers.
CLOSEDQN.PAS	Source code in Pascal for CLOSEDQN.EXE
OPENQN.EXE	Program to solve open multiple-class
	queuing models with LD servers.
OPENQN.PAS	Source code in Pascal for OPENQN.EXE

If you are going to run *QSolver/1* from your floppy disk, type A: first and then load the program. If you have a hard disk, create a directory called QSOLVER and copy the contents of this disk into this directory.

D3. How to get started.   Load the program by typing QSOLVER1. This brings the main screen of *QSolver/1*. You are now ready to interact with this capacity planning tool. The ESC key is used to exit each window including the main one, which takes you back to DOS.

D4. Main screen commands.   The main screen of *QSolver/1* contains the matrix of service demands for the model. In a spreadsheet-like format, the matrix represents the workload and the devices that make up the model. Each element of the matrix corresponds to a service demand, in time units, that a specific workload class places on a specific device. All values must be in the same time unit. Each column corresponds to a workload and each line to a device. There are two command lines at the very bottom of the screen.

[F1] Load: loads existing models. Try this option and load EXAMPLE.

[F2] Save: saves the model shown in the screen.

[F3] Solve: solves the model shown in the screen.

[F4] Results: exhibits the results (graphs/reports) for the model shown in the screen. If the model is not already solved, it is solved before the results are displayed.

[CTRL Z] Clear: clears the current model to allow the creation of a new model.

The commands available at the bottom line can be issued by typing the letter shown in square brackets.

[E]nvironment: edits the environment. For documentation purposes only, the user can specify information about the environment being modeled.

[W]orkload: edits the workload corresponding to the column where the cursor is in the matrix of service demands. The workload specification parameters are: name, domain, priority, type, multiprogramming constraints, number of terminals [TS], average think time [TS], and arrival rate [TP]. When creating a model with non-shared domains, do not input any number in the domain field of the workload. *QSolver/1* will automatically assign different domains to different workloads unless otherwise indicated.

[D]evice: edits the device corresponding to the line where the cursor is in the matrix of service demands. The parameters to be edited are the device name and type: delay [Y] or queuing [N].

d[O]main: edits a domain. The number of the domain will be requested in a separate window. The parameter to be edited is the domain capacity, measured in number of jobs or transactions.

[Ins]ert: inserts a new entity (workload, device, domain). If you key INS, you will be prompted to select the type of entity you want to create. To create a new model, type INS to insert the workloads, devices, and domains of the model.

[Del]ete: deletes an entity (workload, device, domain). If you key DEL you will be prompted for the type of entity you want to delete.

D5. Editing the matrix of service demands. To change any value in the matrix of service demands, just move the cursor (by using the arrows) to the desired position and start to type the desired value. If you type ESC while typing a value, the previous value is restored. The arrows, the PAGE UP and PAGE DOWN, HOME, CTRL+HOME, END, CTRL+END, as well as CTRL+→ and CTRL+← keys can be used to easily navigate on the service demand matrix.

D6. Results of the model. *QSolver/1* generates two types of results: graphs and reports. Load the EXAMPLE model and use the [F4] key to view results. Select one by one the five available graphs. Note that graphs 4 and 5 are per workload class graphs. The workload for which the graph is displayed is the one associated with the column where the cursor is in the matrix of service demands. Reports may be printed or written to a file. If you choose the file option, you will be prompted for the file name. *QSolver/1* automatically attaches the extension .REP to every such file. Try to generate the reports for EXAMPLE.

D7. Miscellaneous.

- All models created with *QSolver/1* receive a .PC1 extension.
- The version of *QSolver/1* contained in this disk is intended for educational use only and accompanies the book "Capacity Planning and Performance Modeling: From mainframes to client-server systems" by Menascé, Almeida, and Dowdy, published by Prentice Hall. *QSolver/1* cannot be sold nor used for commercial purposes. This version is restricted to models with up to 3 workloads, 8 devices, max MPL = 20 per workload. For further information on *QSolver/1* contact:

Daniel A. Menascé
Department of Computer Science
George Mason University
Fairfax, VA 22030-4444
email: menasce@cs.gmu.edu
(703) 993-1537

Index

Bold page numbers indicate term definitions

A

ABA (*see* Bounds on performance, asymptotic bound analysis)
Absolute demands (*see* Calibration, techniques, absolute demands)
Absolute difference (*see* Calibration, techniques, absolute difference)
Absorbing state, 147
Accounting system, **275**, 289, 373
ACM Sigmetrics, 372
  bulletin board, 372
  Performance Evaluation Review, 372
ACMS (*see* DEC, VMS, ACMS)
Active resource (*see* Resource, active)
ADABAS, 26
Aggregation of classes (*see* Workload, aggregation)
Aggregation of workloads (*see* Workload, aggregation)
Agrawal, S., 204, 257, 268, 303
Algorithm:

  decomposition/aggregation, 167
  I/O contention in closed systems, 253
  k-means, 57 (fig.)
  minimal spanning tree, 57 (fig.)
  mixed multiclass model, 201 (fig.)
  multiple-class approximate MVA, 191 (fig.)
  multiple-class approximate MVA (load-dependent), 225 (fig.)
  multiple-class exact MVA, 186 (fig.)
  multiple-class memory queuing, 241–242
  open multiclass model, 196 (fig.)
  open multiclass model (load-dependent), 229 (fig.)
  single-class convolution, 158–159
  single-class load-dependent MVA, 217 (fig.)
  single-class load-independent MVA, 162–163
  single-class memory queuing, 238–239

SWIC priority, 258
Almeida, V. A. F., 240, 268, 393, 397
Analytical model (*see* Model, analytical)
Anderberg, M., 75
Anderson, G., 74
Apon, A., 304
Application Description Language
　　(ADL), **358**
　compiler, 358 (fig.)
Applications,
　data-entry, 85
　development of new, 7, 340
　mission-critical, **20**, 377
Application sizing, **341**–342 (fig.), 373
　example, 344–352
Arrival rate (*see* transaction, arrival
　　rate)
Arrival theorem, **160**, 185, 194, 369,
　　373
Artificial workload model (*see*
　　Workload, model, artificial)
Availability, 33–34, 37, 244, 263, 374
Averaging (*see* Workload, parameters,
　　averaging)

B

Balance equations (*see* Flow balance
　　equations)
Bard, Y., 189, 204
Bare machine, 281
　service demand (*see* Service demand,
　　computation, bare machine)
Baseline model (*see* Model, baseline)
Basic component, **38**–39 (*see also*
　　Workload, characterization)
　identification, 46
Baskett, F., 174, 180, 203, 268, 369
Batch class (*see* Workload, batch)
Batch system, 88 (*see also* Performance,
　　model, batch system)
Batch turnaround time, 37
Batch window, **31**, 89, 374
Bay, P., 268
BCMP theorem, **180**–181, 189, 192,
　　202, 234, 369
Belady's anomaly, 260
Benchmark, **29**, 72, 98, 374

Dhrystone, 29
Linpack, 29
nhfsstone (*see* Network File system,
　　artificial workload generator,
　　nhfsstone)
Perfect Club, 29
SPEC, 29
　SPECmark, 29
　SPECthruput, 29
TPC (*see* TPC)
Whetstone, 29
Best/1 (*see* BGS Systems, Best/1)
BGS Systems, 303, 369
　Best/1, 303, 369–370
　Crystal, 357, 370
Bier, G., 268
Birth–death model, generalized,
　　131–133, 193, 211–215, 387
　flow balance equations, 132
　queue-length, 133
　response time, 133
　state-space diagram, 131 (fig.)
　steady-state probabilities, 132
　throughput, 132
　utilization, 132
Birth–death system, **119**
BJB (*see* Bounds on performance,
　　balanced job bound analysis)
Bodnarchuk, R., 75, 209, 232
Boehm, B., 352
Boole & Babbage, 370
　MODEL 300, 370
Borovits, I., 303
Bottleneck (*see* Server, bottleneck)
Bounded buffer single server, 136–137
Bounds on performance, 167–172, 179
　asymptotic bound analysis, 167–169,
　　172 (fig.), 373, 389
　balanced job bound analysis,
　　169–171, 172 (fig.), 374, 389
Brady, J., 74
Brandwajn, A., 240, 268
Bronner, L., 75
B-tree, 346–347, 365
Buffer pool, 100
　hit, 100
　hit ratio, 100

Buffer pool: (*cont.*)
    miss, 100
Bulk arrivals, 182
Bunt, R., 75, 232
Business plans, 61
Busy time (*see* Server, busy time)
Buzen, J., 138, 157, 174, 268, 303, 369
Buzen's technique (*see* Convolution
        algorithm)

C

C, 29, 99
Cache,
    client, 198–199, 209
    consistency protocol, 209
    disk, 84, 106
    file server, 198–199, 209
    memory, 244 (fig.)
Cady, J., 75, 303
Calibration, 24 (fig.), 97, 114 (fig.), 115,
        140, 304–339, 374, 377
    absolute difference, **309**, 312
    case study, 316–333
    effects, 311–312
    example, 305–309
    objective performance metric, **308**
    percentage difference, **309**, 312
    procedure, **308**
    rules of thumb, 333
    scoring function, 332
    techniques, 312
        absolute demands, **312**, 315
        absolute difference, **312**, 320
        demand at the bottleneck, **312**, 316
        ghost server, **312**, 316, 320
        mean multiprogramming level,
            312–313, 320
        multiclass, **312**, 315, 320
        multiprogramming level
            distribution, **312**, 314, 320
        percent difference, **312**, 320
    types, 309–311
Capacity,
    effective, 27(fig.)–**28**, 376
    theoretical, **26**, 381
Capacity planning, 2, **7**, 19, 374
    common mistakes in, 11–13

    importance of, 10–11
    input parameters, 9 (fig.), 20 (fig.)
    methodology overview, 23–25
    output variables, 9 (fig.), 20 (fig.)
    situations, 3
Capture ratio, **292**, 374
Carlson, B., 203
Central server model, **144**, 196, 374
    visit ratios, 196
Centroid (*see* Clustering analysis,
        centroid)
Chan, K., 74
Chandy, K., 75, 174, 180, 203, 268, 369,
        369
Channel (*see* I/O, channel)
Cheriton, D., 232
CICS (*see* IBM, CICS)
CISC, 29
Class population, **90**, 106, 182, 375
Class priority, 93–95, 178
Client, **207**, 375
    caching (*see* Cache, client)
    delay, 207
    think time, **221**, 375
Client-server paradigm, 22, 102–106,
        112, 205–207, 209, 375 (*see
        also* Performance, model,
        client-server system)
    interaction, 208 (fig.)
    multiple-request clients and
        heterogeneous workload, 222
    multiple-request clients and
        homogeneous workload, 221
    performance considerations, 209
    performance model (*see* Performance,
        model, client-server system)
    single-request clients and
        heterogeneous workload, 221
    single-request clients and
        homogeneous workload, 220–221
    workload charaterization, 209–210
Closed class (*see* Customer class,
        closed)
Closed system, **128**
    number of states, 146
Clustering analysis, 51–60, 375
    algorithms, 56–60

example, 57–60
k-means, 56–57 (fig.)
minimal spanning tree, 56–57 (fig.)
centroid, **52**, 56, 58
data analysis, **53**–54
linear transformation, 53
logarithmic transformation, 53, 58
Euclidean distance, **54**–55
outlier, **53**
scaling techniques, 55–56
z-score, **55**–56, 386
CMS Computer Management Sciences, 371
CP-Expert, 371
COBOL, 99
Comer, D., 368
Command, **85**, 375
Commer, D., 232
Compactness (*see* Workload, model, compactness)
Compiler, 99, 358
optimizing, 99
Compute processor, 264 (*see also* Multiprocessor, loosely coupled)
Computer Measurement Group (CMG), 372
Computing environment, 25, 33, 36
Confidence interval, 115
Convolution algorithm, **155**–159, 182, 235, 374–375, 388
computational complexity, 173
numerical instability, 159
Conway, A. E., 204
Cooper, J., 303
Corporate plans, 20, 22, 24 (fig.)
Courtois, P., 236, 268, 369
CPU,
busy period, 82
queue, 78
service demand estimate (*see* Parameter estimation, CPU service demand)
speed, 79
utilization, 11–13, 31–33, 62
Crossbar switch, 106
CSMA/CD, 103, 208
collisions, 208

Customer class, **5**, 89, 109, 141, 176, 375
closed, **180**
memory-constrained, **240**–241
open, **180**
Cycle time, **161**

D

da Costa, H., 233
Daemon, 235
Database management system (*see* DBMS)
Database relation, **90**
Database server, 77, 102, 239, 250, 253, 316–317
Data collection, 47
DBMS, 26, 98, 273, 276, 353
crash recovery, 101
log file, 101
DB2 (*see* IBM, DB2)
Deadlock, 76
Debit-credit transaction, 29 (*see also* TPC), 34
DEC, 97
DECintact, 26
11/780, 29
VAX, 29
VMS, 25, 49, 271, 303
ACCOUNTING, 275
ACMS, 26, 272, 276, 283
Decomposition/aggregation, 163–167, 182, 236–237, 369, 375
error, 236
example, 237
Deitel, H. M., 112
Delay server (*see* Server, delay)
Denning, P. J., 138, 269, 369
Device (*see* Server)
Dhrystone (*see* Benchmark, Dhrystone)
Digital Equipment Corporation (*see* DEC)
Disk,
access time computation, 30
busy time, **246**
cache (*see* Cache, disk)
controller, 84, 243–244, 376
overhead, 250–251

Disk: (*cont.*)
  utilization, 249
  controller time, **30**, 246, 251
  control unit (*see* Disk, controller)
  latency, 77, 101, 103, 245, 247, 347
  queue, 78
  rotational delay, **30**
  seek time, **30**, 77, 101, 103, 245–247,
    347
  service demand (*see* Service demand,
    disk)
  service time, 247
    basic, **247**
    contention, **247**
    effective, **247**
  transfer rate, 30, 77, 101, 103, 347
  transfer time, 245–247
  utilization, 246
Dispatching, CPU, 77 (*see also* Class
    priority)
Distributed processing, 14–16, 22, 36
Domain, shared, 95–97
DOS (*see* Microsoft, MS-DOS)
Dowdy, L. W., 179, 203, 268, 397
Downsizing, 102, 205
Drakopoulos, E., 76, 204

E

Eager, D., 75, 175, 268
EDP Performance Review, 372
Effective capacity (*see* Capacity,
    effective)
Elapsed time, **88**, 289, 376
Elms, C., 75
End effects, 289
Environmental impact, 341, 376
Ethernet, 30, 37, 45–46, 207, 210
  probability of successful transmission,
    218
  slot duration, 211
  throughput equation, 218
  workload model, 45–46
Euclidean distance (*see* Clustering
    analysis, Euclidean distance)
Event, **277**
Event trace mode (*see* Monitoring
    mode, event trace)

Everitt, B., 75
Execution time, 8, 79, 262, 275
Expansion scenarios, 14
Expert systems, 371
Exponential distribution, 115, 133, 182
Exponential smoothing (*see* Workload,
    forecasting, exponential
    smoothing)

F

FCFS (*see* Scheduling policy, FCFS)
Ferrari, D., 18, 75, 302
FESC (*see* Flow-equivalent service
    center)
File placement, 155
File server, 22, 27, 57, 102, 192, 195,
    208, 278
  availability, 34
  cache (*see* Cache, file server)
  configuration, 28
  performance model, 195–199
  workload characterization, 45, 192,
    196 (table), 209
File transfer program (ftp), 42
First come first served (*see* Scheduling
    policy, FCFS)
Flow balance, **119**–120, 148 (*see also*
    State-space diagram)
Flow balance equations, 120, 129–130,
    140, 142, 147, 149, 171, 376
Flow control in communication
    networks, 190
Flow-equivalent method (*see*
    Decomposition/aggregation)
Flow-equivalent service center, **164**,
    236–237, 376
Forced flow law, **135**, 168, 194
Forecasting business unit, **62** (*see also*
    Workload, forecasting)
FORTRAN, 29

G

Galler, B., 175
Galvin, P., 232
Gardiner, V., 74

Generalized birth–death model (*see* Birth–death model, generalized)
Georganas, N. D., 204
George Mason University, 397
Ghost server (*see* Calibration, techniques, ghost server)
Gibson, G., 268
Gifford, D., 75
Global balance equations (*see* Flow balance equations)
Gordon, K., 268
Graham, S., 139, 174, 204, 233, 268, 303
Gray, J., 74, 303
GreatSPN, 370

H

Hardware configuration, 25, 270
Harrison, D., 233
Harrison, P., 268
Head of string, 84, 244–245
Heidelberg, P., 204, 303
Hennessy, J.L., 74, 79, 112, 268
Herzog, U., 174, 369
Hierarchical modeling, 211
Highleyman, W., 303
Homogeneous workload assumption, 119
Houtekamer, G., 268
Howarth, B., 75, 303

I

IBM, 97, 232, 244
  DB2, 26, 272
  CICS, 26, 272, 276, 283
  CMS, 285–286
  IMS, 276
  I/O technology, 250
  MVS, 25, 96, 112, 275, 285–286, 293, 303, 370
    MVS/ESA, 371
    MVS/XA, 371
  OS/VS, 368
  RMF, 275, 294

SMF, 275
TSO, 292
VM, 25, 285–286
VM/370, 303
VSAM, 346, 368
VSE, 271, 285
ICL,
  VCSR, 357
IEEE, 232
Infinite server, **181** (*see also* Server, delay)
Informix, 26
Instruction mix, **44** (*see also* Workload, model)
Intelligent device, **246**, 250
Interactive (*see also* Workload, interactive),
  response time law, 134–135
  system, 76, 111
    pictorial representation, 85 (fig.)
    qualitative analysis, 87
Interfault time, **259**–260, 377
  function, 392
I/O,
  bus, 244 (fig.), 250–251
  channel, 84, 243–244, 294
    busy probability, 248
    contention, 250, 392
    utilization, 248, 251, 391
  operation, 26–27, 40, 78
    logical, 355, 377
    physical, 208, 294, 355, 365, 378
  path, 244–245, 247, 377
    busy probability, 248–249
  processor, **264**–266
  service demand (*see* Parameter estimation, I/O service demand)
  subsystem, 29, 36, 84, 111, 244–246, 250
    architecture, 244–246
    contention, 250
    delay, 246–247
  subsystem model, 243–254
    abstraction, 84
    in closed systems, 252–254
IOPS, **27**
IS (*see* Infinite server)

J

Jain, R., 75

K

Kant, K., 233
Katz, R., 268
Kelton, W. D., 112
Kernel, **44** (*see also* Workload, model)
Key value indicator, **62** (*see also* Workload, forecasting)
Kienzle, M., 303
Kleinrock, L., 139
Krantz, A., 203
Kunze, J. A., 233
Kupfer, M., 233

L

Lam, S., 74
LAN (*see* Local area network)
Last come first serve—preemptive resume (*see* Scheduling policy, LCFS-PR)
Latent demand, **61**
Lavenberg, S., 174, 204, 303, 369
Lavery, D., 303
Law, A. M., 112
Lazowska, E., 139, 174, 204, 209, 232–233, 240–241, 249, 257, 266, 268, 303
LCFS-PR (*see* Scheduling policy, LCFS-PR)
Lederer, A., 74
Letmanyi, H., 75
Limmer, H., 76
Linear equations, system, 120, 143, 156–157
Ling, S., 75
Linpack (*see* Benchmark, Linpack)
Little, J.C., 138
Little's result, **123**–126, 135–136, 143, 154, 160, 162, 183–184, 193, 214, 369, 377, 387
applications to single-server, 125–126
Lo, T., 75
Load-dependent server (*see* Server, load-dependent)

Local area network, 22, 77, 102, 180–181, 189, 192, 195, 206–207, 278–279
speed, 77
Local balance equations, 149–150 (*see also* Flow balance equations)
Loukides, M., 303
Lowery, C., 304
L&S Computer Technology, 370
SPE · ED, 370

M

MacDougall, M. H., 112
Markov,
assumption (*see* Memoryless assumption)
chain, 317 (*see also* State space diagram)
state-space diagram (*see* State space diagram)
Mean square error, **64**–65, 68, 386
Mean time to failure (*see* MTTF)
Mean value analysis, 182, 235, 257, 369, 377
multiple class, 182–193, 222–226
approximate load-dependent, 222–226, 238, 390
approximate load-independent, 189–192, 389 (*see also* Schweitzer's approximation)
computational complexity, 189–190
exact load-independent solution, 185–189, 389
sequence of calculations, 187
single-class load-dependent, 215–218, 237, 390
single-class load-independent, 159–163, 215, 388
computational complexity, 173
Measurement,
interval, 82
overhead, 277
techniques, 272–278
Medium acess protocol (*see* Network, protocol, medium access)
Memory, 25
constraints, 95, 202

contention, 33
module, 106
partitions, 77
queue, **78**, 234
queuing model, 235–243
    multiple-class, 240–243
    single-class, 237–240
Memoryless assumption, 141, 145
Menascé, D. A., 240, 268, 393, 397
Merges, M., 204
Metron Systems Inc., 357, 370
    Athene, 370
    SCERT, 357
MFLOPS, 79
Microsoft,
    MS-DOS, 25, 393, 395
    NT, 25
MIN (*see* Multistage interconnection network)
MIPS, **29**, 78–79, 102
Mission-critical applications (*see* Applications, mission-critical)
Mitrani, I., 138, 174, 204, 369
Mixed model (*see* Model, mixed)
Model, 76
    analytical, 23, 44–45, 108, 113
        acceptable accuracy, 108
        advantages and disadvantages, 109
        approximations, 108, 115, 235
        exact, 115
    baseline, **97**, 114 (fig.), 115, 197, 311, 374
        calibration (*see* Calibration)
        validation (*see* Validation)
    closed, 182–185, 375
    functional, 76
    mixed, 199–202
    multiclass (*see* Multiclass models)
    open, multiclass load-dependent, 226–229, 391
        example, 228
        stability condition, 226
    open, multiclass load-independent, 192–196, 390
        example, 195–199
    parameters, 76–77

estimation (*see* Parameter estimation)
performance (*see* Performance, model)
prediction, 114 (fig.), 378
principle of minimal complexity, 84, 91
representativeness, 270
simulation, 23, 44, 108, 112–114
    advantages and disadvantages, 109
    statistical analysis, 108
    single-class (*see* Single-class model)
    types, 108–109
Modeling paradigm, 113–117, 305–306 (fig.)
Modification analysis, **97**–102, 115, 126, 377
Mohr, J., 75
Monitor, **274**, 301, 377
    hardware, **274**
    hybrid, **276**
    program analyzer, **276**, 379
    software, 17, 82, **274**, 283
    system, 23, **278**, 380
    transaction, 26, 37, 276, 283, 353
Monitoring mode, **277**
    event trace, **277**, 376
        overhead, 278
    sampling, **277**–278, 379
        overhead, 278
Moving average (*see* Workload, forecasting, moving average)
MTTF, 33–34
Multiclass models, 89–97, 141, 180
    assumptions, 180–182
    notation, 180–182
    parameters, 97
Multiprocessing, 106–109
Multiprocessor, 25, 106
    loosely coupled, 263
        model, 264–266
    performance model, 106–107, 216, 262–266
    speedup, 107
    tightly coupled, **263**
        model, 263–264
    utilization, 107

Multiprogramming, 235
  average degree, **89**, 97, 374
  level, 152, 160, 165, 170, 238,
    261–262, 307–308, 310
    estimation (*see* Parameter
      estimation, multiprogramming
      level)
  maximum degree, 77, 83, 97, 237,
    377
Multistage interconnection network,
  106
Muntz, R., 174–175, 180, 203, 268, 369
MVA (*see* Mean value analysis)
MVS, IBM (*see* IBM, MVS)

N

Natural business unit, **62** (*see also*
  Workload, forecasting)
NCR,
  TopEnd, 272
Nelson, R. D., 369, 372
NetBIOS, 207
Network, 25
  access delay, **103**, 105, 207–208
  bandwidth, **30**, 33, 211, 374
  protocol, 103, 207
    medium access, 208
Network File System, 207–210
  artificial workload generator, 210
    Legato mix, **210**
    nhfsstone, **210**
  requests, 209–210
    create, 209–210
    frequency distribution, 209
    fsstat, 210
    getattr, 209–210
    interarrival time distribution, 209
    lookup, 210
    mkdir, 209
    read, 209–210
    readdir, 210
    readlink, 210
    remove, 209–210
    rmdir, 209
    setattr, 210
    write, 209–210
Neuman, S., 303

NFS (*see* Network File System)
Normalization constant, **152**, 157 (*see
  also* Convolution algorithm)
  computation, 158–159(fig.)
Norton's theorem, 369
Novell, Inc., 232
NT (*see* Microsoft, NT)

O

Observation period, 133, 246, 281
OLTP (*see* On-line transaction
  processing)
On-line transaction processing, 21,
  26–27, 29–30, 68, 111, 262
Open customer class (*see* Customer
  class, open)
Open model (*see* Model, open)
Open system, **128**
Operating system, 25–26 (fig.), 29, 39,
  273, 281, 347
  overhead, 263, 283, 287, 378
  service demand (*see* Service demand,
    computation, OS)
Operational analysis, 133–136, 168, 369,
  378, 388
  basic quantities, 133–134
  derived quantities, 134
Oracle, 26, 272
Ousterhout, J. K., 210, 233
Outlier (*see* Clustering analysis, outlier)

P

PA (*see* Pairing of the arcs)
Packet switching network, 190
Page fault, 259
  rate, **259**, 272
Page frame, 260
Page replacement policy, 260
  FIFO, 260
Paging, 116, 202, 235, 267
  disk service demand (*see* Parameter
    estimation, I/O service demand,
    paging disk)
  modeling, 259–262
Pairing of the arcs, **150**–151, 378
Palacios, F., 174, 180, 203, 268, 369

Parallel processing, 262
Parameter estimation, 287–297, 301
  arrival rate, 288–289, 298
  CPU service demand, 79, 291–294,
    298
  I/O service demand, 294–297,
    299–301
    paging disk, 296–297
    single-class disk, 294–295
    swap disk, 295
    user-disk, 295
  multiprogramming level, 289–290
  number of terminals, 290
  steps to be followed, 288
  think time, 290
Partitioning of workloads (*see*
    Workload, partitioning)
Passive resource (*see* Resource, passive)
Patel, N., 268
Path length, **79**, 378
Patterson, D. A., 74, 79, 112, 268
PAWS, 370
Penansky, S., 75
Percent difference (*see* Calibration,
    techniques, percent difference)
Perfect Club (*see* Benchmark, Perfect
    Club)
Performance,
  goals, 95
  metrics, 4, 77, 109, 115, 143, 153 (*see
    also* Response time, Throughput,
    Utilization)
  model, 24 (fig.), **76**, 77 (fig.), 341
    (fig.)
    batch system, 88–89
    building a, 77
    client-server system, 102–106,
      211–212, 215–219
    interactive system, 84–87
    multiclass, 89–97
    multiprocessor (*see* Multiprocessor,
      model)
    simple computer system, 77–84
  prediction, 7–8, 17, 24 (fig.), 68–72,
    77
Peterson, J. L., 112, 232, 303
Petri nets, 76, 112

Postel, J. B., 232
Power, 138
Printer server, 102
Priority (*see* Class priority)
Priority scheduling (*see* Scheduling
    policy, priority)
Probability, conservation of total (*see*
    Total probability, conservation)
Process, 97, 106, 207
Processor, cycle time, 28–29
Processor sharing (*see* Scheduling
    policy, processor sharing)
Product-form queuing network (*see*
    Queuing network, product-form)
Product form solution, **153**
Program analyzer (*see* Monitor,
    program analyzer)
Program coding, 352–354
Program design, 352–354
Protocol (*see* Network, protocol)
PS (*see* Scheduling policy, processor
    sharing)

Q

QN (*see* Queuing network)
QNAP, 370
QSolver/1, 111, 203, 266, 362, 393–397
Queue, 379
  CPU, 78
  disk, 78
  memory, 78
  pictorial representation, 80 (fig.)
  single-server, 108, 113, 117–123, 387
    queue length, 122, 126
    response time, 123
    state probabilities, 121
    steady-state condition, 121
    throughput, 122, 126
    utilization, 121
  waiting, **79**
Queue length, 122, 131, 143, 311, 379
  computation, 154–155
Queuing network, **80**, 379
  closed (*see* Model, closed)
  customer, 80
  open (*see* Model, open)

Queuing network: (*cont.*)
  product-form, **153**, 180–181, 194, 234,
    254, 310, 317, 369, 379
  single class solution, 153
  state, **180**

R

Raatikainen, K., 75
Random number generators, 108
Regression, linear, 12 (*see also*
    Workload, forecasting,
    regression methods)
Reid, K., 232
Reiser, M., 174, 204, 369
Relative throughput (*see* Throughput,
    relative)
Relative utilization (*see* Utilization,
    relative)
Relative visit count (*see* Visit count,
    relative)
Reliability, 33, 263, 379
Remote Procedure Call, 207
Representativeness (*see* Workload,
    model, representativeness)
Requirement analysis and specification,
    352–353
Residence time, 183, 379
  job, **88**
  paging device, 261, 392
Resource,
  active, **78**, 373
  passive, **78**, 79, 109, 378
    allocation, 79
    pictorial representation, 80 (fig)
    pool, 80 (fig.)
    release, 79
    simplified pictorial representation,
      81 (fig.)
Response time, **3**, 8 (fig.), 14 (fig.), 16
    (fig.), 27, 31, 43, 69, 113, 131,
    182–183, 230, 311, 361, 379
  acceptable value, 4
  evolution, 7–8
  minimum, 82
  single-server queue, 108, 123, 126
Response time law (*see* Interactive,
    response time law)

Reuter, A., 303
RISC, 29
RR (*see* Scheduling policy, round
    robin)
Rose, C., 302
Ross, S. M., 112
Rotational position sensing, **245**–246,
    250–251, 253, 379
  miss, **245**, 248
  reconnect delay, 245–251, 392
Round robin (*see* Scheduling policy,
    round robin)
Routing probability matrix, **156**
RPC (*see* Remote Procedure Call)
RPS (*see* Rotational position sensing)
Rules of thumb, 70–71, 115, 379
  calibration (*see* Calibration, rules of
    thumb)

S

Sampling mode (*see* Monitoring mode,
    sampling)
Samson, S. L., 112
Saturation, **4**, 7–9, 381
Sauer, E., 268
Saxton, L., 268
Scheduling discipline (*see* Scheduling
    policy)
Scheduling policy, **178**, 310, 379
  FCFS, 179, 181, 184, 317
  LCFS-PR, **181**, 184, 377
  priority, 202, 234, 378
    model, 254–259
    preemptive resume, **254**, 378
  processor sharing, 181, 184, 317, 378
  round robin, 179, 181
  shortest job first, 179
  shortest remaining time, 179
Schweitzer, P., 189, 204
Schweitzer's approximation, **189**–190,
    192
SCSI (*see* Small computer system
    interface)
Separable queuing network (*see*
    Queuing network, product-form)
Serazzi, G., 75, 302

Server, **78**, 278
  bottleneck, 9, 12, 17, 28, 180, 187
  busy time, 133
  delay, **104**, 109, 181, 184
  flow-equivalent (*see* Flow-equivalent
      service center)
  load-dependent, **104**, 109, 377
    pictorial representation, 104
  pictorial representation, 80 (fig.)
  queuing, 109
  response time, 154
  saturation, **9**, 12, 111, 376
  service rate, 78, 118
    multiplier, **216**–217, 226, 380
  utilization, 200
Server (in the CS paradigm), 205, **207**,
    379
  delay, 207–208, 375
Service completions, number, 133
Service demand, **5**, 44, 81, 97, 110, 163,
    182, 211, 278, 280–287, 379, 387
  computation, 82, 98–101, 105,
      280–287
    bare machine, 281–282
    OS, 282–283
    transaction processing monitor,
        283–285
    virtual machine, 285–287
  disk, 243, 246–247
    paging, 261
  effect of changing the server speed,
      81
  estimates, 7, 353–354
  matrix, 90
Service level, **4**, 12, 14, 27–28, 32, 34,
    380
Service rate (*see* Server, service rate)
Service rate multiplier (*see* Server,
    service rate, multiplier)
Service request, **26**
Service time, 134, 281, 380
SES, 370
  SES/Client/Server Model, 370
  SES/workbench, 370
Sevcik, K., 138–139, 174–175, 204, 233,
    268, 303, 369
Shadow CPU, **255**–257

Shared domain, 95–97, 380
Shortest job first (*see* Scheduling policy,
    shortest job first)
Shortest remaining time (*see* Scheduling
    policy, shortest remaining time)
Shum, A., 268
Silberschatz, A., 232, 303
Silvester, J., 303
Simulation model (*see* Model,
    simulation)
Simultaneous resource possession, 107,
    109, 202, 234, 380
Single-class model, 119, 141, 178, 380
  equivalent, 179, 197
Single-server queue (*see* Queue, single
    server)
Sinha, A., 112, 232
SJF (*see* Scheduling policy, shortest job
    first)
Small computer system interface, 244
Smith, C., 74, 368
Smith, K., 232
Software development lifecycle, 352
Software monitor (*see* Monitor,
    software)
Software performance engineering, **342**,
    380
  environment for, 356–360
  obtaining data for, 354–356
Souza e Silva, E., 204
SPARC, 29
SPEC (*see* Benchmark, SPEC)
Spector, A., 75
Speedup, 107
SPNP, 370
SPX, 207
SQL,
  request, 211, 215,218
  SELECT, 26
  server, 102, 208, 210
Starvation, 76
State,
  absorbing, 147
  description, **118**, 141, 145
  enumeration, 142, 145
  probability, **119**, 142–143
  steady, **119**

State: (*cont.*)
transient, 148
transition rates, 142, 147
State-dependent arrivals, **128**
State-dependent service rates, **128**
State-space diagram, **118**–120, 136, 140,
148 (fig.), 165, 166 (fig.), 171
finite, 128, 130 (fig.), 213
Steady state probability, **119**, 121 (*see
also* State, steady)
Stepwise inclusion of classes, **255**,
257–258, 380
Stochastic analysis, **133**, 136, 380
Stochastic matrix, **157**
Stretch factor, **163**, 380, 389
String controller, 243, 380 (*see also* I/O,
subsystem model)
Sun Microsystems, 232–233
Sybase, 26, 272
Synthetic program, **44** (*see also*
Workload, model)
Synthetic workload model (*see*
Workload, model, synthetic)
System design, 352–353
System monitor (*see* Monitor, system)
System testing, 352–354
Swapping, 235
SWIC (*see* Stepwise inclusion of
classes)

T

Tandem, Pathway, 272
Tanenbaum, A., 269
Target parameter, **308**, 310, 380
TCP/IP, 207
TeamQuest Corporation, 370
Automatic Model Builder, 370
CMF, 370
Terminals, 25
increasing the number, 4, 85
representation in QN models, 278
Think state, 86, 102
Think time, **43**, 45, 86, 97, 133, 183,
381
estimation (*see* Parameter estimation,
think time)
response time effects on, 86

Thomasian, A., 268, 303
Thompson, J. G., 233
Thrashing, **262**
Throughput, **4**, 12, 26, 82, 89, 130, 134,
143, 165, 182, 213, 219, 241, 262,
311, 313, 381
computation, 154
graph, 314
increase through multiprocessing,
262
relative, 154, 157
computation, 156
Timeslice, 78
Time window, **30**–32, 37, 57, 381
TIP (*see* Unisys, TIP)
Token-ring, 30, 37, 103, 208
Total probability, conservation, **121**,
130, 143, 149, 151, 375
TPC, 29
TPC-A, 29
TPC-B, 29
TPC-C, 29
Track buffer, 250–251
Transaction, 381
arrival rate, **4**, 13, 14, 83, 113, 118
effect on response time, 83
flow of execution, 78
increase in volume, 4
interactive, 6
query, 5, 6
update, 5, 6, 90
Transaction Processing Council (*see*
TPC)
Transaction processing monitor (*see*
Monitor, transaction)
service demand (*see* Service demand,
computation, transaction
processing monitor)
Transarc,
Encina, 272
Transient state, 148
Transition rate (*see* State, transition
rates)
Transmission delay, **103**, 105
Trend analysis, 71–72
Tripathi, S., 180, 203

Turnaround time (*see* Batch,
    turnaround time)
Tuxedo (*see* UNIX, Tuxedo)

U

UDP, 207
Uncaptured time, 291
Unisys,
    MAPPER, 370
    Series 2200, 370
    SIP, 275, 370
    TIP, 26, 272, 283
UNIX, 25, 33, 37, 39, 43, 181, 235, 271,
        370
    cat command, 39
    ls command, 39
    mail command, 38–43
    more command, 39
    system activity reporter (sar), 275
    Tuxedo, 26, 272, 276
    uptime command, 33
Utilization, 9, 11, 126, 130, 134, 162,
        170, 281, 311, 381
    computation, 153–154
    prediction, 12
    relative, 152, 154, 157, 170
Utilization law, 134, 168, 194, 253

V

Validation, 24 (fig.), 97, 115, 117, 140,
        304–339, 377, 381
Vernon, M., 268
Virtual channel, 192
Virtual machine, 281 (fig.)
    service demand (*see* Service demand,
        computation, virtual machine)
Visit count, **134**, 182, 281
    relative, **161**–162, 168
Visit ratio (*see* Visit count, relative)
VM (*see* IBM, VM)
VMS (*see* DEC, VMS)

W

Waiting line (*see* Waiting queue)
Waiting queue, **79**

Waterfall model, 352
Weicker, R., 74
Whetstone (*see* Benchmark, Whetstone)
Wilson, C., 368
Wong, J., 175
Wonnacott, R. J., 18
Wonnacott, T. H., 18
Woo, L., 174, 369
Woodside, C., 180, 203
Workload, **38**, 89, 393
    aggregation, 6, 90–93, 110–111, 179
        batch, 94
        interactive, 94
        transaction, 93
    batch, **36**, 50, 182, 238, 241, 279, 374,
        394
    class, 278–279
    component, **5**, 374
    characterization, **6**, 24 (fig.), 37–43,
        381
        functional, **39**, 376
        resource-oriented, 48, 379
        simple example, 40–43
    evolution, **7**, 13
    forecasting, 24 (fig.), 60–68
        applying, 68
        exponential smoothing, 65–66, 386
        moving average, 63–65, 386
        regression methods, 66–67, 386
    global, **5**, 376
    growth, 6, 279
    intensity, **6**, 81–83, 110, 278–279, 355
    interactive, 6, 36, 50, 84–87, 182, 238,
        241, 279–280, 376, 394
    model, 23, 39, 41–43, 45, 381
        accuracy, 41
        artificial, **44**, 373
        compactness, **43**
        representativeness, **41**–42(fig.)
        synthetic, **44**, 380
    parameters, 23, 46, 118
        averaging, 51
        computation, 51–60
    partitioning, 6, 47–51
        based on applications, 48
        based on functional classes, 49

Workload: (*cont.*)
    based on geographical orientation,
      48–49
    based on organizational units,
      49–50
    based on resource usage, 47–48
    based on type, 50–51
  real, 41–43, 279, 379
  transaction, **36**, 50, 238, 241, 279–280,
    394
Workstation, 102, 189, 219, 305

client, 206
cluster, 221, 375

Z

Zahorjan, J., 139, 174–175, 204,
    232–233, 240–241, 268, 303
Zeigner, A., 75, 302
Z-score (*see* Clustering analysis, scaling
    techniques, z-score)
Zwaenepoel, W., 232